The Power of Ideas to Transform Healthcare

STEVE HOEFT • ROBERT W. PRYOR, MD

The Power of Ideas to Transform Healthcare

Engaging Staff by Building Daily Lean Management Systems

CRC Press
Taylor & Francis Group
Boca Raton   London   New York

CRC Press is an imprint of the
Taylor & Francis Group, an **informa** business

A PRODUCTIVITY PRESS BOOK

Credit on cover photo: Gary L. Hansen, Scott & White Health, 2006: Daytime June 2010

All proceeds to the authors will be donated to the Scott & White Healthcare Foundation. Information on the foundation can be found at http://foundation.sw.org

CRC Press
Taylor & Francis Group
6000 Broken Sound Parkway NW, Suite 300
Boca Raton, FL 33487-2742

© 2016 by Taylor & Francis Group, LLC
CRC Press is an imprint of Taylor & Francis Group, an Informa business

No claim to original U.S. Government works

Printed on acid-free paper
Version Date: 20150511

International Standard Book Number-13: 978-1-4987-0740-4 (Paperback)

Library of Congress Cataloging-in-Publication Data

Hoeft, Steven E., author.
    The power of ideas to transform healthcare : engaging staff by building daily lean management systems / Steven E. Hoeft and Robert W. Pryor.
    p. ; cm.
    Includes bibliographical references and index.
    ISBN 978-1-4987-0740-4 (alk. paper)
    I. Pryor, Robert W., author. II. Title.
    [DNLM: 1. Delivery of Health Care--organization & administration. 2. Efficiency, Organizational. 3. Management Information Systems. 4. Organizational Culture. W 84.1]

    R729.5.H4
    362.1068--dc23   2014048638

Visit the Taylor & Francis Web site at
http://www.taylorandfrancis.com

and the CRC Press Web site at
http://www.crcpress.com

Contents

Foreword

I first met Steve Hoeft in a phone conversation. He described the Lean management system he had been involved in implementing at Scott & White Healthcare, telling me they used the description of the Lean management system in *Creating a Lean Culture* as a template, and with great effect. "Come spend a few days with us, see what we've done, and give us your feedback," he said. I agreed to Gemba the Lean management implementation Hoeft had described. By the time I made the trip, Scott & White had merged to become Baylor Scott & White Health (BSWH).

I've seen hundreds of applications of Lean management systems. No two are alike, so it wasn't surprising that the application I saw at BSWH, described in the pages that follow, was not the same as others I had seen. What was surprising was its effectiveness, exemplified by this hallmark: The Scott & White system, at the time this book was written, counted 2000 implemented ideas for improvement from employees per week from their 16,000 employees, this in an environment that included recent budget and staff cuts. That number is unheard of in my experience outside of a few high-volume, low-variety automotive manufacturers, mainly Toyota and some of its suppliers.

That level of employee engagement is for me the *sine qua non* of a successful Lean implementation supported by a robust Lean management system. You will find descriptions of many elements of both systems here. One thing I've learned after repeatedly being surprised by Lean management implementations described as "taken straight from the book" is this: There are many ways to do it right. The "right" way is the one you have developed yourself that works for you, as long as it adheres to a few principles starting with *focus on the process*. But most applications, even very good ones, do not produce the high level of front-line engagement reported clearly and credibly in this book.

What I saw in late 2014 at the legacy Scott & White hospitals and clinics was the product of a Lean journey begun in 2008. Prompted by accelerating change particularly on the financial side of healthcare, CEO Bob Pryor was looking for ways to get ahead of the curve. He caught a glimpse of the future in a benchmark visit to a Toyota assembly plant with its highly engaged production employees and the thousands of implemented ideas for improvement they submitted annually.

Steve Hoeft is a teacher and coach with firsthand experience in Toyota's thinking and approach. Pryor knew the direction he wanted to go: sustained high levels of employee engagement in improving S&W's performance. Together, they developed an approach to move in that direction. Either would tell you they are far from done. However, the distance they have traversed and the progress they have made stand as significant achievements, chronicled in the pages that follow.

The hardest part of Lean is creating the conditions that engage the hearts and minds of those who do the actual work—the nurses, MAs, techs, housekeepers, providers, and other professionals—in an ongoing improvement process in which "bottom-up" suggestions for improvement are a significant component.

This book documents the path the authors created at Scott & White, now up to the merged BSWH to continue. It started with a familiar approach: creating metrics, defining targets, identifying gaps, and chartering projects to deploy Lean applications to close significant gaps. Many projects were successful, but problems were growing faster than projects could reduce them. Concurrently, many leaders were trained in Lean approaches and tools, but few knew what to do as leaders to engage those they led.

In response, the authors developed their own approach for the next steps. It did not come from a book or a consultant. Instead, they created the next steps based on Pryor's goal of high engagement at every level in the organization: Hoeft's Lean expertise, their experience up to that point, and the gaps they observed in leaders' behaviors and staff disengagement. They combined equal parts of three-tiered accountability meetings, employee idea processes, layered audits, Gemba walks, leader standard work, and visuals for each team in each tier displaying goals and gaps appropriate to the team in five areas consistent across teams and tiers. It is a systematic approach, and it is working.

I believe the single ingredient essential to this success was the example that Pryor, the CEO, set for his team and everyone in a leadership position at every level throughout the organization. This was not something he delegated. It was not the CEO "getting it," or endorsing an approach for others to take. It was—and is—something he personally demonstrates, coaches others on, observes them performing, and gives feedback. It is as simple (uncomplicated) but difficult (to achieve) as this: Pryor insists that leaders learn to lead, first by asking front-line workers to share ideas for how to reduce the gaps between their unit's performance and its goals, visually displayed where teams meet for their daily (or weekly) tier meetings. Then leaders are asked to take steps to be sure those who shared their ideas can tell whether their ideas were acted on, and if so with what results on the performance gap.

Hoeft and his team developed tools, processes, and coaching for leaders on the behaviors and practices that currently yield thousands of implemented ideas. As you read this book, you may think this sounds straightforward. But that does not mean it is easy. What Pryor has insisted on and personally reinforced and what Hoeft and his team developed are rare. They entail taking leaders through a process wherein they persuade themselves of the value of sharing, with front-line staffers, their managerial discretion to define problems worth working on. When that happens, it holds the promise to improve the entire organization's performance in ways others will find difficult to duplicate.

The goal is worthy, the journey is worth making.

David Mann, Ph.D.
Author of Creating a Lean Culture, 3rd ed.

Acknowledgments

What a difference a few years make! Steve's *Stories From My Sensei*[*] was released just over five years ago when he was still a traveling sensei working for a nonprofit health research and consulting organization. Bob went from grinding along as CMO, then added COO, then CEO, then back to CMO/COO after a big merger with Baylor Health Care System.

For Bob:

One thing I must say at this point is that this is not a history book, even though there are historical accounts written in this book. These accounts serve to illustrate teaching points. This is a book about our journey. It started by understanding the gaps in our present state and continues with our desire to move to a future state. The present state is an ever-changing landscape with some pathways well worn and others accomplished only after forging a new way in a new land.

First, I would like to thank my friend, co-worker, and sensei Steve Hoeft. He not only started me on my journey of understanding and practicing the Toyota Production System, but also he was the driving force that made this book happen.

There are numerous people within Baylor Scott & White Health who helped make this possible. I thank the staff of Baylor Scott & White for their patience in allowing us to take this journey. Through several years of learning and implementation, I can say that we are much better off having taken this journey.

---

[*] Hoeft, Steve, *Stories From My Sensei: Two Decades of Lessons Learned Implementing Toyota-Style Systems,* Productivity Press, New York, 2010.

I must thank Kerri Beckham who has kept me organized, mostly on time, and appearing when and where I should for all of the various meetings that I must attend. I also thank Alicia Dunn, my chief of staff. Without these two wonderful women, I could not have accomplished half of what I did.

My senior leadership team at Scott & White is phenomenal. They walked with us on this path and helped us go from a very rudimentary understanding to where we are today. We are only starting this journey and we have a long way to go. It is only through the hard work of the senior team that we have gotten as far as we have.

I need to add a word of thanks to those who have reviewed this manuscript and given valuable input. This, of course, includes the editors, the quality department, the Operations Excellence department, and the STEEEP Institute at Baylor Scott & White. Efficient care is part of the Baylor Scott & White STEEEP Way and the Toyota Production System is at the heart of efficiency. To that end, I would like to thank Joel Allison, chief executive officer of Baylor Scott & White, and Dr. David Ballard, the leader of our STEEEP Institute.

I need to thank my wife, Kay, who has stood by me through many difficult times in my medical and administrative careers, and has unwaveringly supported me. Thanks to my children, Jami, Jarrod, and Jaxon, and to my five grandchildren for making my life worthwhile.

Last, I must thank the chairman of the board, Drayton McLane. He is indeed an inspiration to many and a trusted mentor for me.

For Steve:

There is no way to thank every person who contributed to the improvement toolkit at Baylor Scott & White Health. Even today, it is still growing. Several people were noteworthy contributors to the toolkit and this book.

First, Bob Pryor and the Scott & White Healthcare (S&W) leadership team for actively experimenting, tinkering, and developing new applications in healthcare that did not exist anywhere else. Bob's persistence in building a TPS framework and a culture of continuous improvement guided this effort through its early, fragile years before momentum could be sustained.

Scott & White's Pat Currie (chief operations officer), Glen Couchman (chief medical officer), Cyndy Dunlap (chief nursing executive), and the regional presidents led a war on waste that is still improving today. Presidents Shahin Motakef, Glenn Robinson, Jason Jennings, Jay Fox (Kevin

Smith served as interim), Eric Looper, Dr. John Boyd, and Kim Langston are Lean-thinking leaders. Clinic vice president Colleen Sundquist and George Brown, a director, added much to the toolkit as they experimented with LMS and committed to leading in a Lean way.

The Lean team—thanks a million! There are no better coaches and zealots than you in the battle to help develop all of our great employees into waste-busters and problem-solvers.

The longest standing S&W Lean team member is Marji Henry, a great people-focused training leader. She was chosen to start-up the fledgling Lean effort. Thanks, Marji.

A trio of senior consultants saw the huge challenge in healthcare, joined us at S&W, and now coach our growing system. Dave Scottow led companies, even serving as a CEO, before doing healthcare consulting. His bull-dogged efforts make him first-in as an emergency responder—sort of a "process doctor." Dave helps coach S&W's largest region. Dave's work folders of well-organized huddle board pictures made the examples look good throughout this book. Thank you, Dave.

The next thank you goes out to Dennis Raymer. Dennis is a friend and colleague reaching back to Dr. Jeffrey Liker's consulting firm Optiprise. He embraced the challenge to bring TPS in all its glory to healthcare. Dennis was described again recently as our best instructor. He simplified all of *Daily Lean* into a few words and one quick drawing, and then watched another lightbulb turn on. This was a few weeks *after* this student had been formally trained in the classroom. Good coaching beats hours of training every time. Thank you, Dennis.

Michael Baratz was made to coach leaders through their Lean journeys. He was normally the first to make major changes in training materials or to build a Lean *system* where none existed prior (tracking, layered audits, elevation system, etc.). Many innovations in this book started with him operationalizing the principles. Michael continuously improves the continuous improvement system itself! Thank you, Michael.

Many other current team members added to the S&W Way including Dr. Glenn Kuriger, Sundeep Boinpally, Aaron Liebig, Jarrod Pryor, Amy Stecker, Nicole Hogan, Carlton Ligon, Todd McCann, and Stacey Simonton. Thanks for building something special here at S&W—more Lean thinkers.

The world's greatest senior executive assistant, Jana Huffstutler, spent countless hours of her own time transcribing Bob's and my recorded thoughts. Her organizational abilities helped steer this book through the many details. Thank you, Jana.

Herb DeBarba led the Cancer Treatment Centers of America through their Lean journey. We became friends after several of his staff took my university course. Herb and his team mastered "A3 Waves," and were nice enough to show others and me how to conduct them as well.

Michael Sinocchi, executive editor at Productivity Press/Taylor & Francis Group, was instrumental in leading us through delivery of this book. He encouraged us throughout the process and offered great ideas.

Thanks to my kids, Megan, Erich, and Erin, for your encouragement and inspiration. You have all grown up now, and I am proud of what you have become. Follow Him.

One final acknowledgment is due. To my wife, Gena Hoeft—thank you once again for losing me to the writing chair for many days when other normal people walk and talk. I owe you a non-distracted vacation. But, thank you mainly for being a great wife and our kids' mom. What would I do without you?

A Message to Leaders and Facilitators Outside of Healthcare

While this book was generally written for healthcare, the *management systems* described in detail here can and will work outside of healthcare environments. In fact, Steve and others built on top of what they learned and deployed in multiple industries and consulting careers. They are included in this book.

If your organization is non-manufacturing, people- or business process-oriented, the authors feel you will find a connection to the ways S&W tailored the Toyota Production System (TPS) to work for them. Healthcare processes are some of the hardest to systemize, standardize, and, quite frankly, just manage. This should give leaders outside of healthcare hope—and a challenge.

In some ways, a healthcare enterprise includes more high-tech, billing, business, "engineered," one-off, scheduling, information technology (IT), transportation, supply chain, and people systems than many other industries. Outside of patient interfaces, healthcare's support processes are similar in many ways to these other industries.

The path S&W followed can benefit nearly any organization. Its flight plan was not perfect by any means. Many TPS tools were adapted, some substantially. Key take-away: transforming and sustaining is not about Lean or TPS tools. It was who learned them, who used them first, and how they were sustained and spread throughout a fast-changing system.

And, it works. The principles and key learnings can be translated to nearly any type of operation. The tools and systems can be adapted to your industry and work processes. Just start. Commit to trying these concepts as a system. Focus on the higher principles written here, and then ask, "How can we adapt this way of thinking in our organization?"

Throughout this book, there will be call-outs and indented boxes to help you focus on key points and important principles. Some of these will be questions. When you reach one of these boxes, please stop and think.

The Japanese word *Hansei* means deep self-reflection.* So, do the Hansei. Ponder a bit. Answer the questions yourself and then seek out other leaders and staff members to see how they would answer. Involve your team members. Your team time and discussions will provide even more tips and practical improvements on top of those contained in this book.

There is power in a single idea. Something changes when a staff member brings up, tries out, and sees impact from a single idea. Multiply that times every staff member, every day. Unleash ideas.

---

* Lean Enterprise Institute Online Lean Lexicon, *Hansei*, Lean Enterprise Institute, Cambridge, MA. http://www.lean.org/Common/LexiconTerm.cfm?TermId=223

Chapter 1

Introduction

Bob Pryor was told that he needed to be *the* physician leader in an organization that was physician-led. But, what did that mean? Physician leadership has been likened to "herding cats." Also, in some physician groups, their democratic process holds that a single dissenting vote is a tie! Then, all changes being contemplated just stop.

His new role would be easier to define in a manufacturing company. He knew what this meant in his prior roles. Bob had been the managing partner of a large group practice, start-up Medical Director of a new Children's Hospital, and then regional Chief Medical Officer of a large healthcare system. But, to tell the truth, he didn't really know what it meant to be a leader of leaders. So, he did what most smart people do— he went back to school to learn, and learn and learn...

After 30 years, Bob felt he had tried everything. In retrospect, it probably looked like one very long Plan–Do–Check–Act (PDCA) experiment. He got some spotty results but eventually, changes slid right back to the "old way" as his leaders turned their focus onto the next new crisis. In fact, one 30-plus-year employee told him, "All I need to do is outlast *you*, just like I have outlasted all the previous leaders. Nothing ever really changes."

There must be something missing in all the management fads he learned thus far! He even went back for his MBA, and took barbs from students calling him the "old dude." Then, he started to adapt his own way of thinking.

He was slowly developing a philosophy in his head that worked. Then, rapid changes in health care—especially reimbursement systems—drove him to try Lean production techniques. Could it be? Could something as simple as empowering all staff to identify and remove *waste* be the transformation methodology his organization desperately needed?

One theme that threads this book together is *ideas*. This single word weaves together much of the fabric of *The Power of Ideas to Transform Healthcare*. Another theme is *"two hats."* As in, "Everyone hired at S&W Healthcare has two hats. You are to *do* your job well. And, you are to *improve* your job— every day." Both are equally important.

Starting in early 2013, this mantra was modeled to every new employee entering S&W's renovated orientation process. This seemed to create another inflection point on their journey to build a culture of continuous improvement (CI). More on two hats in Chapter 4, Step 1.

Ideas and two hats for everyone. Put the two together and what do you have? Chaos?! The authors believe there is great innovation and even job fulfillment on the edge of chaos, if changes are guided properly. You just need to have the right guardrails. More on that in Chapter 5.

The new "currency" for 2015 and beyond will be *ideas*. This is what organizations will need more of to survive and thrive in the coming decades. Not just ideas spinning around in someone's head. It will be ideas that are *incubated*, sought out, grown, guided, and encouraged.

Ideas on their own are not enough. You also need to build systems by which great staff members can *check* to see if their ideas *worked*, and elevate those out of their span of control. Leaders need to build these systems! In fact, it may be their most important job. Why? Because *they* control the faucet for ideas. Leaders must ask for them. Moreover, leaders control whether staff ideas "stick" and "spread!" The truth is that most supervisors and leaders do not even ask for staff members' ideas.

The authors first set out to write a book about a missing topic from healthcare literature—building systems for *Daily Lean* and *huddles* in healthcare. The book became much more. First bigger, then wider, and then (hopefully) deeper. Huddles cannot be taught or implemented apart from the management systems that support and accelerate them. Thus, the most significant concept in this book is not huddles. It is who builds the *systems* around them, and why!

> The most significant concept in this book is not huddles. It is who builds the *systems* around them, and why!

This book may *not* be what you think. It is neither a *how-to manual* on implementing part of a Lean Management System called huddles, nor is it a manual on how to get your teams engaged, even though it includes a lot of each.

The authors believe a step-by-step boilerplate manual is a trap. You can borrow a trailblazer's learning curve, but you cannot borrow what he or she has *personally learned* each step of the journey. You need to make it your own. Sometimes, you must *trust the process* and try out a new concept by challenging your staff with, "How can we make this work in our organization?"

This also applies to organizations that seek the *easy* way out, rather than go through the slow process of developing leaders and staff that *think* Lean for themselves. You can't *microwave* Lean-thinking leaders!

True, some outsiders promise quick training or impact. It is easier to pay some big-talking consultants, who provide a few classes offering belts of all colors. However, where has this worked? The *journey*, the personal process of discovery, is more important than the tools or even quick financial wins that are neither sustainable nor repeatable by your staff.

It is often said that character is what you do when you think no one is watching. Similarly, Lean is what you *do* and *think* daily to solve problems and improve broken processes—especially when you think no one is watching. By the way, if you are a leader, your staff members are always watching!

The Law of Entropy* works *against* processes every day. Just look at your teenager's room! Unless you put energy and effort into them, they get worse. You either make them better, or they make you (and patients) bitter. Los

> The *journey*, the personal process of discovery, is more important than the tools or even quick financial wins that are neither sustainable nor repeatable by your staff.

---

* Merriam-Webster Online Dictionary, *Entropy*; (2b) a process of degradation or running down or a trend to disorder. http://www.merriam-webster.com/dictionary/entropy.

Angeles Lakers Coach Pat Riley once said, "If you're not getting better, you're getting worse."

Your efforts to continuously improve work processes need to become as automatic for staff as a *morning routine*: like getting ready for work. Like a fence-builder picking up his or her post-hole digger, or a firefighter donning his or her gear, or an airline crew doing their pre-flight checklist. Without delay, and without mental gyrations, techniques taught in this book *can* and *do* become automatic. In addition, this way of thinking can be spread system-wide.

This book *is* about people, and how a culture of continuous improvement can be intentionally built and sustained. And, this book is about the journey thus far for staff members and leaders at Scott & White Healthcare. It is a fun and impactful story about how one small but resilient healthcare system found its way through an obstacle course of bear traps, set a people-focused course for the future, and stuck with it for some success.

The authors want to share some of these successes with you. And yes, they share both good and bad stories, along with their forms, tools, and tips.

It is also a revealing window inside the most recent decade of S&W's 120-plus-year history. You will enter the boardroom to see how leaders wrestled with major changes in healthcare starting around 2005. You will also enter the huddles of some top-performing teams as they helped steer their organization clear of some rocky shoals that cut up larger health systems in this same period.

How did this organization go from just one-of-many to one-of-the-best idea generating, staff engaging, Lean Management System building healthcare organizations in the world? We hope that the candor and humility of the authors reveal they are not there yet, nor feel they are even far along in their Lean journey. However, they will give you as much as they can of their journey and tools. Maybe their tips will keep you out of some "bear traps" they and others hit.

Throughout this book, some powerful learning points will be highlighted. WARNING: At times, the application of learning points in this book may show little early promise. Other times, it will yield quick results. Nevertheless, stay with it. *Lean Thinking* is based on common sense, but it is neither common, nor consistent with what made sense in earlier improvement attempts. You will need to think differently, mainly about people.

If there were one small tip the authors could give you now, it would be this: "*Sometimes you have to go slow to go fast.*" Yes. It can mean what you just thought. It could also mean *timing is everything,* or *do it right the first time*, or *don't jump to conclusions*, or *don't skip steps*, or *don't give up*, or *build people* (train, invest) *before they treat patients*, or literally dozens of other great applications.

This book discusses some deep *Lessons Learned* for Bob and his team as they tailored many TPS principles to their health system. The *process* they went through is the key.

Learning what Bob and the S&W leadership team learned on their journey is just as important as their outcomes. If you merely copy the exterior trappings of his *Daily Lean* systems, you may only achieve partial results and struggle to sustain them. *Reading* some of what Bob and his leaders tried on their journey may make you laugh, but then hopefully think deeply about what you would do if faced with the same set of conditions. Personal learning sticks. Quick results often quickly slide back.

The title of this book begs some questions. What ideas? Whose ideas? And, do you mean daily, as in every day? The authors offer some brief answers to get you started, but most of the real solutions are in Chapters 4 and 5. Please keep reading.

The *What* will be ideas, and two hats. The *How* will be to prepare and task leaders to build systems that fully engage and utilize all staff's ideas. The *Why* is survival. Yes, survival. Few efforts can bend the cost curve like thousands of everyday ideas by every staff member. The *Who* for this book is leaders, but the key actors in this new play are front-line staff members. This book is for leaders at all levels. This book elevates and celebrates them.

The authors will also detail how they built daily Lean management systems. This has made a world of difference.

In brief, the authors hope this book accelerates and speeds up your journey by helping you avoid the pitfalls and bear traps normally associated with large, system-wide changes. You are welcome to yell at, argue with, and even try the opposite of what the authors did. Just have a *bias for action*. Welcome to the journey that never ends!

As Bob shares with other healthcare leaders in America, he is astounded by a common thread in their conversations—all of them seem to have the same strategy! All are pursuing cost reductions, staying ahead of reforms, and planning for population health. The key will be who will *execute* the best! This book lays out a solid framework for deploying and executing your strategy.

What Can Lean Do for My Organization?

Great question. Why not publish possible results first? That would be like reading the end of the book first.

Good news: deploying Lean pays off! However, it is not recommended that you judge your Lean journey with return on investment (ROI) every single step of the way. It is difficult to isolate and quantify the hard green-dollar savings of every single idea. In addition, there are building block investments needed to prime the pump or grease the skids for the next big set of changes.

Example: What is the ROI at the end of a multi-day training class? Zero. Negative. However, this building block lays the foundation for staff to think differently, which they immediately start to apply in their own work processes. That is where S&W and others get results. Lots of them!

In *Going Lean in Health Care*[*] Jim Womack and some great Lean leaders reported large gains were possible if organizations committed to Lean thinking and kept the improvement projects rolling. The most dramatic were cost reductions—an average of 30% or more, as shown in Figure 1.1.

Dr. John Toussaint, then CEO of ThedaCare, reports similar numbers by applying Lean systems throughout his health systems over a 3-year period. They saw increased productivity by 12%, decreased costs by 30% (per stay, visit, or service), an amount equal to 5% of their annual revenue, and

• 25–55% Cost Reduction
• 60–90% Throughput Increase
• 50–90% Less Errors
• 60–90% Inventory Reduction
• 35–50% Space Reduction
• 50–90% Lead Time Reduction
• 45–75% Productivity Increase
• Greatly Improved Morale

Figure 1.1   Typical improvements when applying Lean for more than two years.

---

[*] Womack, James, Arthur Byrne, Orest J. Fiume, Gary S. Kaplan, and John Toussaint, *Going Lean in Health Care*, Institute for Healthcare Improvement White Paper, 2005.

Scott & White (2009–2013) Annualized Improvement Amount (tracked projects only)
✓ Cost Avoidance of $120,455,561
✓ Cost Reduction of $2,300,000
✓ Increased Collections by $4,533,480
✓ Increased Capacity by $18,647,340 (if filled, freed up staff)
✓ Patient Throughput ↑ by 809,020 patients
✓ Productivity ↑ by 944,580 min (per FTE)
✓ Lead Time ↓ by 253,354 minutes
✓ Process Time ↓ by 504,212 minutes
✓ Staff Walking Distance ↓ by 317,260 feet
✓ Patient Wait Time ↓ by 93,510 minutes
✓ Staff Wait Time ↓ by 1,088,060 minutes

Figure 1.2   Scott & White Lean improvements from 2009 through 2013 (tracked projects only).

doubled operating margin.* John also summarized his Kaizen projects typically remove 40% of the waste each full cycle. The United States spends approximately $2.4 trillion annually on health care, so removing 40% of the waste would save our nation $1 trillion!†

S&W also saw similar gains in their first few years of CI projects, as seen in Figure 1.2.

Although it is nearly impossible to isolate Lean savings from other efforts and hard work in each department, S&W leaders believe Lean played a significant role in keeping the organization positive when many others their size lost ground. The main reason: waste reduction.

When someone removes waste from his or her own process, it frees up time each day to take on more value-added work. These are tasks that healthcare professionals went to school for and are fulfilling for them. This always improves productivity—eventually. S&W maintained steady productivity improvements in clinics and hospitals each year over this same period.

---

* Toussaint, John, "Writing the New Playbook for U.S. Health Care: Lessons From Wisconsin," *Health Affairs*, 28(5), September/October 2009. http://content.healthaffairs.org/content/28/5/1343.long, accessed August 2014.
† Ibid.

However, the biggest gain S&W made in a single year was the non-replacement of 500+ staff members while gaining volume and visits in nearly every service. There is no way this would have been possible without S&W's extensive Lean effort. Again, no across-the-board layoffs were made.

In addition, one of the most significant new interventions the S&W Lean team added was Work Balance/Risk Share in the huddles. S&W leaders expect big gains as staff learn to balance their own workloads, cross-train staff to cover peak work periods for each other, and learn to run as a team. See Chapter 5, "Rebalance and Workshare in Huddles."

Bob's Background

So here Bob was, Chief Operating Officer and Chief Medical Officer of Scott & White Healthcare. How did he get there? Bob wonders that himself. In high school, he started working at the S&W morgue after-hours as a technician. He helped the pathologist, and then stayed behind in the basement after midnight cleaning up the morgue. That gave Bob his first ideas about how healthcare worked. What Bob saw was the opposite of healthcare "success." As he learned to see it, the job of healthcare was to prevent morgue dwellers.

Bob continued on to medical school, where he learned the diagnosis process for physicians. They started with a wide variety of possibilities called the *differential diagnosis*. Then, they used data of all kinds to hone the differential diagnosis down to the most logical conclusion. Then, they started therapy based on the conclusion. Sometimes the therapy worked, and sometimes it did not. However, it was important to know at the earliest point in time if the therapy was not working.

Bob spent 20 years in an intensive care unit (ICU) environment. In the ICU, Bob was fortunate enough to have all the data at his fingertips, updated quickly if the data changed. That was when Bob learned that data from yesterday was as bad as yesterday's fish. It stunk!

You need data for very ill patients in *real-time*. By presenting data to providers promptly, they could make people better. Anything later was like steering a car by watching a camera with a 1-hour delay!

Bob reached his last day in the ICU in Dallas, Texas. The next day, he was on the road to Phoenix, Arizona. He became the Chief Medical Officer for a system there. He needed to learn more about running the business of

> Bob learned that data from yesterday was as bad as yesterday's fish. It stunk! Doctors need data for very ill patients in *real-time*.

healthcare, so Bob also became an older student in a master's of business administration (MBA) program.

He learned a great deal. As he interacted with younger colleagues, all executives in their own right, he learned that their businesses required up-to-the-minute data as well. However, very few of these industry leaders were pleased with their feedback systems either. During his MBA, Bob was also exposed to operations management and the Toyota Production System. He filed that away in the back of his mind.

Bob was very happy in Phoenix. But one day, a recruiter approached him about the "perfect" job for his skill set in a small town in Texas. They asked if he would apply to be the Chief Medical Officer for Scott & White Healthcare in Temple, TX. The recruiter was amazed that Bob knew anything about S&W and their flagship Memorial Hospital.

He competed for the position, won it, and rejoined friends and family in central Texas. Two years later, Bob arrived at his dilemma (see beginning of Chapter 2) as the Chief Operating Officer and Chief Medical Officer, wrestling with how he would help make this good health system better. How would S&W become the healthcare system they all desired it to be? Moreover, how would they best manage their operations?

Bob was reminded of his operations management courses and TPS when then Chairman of the Physician Board, Dr. Paul Dieckert, showed him an advertisement for a university's Lean Healthcare certificate series. Paul and Bob went. They drank the Kool-Aid. Bob still describes himself as somewhere early in his Lean journey.

Steve's Background

The easiest way to understand Steve's background is to read his book, *Stories From My Sensei: Two Decades of Lessons Learned Implementing Toyota-Style Systems.** It won a 2011 Shingo Award for Research and Professional Publications. It is a story about a learner, or better, someone who quickly learns from mistakes—including his own.

---

* Hoeft, Ibid.

In brief, Steve is an engin-nerd, heavy in operations management, with an MBA and PMP certification. He was blessed to be taught improvement techniques first by Eli Goldratt while at GM, then he learned from a few great sensei, deeply rooted in the Toyota Production System.

He is the son and grandson of hard-working automotive industry workers from Detroit. From his earliest memories of layoffs that harmed his family to his first visit to a Toyota plant, Steve always believed there was a better way to manage work. Then, he saw it. In many ways, Steve is still a "car guy." Better, he is and always will be a *process improver*.

Chapter 2

Why Lean? Why Now?

It was my first day as Chief Medical Officer (CMO) and Chief Operating Officer (COO) for the health system where I grew up. I arrived at my desk overwhelmed by the sheer number of issues to fix. But, I had no clue how the Scott & White Healthcare *Operating System* worked, or even if there was one.

How were decisions made around here? What was my level of authority and responsibility? How and where should we grow? Where was the restroom?!

More questions swirled:

"How do we communicate with each other?"

"What is the common language we use to solve problems?"

"Why do the same problems come up day after day?"

"How do I direct and coordinate our geographically sprawling provider community?"

I thought, "There must be some way to get my arms and head around all of these issues, and then get our leaders to all row in a common direction!"

I kept looking for a people-based solution. It was more than just a "want." I needed a common way of getting things done across this fast-growing system with fast-growing issues.

—**Bob Pryor**

Simon Sinek states in his classic speeches* that one should always start with "Why?" So, why? Why Lean? Why now? Some answers: need, strong desire, belief in people, nothing else worked, maybe all of these things and more.

For Scott & White Healthcare, Bob's needs coupled with a healthcare storm on the horizon created the right mix of fear and desire that greases the skids for major changes to occur. In many ways, Bob and his leaders acted more quickly than other health systems to "turn on the faucet" of ideas that were pent up in their staff members' heads for many years. However, healthcare in general has been the slowest industry to do this *en masse*!

Steve saw this firsthand. He describes his career as one long roller coaster ride—all in the same car or seat. He worked in or for hundreds of great organizations in nearly every business sector through his 30-plus year engineering and consulting vocation. However, his role or title always had *continuous process improvement* (CPI or just CI) in it.

After serving auto manufacturers of all kinds and tiers, liquid/paint, energy (including nuclear fuel), business process and transactional firms, Steve committed his Lean toolbox to the military men, women, and weapon systems that protected our country for several "up tempo" years. After that, he continued to apply Lean and process improvement to government entities. Yes, even the U.S. government applied Lean on a few good "islands" before the last holdout from leader-led process improvement—healthcare.†

Starting around 2006, Steve was determined to apply Lean and process improvement to healthcare. He describes it as the greatest challenge of his career. And, it has made a difference, as you will see in the next few chapters.

The Healthcare Desert Oasis

For the times they are a-changin'.

—Bob Dylan
(title track), Columbia Records, 1964

---

* Sinek, Simon, *How Great Leaders Inspire Action*, Filmed Sep 2009, TEDx Puget Sound, http://www.ted.com/talks/simon_sinek_how_great_leaders_inspire_action.html accessed August 2014.
† Steve refers to system-wide process improvement efforts, led by top leaders. He recognizes many improvement efforts in healthcare were well advanced, like the application of Industrial Engineering starting in the early 1980s. Steve studied under Dr. Vinod Sahney, an early pioneer in this field. He also affirms early continuous quality and safety improvement efforts that transformed healthcare in many locations.

An analogy can help answer the *Why* questions. For the past few decades, healthcare as an industry has been at a lush, plentiful oasis in a friendly desert. The herds came on schedule and there was plenty of water to drink. Herd leaders grew in size and weight in the safe shelter of the oasis. All was well.

However, the winds of change started blowing, imperceptibly at first. With each foray into different forms of payment capitation (HMOs, government-paid care, fixed payments based on diagnosis, etc.), the wind blew harder. With the passage of the Affordable Care Act and related legislation, the wind blew even harder. The sands shifted.

Some herds merged for protection. Some herds skimmed off the best of what the oasis had and left the weak behind. The wind howled. Sand flew everywhere. When many herd leaders finally looked up, they saw the water holes drying up, and the sands literally taking over. Their oasis was gone!

It would be nice to wrap up this analogy with a happily-ever-after ending, but the current state of healthcare is nothing but sand for miles. Healthcare leaders need to choose a different path. They need to move from something and toward something altogether different. A new way of thinking is desperately needed.

Throughout the history of healthcare, leaders were able to use heuristic rules that reinforced their thinking, which was, "What has worked in the past, will work again now." Coin in, gumball out. However, as healthcare environments changed even faster, what worked in the past would not work in the future. Think of how quickly healthcare finance and payments have already "reformed."

Therefore, we entered a survival period. Wandering a rich savannah of plentiful grasslands with well-worn paths of problem → response is now replaced by desert sands, shifting fast to cover the old paths. No paths are visible or familiar anymore.

Healthcare leaders need to shift from the simple heuristic thinking that worked in the past to new ways of thinking that are more nimble—ones that use more brainpower. The brainpower of just you and your executive staff is not enough. To survive and thrive, the brainpower of your whole staff can and must be harnessed. Look ahead. Decide *what* and *where* you really want and need to be. Move toward the next oasis along your new path.

A clarion call is sounding. The smart herd leaders are now saying, "Move! Find another path and move, *fast*!" The water holes are drying up. The old ways of thinking just leave us in shifting sand. For healthcare, a *new path* is needed to survive the changing environment—both internal and external.

Healthcare Challenges Nationwide

Healthcare costs too dang much! Since employees pay up to one third of the total costs in any given year, this problem affects all of us. Because of this, most healthcare systems started seeing a decline in utilization of *non-emergency* treatment and procedures as costs rose at a frenetic pace. We simply cannot afford the system we have.

The challenges for any company today are great. For healthcare organizations, they are compounded. Walgreens, CVS, and other retail establishments now provide a growing number of health services. Companies are approaching healthcare organizations directly to provide on-site services. Some of these companies are thousands of miles away from the sites.[*]

Healthcare was once considered immune to competitors at a distance. Now with electronic medical record systems, telemedicine,[†] medical tourism,[‡] and new types of competitors, there is no immunity.

Futurists describe a phenomenon called *disruptive innovation*,[§] where a product or competitor unknown to the big players changes the rules and takes market share before the big players can react to the changed playing

---

[*] Diamond, Dan, Health care for $4: Are you ready for Walmart to be your doctor?, Forbes.com, August 8, 2014.
[†] The Free Dictionary, *Telemedicine*; http://www.thefreedictionary.com/Tele+medicine.
[‡] The Free Dictionary, *Medical Tourism*, http://encyclopedia.thefreedictionary.com/medical+tourism.
[§] The Free Dictionary, *Disruptive Innovation*, http://encyclopedia.thefreedictionary.com/disruptive+innovation.

field. Author Clayton Christensen moved this body of knowledge forward in his books. See the next section.

So why are healthcare organizations still building large, inaccessible buildings to house their brand of healthcare? Making this question even more concerning is the fact that inpatient beds will decline as population health experiments expand and out-of-pocket costs continue to increase.

Declining utilization of many health services is not new. Utilization has been trending downward for the past decade. A multistate study conducted by Kaufman Hall inclusive of nearly half of the nation's population shows inpatient use rates per 1000 declined significantly between 2006 and 2011.* Yet, more hospital inpatient towers rise out of the ground every year.

One of the biggest shifts nationwide is toward smaller, single-purpose facilities like ambulatory surgery centers, urgent care centers, stand-alone emergency departments (EDs), imaging centers, and others. The reason is simple—focusing on just one or a few processes makes it faster and more convenient for the patients. For healthcare organizations, it is a way to generate more admissions to their hospitals and reduce crowding at their emergency rooms in their hospitals. However, it is also a way to expand into new markets without the huge cost of building a full-service hospital.

Many believe these "stand-alones" only drive healthcare costs up and skim off insured patients. Of the 400+ freestanding EDs built between 2010 and 2013, many are located near high-end shopping centers and target consumers with private insurance. Unlike urgent care centers, these EDs can cost close to $1000 per visit, even though many of these patients could have been cared for in an urgent care or regular clinic[†]— if they were open!

Sticking with the construction of healthcare facilities, why build a multi-million dollar clinic building only to close it 16 hours per day? Steve saw how manufacturing and other industries solved this dilemma. If a manufacturer spent millions of dollars on a large piece of capital equipment, they sure as heck would find a way to keep it running longer! It would not be "unavailable" 16 hours each day and all weekend.

---

[*] Grube, Mark, and Kenneth Kaufman, Decline in utilization rates signals a change in the inpatient business model, HealthAffairs Blog, Mar 8, 2013, http://healthaffairs.org/blog/2013/03/08/decline-in-utilization-rates-signals-a-change-in-the-inpatient-business-model/ accessed August 2014.

[†] Galewitz, Phil (from Kaiser Health News), Stand-alone emergency rooms popping up, *USA Today* (online), July 14, 2013.

And yet, that is the typical utilization of clinic and some specialty provider buildings. Future-focused healthcare leaders must throw away most "Closed" signs on their doors.

All clinic building signs should say "Open" on one side and "Urgent Care—Now Open!" on the other side! Or, at least some thought should be put into building utilization before more are constructed.

Today, consumers expect more. It is getting harder, not easier, to meet their timeliness expectations. Maybe it is because there are fast food and drive-through drug stores on every corner. Maybe consumers are experiencing faster service everywhere. Patients are no longer willing to wait weeks to see a healthcare provider. They want same-day, right now access and they do not want to walk or wait.

At the same time, healthcare is getting very "local." People want to park their front bumper against the front door of the store, and they don't want to wait at check-out either! This is why pharmacy in-store clinics are growing. This is also why the Dollar-type stores are digging into Walmart's once untouchable market share. Customers want service—now!

One of the best examples of disruptive innovation is Theranos. Founder Elizabeth Holmes developed a way to quickly diagnose a few drops of blood at a fraction of the price of commercial labs. Walgreens plans to roll out Theranos Wellness Centers inside its pharmacies.[*] Theranos plans to charge less than 50% of standard Medicare and Medicaid reimbursement rates—under $3 for blood typing, cholesterol, and others. If all tests were done at these lower rates, it would save Centers for Medicare/Medicaid Service (CMS) $200 billion over the next decade![†]

In addition to new upstart competitors, healthcare organizations had many other increasing challenges:

---

[*] Moukheiber, Zina, Elizabeth Holmes, who wants to shake up the blood testing industry, is a billionaire at 30, Forbes.com, July 17, 2014.

[†] Roper, Caitlin, This woman invented a way to run 30 lab tests on only one drop of blood, wired.com, February 18, 2014.

- Decreasing reimbursements from government and private payors
- Increasing costs
- Increasing government and third-party regulations

Rather than doubling-down on process improvements over the past decade, all of these challenges nationwide caused healthcare organizations to focus in areas *outside* of continuous improvement. They just did not feel they could "free up" staff members for "improvement projects."

Many reasons for avoiding continuous improvement workshops have been offered:

- Staff time limitations
- Continued pressures to improve productivity
- Staff unavailable to work on continuous improvement (can't backfill)
- Difficulty in implementing large action plans and projects
- Time needed to properly set up and collect data
- Staff moved along to the next big crisis
- Pay-for-performance and utilization metrics prevent providers and others from choosing to be involved
- Leaders and staff often wait for improvement workshops to fix persistent problems, but workshops are limited by facilitators and time away from work for team members
- Some leaders infer to staff that improvement workshops are "just one more thing to do" on top of their regular job, rather than a key part of their job

These problems were well known and understood by front-line staff, supervisors, and leaders. However, most leaders did not feel empowered to fix these challenges.

New Challengers: Non-Traditional Healthcare Providers

Healthcare must change. Change is coming. New and nimble competitors are already in the marketplace. Moreover, they are following the example of innovators of the past that disrupted powerhouses stuck in their ways. Some of these innovators were Apple, Walgreens, FedEx, and others. They start in a narrow niche. As they get a foothold, their markets become wider and larger. Soon, the behemoths that laughed at their presence are now chasing their tails. Some behemoths became like wooly mammoths and faded away.

One example of a disrupter is the BlackBerry smartphone marketed by BlackBerry Limited, formerly known as Research In Motion Limited (RIM). The smartphone started as a narrow niche. It was just a phone with a few other functions. However, it was cheaper than a computer and easier to carry. The operating system was different. In no way could you call it a computer, right? Smartphone companies added quickly features and applications to their open, nimble systems.

Computer companies miscalculated. They denied these new products were substitutes for their entrenched items. They did not see the threat because they started in such a small niche. They did not look and feel enough like their products. Entrenched big players ignored them. That is, until it was too late. The upstarts had eaten much of their market share.

Observe all of the other electronic devices that today's smartphones replace. You no longer need a separate phone, calendar system, email device, watch, digital camera, camcorder, GPS device, TV (albeit small), laptop, digital reader, or even books for that matter! All the while, it adds many impressive ways to connect to what every young person wants—their friends. The smartphone is a handheld computer and more.

A company making single-purpose digital cameras is as obsolete as one making buggy whips at the turn of the twentieth century. Popular firms making GPS devices are struggling.

Similarly, Figure 2.1 shows what the marketing department of one large personal computer-related company thought of Apple's iPad when it first came out. They called their analysis a "tie," but clearly preferred the rock. This type of denial only speeds up the demise of the once-dominant market incumbents.

The same process is playing out in healthcare. For many decades, hospitals and physicians had huge barriers for competitors to entry into their world of the healing arts. Now, Nurse Practitioners (NP), Physician Assistants (PA), nurses of all certification levels and even medical assistants (MA) with clear protocols and training are changing healthcare processes.

In the near future, we will see mobile clinics, tele-medicine, 3-D printing of transplantable organs, computational biology, health clinics in local grocery stores, immediate-result lab kiosks in public places, and much more.

	Rock (old)	iPad (2010)
Camera	✕	✕
Multi-tasking	√	✕
Changeable Battery	✕	✕
Standard Ports (USB, SD Card, etc.)	✕	✕
Touchscreen	✕	√

Figure 2.1 Personal computer marketing department's assessment of the iPad.

Another big concern for traditional health systems is best called *co-opetition*. Insurance companies are now starting to offer health services. Physician groups are buying and managing their own stand-alone ambulatory surgery and diagnostic centers. Once devoted partners, organizations now compete for scarce revenue. Some competitors skim off fully insured customers, making the playing field even more stacked against those determined to improve health for entire populations.

Why should healthcare organizations be concerned about competitors and disruptive innovators? The answer lies in another question. Do healthcare organizations really listen to their customers? Why does a patient complain about a $30 co-pay at a specialty clinic, but will pay four times more to a health food store that sells products promising health, but are "not intended to diagnose or treat illness?" The physician visit should be value-added and offer scientifically, well-proven methods to diagnose and treat illness.

However, what hoops was the patient required to jump through on his or her last visit? In addition, who does the patient usually see last? In the chain of hand-offs, who spends the least time with the patient? Who did the patient come to see? Hmmm. Sounds like healthcare processes really need change, and Lean! Otherwise, someone more innovative will solve patients' health needs in a much different way.

Keeping Up with Change

So, what keeps healthcare leaders up at night? In a word, change. Lots of them, inside and outside of their organization. Figure 2.2 shows a simple way of thinking to escape the reactive death spirals that usually accompany major changes.

In the face of rapid change, healthcare leaders search their memory banks for what has worked in the past. If it is a new or unknown change, there may not be a "usual" response. However, that does not stop leaders in healthcare. They will still tend to use more comfortable solutions that worked in the past but have no relevance to today's challenges.

In fact, healthcare leaders will generally resist new ways of thinking. Typical excuses include: Don't micromanage me, this takes too much time, we know what to do, and, don't bother me—I'll do something about it soon. While just-do-something is an important concept when problems and solutions are simple, it does not work in today's complex healthcare environment. What is needed is *slow thinking*, utilizing root cause analysis, analysis, and then rapid Plan, Do, Check, and Act (PDCA) cycles in teams to prove that their new solutions are working.

Leaders know they need to make changes, but what and how? A better question is that they need to change quickly from what and to what?

Most leaders attempt some root cause thinking, or at least guessing, to get back on track. Some develop strategies, frameworks, and structures (e.g., a new service line) to respond to change.

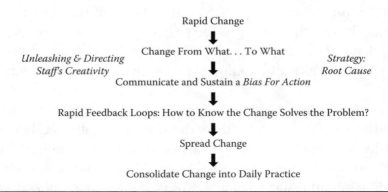

Figure 2.2 A simple model for executives dealing with change.

Once leaders seize upon the changes needed and strategies to guide them the harder part of leadership begins. Not only must they now deploy those strategies, they must also communicate and sustain a *Bias for Action* throughout their organization. Leaders must show respect for workers by telling them why the change was needed. Sustaining them requires leaders to frequently audit that changes are happening. This requires being in the workplace much more.

Most healthcare organizations are good at making plans. In fact, most healthcare organizations have the same strategy. Execution is lacking. Few are good at executing them in an intentional and well-communicated way.

Chapter 4, Step 4 Daily Lean offers a tremendous vehicle for this in huddles. General Dwight D. Eisenhower put it this way:

> In preparation for battle, I have always found that plans are use-less. But, planning is indispensable!

From Figure 2.2, the next step in responding to major changes is to install rapid feedback loops so leaders at all levels can see if their changes or improvements are working.

The last two steps on the figure seem easy in principle, but actually, they are the most difficult. Any change, once proven to have great benefits in a pilot or focused area, should be easy to spread to another area, right? Not so. Even in the face of numeric improvement, *not-invented-here* syndrome resists changes—especially those from "another area."

However, with steady, visible leadership and respectful two-way communication, even stubborn staff can be encouraged to try new ways. With broken processes in healthcare (and outside of healthcare as well), what could it hurt?

S&W leaders encourage many changes with a simple request, "Just try it!" With enough trials, it can become the norm. Once staff no longer can say, "This is how we always do it," positive changes get easier. Just try it. The good news is that processes with less waste "feel" better, right from the start. Leaders then help all staff consolidate the working changes and improvements into their daily practices.

S&W's Particular Challenges

Video: Bob Pryor presenting the President's Award for best Lean project, Continuous Learning & Improvement Program (CLIP) Fair, November 3, 2011

Scott & White has always been known as the place people would come when no one else could figure out what was wrong with them. When I travel, many people share stories about how Scott & White served as the "last hope" for a family member.

Since Scott & White has been in existence for almost 120 years, it isn't unusual for someone, even well-outside Texas, to tell a story of how their great uncle in 1910 had a ruptured appendix and was transported here on a wagon, operated on by Dr. Scott, and survived because of great care. Remember, this was a time before penicillin was available.

Our history and heritage of innovation at Scott & White, doing the right thing at the right time for our patients, is engrained in our culture. It is what Scott & White does!

S&W's Growth Era

Beginning in 2005, change came rapidly at S&W. Whereas S&W had historically been on the forefront of innovation, it eventually gave way to a single-minded strategy—growth! During times of rapid growth, innovation seems to be put on the back burner. Figure 2.3 shows many years of innovation, followed by a decade of acceleration! If the first 108 years were the (slow) years of innovation, then the next nine years were the (fast) years of acceleration!

In their years of innovation, S&W had many "firsts" including:

■ First to use electro-cautery for hemostasis in the operating room (1908)
■ First health system in Texas to have a certified program for graduate medical education (GME)
■ Establishment and integration of the Scott & White Health Plan; became one of the first in the country to have a truly integrated delivery system for healthcare

In Figure 2.3, the years 2005 through 2014 marked a decade of incredible change for S&W. The organization needed to grow—and grow it did! S&W

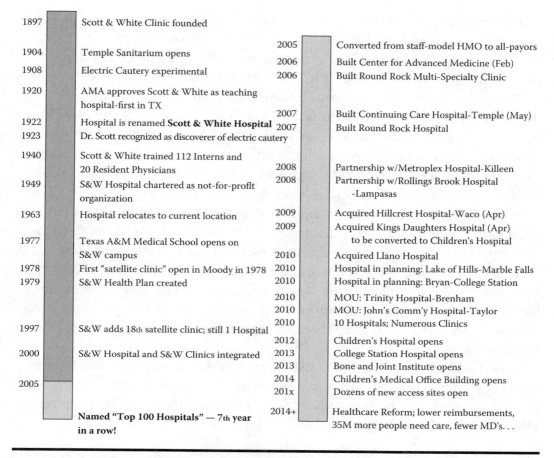

Figure 2.3 A century of innovation followed by a decade of acceleration.

brought online over $1 billion worth of buildings and capital projects in this 9-year period. Given the borrowing limits of non-profits, this was amazing.

This also drained the coffers normally in place to absorb the body blows of revenue-reductions sweeping healthcare. It is a Catch-22: Don't grow enough, you die. Grow too fast, you die.

S&W's Financial Model

As the pace of change accelerated greatly, S&W was faced with challenges that few other healthcare systems in the country faced. The biggest struck to the core of who S&W was, and what they would become. For years, their employed physicians served members of their own Scott & White Health Plan and just a few other payors.

However, beginning in 2005, S&W started rapidly converting its financial model from a closed-model staff HMO[*] to an all-payor strategy. That decision was carried out through contracting with other insurance companies besides the wholly owned Scott & White Health Plan.

When you own your own health insurance plan and all services are delivered under it, you really do not need to bill or invoice many outside entities. You essentially just keep what is left. As S&W rapidly added other insurers, it did not ramp up their back-office revenue recovery services at the same pace. Learning the ins and outs of payors does not come quickly. This challenge put S&W in a disadvantageous position early.

Also during that time, department leaders developed many new managed care contracts, but the infrastructure was not built to efficiently invoice insurers and patients in the new reimbursement paradigm. At the same time, early contracts were not written specific enough to be paid at the "full" contract rate—they often slid to the "lesser of" rates. Several years later, when the contracts were evaluated, almost half the time under the managed care contracts, S&W was paid the "lesser of" rate rather than a rate the contract would have suggested.

When added to S&W's traditions, express desires and public teaching of medical students to avoid defensive medicine, over-testing, unnecessary surgeries, and non-generic prescribing, S&W's revenue hit the skids long before other traditional health systems felt the changes.

S&W's Secret to Low Costs—Integrated Health Delivery

The Dartmouth Institute for Healthcare Policy and Clinical Practice publishes the *Dartmouth Atlas* for healthcare spending across the United States. In several books and articles at that time, Atul Gawande sought answers to why certain areas of Texas like McAllen were among the highest in the country for Medicare per visit spend.[†] Yet, he states, "Scott and White Memorial Hospital has brought Temple, Texas, higher Medicare quality scores than McAllen hospitals, higher patient satisfaction, and the *lowest* costs in the state ($7,015 per enrollee) by building an accountable care organization that we could learn a great deal from."

---

[*] Hunter, Rachel, HMO insurance, *Mama's Health,* http://www.mamashealth.com/insurance/hmo. asp, accessed August 2014.

[†] Gawande, Atul, The cost conundrum redux, *New Yorker,* June 23, 2009.

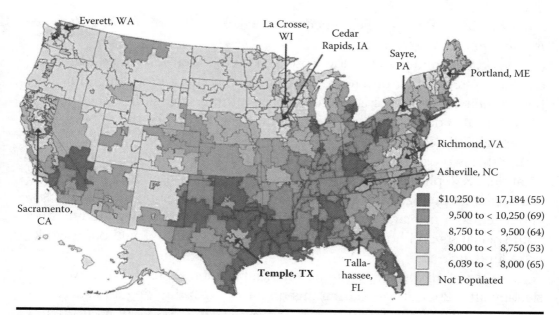

Figure 2.4 Price-adjusted per-capita Medicare spending in The Dartmouth Health Atlas. (From *The Dartmouth Atlas of Health Care*, Dartmouth Institute. With permission.)

As seen in Figure 2.4, the region around Temple, Texas, S&W's home headquarters, remains one of the lowest Medicare per capita cost areas in the state and country. Just two to three years later, a similar study was published looking at the commercial insurance spend per member. Temple, Texas, once again was one of the lowest cost areas.

Most of the areas lower in Medicare cost per capita were higher than average for commercial payors. The assumption is that organizations must offset low-rate business with higher-rate. However, S&W was low on both.

Joe Flower summarized the difference and challenge well when he wrote, "Think about what it means that it costs twice as much for patients in the last six months of life to be involved with Cedars-Sinai in Los Angeles, UCLA Medical Center or New York University Medical Center than it does for them to be involved with Mayo Clinic in Minnesota or the Cleveland Clinic; or that Medicare spends half as much per patient per year in Temple, Texas, as in McAllen or Harlingen or Brownsville, Texas; or why Medicare spending per patient per year in the top and bottom quintiles of hospital catchment areas *differ by 60 percent.*"* He headlined this section of the article *The Difference Is Integration.*

The S&W commitment to low costs starts with their integrated health delivery system. Their difference was integration and a prevailing philosophy in their teaching hospital to do the right thing. The clinic structure of S&W was also designed to do the right amount of care for the right reason at the right clinical site.

In other words, during the years of practicing as a staff-model HMO organization, S&W physicians learned to have a high adoption of generic prescribing, a low utilization of expensive, unnecessary testing for a diagnosis, and a series of primary care clinics that functioned in an integrated manner with specialists and hospitals that provided additional care without rework or redundancies.

Because of all these factors, the financial challenges for S&W grew steadily after 2011. It was during this time that Lean thinking and successes started to penetrate more areas. So, year over year, costs were reduced and productivity increased.

The authors do not want to paint the wrong picture at this point. Lean interventions did not save S&W without hard work and good management during this period as well. However, it was a significant part of it.

How S&W's "Secret Sauce" Helps Improve Population Health

S&W's secret sauce grew out of their beginnings. As opposed to most hospital systems that attempt to become an integrated delivery system,† S&W started as a group practice of physicians that ran hospitals. This is very different from a hospital system that contracted with physicians. While this may seem like splitting hairs, their root practices are light years away from each other.

Scott & White was a physician-led organization. This meant a group of physician-managers managed it, and then the professional management staff worked for the physician managers. Physicians look at businesses completely different from other types of leaders, even those in for-profit healthcare companies. Whereas many healthcare companies focus on the balance

---

* Flower, Joe, How the future of healthcare will actually work: nuts and bolts, *The Healthcare Blog,* September 26, 2010, http://thehealthcareblog.com/blog/2010/09/26/how-the-future-of-healthcare-will-actually-work-nuts-and-bolts/#more-19894, accessed August 2014.

† The Free Dictionary, *Integrated Delivery System,* http://medical-dictionary.thefreedictionary.com/Integrated+Delivery+System.

sheet, physician leadership at S&W focused on "plowing" any earned margin immediately back into healthcare services and providing more healthcare to the population. This was their training—at least at S&W.

This created an interesting dilemma. When population health* became a common term in many healthcare strategy circles, the physicians at S&W recognized it as merely what they had done and taught for decades in their group practice and hospitals. Looking backward, as the country continues to shift from a fee-for-service model to a pay-for-performance model, S&W may have been too early on that part of their vision and strategy.

For S&W physician leaders, it was relatively easy to understand how to deliver population health. However, it was much more difficult to be paid for doing the preventive work, when all reimbursement and billing systems are totally geared to reimburse fee-for-service only. It paid only based on how much "sick care" you do, not how healthy you make your communities. It is often said that reimbursements in the past were only for sick care, not health care.†

Therefore, S&W continued to reduce non-effective services and missed a big chunk of fees other organizations continued to charge. In addition, S&W moved quickly toward a new currency of "covered lives." Their well-trained staff kept their populations out of the hospitals, but few of these additional actions were reimbursed! It seems that S&W and many other great healthcare institutions across the United States were being punished for keeping populations healthy by not billing for the "maximum allowable" services on patients, whether they needed them or not!

Rapid Growth and Pride

There are two vulnerable times in the history of an organization. The first is during rapid growth. During rapid growth, the accrual accounting may look good but you can become cash poor during this time as reimbursements and full utilizations lag hiring and start-up costs.

The second most vulnerable time for an organization is when you are on top of the world and everything is working well. When everything is working well and you are on top of the world, innovation and pressure

---

* The Free Dictionary, *Population Health,* http://encyclopedia.thefreedictionary.com/population+health.
† Google search finds over 83,000 hits on "sick care health care." Great short read is Marvasati, Farshad Fani, and Stafford, Randall, From sick care to health care—reengineering prevention into the U.S. System, *N Engl J Med* 367:889–891, September 6, 2012.

to innovate ceases. This is one of the reasons that S&W became lethargic. In the 2005 timeframe, things were going so well at S&W that innovation driven by "need" seemed to cease. As stated earlier, this need to innovate was replaced with a single strategy of growth.

In population health, a healthcare organization needs to be doing the right thing for the patient at the right time for the right reasons and only in the amount that they really need. From a patient's perspective, this is sometimes hard to discern. If their doctor says they "need" a test or procedure, they need it. Right?

Asymmetrical information from healthcare providers has a risk of causing patients to utilize more than they need. Making quality and outcome metrics transparent can help produce superior outcomes and remove the fear of under care. Major changes are still needed to get health systems in the United States closer to the realm of appropriate care.

S&W leaders knew population health was coming. However, they also recognized health systems that did this too well were punished financially for doing the right thing.

S&W ran its own health plan and served as the largest teaching hospital in central Texas. This, combined with a tight-knit community focus, kept it from cranking the overuse wheel in a fee-for-service sick care reimbursement model. To most S&W physicians, S&W's philosophy of "do the right thing" seemed like the right way to do medicine.

S&W continued to reduce even more Unnecessaries:

- Scans
- Tests
- Defensive medicine[*]
- Consecutive specialists doing additional exploratory procedures
- Surgeries

All of this reduced S&W's length-of-stay in hospital areas and resulted in low costs per visit for both Medicare and commercial insurance claims. However, S&W was missing the revenue that less-strategic competitors were gaining by maximizing fee-for-services.

As a result of these effective practices, S&W partnered with a large national retailer to provide certain complex surgeries directly to its

---

[*] The Free Dictionary, *Defensive Medicine*, http://encyclopedia.thefreedictionary.com/ Defensive+Medicine.

employees. One of them is spine surgeries. Large employers know that S&W physicians choose the best pathway for patients, even if it is <u>not</u> to do surgery.

A common story related by S&W staff is that their orthopedic and spine specialists have told overweight patients, "You don't have a *back* problem (pointing to their back); you have a *front* problem (making a curving motion around their belly)!"

In other words, spine surgery will not help in some cases when the root cause is a belly weighing more than two bowling balls pulling on the spine. In these cases, the right thing is first to give the patient guidance in exercise and eating skills. It is difficult to get reimbursement for these services in today's healthcare reimbursement model.

If there is nothing structurally wrong with your spine, the likelihood of spine surgery curing your back pain is low. In addition, if the back pain continues after the first surgery, there is an increased likelihood of having a second surgery. This negatively affects the quality of life for the patient.

Confusing Leaders—Management Systems and Gurus Everywhere

Management books, "experts," tips, techniques, articles, magazines are everywhere. There is an opinion on every corner, especially if there is a business school or large consulting firm nearby. However, there seeming to be few pontificators who can prove that what they say actually works.

Something was still missing. Bob wanted a management system, a path to follow. But, which one? How does one manage? There are many theories in business school about how to manage. But, what if it does not tailor or scale up to healthcare? Moreover, what if S&W needed to exit or change from one management system to another? Would this create more chaos and fear than the original problem?

Bob had seen first-hand how staff members, even good ones, used many ways to block new programs and major changes. The root was fear. These fears often keep leaders from acting until it is too late.

It is a learned thing. Most people are afraid to change because the new or in-process state *might* be worse than where they are today. Therefore, people apply many tired excuses to avoid change. Leaders do too. It is really fear that is preventing them from changing.

The first type of fear is revealed by statements like, "I don't want to be a micromanager or be micromanaged." This is the most common change-blocker by managers in healthcare. The second is more subtle. It sounds more empowering and even executive-like. It says, "I trust my people! Why should I be involved in what they do day-to-day?" The third type of fear is very common and actually covers up other problems. They say, "This data about my department looks bad (or makes me look bad), so it must be wrong."

Steve's rant: In the manufacturing world, a leader "owns" his or her processes *and* the data by which they make decisions. It is the leader's decision to make. If a leader says to his or her data, "This can't be right. There is no way my area is that bad," the leader would be summarily fired before these words left his or her lips!

It is the leader's job to answer the question "Why?" when the boss probes into a "missed" metric or goal, and to have an action plan already in place—before anyone asks. The leader must also fix his or her own data pipeline by which he or she makes day-to-day decisions. The leader owns the decision, so he or she must also own and correct the data used to make it, no matter how scattered the original data is.

Steve argues this is perhaps the biggest difference between manufacturing and healthcare processes.* When an issue would arise, sometimes with inaccurate or missing data, Steve's first sensei would point to a cot, always visible in the corner of the manager's bullpen.

Sounds draconian. However, the intent was clear. Fix it! Or, sleep here until you do. Who must make the decisions? Who else will build these feedback systems? The workers? Sure, they can and do collect data and document issues—as directed. However, when would they design and build the management systems for collecting and feeding it back? While they are working?

---

* Steve also answers manufacturing leaders with another key difference, "Your 'product' doesn't yell at you, or complain when it waits!" This difference is proof that healthcare needs Lean principles even more.

True, there seems to be a more pronounced data "lag" for decision-making in healthcare. Developing a "pipeline" of accurate and quick feedback data is hard. It takes effort. However, what are the alternatives?

The problem is much worse in healthcare than just poor data. It is said that culture eats strategy. Well, culture can eat root-cause problem solving as well! Here are two ways:

1. If a leader is allowed to attack any data that makes him or her "look bad," it is likely that organization will either do nothing or (worse) overreact based on anecdotal data and develop time-consuming work-arounds.
2. If a leader attacks not only the data pointing to a problem but also the messenger bringing up the problem, it is likely that organization is building *a culture of blame and shame*, rather than a culture of accountability and problem solving. Staff quickly learn <u>not</u> to bring problems forward.

Most health system leaders say they have great people working in broken processes. For that reason, Lean thinking as a system seems to be common sense for health systems. However, it is not common.

According to a benchmarking study of 77 hospitals by the American Society for Quality (ASQ):[*]

- 53% of hospitals report some level (minor, moderate, or full) of Lean deployment
- 42% report some level of Six Sigma deployment
- Only 4% of hospitals reported "full deployment" of Lean

Have you heard these statements? What can you do to counter the fear that underlies them? Whose job is it to fix the processes? What about the data pipeline by which leaders make daily decisions, with frequency and accuracy? Whose job is that?

Answer the questions what, by whom, and when for each data stream—hopefully it is daily or frequently for direct performers.

---

[*] Pizzi, Richard (Editor), Hospitals embracing Lean and Six Sigma strategies, *Healthcare Finance News*, March 24, 2009.

In order for Lean management to truly be effective, all staff need to know and think Lean. The same ASQ study showed that reasons for lack or delay in deployment in Lean or Six Sigma were:

- 59% lack resources
- 41% lack information
- 30% lack leadership buy-in
- 11% are not familiar with either method

Systems Thinking: Big and Small

Some programs that swept through management ranks early on were good. In Peter Senge's seminal management book *The Fifth Discipline*[*] he furthered the concept of the *learning organization* as well as *systems thinking*. In systems thinking, the fidelity between an action and the data resulting from that action needs to be as soon and as close as possible.

A good example of quick feedback loops is driving a car. You notice that you are passing the other cars on the freeway. A glance at the speedometer gives you an instantaneous data feed that you are way over the limit. You remove pressure on the accelerator, and watch the change in the data feed until you are back at the speed limit.

As systems get more complex, the feedback mechanisms need to become more and more robust. A good example is your own physiologic system. If a person decided to walk a path through a park, he or she needs continual feedback on the journey.

To stay on the path requires numerous feedback loops. For instance, the brain has to decide you are going to go from here to there. The brain has to say, "Right foot, move!" Then it needs feedback from the proprioceptors and the pressure receptors whether the right foot moved, if the body is balanced and if it moved into danger.

Then, you have to use your eyes to see if you are still within the boundaries of the path. Each time your senses show you are off the path, all of the prior systems react in order to get you back onto the path. What if the path forks halfway down? The brain needs to decide which path, and then follow the processes again. Quick feedback mechanisms are vitally important in life. Why would your organizations and work processes be different?

---

[*] Senge, Peter, *The Fifth Discipline: The Art and Practice of the Learning Organization,* Doubleday, 1990.

In management, there are many paths from which to choose. It is the job of management to make sure the organism or organization is on the right path, headed in the direction, with quick feedback and at the pace that will keep it out of danger.

Think about how hard this would be on a path if your feedback only came months after each "step" occurred! In healthcare, leaders change a process, but then typically do not get results for months or even a year later. You would never do this with a patient. However, healthcare processes are often hidden. And, processes outside of a leader's line-of-sight are someone else's problem, right?

Lots of Operating Systems: Which One?

In the same book, Senge introduces the concept of a *learning organization** where staff members continually expand their ability to create results by introducing and using new ways of thinking. One way they do this is by nurturing and setting free good ideas. This allows staff to continually try small changes and learn from them. Senge concludes only those organizations able to adapt and respond quickly and effectively will excel in their markets.

Another management system theory is *management by walking around* (MBWA). If you never get out of your office to see what is happening do you really know how your organization is functioning (or dysfunctioning)? However, is it enough to walk around?

Leadership author and speaker John Maxwell likes to say, "He that thinketh he leadeth, and hath no one following, is only taking a walk."[†] The authors' version of this is, "If they ain't following, you ain't leading." You will see in Chapter 4, Step 4: Daily Lean (LMS) how a leader Gemba walk takes this to the next level.

Yet another theory is *management by objectives* (MBO), or goal setting. With typical goals, leaders often do not know if they obtained the goal until many months has gone by. Is that rapid enough to make the changes and adjustments necessary to course-correct? In today's fast-changing environment, probably not.

---

[*] Senge, Ibid.
[†] Maxwell, John, *21 Irrefutable Laws of Leadership*, Thomas Nelson, Nashville, 1998.

MBO also has an unintended consequence. Sometimes, leaders will hit one or two goals at the expense of several other key categories that are not measured (or rewarded) equally. In healthcare, this can be disastrous. See Chapter 6, "*What You Measure is What You Get*" for a similar story. Goals need to be balanced. This should create some tension for leaders. They cannot maximize all balanced goals at once. The right sweet spot must be found—and it moves.

With all of these management systems, Bob had another question. He thought, "If I am walking down a well-worn path, is the path well-worn because it is over-used (lemmings?), or is there a better path?" This is where leadership comes in. Leaders need to know which path to move down and how fast in order to lead their organization away from danger and toward a place they can survive and even thrive.

A System That Ties Together Other Good Micro-Systems

Bob learned about the Toyota Production System (TPS), aka Lean Manufacturing, briefly in business school. Bob likes to say that TPS principles *hard-wire* every successful management technique into a leader's daily work. Granted, knowing these principles is not enough. You must also practice them—daily.

Bob also reminds us that you cannot implement just one or two tools. You must implement the whole system. The system is a more important concept than the parts or tools. Today, S&W does faster and faster PDCA loops using Lean thinking plus many of the above theories. To this, they add good goal-setting, strategy, organizational development, and problem solving micro-systems. The overarching construct is a common way of thinking—an operating system.

Imagine PDCA cycles, faster and faster, deployed by more and more staff, fixing your processes for decades. What would you get? You would get something akin to Toyota's ribald production systems.

It is a system. A bunch of individual automotive parts lying on the ground will not get you to the church on time. Nor will a football team that only knows offense make the playoffs. Successful Lean transformation is a continuous process. It requires effective teaching and discipline to follow through. It is a system.

Have you ever visited a Toyota assembly facility? Most have an on-site museum demonstrating TPS principles. They also offer free tours every day. Why do they give it away free? What is in it for them?

On a different note, how much preparation did you do the last time a top leader or dignitary visited your facility? Toyota workers keep their facility clean because *they* work there, not because an outsider will visit. Workers are the key part of any system. How involved in daily management and improvement are your workers? Why? TPS holds much promise for healthcare.

Bob's Bold Statement

Bob made a bold statement in early 2012. After seeing Toyota assembly workers with his own eyes, Bob was introspective. After his tour, a question-and-answer session with Toyota leaders and workers highlighted a "gap" and ignited questions in his mind. The gap he saw was total vs. spotty engagement.

Steve asked Dennis Raymer, a senior Lean coach and former employee at Toyota Motor Manufacturing in Kentucky (TMMK) to help arrange a tour. Dennis not only arranged the tour, he also introduced them to samples of Kentucky's finest industries—bourbon, healthcare, and of course auto manufacturing!

A bourbon-tasting seminar was put on by a local distributor—a big hit with the leaders. They first honed their listening and reasoning skills as a

Getting into the mind of a healthcare CEO:

For three years, Bob felt a growing need. After a few years of focused Lean efforts, ideas were flowing nicely from team members in the dozens of facilitated Lean projects each year. Ten to fifteen team members would go on a fantastic journey. But Bob often thought, "How do the hundreds of other staff in this area, and the thousands of others in our growing organization, participate?"

True. In every workshop, S&W facilitators posted flip charts and asked for outside input. But, how? Bob also thought more than once, "Why do these projects take so much time?" Time for teams to get to a stabilized future state and time away from their work.

local brew master expert explained the different ingredients, process steps, and precision that go into making some of Kentucky's premier products.

The next day, Bob and his leadership team toured the Toyota factory first to see TPS in action. They saw Toyota's museum area, then viewed a wide assortment of team huddle boards throughout the factory on a moving tram. After, they cornered their tour guides and a very helpful Public Affairs Manager with questions like:

- Why do team members seem so happy at what seems like mundane, repetitive jobs?
- How do team members get time to work on problem solving and continuous improvement?
- How, where, and when are so many ideas generated?
- How are team members rewarded for their ideas?

The guides explained they rotate jobs every two hours for safety and extensively cross-train workers. A guide also said, "Toyota hires every team member for their brain, not just their hands." Even better, the Public Affairs leader said Toyota's philosophy is that every employee is seen as a future vice president. They can choose not to become one, but every employee is seen as much more valuable than the job they hire into. Guides gave examples where nearly every promotion came from within. Even their highest-level leader, the General Manger, was promoted all the way up from a Production Team Member.

The leaders heard of Toyota's low turnover, extensive hiring process (12 rigorous steps while being evaluated closely as a temporary employee for months) and development plans (six or more weeks for every 60-second set of tasks at a workstation). One surprised leader asked, "Why train them for so long when they are just shooting screws?" The guide turned the question on him asking, "You deal with lives, so how long do you train your typical workers before they start?" Silence!

The leaders heard the number of ideas that Toyota employees try out each year. It was much more than a few ideas per staff member each year. They get thousands per year, mainly during their huddles.

Bob looked like he was about to burst. Answers came so easily from the shop-floor guides. They actually lived the TPS philosophy he read so much about. This was going to be a fun reflection session when the management team met after the tour.

After seeing Toyota, they toured a local hospital in Lexington. This facility used Lean principles and had just improved the flow through their emergency department. They engaged staff in a redesign of door-to-door patient flow. The result was a dramatic drop in ED length of stay (LOS) times—from hours to minutes! When asked how they accomplished this, they got the same responses they heard while at Toyota. They just involved staff to remove waste and improve flow.

A connection was reinforced in the minds of the S&W leadership team. Having all staff involved in continuous improvement was the key to success. Moreover, staff do not push back on their own ideas. There is ***buy-in through involvement***.

As the team gathered to reflect, S&W leaders gushed about what they saw and heard—mainly at Toyota. However, they were not making the leap to S&W processes and people. Bob asked his question again, "How can all our staff try their good ideas out every day?" Silence. Bob added, "And why do our Lean projects take so much time?"

Bob clarified, "Our ideas come mainly from our Lean projects, right?" Yes. "How many ideas do we actually implement in a typical project?" Maybe 10 to 20 for a small A3 Problem Solving team and up to 100 for a larger Value Stream team, so maybe 30 is a conservative average. "How many projects do we do in a year?" About 40 to 60. "And, how many employees do we have?" Around 14,000. "So, at the end of every year, we only implement about 1 idea for every 10 staff members per year?! Do we even ask them?"

Bob saw it. Sheepishly, the other leaders did too. Leaders must "allow" ideas to flow. No one even asked most staff members for their ideas! Making matters worse, if ideas were somehow brought forward, management provided no quick feedback systems for staff to see if their ideas worked (the *Check* step of PDCA). Worse yet, staff members were often told, "Just wait until next year's Lean project starts. Maybe you can bring your idea forward at that time!"

It was hard for Steve to hear this. S&W's current management systems and Lean projects were actually limiting the flow of ideas. Like "hooks" on an overhead conveyor, S&W's team members had few opportunities to formally bring up and try out their ideas. In most cases, no one even asked. Depression set in!

Every great solution starts with a strong or urgent need! This need was huge. They say necessity is the mother of invention. Well, S&W needed a big mother!

> Bob made a bold statement to his leaders that night. He said, "I know our staff members have just as many ideas as these good factory workers." Here it comes. "I need *ten times* the number of ideas from all staff implemented this year! And, they need to do this without spending time away from their work!"

Steve saw daily idea-generating systems at Toyota, and then helped develop them at auto suppliers and as a consultant to many great firms in the 1990s and 2000s. Steve also helped teams win multiple Shingo Prizes at Air Force Repair Depots utilizing huddles and daily Lean ideas.

However, this was healthcare. Data was inaccurate and rarely fed back to staff quickly enough for analysis and decisions. In addition, this was healthcare! Could it work there?

Because you are reading this book, you know the answer. In fact, Bob and Steve believe it works even better in healthcare than in other industries. Why? Need! Moreover, there is a natural desire to engage in healthcare, to offer opinions and ideas. Somewhere over the past three decades, healthcare systems adopted Sloan-style, management by objectives (MBO) systems that told workers to "check your brains at the door and just do what we say." What a waste!

Bob and Steve are happy to report that they have maintained a pace of ten times the number of implemented ideas without even one more minute away from their work! In addition to great Lean projects, they now huddle and try out ideas while they work! It is not magic. It is Lean Management Systems!

Toyota Changed the Value Equation (aka Only One Way to Thrive)

Toyota's initial entrée into the U.S. auto market was ugly. A little export vehicle called the Crown (sold as the Toyopet Crown; Toyopet because of their very small size) had reliability and other image problems.[*] Dr. Edwards Deming was brought to Japan not only to fix quality problems, but also to build quality into the processes. Toyota in particular quickly learned to reduce variation and solve problems—deeply. Natural resources were scarce

---

[*] Truett, Richard, The Toyopet Crown: Rocky start for a future giant, *Automotive News*, October 29, 2007.

on most islands, so getting it right the first time was more of a need than just part of an operating philosophy.

Toyota once again ramped up their export pipeline to the United States. As more Corollas and Camrys were driven with very few problems, the American appetite for well-built small cars increased. When gas prices soared, Toyota was there in a new sweet spot with well-built, fuel-sipping small cars. However, Toyota's *financial* innovation caught U.S. Big 3 automakers by surprise. Their equation of how a business earns profit or secures its future was most profound. In addition, it applies to healthcare.

As Toyota ramped up to sell cars in the United States again, they were confused by the application of an inflated sticker price on the window of each model. The cars Toyota sold back home were "market" or "no haggle" priced. However, U.S. Big 3 automakers used "Cost-Plus" for the most part. The difference could not be greater.

A Big 3 automaker determined the sticker price of a new vehicle by first adding up its costs.* All costs! Even the costs you would not ever pay for if you knew. We would all agree that rubber, steel, and tested electronic components were valid costs to pass along. Direct labor was part. However, would you pay for excess inventory, kept just in case, rather than delivered just in time? What about bad parts made?

How about the costs of hundreds of employees that did not add value for various reasons (inventory counters, "light duty," hiders, seekers, union officials, and workers under contracts that required certain numbers to be on a factory payroll but actually did not build cars)?

What about the thousands of vehicles headed for sales lots? Are these costs just "passed along" too? What about inflated wages, even when these companies were headed for bankruptcy? They couldn't possibly be passing along all those costs to consumers. Yes! Someone needs to pay for them, right?

Now, on top of all those costs, an automaker also applied a "plus" factor. You know, to cover the other things not mentioned above. Things like new product launches, and for correcting all the launch mistakes that invariably happen. Other items in the plus factor might be advertising—those Super Bowl ads are darned expensive—cost-of-living and pay increases for next

---

* This example is based on some knowledge of the auto industry, but is only an estimate. The authors believe most products sold in America with discounts, heavy advertising, and constant "sales" are still priced in a similar way.

year, and gosh, those top leaders need big bonuses, just like the leaders in other industries.

An example may help this hit home for you. Let's say you want to buy a basic crew-cab pickup truck. The costs—all in—for one built in my old hometown near Detroit might be $24,000. The plus factor might be another $6,000. That leaves a sticker (shock) price of $30,000. Over twice the price of my parent's first home in a Henry Ford factory town subdivision bought in 1964.

Now, you are not going to pay $30,000 for that pickup truck are you? What does the company need to do to trick—sorry—to encourage you to buy its vehicle? That's right. Rebates. Discounts. Big ones!

Let's say this truck was purchased when gasoline prices were high. Do you know how much the total givebacks or rebates were? Usually $8,000 to $10,000! Are you doing the math? What was the base cost? What would be the profit or lack thereof? Do you understand why bankruptcy was the "only option" for a few of them? Do you think it could happen again?

Toyota, and now several other automakers, changed the equation when they started selling vehicles in the United States. They used market pricing. Even today, it is unusual to see large discounts, even at the end of a model year. Most Toyota dealers are independent, so this varies.

The truth is, "The market determines the price of a good or service!" Thus, Toyota believes the only thing they can do is teach all employees how to identify and eliminate waste. Each employee must come to work every day with two hats. They are to do their job very well (first hat). And, they are to improve their job and work processes (second hat). Or else…

It starts with the market price. The market determines the price of a good or service! The market. Do you see where this equation leads you? It changes what was thought to be fixed and what was variable. Next, all employees must be taught and encouraged—no, expected—to remove waste from their work processes every day! So, do you? How many ideas were implemented last week? How about the week before?

Only after waste is removed can a profit (or a "viable future") be earned. In summary, the only equation and the only way to thrive and ensure the

How much urgency for cost reduction is there when all costs are passed along to the customer (or at least attempted)? How hard is it to wean oneself off this type of system? Who benefits from inflated revenue and the inevitable "yard sale" pricing discounts to move the vehicles? Who loses?

Here is Toyota's innovative equation:

Sales (market) price – reduced controllable costs (by eliminating all waste) = profit (and viable future)

organization's future relies heavily on the secret weapon—ideas in the heads of good employees.

So why walk through this auto example in a book about healthcare? Cost-plus. Around the same time that Toyota started market pricing and blasting away waste, a major "pricing" change was also occurring in healthcare. It started with Medicare and raced through most forms of reimbursements for healthcare services.

There once was a time when healthcare billing was cost-plus. Find an old hospital bill from a birth that took place pre-1980s. The numbers look low compared to today's standards, but *all* costs were passed on to the customer.

Cost-plus reimbursements actually stifle innovation. Some early attempts to curb runaway costs happened in the 1980s—first in the form of Diagnosis-Related Groups (DRGs). DRGs were first tested in New Jersey in 1980, with reimbursement changes spread across the United States starting around 1983.[*] Medicare paid for DRGs, not for every nickel and dime someone dreamed to pass on as costs. Insurers followed with their own versions of DRG-based reimbursement. Like it or not, this is market pricing. The sands shifted.

Next came the Health Maintenance Organization (HMO) experiment. HMOs were designed to do the right things for the patient in just the right amounts. However, did this experiment work? Although it did bend the cost curve somewhat, patients hated HMOs because they restricted their access to what they wanted from their healthcare providers. In addition, profit (margin) can increase under HMO capitation by withholding services. If the services were necessary and withheld, outcomes (especially those that were not measured accurately) could suffer.

In the era of HMOs, the payment structure for the first time changed from fee-for-service to a capitated payment. With capitated payments, a health system was paid on a per-member-per-month basis. This fee over a

---

[*] The Free Dictionary, *Diagnosis Related Groups,* http://encyclopedia.thefreedictionary.com/Diagnosis+related+group.

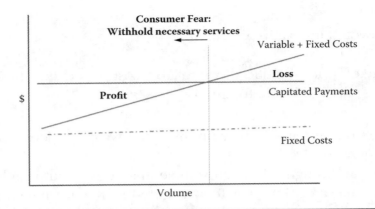

Figure 2.5   HMO capitation—crossing the line.

period of time, say a year, remains constant—no matter how many health services the patient utilized. Since the total cost is a sum of the fixed cost plus the variable cost, as volumes increased, costs went up.

Therefore, in Figure 2.5, when the volume causes expenses to cross the line of capitated payment, then profit turns to loss for a health system. During the HMO era where quality was difficult to define precisely, it was a perception that HMOs made money by withholding necessary services. As our nation moves forward rapidly into population health with capitated reimbursements, this is a perception healthcare leaders must combat with proper rewards and a balanced set of outcome measures.

After unraveling HMOs, change and pressure for innovation quieted down for about a decade. Some healthcare entities once again saw the outline of their "old paths" through the sand. Healthcare costs skyrocketed again. The United States spent 17.9% of its GDP on healthcare in 2011, by far the highest in the world.[*]

Health and Human Services expects total healthcare costs to continue their upward march, reaching 19.5% of GDP by 2017.[†] In 2012 U.S. health care spending increased 3.7% to $2.8 trillion, or $8,915 per person.[‡] This

---

[*] WHO, *World Health Statistics 2011*. Geneva: World Health Organization, 2011.

[†] Keehan, Sean, Sisko, Andrea, et al., and National Health Expenditure Accounts Projections Team, *Health Spending Projections Through 2017: The Baby-Boom Generation Is Coming to Medicare*, Health Affairs Web Exclusive, February 26, 2008.

[‡] Centers for Medicare and Medicaid Services, http://www.cms.gov/Research-Statistics-Data-and-Systems/Statistics-Trends-and-Reports/NationalHealthExpendData/downloads/highlights.pdf, accessed August 2014.

is 4.6 times the entire defense budget, including all overseas contingency operations (wars) and is still growing!* Innovation is desperately needed!

Since Toyota started market pricing and teaching staff to remove waste daily, two very good U.S. automakers went bankrupt. Why? One reason was that not all employees were removing waste every day. Were they allowed or asked to remove waste? Another reason could be that their *cost-plus* pricing model hides waste. In addition, their financial model rewarded them. Since all costs were passed on to the customers, reducing them lowers revenue, right?

Now, let us look back at healthcare. In nearly the same year that Toyota started driving these two great automakers bankrupt with their value equation, healthcare was also changing to market pricing. However, what has the healthcare industry done in the past three decades to respond to these major changes? Has cost-plus thinking gone away? Is healthcare "immune" to this type of cost pressure?

Toyota feels the only equation that works is to teach all employees to identify and eliminate waste. Every employee comes to work every day with two hats. There has never been a greater need for this type of thinking in any industry in any time than in healthcare now.

The Promise

It has been said, those things that can't go on, won't! We are at a crossroad where healthcare costs must come in line with what the American people can afford. The promise of Lean thinking in healthcare, if deployed widely, is that we can take out 25% or more of total costs by removing wastes.† To illustrate, 25% of $2.8 trillion is $700 million year over year!

This will allow us not only to afford the best healthcare in the world, but also the most effective healthcare in the world. Lean thinking allows us to capture creative ideas that every employee has within himself or herself. Ideas must be requested, encouraged, and operationalized with discipline to make them real. This is the job of leaders. Leaders must build these systems.

---

* Amadeo, Kimberly, U.S. military budget: components, challenges, growth, http://useconomy.about. com/od/usfederalbudget/p/military_budget.htm.
† Pear, Robert, New health official faces hostility in senate, *New York Times*, July 26, 2010.

What Percentage of Your Creative Brainpower?

Steve met Dr. Edward Marshall a few years after his book *Building Trust at the Speed of Change** came out. In one group meeting, he asked Steve and other leaders, "In the form of ideas, what percentage of your creative brainpower is your organization asking you for and implementing daily?" Dr. Marshall paused for effect.

Steve thought hard. He served as sensei to dozens of industry leaders for their continuous improvement efforts. What would these leaders say? What would their staff say? Their percentage estimates were likely very low—even for those who led Lean teams!

As stated earlier, Steve helped build *Daily Lean* idea systems in manufacturers, and even helped Air Force repair sites win coveted Shingo Prizes with these systems. Many organizations tried types of *Suggestion Systems*, some even tried to automate them. However, Steve had not seen any healthcare organizations get close to the successful daily idea generation of Toyota. Not even close. Why are these seemingly simple systems so difficult to deploy?

These questions would hound Steve and other Lean healthcare coaches. Try as they might, large improvement projects led by professional facilitators were still the most common way for staff to bring their ideas forward. However, there were only so many large projects that a healthcare organization could "stomach" in any given year!

In these large projects, 12 to 15 project team members would have an incredible experience. They would learn much. However, how would the other 99% of staff in that building bring forward their ideas? What was the vehicle by which *they* could learn and experiment with their work processes?

Need. There was and still is a great need for staff to bring forward improvement ideas daily. However, there was scarce time for every single staff member to go through a facilitated project. This natural tension helped S&W create its version of a Lean Management System—a system to generate and try out daily Lean ideas by all staff. You will read more about this in Chapter 4, Step 4: Daily Lean (LMS).

---

* Marshall, Edward, *Building Trust at the Speed of Change: The Power of the Relationship-Based Corporation*, AMACOM, 2000.

Countering the Two Biggest Excuses

Steve marvels at corporate mottos and vision statements that say they desire to be the leader in their industry. However, the first thing executives say is, "Which of my competitors is doing this?" In addition, if he only had a nickel for every time he heard, "*It won't work here!*"

The litany of excuses grew old for Steve as he engaged healthcare organizations. It was the same story as manufacturers and other industries earlier. "That's OK for widgets and cars, but this is healthcare." "Our patients are sicker." "We are an academic medical center." "My supervisor doesn't believe in this stuff." And the ever-present, "We've tried improvement workshops before—the changes don't stick here!"

One big tip the authors have for readers encountering these arguments is this: Just try it! Try it again. This time, add effective huddles and some leader time in the Gemba to your deployment plan. After just a few weeks of huddling at Scott & White, leaders still heard detractors saying, "It won't work here!" They would say, "Come and see. It can, and it is!"

The second big excuse is, "*This is more work!*" The peanut gallery rallies around this excuse a lot in healthcare. The authors wonder if these leaders realize they are saying it. Many leaders have become so mired down in fire fighting and work-arounds they feel they do not have time to actually solve problems and eliminate waste. Is there a better investment of time than to take 15 minutes today to solve a problem that will save a team 15 minutes per day for the rest of their careers?

Bob frequently told his staff, "It's not extra work—it is **the work**!" The authors are not even certain themselves how it happens, but when leaders start huddling daily and doing Gemba walks, they have more—not less—time! For lack of a better term, the authors call it the *Meeting Buster Principle*. What would normally be a 60-minute meeting request with the leader shrinks to a brief question while on a Gemba walk or in a huddle.

Leaders often need to quickly discuss and decide on key issues. But, when? Everyone you need to discuss options is present at the huddle, so the mini-huddles that "break out" after every team huddle are *Meeting Busters*. Don't schedule separate one-on-one meetings. Just huddle! It is the work.

You will read about Gemba walks in more detail in Chapter 4, Step 4: Daily Lean (LMS). In these Gemba walks, the leader makes him or herself available for continuous improvement, to build Lean Management Systems and to ask and answer questions. Leaders ask the *Four Questions* to reveal the absence or presence of Lean Management Systems, and they follow up. They always follow up.

After conducting weekly Gemba walks for a month or two, most leaders concur this *is* their work! Moreover, it is fun to see quick impact as you unleash your staff's creative brainpower!

> How many ideas have your departments implemented today? How about this week? Why? Ask them.

Chapter 3

Philosophy

To me, there's always a better way to do things. I was always looking for a way to improve. The most exciting part of medical practice is creating opportunities to improve.[*]

—Everett Veirs, M.D.,
Director of Ophthalmology, Scott & White, 1945

Oxford Dictionaries define *philosophy* as (1.3) a theory or attitude held by a person or organization that acts as a guiding principle for behavior.[†] The guiding principles S&W prescribes for work processes are those promoted and used by Toyota called TPS. One guiding principle is to maximize value to the customer while minimizing waste. This means creating more value for good customers using fewer resources by eliminating waste. Thus, a perfect process would have zero waste.

Lean thinking is an outcome or major goal of S&W's Continuous Improvement (CI) philosophy. Lean thinking changes things. It is not a course. It is not a department.

One big philosophy shift where leaders focus. Management typically focuses on controlling silos, command-and-control, organization charts and, loosely, power. Leadership in the new way of thinking focuses on end-to-end processes by which customers get what they need. They empower staff to fix broken processes. Work processes cut and slice through the silos and departments. Is it clear who does what and when?

---

[*] Benoit, Patricia, *Scott & White Beyond 'The Hill:' The Quest for Quality 1988–2012*, S&W Healthcare, 2012.

[†] Oxford Dictionaries, *Philosophy*, http://www.oxforddictionaries.com/us.

> Who manages the patients from end-to-end through their continuum of steps? The short answer in healthcare is no one! Moreover, in healthcare, this results in multiple hand-offs. Hand-offs can be sources of patient safety issues.

One warning: Some readers may want to skip this section on philosophy and maybe the next on how Scott & White applied it early on. This would be a mistake. Many organizations and leaders have visited S&W in the past few years. All leave vowing to whip up a few huddles and repeat the successes they saw at S&W. Bob and Steve marvel at this thinking.

Maybe it is possible. More likely, they will fail. Then, they will declare that TPS does not work in their organization. This is not true. There is an underlying philosophy, a way of thinking that needs to change. And, it changes slowly. Just ask Bob and his team of leaders.

Toyota's Philosophy

> Excellent firms don't believe in excellence—only in constant improvement and constant change.
>
> **—Tom Peters**

Is it possible for a leader to communicate a simple philosophy to all staff, and then have future leaders live out that philosophy in their day-to-day decisions? For how long? Decades? Toyota seems to have done so, if you consider some quotes from founding leaders, in chronological order.

> "Everyone should tackle some great project at least once in their life. I devoted most of my life to inventing new kinds of looms. Now it is your turn. You should make an effort to complete something that will benefit society."
>
> **Sakiichi Toyoda,**
> *Founder of Toyoda Loom Works, 1926*[*]

---

[*] Liker, Jeffery, *The Toyota Way: 14 Management Principles from the World's Greatest Manufacturer,* McGraw-Hill, New York, 2003.

"I plan to cut down on the slack time in our work processes... As the basic principle in realizing this, I will uphold the 'Just in time' approach."

Kiichiro Toyoda,
Founder of Toyota Automotive Co., 1937[*]

"All we are doing is looking at the time line from the moment the customer gives us an order to the point when we collect the cash. And we are reducing the time line by removing the non-value-added wastes."

Taiichi Ohno,
Founder of the Toyota Production System (TPS), 1940s–1970s[†]

"The key to the Toyota Way is not any individual elements... But what is important, is having all the elements together as a system. It must be practiced every day in a very consistent manner—not in spurts... We place the highest value on actual implementation and taking action."

Fujio Cho,
CEO, Toyota Motor Corp., 1999–2005[‡]

Can you hear the same, simple philosophy cascading down a long line of leaders for the past century? Sakiichi spoke of building something more beneficial than just a factory. He speaks to his associates. Kiichiro speaks of cutting slack or waiting time. Waiting time for his associates and customers.

Taiichi speaks of removing non-value-added wastes to cut down time more and more to the benefit of the customer. He used "we" a lot. We the people. In addition, Fujio speaks of the Toyota Way as a system, practiced consistently every day by his leaders and associates. He calls for action. Action from Toyota's secret weapons—their people.

---

[*] Ibid.
[†] Ibid.
[‡] Ibid.

What is the single-sentence philosophy that is communicated to all staff from your Chief Executives? If they can't state it, why not? Do your executives "walk the floor?" Do they know names? One of the biggest shifts in building a culture of continuous improvement is to believe "It's all about people!"

Long-time employees at Toyota in Kentucky all tell Steve the same things about Cho-san:

- "He was always on the shop floor, dressed in a Toyota team member shirt. Some thought he was a production worker or a team leader."
- "He greeted many associates by name. How did he remember all those names?!"
- "Just before Christmas, Cho-san would walk the entire factory, smiling and shaking hands with every associate, thanking them for their service, and wishing them a Merry Christmas. All 5000 of them!"

Toyota has been blessed with a series of unremarkable but consistent leaders who live out and communicate the same consistent philosophy, every day.

Patient Centered

A physician does not derive much satisfaction from the practice of medicine unless he has learned the art of medicine. The art of medicine is the ability to win and keep the confidence and esteem of the patient. [Dr. Scott and Dr. White] appreciated that this was accomplished by a sympathetic interest, a ready availability, a thoroughness of service, a consistent dependability, a gentle sincere conduct and a practical knowledge of medicine. They knew that if you manifest and exercise these properties, your patient will trust you, and with confidence, will accept your diagnosis and treatment.

—Dr. G.V. Brindley,
Who worked with Drs. Scott and White in the early 1900s[*]

---

[*] From the S&W surgery website, http://www.sw.org/surgery/history-surgery-dept, accessed September 2014.

Every health system in the world talks about becoming patient centered. So, what is it about patient-centeredness that is so hard to understand? A big one is that the patient is the center, not the provider, healthcare system, or payor. What patient or family wants to come to a clinic and wait? What patient wants to wait in an emergency department only to be placed in a hallway after some evaluation? What patient wants to arrive on time for a surgery, only to be told that it will be a few more hours because they started late again?

Is initial ED wait time important to the patient? Many billboards advertise this! Steve calls this phenomenon "billboard wars." The authors emphatically state the total process time, from arrival to discharge, is what really counts to patients.

Figure 3.1 shows two billboards directly across the highway from each other around 2009, when "billboard wars" swept over the metro area of a rust-belt city. The backstory with these images is quite funny. These two organizations, and a third that followed with its own billboard, argued in public about the accuracy of each other's advertisements.

The advertiser of "zero wait" turned off the waiting clock when the patient saw a nurse inside one of their many rooms. However, the other two facilities insisted that the clock could not stop until the patient saw a physician or mid-level provider. The sad part about "billboard wars" was that, possibly, none of these organizations actually reduced the overall length of stay in their EDs. The authors again emphatically state the total time is what really counts to the patients. This requires a new, Lean view of the end-to-end patient flow and support processes.

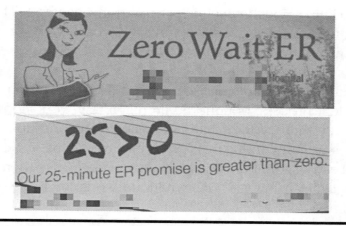

Figure 3.1 "Billboard wars" on opposite sides of the highway.

> The authors again emphatically state the total time is what really counts to the patients. This requires a new, Lean view of the end-to-end patient flow and support processes.

Once we drop all pretense that a provider or company is at the center, then patient centeredness actually becomes quite natural. We just ask, "What adds value in the eyes of the patient?" Then we find better ways to deliver value without all the waste and delays. We use the collective wisdom of the team to focus entirely on the patient.

This is Lean thinking. It starts with a focus on what the *customer* values. Lean principles applied by teams create patient-centered processes. Any approach focused on the provider, training, or "scripting" will pale in comparison to blasting away at issues and waiting times. Whose waiting times? The patient's! Lean greatly improves flow. Whose flow? The patient's!

> Listening to customers must become everyone's business. With most competitors moving ever faster, the race will go to those who listen (and respond) most intently.

> **—Tom Peters**

Another critical part of TPS philosophy is it is a system. Again using Oxford, a system is a set of connected things or parts forming a complex whole, in particular, a set of things working together as parts of a mechanism or an interconnecting network.* The system is best described in general in the Toyota House Model, which is discussed in Chapter 3, The Toyota House. You cannot use a tool or two and say you are done, or that you built your Lean system. In fact, you can use TPS and the phrase continuous improvement system synonymously.

The sad truth is that leaders, disconnected themselves from the continuous improvement process, bought the lie that a few workshops done by staff would make their system Lean. Steve heard the question from leaders many times in many industries, "When are we going to be done with Lean?" Since Lean is continuous improvement, Steve asks them to repeat their question again using CI. "OK, when are we going to be done with contin…" Hmm.

---

* *Oxford Dictionaries*, Ibid.

When you eliminate waste in an end-to-end process, it creates new ways of serving customers that need less space, capital, human effort, and time. Customers love the results. Moreover, you can make your products and services at far less costs and with much fewer errors.

With these results, your customers will applaud and you will have fewer real competitors in your region. Better yet, your organization will be able to respond to the rapidly changing healthcare (or any other) environment with ever-improving quality, cost, access and very fast end-to-end process times.

The Improvement Philosophy for Healthcare

The authors need to bust a popular myth. It is that Lean thinking is only suited for manufacturing. Lean applies to all processes. Do you have any work processes? Are they perfect yet? All industries have processes, and none is perfect yet. As an improvement philosophy, Lean thinking works.

It is also useful to state some things that Lean is not. It is not a cost reduction program, although it does reduce costs. It is certainly not a head-count reduction program, although it does free up staff for more value-adding work. It is not a program. Its main purpose is not short-term cost reduction. Rather, it is a way of thinking and acting for your entire organization. It is the way the organization operates and gets work done.

Sometimes, a sensei will add transformation after Lean because the philosophy is to be applied to more than just a few tools or processes. It is a new way to conduct business. Because this requires a change in the way all staff think about work and processes, it takes longer, sometimes a lot longer. This will require a long-term perspective and perseverance by leaders, board members, and staff.

Organizations in all industries, including healthcare, are using the principles of TPS to improve all processes. Even the U.S. government is applying Lean thinking to its work processes! So is Scott & White. Their philosophy is to teach all staff to think Lean for themselves. Then, they will apply Lean in their daily work processes. TPS creates Lean thinkers, who reproduce more Lean thinkers, who continuously improve all work processes.

Bob Finds His People-Based Lean Philosophy

Video: Bob Pryor presenting the President's Award for best Lean project, CLIP Fair, November 3, 2011

How would a competing healthcare organization go about getting these same improvements? I have been in many, many hospital systems. I know. They would have found the best consultants to help them in a particular area like the OR. Then they would have sourced them with a big contract. They would have taken the "high value but low bidder" and it would have cost them, say, $100,000 per area.

After promising a lot of efficiencies, the consultants, who know nothing about the hospital system, would take the *plan du jour* from their previous client off their word processors, add a few recommendations they heard from our people, hand it out, and then leave. By the way, most of these $100,000 engagements never achieve the promised savings because leaders do not really understand the changes proposed.

So, what is the alternative? We bring in the people who really know what is to be done. These are the people who are working on the front lines. It's you. You know the people. You know the speed bumps and obstacles. You know your processes. You know how to make them better. You know what the future state should look like.

We turn you loose and what do we get? We get the results you all showed in this year's projects. Good news! We didn't pay $100,000 each project for useless consultants. And, we had absolute change for the good! Thank you for doing what you do best!

There are well-worn old paths to cut costs. One way is to use outside consultants to remove a fixed amount of cost. The easiest and quickest way to reduce costs is to cut people. However, when you cut people without improving their underlying work processes, you end up with a design that makes everyone equally unhappy—patients, staff, physicians, and administrators.

The easiest and quickest way to reduce costs is to cut people. However, when you cut people without improving their underlying work processes, you end up with a design that makes everyone equally unhappy—patients, staff, physicians and administrators.

Hiring Process *(12–18% turnover in healthcare)*	*Redeploy Good Staff* *(12–18% turnover in healthcare)*
• Sourcing candidates (recruiter)	• Redeploy and cross-train known good employees
• Interviewing candidates	
• Second round interviews	
• Job offer (negotiate)	
• Offer accepted	
• Notice period	
• Relocation expenses	
• Training	
• Start-up and on-boarding	
• Productive new employee	

Figure 3.2   The common sense of redeploying good staff.

The authors admit that organizational expenses can be lowered through layoffs. However, here is what often happens to healthcare organizations using "layoffs" in small downturns. Over time, because processes have not changed, they are forced to add people back because they do not know any other way of working. Lean thinking changes work processes, which adds more value to more patients with the same or even less staff.

Traditional cost management says cut staff. Lean says change the processes and free staff up to add even more value in this area and elsewhere. Without changing the processes, cutting staff only shifts work tasks from those laid off onto the providers and nurses—and that really ticks them off!

Figure 3.2 shows the common sense of redeploying good staff. This does require an active Human Resources team and cross-training. However, redeployed staff members do not need orientation or training about the company systems—they are already on board. The right side yields increased staff morale and feelings of job security, but more importantly, trust. Staff turnover costs much more than any simple financial analysis can show.

How about you? Have you seen situations where layoffs only added more work onto frontline staff like nurses, technicians, and providers? Did some high-performing workers leave because of this? List as many costs of a single turnover as you can.

Read the bullets on the left side of the list in Figure 3.2. There is a cost to each of these. The cost is sometimes called "hidden" by a finance leader. To staff leaders in areas of high turnover, there is nothing hidden about these wastes. Someone needs to do each of these tasks. At what price? Usually, developmental and continuous improvement activities suffer, and that yields more turnover.

Earlier, we discussed Bob's great need as he started again at Scott & White. Here is how he stumbled upon a new way of thinking.

For months, Bob looked for a change effort that matched his needs and set of circumstances—his philosophy. One thing was certain: he knew what *didn't* work!

Before Bob returned to S&W, they agreed to the services of a consulting firm that promised quick financial results. The consultants charged a lot of money, but promised a plan that quickly returned three times their costs. After a few weeks of talking to staff, S&W departments were told to rank all staff and then cut a specific percentage of them as noted in the consultant's report.

The percentage of immediate layoffs matched their 3-to-1 return promise. Ta da! The consultants left, cashing their large check. Layoffs were announced. Many families in central Texas cried that night.

Within a few weeks, it was clear these layoffs cut a little "fat," but also some muscle, sinew, and bone to use a human body analogy. Within a few months after the consultants cashed their check, most laid-off staff members were hired back, at least those willing to come back. Factoring in the consultants' fees and staff overtime in the interim, actual costs went up after staff was added back. In addition, a "trust" bond of sorts with staff was broken.

Bob was determined to find a change effort that better matched his philosophy and maybe that of Central Texans in general. Bob believed in people. People were the answer, not the problem! S&W could not do patient care without them. Bob was searching for a change effort that would help them build a culture of continuous improvement.

Bob believed S&W staff members had something to say, that they had ideas for improvement. Without knowing much about TPS or Lean, Bob's personal philosophy was drawing him toward TPS. Bob believed in people, and the center pillar of TPS is *Respect for People*. Bob learned that layoffs were a last resort. Toyota hires most full-time staff for life.

At a meeting of healthcare leaders, Bob met an executive who pioneered the application of Lean in his healthcare system. Bob asked him if he could see Lean healthcare in action and implement those at S&W. He said, "No. You can't begin to understand at that low level of involvement."

Bob was disappointed at that time. However, the leader was right. A superficial engagement never sustains. A transformation effort where leaders delegate system building to Lean coaches, low-level staff members, or consultants never works.

As Bob considered Lean principles for S&W, many consultants came knocking at his door. He asked if they would teach Lean tools to his S&W staff. Every one of them, "guaranteed" Bob they would train and implement Lean across his entire organization in a year or two.

Bob and Paul Dieckert looked for a seminar on process improvement. There were dozens if not hundreds of seminars—most very technical and statistical in nature. Some were taught by consultants, some by universities, but few by actual practitioners and leaders. Part of their decision was to choose best-in-all-industries vs. best-for-healthcare for Lean training.

In addition, Bob did not want to attend a change program led by speakers in white coats, other MDs. He wanted to learn from engineers who had deep experience fixing broken processes, and who were successfully practicing these techniques. Bob and Paul chose a university-based Lean healthcare program where Steve was a lead instructor at the time.

Steve taught two days of the program for Bob's group. After the first day, Bob and Paul were very excited. Bob called and emailed nearly all of his leaders about what he was learning. He believed he had found the philosophy to build a culture of continuous improvement at S&W.

He commented, "Maybe it was just the cold and snow, or the wine we had at some great restaurants, but I really believed applying TPS to healthcare was the answer!" After class, Bob and Paul spent their evenings thinking about and discussing how to apply Lean thinking to the work processes at S&W.

After class, Bob confidently stated his plans to Steve—Lean training, top-down with leaders for a whole year or more to get a "critical mass" of Lean thinkers. He asked Steve, "What do you think?" Steve said, "You have 0% chance of success by just teaching Lean! You need to ensure every staff member also quickly applies these tools."

The key to making Lean "stick" is not just teaching tools, it is doing them. It would be like learning to fly a plane from a book. You need to try it out, chunk-by-chunk, usually at the elbow of someone who knows what they are doing. In addition, you need to allow staff to make small mistakes and learn from them.

It is a lot like learning medicine. It is a philosophy or a way of thinking. In the immortal words of Mr. Miyagi, "Either you karate do 'yes' or karate do 'no.' You karate do 'guess so,' [makes squish gesture] just like grape."*

Steve offered to help any leader in his seminars if they just called, promising he would not charge them for phone calls. Bob and Steve hit it off immediately. Steve agreed to serve as a sensei to Bob, a relationship that continues to this day.

If Lean were to take hold at S&W, their philosophies had to match. Expectations and timeframes for change had to match. Steve had learned from great senseis. He felt he could serve in a similar fashion for healthcare leaders like Bob.

It all starts with people. Bob had a belief in people. Like many leaders reading this book, Bob felt he had good people working in completely broken processes! When you have good people working in broken processes, then the TPS philosophy will fit well. If you start with the philosophy that continuous improvement is all about people, that people are the solution, then applying TPS will make sense.

It is a lot like learning medicine. It is a philosophy or a way of thinking.

Like many leaders reading this book, Bob felt he had good people working in completely broken processes! When you have good people working in broken processes, then the TPS philosophy will fit well.

---

* *The Karate Kid*, Columbia Pictures, 1984.

Go, No-Go #1: CEO-Driven

If you choose to head down a people-based Lean path, it will require new ways of thinking by leaders at all levels. The authors feel it is impossible to do this unless the highest levels of an organization are completely engaged. The only model that seems to sustain in healthcare is when the CEO, or at least the highest-level leader in a large division or region, is driving and directly in charge of the change effort.

Bob says, "Unless the CEO is willing to humble himself or herself, take Lean and Lean leadership courses, and then apply them, it will not work!" False levels of commitments are when the CEOs say they "won't get in the way," give their "permission," or worse, say they will attend a few "steering committee meetings." Unless the C-level leaders roll up their sleeves, you have no chance of sustaining daily improvements. Leaders must build and spread. It is worth repeating. Leaders must build systems by which ideas are requested of all workers, tried out, then checked. And it's their job to "spread" good ideas they discover on gemba walks and during audits.

Go, No-Go #2: No Layoff Policy

One item Steve and Bob discussed early on was a no layoff policy. Once started, there should be no layoffs in the areas collecting staff ideas and applying Lean. Barring any major business downturn, no one should be laid off because of Lean improvements in that area. You do not lay off people who are bringing forward ideas. The process under study should be considered immune to layoffs. Steve said the flow of improvement ideas would stop if workers trace their ideas to layoffs, even if it was a colleague.

Steve describes this unintended consequence using a hockey analogy. If you rough someone into the boards, you get two minutes in the penalty box. If you lay someone off in an area where you have been actively implementing staff ideas, you will be in the penalty box in that area for two years!

As Steve walked through hundreds of healthcare facilities, he could often "feel" the workers' apprehension. Leaders would confess that they recently had layoffs or reductions in force (RIFs). Steve would shake their hand and leave, stating, "See you in a few years."

How would this work in your organization? Could your CEO or C-level leaders write this? What would happen if they did? What would happen if they did not? Why is this important?

However, Steve emphatically states that Lean ***always*** frees up staff. There is no conflict in this truth. As you remove waste, worker time will be freed up. It is best to prepare for this in advance with a clear *plan for people*. What would S&W do with freed up staff? Growth and turnover exceeded productivity improvements at S&W for decades. In addition, Steve guessed there would be few staff members at S&W freed up at first, but this would increase over time.

The leaders agreed they would strategically avoid replacing some staff that leave in an increasing trend over a multi-year period. With a *plan for people* around turnover and growth, Bob confidently wrote a key **COO/ CMO Corner** message on the company intranet: "There will be no layoffs due to applying TPS/Lean in your work processes!" Something was different in the air at S&W!

While it is true that a no layoff policy is needed, the authors recognize the black-and-white world that a CEO, CFO, or accountable leader lives in. Return on all investments is needed. The only way to get hard dollar savings is to remove cost permanently from an operation. However, you <u>can</u> have it both ways—no layoffs and eventually big cost reductions. Lean thinking actually works on both sides of the financial coin—increased capacity and decreased cost.

Here is how. Lean greatly reduces waste in processes by having all staff implement improvement ideas. The net effect of removing waste from staff members' days is more capacity. Sometimes an organization can capitalize on that increased capacity to add patients and services (with the same staff). S&W started a very successful Same-Day Appointment effort to capitalize on this effect.

However, sometimes an organization cannot add more patients or services immediately. In this case, staff can be freed up to work elsewhere. There are great employees at S&W. One characteristic of a great employee is his or her ability to improve work processes daily and focus on the customer. Staff who do Lean make great leaders in other areas.

What is your turnover rate by all position types? Do you sometimes struggle with getting good workers replaced? Do you have examples where staff were promoted from within? Why or why not? Lean provides a great answer—keep, cross-train, and promote all good workers internally!

It's All about People

A mediocre person tells. A good person explains. A superior person demonstrates. A great person inspires others to see for themselves.

—Harvey Mackay

It starts with a belief in people (Figure 3.3). Some healthcare leaders say, "Hey, we involve some workers, too." *Some* workers? It is *all* about people. It starts and ends with people, from beginning until, well, it never ends.

Figure 3.3   It is all about people.

As news of Scott & White's early successes spread word-of-mouth and through Steve's university seminars, healthcare leaders would ask, "How does Scott & White engage its staff so well?" This may sound funny, but Bob and Steve say, "We engage our staff… by engaging our staff!" S&W leaders build systems for PDCA and then ask staff daily how they can improve processes for their customers. They listen, and then let workers try out their own ideas.

Staff will eventually demand to have their ideas heard. Staff feel it is right and natural to be asked for their opinions and ideas. If encouraged only briefly by leaders early on, staff will demand involvement. S&W has a high-level leader teach this principle (two hats) in day one of their orientation. Imagine what new S&W staff members would say to their supervisor if they were told to keep their ideas to themselves!

Bob and Steve also get questions about training programs, consultants, or even rewards programs. The answer to successful engagement is not training programs, consultants, or rewards programs. They engage staff by directly involving them in change activities using their own ideas.

Figure 3.3 shows a few of S&W's different change activities. Clockwise from top-left, you can see Lean course participants being led through a value stream mapping exercise by instructor Sundeep Boinpally. Most students take their classwork back to their offices to start another great Lean project.

Next is a nursing huddle in S&W's Memorial Hospital ED, followed by a 3P Lean layout workshop. These workshops reduced up to 20% of new floor space if done before locking in the shell of the building. How much would that save your organization?

Next is some try-storming on the floor with masking tape and then an effective leadership huddle in Temple. The 6-North nursing huddle on the bottom left is led by staff member Domingo Parra and Director Gale Baumgartner, followed by Dr. Mark Holguin at his huddle board (more on his team in Chapter 4, Lean Project Example—Chemo Infusion). The center picture shows a 5S exercise in a storage closet in Brenham.

How does S&W engage its staff? By asking. And allowing. And building systems that encourage and help check ideas. And daily huddles—lots and lots of huddles. Engagement shows more on the faces of staff than in any number. S&W's annual survey "Highly Engaged" scores indicate they are doing something right! More on that in Chapter 4, S&W's Employee Engagement Outlier.

The Goal: Building a Culture of Continuous Improvement

At S&W, there is something larger than its Lean or TPS effort. The goal is not to do Lean or use Lean tools. Rather, they are building a Culture of Continuous Improvement. There is such a thing as a Culture of *Safety*, just as certainly as there is a (negative) Culture of *Blame and Shame*. There are work cultures that encourage quality improvements, and even ones that focus on implementing ideas to improve the health of S&W staff.

In David Mann's book, *Creating a Lean Culture*, he defines culture in a workplace as the sum of the habits people rely on to get things done; "The way we do things here."*

S&W leaders desire to create their own culture—the S&W way of doing things—and tap the reservoir of ideas in the heads of staff just waiting for a chance to be heard. The authors encourage the readers as well to seek their own culture. Make it your way. Do not just copy the exterior trappings of the Toyota or S&W way.

A useful tip in David's book is that bad habits must be "extinguished" rather than broken.† Most leaders achieved their levels by acting in ways that worked for them in the past. However, some of their old, well-worn paths lead in a direction opposite of TPS principles.

TPS does not reward "do whatever it takes to get through the day." TPS condemns it. Rather, a *find it-fix it* culture, a leader as servant culture, and a continuous learning culture must trump some habitual reactions by leaders. It is not easy. However, it can be extinguished by practicing the simple concepts found in this book.

S&W is on a journey that includes all of these important ideals. But in the beginning, it focused mainly on work process improvement. As Bob noted earlier, he had good people working in completely broken work processes. This needed to be their priority.

The interesting thing is that S&W also achieved quality and safety improvement, as well as staff and patient satisfaction improvement as it dramatically improved its processes. A great example of this was when S&W improved waiting times enough to kick off their Same-Day

---

* Mann, David, *Creating a Lean Culture: Tools to Sustain Lean Conversions*, Second Edition, Productivity Press, New York, 2010.
† Ibid.

Appointments effort (see Chapter 5, Same Day Access Effort Using Huddles).

The Japanese word for continuous, small improvements is Kaizen. Kaizen means change for the good. Thus, continuous improvement is a way of thinking, of always being alert to the opportunity to make improvements. If you put these two together, what do you get? Our habits, the way things are done around here is for all staff to be alert to opportunities to make changes for the good.

S&W asks staff to find ways to improve, then listens and helps them make it happen. Leaders are alert in every way possible to bring forward a maximum number of ideas, involving as a many people as possible in this never-ending process. That is a culture of continuous improvement!

Investing in People

In Figure 3.4, people do not come out of school or other workplaces thinking Lean. They start at *Today* feeling like "slump man." His shoulders are slumped. He may have been told many times, "Just get back in your hole… we don't want to hear your ideas!" If he becomes a leader, he may not feel equipped to lead process improvements and problem solving for the team.

Tomorrow man has some swagger. And, more important, he has a key. Think of this key as being the key to his work process. If you can somehow transfer ownership, with the improvement tools, to the workers to change their processes, it is like giving them the keys to their own car!

How do good staff members get from where they are today to tomorrow? The authors like the quote, "If you always do what you've always done, you'll always get what you've always got." It has been attributed to Abraham Lincoln, Albert Einstein, Henry Ford, Drayton McLane, Susan Jeffers, Tony Robbins, and many others. No one is certain who said it first, but it is true.

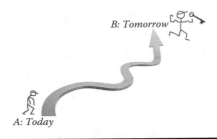

Figure 3.4 Investing in people—what is your plan to get them from today to tomorrow?

> We know inherently that it is not one change, but hundreds of improvements daily that are needed to fix our broken healthcare processes.

Something has to change! Max DePree made a similar quote. He said, "We cannot become what we want to be by remaining what we are."

You will get the same results every time if you do not change and improve the process. Moreover, we know inherently that it is not one change, but hundreds of improvements daily that are needed to fix our broken healthcare processes.

Something has to change to get from where we are to where we need to be. The question for you is what needs to change? These changes are not going to come through training, although we need to train the minds to think differently. It is not going to come through brute force or the strong will of dynamic leaders. It is not going to come from staring at metrics, or spending a lot of cash on consultants. The first change is to release something. Leaders must act to release ideas from their staff.

Healthcare and knowledge workers are natural problem solvers. They have opinions. They want to discuss ideas. For goodness sake, they run local PTAs and coach Little League teams. They want to be heard. Leaders just need to allow them.

Lean provides a way to do more and more with the same or less human effort, less equipment, less time, and less space. More value with less waste. Lean is a *behavior*. Lean is a *way of thinking*. Lean is a *mentality*, and more importantly, Lean is a learnable *culture*.

It would help, at this point, to define Lean better. The phrase "Lean" is often distorted, especially as consultants add "Lean" to their services, with few changes in philosophy.

So, what is Lean Production and where did the phrase come from? There have been many, many books written about continuous improvement since the mid-1980s. One of the first books that documented Lean Production was Dr. Jim Womack and Dan Jones' *The Machine That Changed the World*.[*] It started as an MIT study commissioned by Jim. He and his graduate students studied the best companies in multiple industries in both Japan and the United States.

---

[*] Womack, James P., Daniel T. Jones, and Daniel Roos. *The Machine That Changed the World: The Story of Lean Production*. HarperPerennial, New York, 1991.

The students compared the best companies in Japan with the best in America on a few key metrics. They found some consistent results. They found that the best in Japan made their product type with roughly half the floor space, in half the time, with half the people-effort and at half the cost!

It was almost as if they all used a common production system. They asked Jim what they should call this phenomenon. He said he would call it Lean, Lean Production. Some popular diet programs were designed to reduce daily calorie intake by half. It looked to Jim like these were production systems on a diet—half the space, half the calories, with the same or better output.

The phrase Jim used in his book stuck—the differentiating techniques Toyota and others used would be called Lean Production or just Lean. Since Jim's book, Lean has been commonly used to describe the principles and practices of the Toyota Production System.

Lean Production. The authors like one of these words for health-care, but it is not what you think. They like the word *production* for health care. They believe every individual produces something of value for patients or internal customers. A research worker produces valuable research and information for an internal department. A nurse produces something as small as patient comfort and as large as life-saving interventions.

The word they do not like is *Lean.* If you listen to workers from the auto industry or from any of the rust belt states, Lean somehow equates to lay-offs, downsizing, outsourcing, or at least, working harder. If you ever hear a CEO or a leader say, "We need to get *lean* around here; need to do a little belt-tightening," what is that code word for? That's right, it usually means lay-offs, downsizing, outsourcing, and working harder. However, visit a Toyota facility. Ask them about layoffs.

So, what is Lean Production? Lean Production, as used throughout this book, follows the increasing body of knowledge and way of thinking called the Toyota Production System. TPS at its core seeks to eliminate waste to optimize value. Lean thinking then is using TPS principles to rethink your entire business. In this book, TPS, Lean and Lean thinking are used in synonymous ways.

Philosophy—Inclusiveness

Good ideas are borne, not by suppression but by inclusion.

—State Rep. Roland Gutierrez, Texas

Why do leaders often throw out the baby with the bathwater when it comes to change efforts? The authors think some blame lies with consultants, or as they call them, insultants (spelling correct). When consultants "sell" services to a leader, they need to make their services seem unique or different. This requires, delicately, challenging prior change efforts at the "prospect" organization. Their "assessment" will likely conclude that prior efforts' tools and techniques were ineffective. The consultant dangles a few "success stories" from competing clients, and voilà. New insultant in, prior change effort out.

Sometimes it is easier to give up than to fix all of the governance, people, and process issues that encumbered prior efforts. So, the new consultant team charges in with a new set of terminology, making the same missteps as previous efforts. The organization experiences a similar, slow learning curve for a year. However, the organization still lacks proper governance, people, processes, and self-sufficiency to make and sustain changes. Wash. Rinse. Repeat.

There is another way. A key difference in S&W's philosophy after *all about people* and aiming for the higher goal of *building a culture of CI* is *inclusiveness*. Figure 3.5 shows three prevailing continuous improvement toolkits. There are many more toolkits or slices of CI tools, but these three will suffice to make the point. Organizations often make a mistake of swinging the pendulum from one side to another, as if they needed to choose one toolkit or the other.

S&W leaders do not believe one needs to choose toolkits. Only how much of each and when. Six Sigma is placed on one side of the pendulum, Theory of Constraints (ToC) in the center, and Lean or TPS on the right. ToC is a toolkit first made popular by Eliyahu Goldratt in his book, *The Goal.* Leaders often ask Steve, "Which one are you?" Steve answers, "I ordered a cheeseburger." In other words, the question is silly.

Steve often jokes in his training courses, "Leaders pay good money for what you are going to hear next!" And, they do. Let's look at the focus of

---

* Goldratt, Eliyahu M., and Cox, Jeff, *The Goal: A Process of Ongoing Improvement*, North River Press, Great Barrington, MA, 1984.

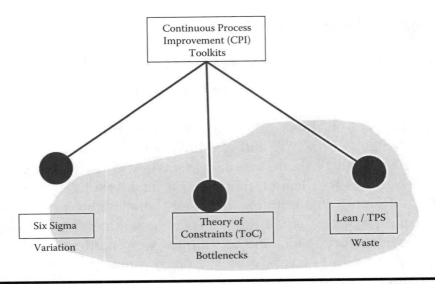

Figure 3.5 Continuous process improvement toolkits. S&W focus for all staff is highlighted.

each of these toolkits in a nutshell. Each toolkit, philosophy, or way of thinking can be explained with a single *focusing* word. Six Sigma can be summarized as the constant identification or elimination of variation—variation in all of its forms. Errors are a form of variation, as is using different work methods with varying results, or veering from the target in some way. In healthcare quality improvement, one goal is to eliminate all unintended clinical variation. You can see how needed this toolkit is.

Now, let's consider Theory of Constraints. Most people do not know a lot about this body of knowledge, but it is important in any transformation. Theory of Constraints can be summarized as the constant identification and elimination of bottlenecks or constraints in a process. Imagine making improvements in a single process step or department that is not the bottleneck. What is the net flow or overall time improvement for the patient or staff member? Usually, there is no impact. In fact, the patient, lab sample, or pile of paper will likely just wait longer before the bottleneck step, which has not been changed. Therefore, Theory of Constraints is the constant identification and elimination of bottlenecks, one at a time, using the thinking steps popularized by Goldratt. Again, much needed.

Variation for Six Sigma, bottlenecks for Theory of Constraints. For Lean, you can summarize it in one word as well. Lean is the constant identification and elimination of—you guessed it—waste! Waste in all of its forms. A short definition for waste, especially in healthcare, is the stuff workers hate

A short definition for waste, especially in healthcare, is the stuff workers hate to do, like walking, searching, waiting, and filling in the same information repeatedly. Waste sucks the life out of people. They did not go to school to do non-value-adding tasks!

to do, like walking, searching, waiting, and filling in the same information repeatedly. Waste sucks the life out of people. They did not go to school to do non-value-adding tasks!

If you look at all three of these "competing" toolkits, people often ask us, "Which one does S&W use?" They ask, "Are you a Six Sigma or a Lean house?" What are you?

The answer lies in purpose. What is the purpose of the tools? Is it merely to use each tool or keep them from getting rusty? No, tools have more than one application, but they have only one purpose—to build or fix something, like a house.

S&W's purpose is to build the strongest possible healthcare delivery and support processes. It is building a strong healthcare house at S&W. If the tools help, it uses them. If they do not, they are set aside for now. Would a master builder throw out finish carpentry tools because they are roughing in the frame right now? Would he throw out hand tools and only use fancy new electric gadgets?

Why would you ever argue that part of a transformation toolkit be un-used? The TPS and S&W philosophy is to use the right tool for the right situation. In this way, it is very inclusive. Maybe that word is too small as well. Mature organization-wide transformations use <u>all</u> of these tools in some way, shape, or form at some point in "construction." As noted earlier, the construction process can also be called transformation to denote the higher goal.

Look back at Figure 3.5. You will see a highlighted area around most of Lean with quite a bit of Theory of Constraints and a little bit of Six Sigma. This describes the S&W toolkit for the first few years and what is taught in core curriculum for the "masses"—all staff—at S&W.

S&W's purpose is to build the strongest possible healthcare delivery and support processes. It is building a strong healthcare house at S&W. If the tools help, it uses them. If they do not, they are set aside for now.

The reason why S&W trained all staff members in this highlighted area first is simplicity and applicability. Some of the statistical portions of Six Sigma did not translate well to all staff. Neither did the monetary and scheduling portions of Theory of Constraints, and some advanced concepts from the Lean house. Eventually, all were taught and deployed.

This is not to say they are not important. On the contrary, safety, quality, and reducing variation are of the utmost importance. Quality is everybody's job in healthcare. If you get quality, you get cost and many other improvements as Brent James demonstrated in his popular Advance Training Programs for healthcare.*

S&W teaches a lot of CI principles to the masses. However, like great specialists in healthcare, it is usually better to have just a few internal experts who master the advanced quality, safety, Six Sigma, and scheduling concepts, and then help all staff apply them. To accommodate the other areas of the toolkits, S&W employs some full-time Black Belts, scheduling, and advanced Lean tool experts on staff who have mastered these deep toolkits.

S&W's philosophy is to teach all staff to use basic Lean tools and to think differently. S&W expects all staff to know and use the principles in the highlighted area. In addition, they expect them to apply these principles without outside facilitators.

Dilbert cartoons are funny because they ring true. One particular cartoon was funny because the boss said they decided to try something new—Six Sigma. Dilbert said it was developed in the 1980s, and then pulled out his smart phone and read that most companies using Six Sigma trailed the S&P 500. The boss fretted.

It is easy to tease the "partial toolkit" efforts, because alone, they cannot fully transform. Trying to build a house with a partial toolkit is similar to throwing the baby out with the bathwater. This is opposite of the inclusive philosophy that fuels improvements at S&W.

The Toyota House

That brings us to the Toyota House. A change agent (that's you) must spend enough quality time on this important model to understand what it is and

---

* Institute for Health Care Delivery Research, Intermountain Healthcare, https://intermountainhealthcare.org/qualityandresearch/institute/courses/atp/Pages/home.aspx accessed August 2014.

why. This book was not meant to be a primer on Lean. However, it is important that the reader understand the timeless unchanging principles so that you can apply them properly, and avoid making the usual mistakes by skipping important steps.

S&W uses the Toyota House as a way of developing work processes and then constantly improving them. They use the house model because it reminds staff of the sequence and importance of TPS principles. It also reminds staff that it is a system. As such, there are few short cuts, work-arounds, or microwaved learning options. The Toyota House model for S&W represents how Lean tools and Lean thinking fit together.

At Johnson Controls, Steve had the opportunity to sit under some very good mentors. One of them was Mr. Phil Beckwith, a general manager. This period of time also allowed Steve to learn from one of Toyota's more famous senseis. His name was Hajime Oba.

This story will help you see TPS in a new light. In one of their first meetings, Steve had the opportunity to ask Oba, "What is the Toyota Production System?" Oba-san pulled out a piece of 11 × 17 inch (A3) paper and started drawing the Toyota House model. Steve saw this method repeatedly with his mentors. There is much here to learn.

You may have seen different house models. Figure 3.6 may look like yet another. However, this is how it was described to Steve. This is still the model that leaders use at S&W today to build strong processes.

Oba-san drew a foundation box first. He said it all starts with a foundation of operational stability. You cannot improve a process unless it is stable. People make this common mistake in implementing Lean or TPS. You cannot improve a process unless it is stable. In addition, you cannot improve unless you have a baseline for key process metrics. Stabilize first.

Oba said the foundation includes many timeless, unchanging, unwavering principles. They are always implemented. Oba wrote several principles on the foundation of his drawing such as Standardized Work, Kaizen, and Waste Elimination. He said, "You are never done! But, you have to get a start on these things, or the remaining principles in the house will not work." Steve shook his head eagerly, waiting for more.

After that, Oba drew three pillars. Figure 3.6 uses Americanized words. The first pillar is labeled Just In Time (JIT). Oba said, "You must build everything Just In Time; never early, never late!" Never late made sense, but never early? He went over to the far right pillar and wrote

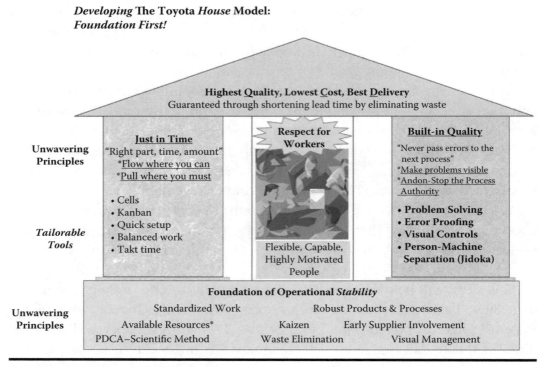

Developing The Toyota *House* Model:
Foundation First!

Figure 3.6   **The Toyota House model.**

"Jidoka." The authors use literary privilege to call this pillar Built-in Quality.

Oba said, "As you start to improve flow, you quickly eliminate waiting and much waste. As you do JIT properly, you're going to go much faster. When you go faster, the tendency is to make more errors. No good!" He said, "For every *one* ounce of energy you put into JIT, you must put *two* ounces of energy into Jidoka (Built-in Quality) or you will only make junk quickly. And, you will not ship me junk seats!" As he started to unveil the Toyota House model, there was something beautiful about it. It fit.

The center pillar was Respect for People. It is also called the People pillar and sometimes adds "flexible, capable, highly motivated people." He said, "All of these things, foundation of stability, doing all things Just In Time, and Built-in Quality must be built around the people that do the work every day. They have to understand and use these principles," not some experts or consultants. The workers need to know and use TPS daily.

The whole house is centered around people. It might be better portrayed as surrounding, supporting, or behind every piece of the house. The foundation of stability, pillars of Just In Time and Built-in Quality, and the whole house is wrapped around people. Results come through people, rather than from management or the system itself.

What you get at the top of the house is a key. Obviously, you cannot put the roof on a house until it is done. Oba drew the roof of the house. What he said was powerful. He said, "I guarantee you, if you build your production processes this way, your company will have the highest quality, the lowest cost, and the best delivery in the business!" He added to the roof, "guaranteed through shortening lead time by eliminating waste." The Toyota House. He was so confident about its outcomes.

Oba-san looked Steve in the eye and gave one more guarantee as well. He said, "If you do not build your production system this way, you will fail." He said, "I want you to remember, it is not TPS that failed. You failed!" He said, "Steve-san, you are going to fail." Steve thought to himself, "We are Johnson Controls. We can't fail!"

Steve asked, "How will we fail?" He said, "You will skip the foundation. You will move on to something sexy like cells and Kanban. And, when it doesn't work, just remember this: You skipped something important in the foundation!"

He said, "Steve-san, you are now a very dangerous man. You have only partial knowledge of TPS. You must promise me that you will do nothing until we meet again." Steve said, "Okay, I promise..." with his fingers crossed.

Steve headed back to the JCI Headquarters in Plymouth, Michigan. As soon as Steve got back, a component plant leader on the East Coast called. He said, "Steve, we heard you are a Lean expert. Can you help us Lean out a seat track line?"

Steve flew out immediately. He walked to the production floor with the Director of Manufacturing who called him. They saw production departments separated by great distances with piles of inventory—a perfect application for a one-piece flow cell. There were five welding machines in separate departments that welded a seat track (slider). These machines could be picked up with a forklift and moved together quickly to create a cell.

Steve drew a sketch. Pleased, the Director of Manufacturing had skilled maintenance people scramble to slap together the most beautiful one-piece flow cell ever made! It flowed clockwise in a tight cell. Workers were close together. Their work would be well balanced. It was a beauty.

The next morning was Friday. With great anticipation, and many on-lookers, they watched as the new cell coughed out assemblies in fits and spurts. It looked like Lean, it smelled like Lean, but it ran like crap! After one full shift, they could see something was wrong. Their "perfect" one-piece flow cell was down, not making anything, for more than half of the shift.

Steve remembers the Plant Manager approaching him yelling, "I told you this Toyota stuff wouldn't work around here! I told you!" Steve disappeared into a nearby office and called Hajime Oba. He said, "Oba-san, help! Plant Manager is trying to kill me!"

When he discovered who was calling him, he said, "Steve-san, what did you do?!" Just then, it hit Steve—the promise. He promised he would do nothing until the next week. Steve confessed saying, "I created a one-piece flow cell at our seat track plant. And, it was down half of the shift."

He said, "Steve-san, you failed. You failed big time. Just like I said. You big failure!" Steve said, "What do I do?" He said, "Change back." Change it all back?! So, with maintenance and forklift drivers smirking because of Steve's "mistake," all five welders were moved back to their original departments. Dejected, Steve headed back to Michigan.

When he met Oba the following week, Steve asked, "Oba-san, what did I do wrong?" He said, "You failed. You skipped the foundation, just like I said." Steve said, "How did I skip the foundation?"

Oba said, "You skipped a foundation principle—Preventive Maintenance." He took Steve's cell sketch and asked, "What is the uptime (opposite of downtime) for welder 1?" Steve said, "About 88%. Sometimes we forget to change weld tips, we run out of wire, the air and water supply lines are dirty in our old pipes, and, well, workers are not always back from breaks on time. So, 88% is not bad for this type of welder." Oba frowned.

Oba asked the same question for the next four machines, and wrote percentages of uptime ranging from about 86% to 91% on the drawing. Oba said, "Steve-san, your cell is doing exactly what you designed it to do— break down!" Oba continued, "When you put these machines in series, the whole cell goes down when one machine is down. Thus, you can multiply the uptimes together, and what do you get?" Steve saw it. It was exactly the down-half-the-shift result they experienced.

Oba said, "Until each piece of equipment is up and available 99% of the time, do not pick them up and slap them into a one-piece flow cell! It is not TPS that failed, it is you that failed. You skipped the foundation!" Depression kicked in for Steve. JCI had never achieved 99% uptime for a welder. Heck, in those days the workers were not even at their workstations 99% of each shift!

Most leaders at that time did not feel 10 to 12% total lost time was a big deal. When they produced parts in large batches with excess equipment in the old welding departments, they covered up the fact they were down a lot for small issues. When a welder was down, they just moved production to an idle machine next to it. Or, they just grabbed inventory from the large stockpiles, to be overfilled again later. The accounting team was supportive of this as well. Inventory was an asset. You could borrow against it. It puffed up ratios that included assets. And, you could always sell the stuff, right?

In a cell, when equipment is placed in series, you can calculate the net system uptime. Multiply the percentage up time from each of Steve's machines together $(0.88 \times 0.86 \times 0.90 \times 0.89 \times 0.87)$ and guess what you get? Workers sitting on their hands for half of the shift. No products for customers for half of a shift. Not stable.

If you do not get a good start on the key principles in the foundation, the bigger impactful parts of the house will not work. It is guaranteed. However, if you do get a good start on any key foundation principles, and if you put the walls up at the same time (Just in Time, Built in Quality), and build all these tools and thinking around the people, guess what you get? You get the same guarantee Oba gave to Steve. You will get the highest quality, the lowest cost, and the best delivery in the business. Guaranteed.

This is called the Toyota Production System House. It is not about the tools. The tools either do or do not help you build strong processes. So, build a strong house!

There is a sequence to the way you build. You lay the foundation first. You cannot put the walls up before the foundation is in place and cured. You cannot put the walls up before the foundation is cured. You have to get a start on all foundation principles, and then you put all three walls up at the same time. They must be true to each other. They must support each other. They are inseparable.

In addition, you cannot put the roof on without all the walls, can you? It will fall in. This house model demonstrates both the sequence and the

Note: In Figure 3.6 in the foundation, the authors use a more generic phrase "Available Resources" because it fits better for healthcare. In the Toyota Production System, this critical principle is called "Preventive Maintenance" (PM). This is the basic availability and uptime of key pieces of production equipment.

In healthcare, it is not pieces of equipment that create value for a customer; it is people. People are the caregivers. To create a one-piece flow cell in healthcare, leaders and change agents would cross-train and co-locate people together to minimize walking and movement for patients and staff. Therefore, *available resources* is a better name for this foundational principle.

Here is how this works with people instead of machines. If you need a one-piece flow cell to do billing or coding in healthcare, the purpose of getting them together is so that they can reduce handoffs and help each other. If their fellow cell workers are not there, if they are not on the same shift, if they show up late, if they are not cross-trained to minimally help others, then don't arrange them in a one-piece cell! It will be worse than it was before! Stabilize first.

philosophy of the Toyota Production System. This is also the key to the Scott & White Way philosophy.

The Toyota Way Principles

Steve thanks Dr. Jeffrey Liker for his wisdom and knowledge of TPS principles. Jeff had a big influence on his philosophy. Steve taught in Jeff's world-class Lean seminar programs for over a decade at a university and also worked for Jeff's consulting company. Thus, you would expect the continuous improvement philosophy S&W adapted for healthcare to follow Jeff's Toyota Way model.

In Jeff's book, *The Toyota Way*,[*] he introduced a pyramid model with four layers, largest at the base. He called the layers (bottom-up) philosophy, process, people and partners, and then problem solving. He listed 14 Principles

---

[*] Liker, Jeffrey, Ibid.

of the Toyota Way off to the side of each layer. The focus of the first layer, *philosophy*, is on long-term thinking. Toyota's Patience story in the next section demonstrates this well.

The focus of the second layer, process, is on eliminating waste. This includes most of the TPS toolkit like making processes "flow," which surfaces problems. It also includes balancing workloads, *Stop the line* authority for quality and flow issues, simple pull systems, visual controls, and standard work. A final process principle is using only reliable, thoroughly tested technology. Healthcare seems to miss this principle, as it remains a guinea pig for high-tech equipment and IT vendors.

Jeff's third layer after process is *people and partners*. This includes growing leaders internally who daily live out the philosophy. True to the middle pillar of the Toyota House, it also includes respecting, developing, and challenging staff and teams. And, it means respecting, challenging, and helping your suppliers. Yes, even those outside their organization need to fully grasp TPS because the weakest link can cause an entire value chain to break! Steve was one of those suppliers Toyota invested in and influenced.

Question: How is your organization doing on this short list of process principles and tools? Do all of your processes flow smoothly without stop? Which ones do not? Why not? Is there a prioritized list of processes somewhere with flow issues? Did you know making processes flow surfaces problems? If that is true, what else do you need to do while making processes flow?

True non-stop flow might be harder in healthcare because of this. When staff experience a problem (e.g., out of bed sheets), they often quickly develop time-consuming work-arounds (store extra in various places, grab from another floor, etc.), which dampen the "urgent" impact of flow problems and thus prevent attention needed to get to the root-cause of the problems.

*Healthcare staff might need to stop and solve (root cause), rather than allow work-arounds. What are your thoughts on work-arounds? Discuss this with your staff.

Like a chain with just one broken link, teamwork deteriorates if even a single dysfunction is allowed to flourish.

—Patrick Lencioni,
The Five Dysfunctions of a Team[*]

The top layer after people and partners is *problem solving*. It is unique to elevate problem solving to the top of any pyramid. The leaders at S&W are just now starting to grasp this simple yet deep concept. This layer includes continual organizational learning through small, continuous improvement (PDCA) cycles. It also elevates the concept of Gemba, "Go see" for yourself to thoroughly understand the situation. In addition, it includes perhaps the most misunderstood part of TPS—Nemawashi.[†]

Toyota makes decisions slowly by consensus, thoroughly considering all options and vetting the decision through key stakeholders. Then, it implements decisions very rapidly. In healthcare, leaders make snappy decisions, which are then resisted and ground to a halt by stakeholders who were not informed. Which is better?

Steve knew firsthand how slowly Toyota engineers and leaders made decisions. They vetted ideas across departments and then up and down the chains of command to get buy-in. However, Toyota then quickly implemented the change or decision. In fact, there were rarely arguments or pushback when the change started. This process of gathering input "from the roots" is called Nemawashi.

Because Jeff sees organizations from a socio-technical perspective, the authors feel his pyramid is even more applicable to healthcare. At its core, healthcare is a series of patient-to-provider, person-to-person interactions toward improving patient health.

Jeff says most American companies are stuck applying Lean principles to just a few processes. They are stuck in the process layer. They do not elevate to people and true problem solving. This is true of healthcare as well. For the past decade, Lean projects have yielded significant improvements in isolated processes. However, the tendency is still to "fix" daily problems by using a work-around that takes time every day, rather than eliminate the root.

---

[*] Lencioni, Patrick, *The Five Dysfunctions of a Team*, Jossey-Bass, San Francisco, 2002.
[†] Lean Enterprise Institute Online Lean Lexicon, *Nemawashi*, Lean Enterprise Institute, Cambridge, MA. http://www.lean.org/search/?sc=nemawashi accessed August 2014.

Problems are like weeds. You need to get rid of the root or it will return.

—Unknown

Toyota's Patience—San Antonio

The first layer of Jeff's pyramid, philosophy, contains only one principle. It is that important. It says, "Base all management decisions on a long-term philosophy, even at the expense of short-term financial goals."[*]

Here is an example demonstrating this philosophy at Toyota, and then a practical application in healthcare. Toyota Motor Manufacturing has grown in Texas from an idea to something bigger than just an assembly plant. It has become part of the community of San Antonio. Toyota makes trucks there—good ones. It needed to screen, hire, and extensively train thousands of workers for months and months in advance.

Toyota started making the large Tundra pick-up in late 2006. The first vehicle rolled off just before the largest decline in the U.S. economy since the Great Depression. There could not have been a worse possible time to start up a new manufacturing facility. Toyota had workers and a great product, but lower-than-expected sales. The volume just was not there at first. People were not buying *any* vehicles with the stock market crashing, economy in turmoil, and high gas prices.

So, what did Toyota do as demand for vehicles crumbled across the United States? Any warm-blooded MBA graduate knows what they were trained to do. You lay them off until you are profitable. You downsize, right? No. They did not.

Toyota paid its full-time staff. All of them. Some of them went into the community to paint classrooms. Some of them even harvested grass in the green spaces around the facility. Toyota paid them rather than lay them off through this temporary downturn because they were valuable. Toyota also deeply trained them, and then cross-trained them to do many tasks to help each other. Toyota invested in them and made a pact with them. Its employees would be its future.

Please visit this great facility. They will tell you about Toyota's long-term philosophy. "All management decisions based on long-term philosophy, even at the expense of short-term financial gains." This philosophy begins and

[*] Liker, Jeffrey, Ibid.

How does this apply to healthcare? How many times have you seen or heard of short-term, knee-jerk reactions because costs needed to be cut? Got a small dip in volume; cut loose a few people. It comes back; hire people back. How's that working for you?

ends with Toyota's workers. It is about people first and strategic decisions second.

Just to be clear, the authors are not saying you can never have lay-offs. However, in areas where Lean ideas from staff are being requested and tried out, you just can't do that. The ideas will stop. Period.

The authors see another use for Jeff's pyramid model and 14 principles. These can also be used as a decision filter. If you "rake" any decision across these 14 principles, what would happen? Good decisions should get through, and the bad ones are screened out. Let's try an example.

Let's say you wanted to start up a whole service line based around managing patient pain. You would be faced with a series of tough decisions and questions. The first screen or filter asks, "Are our plans based on long-term philosophy? Does it move us toward the strategic goals we have for our community and organization?" If yes, then it drops through to the next screen, "Will it use and rely on only reliable, thoroughly tested technology?" Reliable, thoroughly tested. It says do not become the bleeding edge guinea pig for some equipment or software-maker. Don't let the insultants and the sales people try to sell you vaporware.

Maybe your recommended solution makes it through 12 screens up to #13, "Go see for yourself to thoroughly understand the situation."[*] Jeff adds *Genchi Genbutsu*, Japanese for actual thing in the actual place where it is made. In layman's terms, "Get out of the ivory tower conference room and go see for yourself!" A Texan would say, "Get your boots on!"

Have you visited with staff who currently serve patients with chronic diseases and pain? Have you spoken to patients about what they want? Yes, the consultants said they would email the results of their focus group. OK, how is that working for you thus far?

Jeff Liker's Toyota Way 14 principles pyramid and the Toyota House are both useful models. S&W uses them both to teach and to understand a

---

[*] Toyota Way, Ibid.

philosophy about how to build stronger healthcare processes. Continuous learning is a key part of the S&W philosophy. Learning to apply TPS principles daily takes time.

It takes repeated practice with corrective feedback when you get off target. Staff need to do this without impunity. They do not absorb the entirety of TPS in one sitting, seminar, or workshop. Just like learning medicine or flying a plane, they learn the pieces, applying them little by little. They build their skill sets and grow through practice and application, not courses or being "told" what to do.

Staff can and will assimilate this new way of thinking. It is the leader's job to allow them and to be consistent cheerleaders in this valuable learning journey. Thus, top leaders must learn TPS first. This long-term philosophy must be engrained in their DNA and daily practice because it will be "caught" by, not "taught" to, their staff.

All Staff Need to Develop "Eyes for Waste" (DOWNTIME)

Another key principle in the foundation is waste elimination. All staff must develop eyes for waste. So, what is waste? The short definition again, particularly in healthcare, is everything the worker hates to do. It is everything the patient does not like about healthcare as well: waiting, walking, searching, filling out forms in triplicate, asking for information that we already have, re-doing or re-entering things, etc.

S&W, like many organizations, uses an acronym to help its staff remember the categories of waste. They use DOWNTIME. Some examples from each category of waste are shown in Figure 3.7.

Defects, Errors, or Rework of Errors: A good example of this category of waste is medication errors. Another is missing information provided to the next person. Wrong labels and re-draws of blood are others. Whenever you hear the prefix "Re" in front of a word, it usually falls in this category. Any process with "Re" in front of it is sometimes called the "hidden hospital." Defects, errors, and all the rework to fix or document errors are huge wastes and very important in healthcare. Neither staff nor patients like this.

Overproduction: Overproduction is harder to see and experience. This can be when workers prepare or make anything well in advance of need.

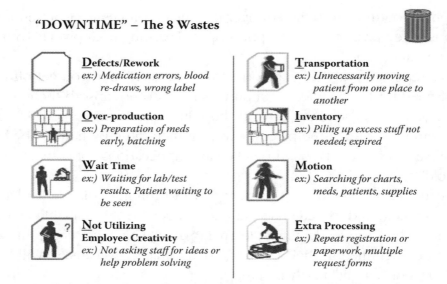

"DOWNTIME" – The 8 Wastes

Defects/Rework
ex:) Medication errors, blood re-draws, wrong label

Over-production
ex:) Preparation of meds early, batching

Wait Time
ex:) Waiting for lab/test results. Patient waiting to be seen

Not Utilizing Employee Creativity
ex:) Not asking staff for ideas or help problem solving

Transportation
ex:) Unnecessarily moving patient from one place to another

Inventory
ex:) Piling up excess stuff not needed; expired

Motion
ex:) Searching for charts, meds, patients, supplies

Extra Processing
ex:) Repeat registration or paperwork, multiple request forms

Figure 3.7 DOWNTIME—Acronym for the eight categories of wastes.

A key word to watch for with this category is *batch*. All batches cause over-production. Many people say, "We don't batch in healthcare." This cannot be further from the truth. Nearly every process in healthcare has batches.

Any time something is done in advance of the need is overproduction, and any quantity delivered to the next step greater than one is batching. Here is a good example. How do you enter data into a computer or database system? Do you enter it immediately at the time of transaction? It is likely that you store up a few and then do them as you are able to. There are valid reasons why people do this. However, the batches for these valid reasons can be reduced as well.

Consider the OR. Every worker in the team needs to enter or log information into the computer system. Yet, how many computer terminals are there—one or two? Go into an operating suite in your mind for a moment. Here comes the surgeon and she is busy. However, there is a nurse currently on the computer.

The surgeon hip-checks the nurse off the computer because she must enter the information at the end of every case. The surgeon first needs to looooog (exaggerated to show delay) the previous person out, then loooooog herself in because her screen has certain fields only visible for security reasons. This process takes, let's say, 6 or 7 minutes. Then, she does about 30 seconds of entry.

Does it make sense for the surgeon to spend 6 or 7 minutes waiting and then do 30 seconds of entry? She doesn't think so. What she will do is queue up a few, and then enter all of them the next time she is logged in. Good workers are actually trying to calculate in their mind some sort of economic order quantity (EOQ).*

In layman's terms, the economic order quantity is the size of the batch a person uses to avoid too much pain of setup or ramp-up to do it one item at a time. In their heads, they balance the pain experienced by doing things one at a time with the pain of not doing so (batches). If no one is hollering for completion, the result is usually bigger batches.

The main reason healthcare workers batch is because it is easier for them. It sub-optimizes the process for just one person, while others downstream (who can only do things one at a time by the way), wait and wait for the whole batch. Then the batch comes in like a tidal wave and overwhelms them. Now, they are behind and start thinking batching as well. Repeat.

In the OR example, another option to reducing the login/logout pain is to allow multiple secure "sessions" with no login delay (fingerprint or disk/key).

Waiting: It is very easy to see waiting. You can see a doctor waiting for labs or test results, patients waiting to be seen, rooms waiting to be cleaned or filled with the next patient, etc. All waiting is waste.

Not utilizing employee creativity: This was not in Toyota's original group of wastes. Toyota used seven categories of waste or Muda. That is a Japanese word for waste. This can be *not* asking staff for ideas or to help solve problems. We must use their minds—not just their hands (two hats). It can also be staff members not working at the highest level of their certification.

Transport and motion: It is easier to discuss these two categories of waste together. Transport is the movement of *things*. Motion is any movement by *staff*. Transport waste can be unnecessarily moving a patient,

> **Key point:** If the pain of the "setup" reduces, then the size of the batch can be cut down. Again, batches create overproduction waste.

---

* The Free Dictionary, *EOQ*, http://encyclopedia.thefreedictionary.com/eoq.

unnecessary movement of blood through a system, or unnecessary movement of some kind of samples or inventory.

Inventory: All inventory is waste. However, you need to balance this. For example, you may choose to carry a little more inventory at the point-of-use so that nurses in the unit do not need to walk so far. Rather than dozens of nurses in a building walking to centralized storage areas, you may store items closer to each team of nurses. The goal is not reducing any one category. You must reduce the total system waste! This is important to remember, as stock runners are often the first to be cut. If they go, how much extra walking is lumped on all nurses?

Motion: Staff members may be walking while they are transporting patients or things, but walking, searching for meds, searching for patients, or trying to fetch supplies are all waste. Note: you cannot reduce one of these categories of waste by just shifting it to another.

Extra processing: This is very hard to see. This happens in nearly every administrative, transactional, or knowledge-worker process. A staff member in department A will do his job. Then, he hands (or sends) it to his supervisor who checks his work. Sometimes, the supervisor does little work at all. Then, the supervisor from department A hands the package over to department B. Guess what happens there? Department B supervisor also checks the work because back in 1904, department A did something wrong and we never got to the root cause of their error. Department B supervisor will then hand it to the next available value-added worker.

Questions for leaders: Why are we doing these four sequential steps separated by a day in each in-basket? Who divided this work into four mundane tasks in the first place?! Why can't one person do both A and B tasks with no waiting?! Extra processing can be a very serious form of waste.

Lead Time and Value-Added Time

In the Scott & White way, all staff reduce work, also called non-value-added work, as seen in Figure 3.8. Did you know that the Leanness of an process can be measured in time? It can be measured. And, it can be measured in time.

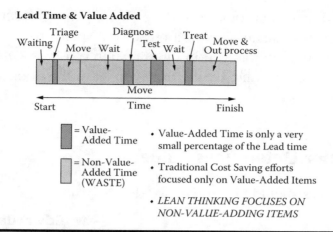

Figure 3.8 Lean thinking focuses on the light grey sections of the process—the non-value-added portions.

It is not the time it takes for any one person to do his or her job. It is the end-to-end time, or what is called lead time. An example is from the time a person comes into the emergency room until he or she leaves. From walking in saying "Ouch," to walking out saying "I'm healed!" With roughly equal volumes, if the end-to-end time is getting shorter and shorter, then this process is getting leaner. However, if it is getting longer and longer, then the process is getting fatter.

Here is some proof in Figure 3.8. Think of an emergency room visit. The graphic represents your last 6-hour marathon waiting with your child. Now it is personal. The lead-time is 6 hours. This is all the customer really cares about. The time required for any sub-task is meaningless if the customer is still waiting.

What are the typical steps? You sign in, and then wait. You are called back for triage and vitals, and then wait. Sometimes you are placed in a room, and then wait. Another nurse comes in, checks symptoms and vitals, enters them into the computer, and then wait. After a long wait, a doctor finally sees your child, orders some tests, and then you wait before each testing station. You make it back to a room, and then wait.

Finally, the tests come back, or worse, only one test result comes back. The doctor pokes his or her head in, realizes the second test result is still pending, and then disappears quicker than an elusive whale. More waiting. Two more head-pokes and then the doctor has all the pieces to put the puzzle together.

The doctor documents some sort of treatment plan or orders some medications, and you wait again. Finally, a nurse or helper arrives, tells you some information, and then points you in the direction of *Check Out*, where there is another line. More waiting! By the time you leave the door, you are frustrated and older!

The Customer Determines Value

The emphasis should be on *why* we do a job.

—W. Edwards Deming

In Figure 3.8, what steps or parts of the process would the patient and family member say is "value added" to them? On the time-scaled emergency department visit graphic, let's say the width of the darker-colored boxes (green on Steve's teaching slides) represent the amount of time value was added in their minds. They might say it is only their "face time" with the nurses and doctor and maybe with the lab or X-ray tech. This is the green-bar time shown. The rest of the time, the patient is waiting. This is the light grey-bar time.

The light grey areas are non-value-added tasks and time, what is called waste, and the darker green chunks are the value-added tasks and time. If you squint, you notice that most of the 6-hour visit is the lighter grey color. What would you work on first? Hold that thought.

If all the customer really cares about is the lead time, then you need to take a big chunk out of the total time. What would you work on first? Would you work on the value-added tasks and time (green) or would you work on the non-value-added tasks and time (light grey)? You would work on the light grey. Why? The main reason is that there is more of it, right?

If you squint at Figure 3.8, the smaller chunks of dark grey bars are probably only 10 to 20% of the total time. There is obviously more light grey to cut out. Think of what the light grey represents. It is the stuff everyone hates! Everybody hates the waiting. They hate the walking, the searching, the waiting, and re-doing.

So, let's evaluate the past 30 years. What have their consultants, improvement specialists, analysts, and engineers focused on? They have taken stopwatches, slid up behind workers while they are adding value (green-bar time), and tried to make them work harder. After 30 years of doing something a certain way, we should evaluate. How is this working?

Do you understand this key difference in Lean thinking? Lean thinking says, "while workers are adding value, leave them alone. Focus on the light grey areas." In healthcare, you do not need a stopwatch to study the grey-bar areas, a calendar works just fine! Lean thinking focuses *first* on the

---

Time Study: Steve learned how to do a formal time study in an Industrial Engineering course at Wayne State University. His professor allowed students to practice what they learned "in real life" because he worked at a large hospital in downtown Detroit. Steve learned the methodology in the classroom from a video.

Then, the professor drove the students to the hospital, and gave them a stopwatch and a clipboard with a list of standard, repetitive tasks the worker was expected to do. Steve's list had about 10 or 12 tasks the nurse typically did in each room. Steve was to capture a few task times using the stopwatch in each room, and then calculate the average.

The professor pointed and said, "There she is, Steve. There's your nurse." Steve walked right up behind the nurse, stopwatch and clipboard in hand, and started the watch. Once she saw that Steve had a stopwatch, she grabbed a sharp object and chased Steve back down the hallway!

Why do you think she chased Steve down the hallway? What was the result of every single time study done during the 1980s and 1990s? What happened to the nurses? That is right. Their workforce was cut, or at least there was more work piled on them.

Think about this. How could a young engineer in a 2- or 3-hour period possibly see all of the various things the nurse was required to do on a shift? In addition, was the time spent doing the green-bar tasks really the problem? The whole concept of stopwatch studying green-bar tasks seemed useless to Steve. He was still hiding when the rest of his class rejoined him with similar experiences.

Steve realizes he may have oversimplified the field of industrial engineering applied to healthcare—roughly called management engineering. However, given his experience, it is no wonder some healthcare workers call it "manglement" engineering. Steve does recognize the value of time observations. But, now he teaches staff members to use the stopwatch on their own to balance work or make improvements.

Non-Time Study: Steve remembers having a stopwatch in his hand one day with his sensei. His sensei took the stopwatch, set it on the ground, and then crushed it! He said "Steve-san, never, ever study somebody while they are working. While they are adding value, leave them alone! Go fetch them some water. Tell them they look nice. Don't study them! The entire organization is riding on their back at that moment."

He continued, "If you want to do some good, if you want to help your fellow employee, help them study when and why they *stopped* working, why they needed to walk and search and look for things (grey-bar times). Talk to them. Help them solve the reasons they must walk, search, and wait!" He added. "You do not need a stopwatch to do this. A calendar works just fine!"

non-value-added tasks. Steve likes to call this slide the "sign-up" slide in his seminars. This thinking is critical for TPS and the S&W Way.

Types of Work

First, let's define value-added work (VA). VA is activities that transform material or information into something that the customer cares about, or roughly, what they are willing to pay for.

There are only two types of work in the study of waste, or waste-ology. This is critical to the S&W philosophy and all staff must understand it. The first is VA. In Figure 3.9, the pie represents the typical healthcare worker's day. Maybe it is a 10-hour day. Notice the little sliver at the top says value added. Roughly, only one-tenth of this worker's day is spent doing value-added tasks. Some do more, some less. The average is about 10%. The authors have studied healthcare tasks enough to conclude this drawing is pretty accurate.

The other category is non-value-added work (NVA). Taiichi Ohno, the founder of the Toyota Production System, would roll over in his grave if he heard this. But in healthcare, this category needs to be broken into two different types of work: Unnecessary NVA tasks (pure waste), and those tasks that are (currently) necessary but still NVA.

Types of Work

Value-Added Work:
Activities that transform material or information into
something that the customer cares about ($)

Non-Value-Added Work:
* Necessary (Currently)
- Room changeover
- Testing

* Unnecessary (Pure Waste)
- RE-TESTING
- WAITING FOR TEST
- WALKING

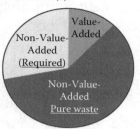

Figure 3.9   Types of work.

Let's look first at NVA that is unnecessary (pure waste). Every time you hear "Re," as in re-do, re-draw, or re-enter, it could have been done the first time. This is pure waste. Waiting and walking is pure waste.

The other type of NVA is still NVA, but it is currently necessary. Healthcare systems need to do these tasks, sometimes because of regulations. It includes documentation, testing, and even mundane things like room cleaning and auditing. These tasks add cost, but not value in the customer's mind.

The reason for two categories of NVA is that they require different thinking. For NVA pure waste tasks, S&W staff know the goal is to completely eliminate it! However, if the NVA is currently necessary, the only thing you could do today is to greatly reduce the time it takes. Do you see the difference?

All tasks can be placed into one of these three categories for improvement. It is either adding value or it is not adding value. That is the non-value-added work focus in TPS.

Remember, if the task adds value, what do you do? Leave it alone, for now. If the task does not add value, what do you do? If it is unnecessary pure waste, you come up with ideas to eliminate it. If it is NVA but currently necessary, you come up with ideas to greatly reduce the time and pain it takes us to do it.

Scientific Method

Another key principle in S&W's continuous improvement philosophy is related to inclusiveness. It is that they are just teaching the scientific method. You may need to blow the dust off your 9th grade science book, but this is just PDCA. You Plan to make a small change, usually in the form of an idea. Then, you Do it. Then, you Check to see if it worked. And then, if it worked, you Act. You take some sort of action to raise the bar and let all staff experience the benefits of this improvement. PDCA, Kaizen, and Six Sigma all use the scientific method.

Here is how this works in healthcare. The scientific method starts by identifying a real problem in its most simple terms. It helps to write it down or make it visual. Then, you find the most likely root cause of it, sometimes using the Five Why's. Then, you make a hypothesis. Screech. Stop the bus. Good healthcare workers' eyes glass over when they see the word hypothesis.

Let's use a real example instead. Very little is on paper anymore, but let's say paper test results were sent back to the wrong emergency room. What is one way to get them back to the proper room? You could clearly label the room, the sample, and the result. The hypothesis is very simple, then. The problem is results getting back to the wrong room. The hypothesis is if you label everything, then you have a better chance of eliminating that error.

So, what do you do? PDCA. Plan to do the change. Then, do it. Then, check to see if it worked. If so, then act or adjust the standard so everyone can benefit. Guess what? It worked. Now what? Identify another problem. Repeat.

In any process like those in an emergency department, there are literally dozens of problems. The good news is that there is a Lean tool that greatly reduces the pain of each one! In the green-bar grey-bar emergency department timeline in Figure 3.8, you can reduce the grey areas systematically with this idea. Pick a problem, any problem. Think of a way to reduce the root cause of it. PDCA. Repeat.

Here is a guarantee from the authors to you. We guarantee you that the application of TPS/Lean thinking will, in fact, fix the flow, reduce the non-value-added time, and improve patient satisfaction and staff satisfaction of all of your processes. Why so confident? Because it works.

What works? The application of a systematic way of thinking. You do not do one workshop. You fix problems. If you teach your staff to do this every day, what do you get? Waste and problems removed every day. If you have 10,000 staff members, then you create 10,000 waste-busters and problem solvers! They all have two hats!

So, how can healthcare leaders fix their many end-to-end processes? It is not with one silver-bullet solution, nor by the purchase of a new computer system—sorry, Mr. Salesman. The way to fix them is to encourage staff to come up with ideas, then to try them out in PDCA "loops" every day.

If you have a dozen problems in the process, then you will likely have a dozen small, rapid PDCA loops to fix them. How will you fix every one of your organization's key value streams? Hundreds of ideas are tried out in PDCA experiments, every day. Who is going to do them? The employees. Whose ideas are they? The employees. The reason why this methodology sticks so well is that employees do not argue with their own ideas!

Lean Thinking Penetrates Every Part of the Organization: Baldrige Framework

Lean thinking needs to penetrate every part of the organization. One way to show this in the S&W Way is to use the Baldrige framework model. The framework helps you see your organizations as a system. It is also useful for focusing improvements. The authors added some "efforts" and focus areas in the call-out boxes where they felt Lean thinking could help. There will be more about that later in this section. It shows how Lean thinking can be used in every area of the organization.

Figure 3.10 shows the Baldrige framework,[*] sometimes called the sandwich model because of its shape. It shows a logical flow from one to seven. Two-way arrows link them together to show flow of strategy/goals to the other boxes and then feedback back. At the top of the sandwich, is Organization: Environment, relations and challenges. This is a model of your organization, including key influences on how you operate and challenges you face. Several good self-assessments are available on the NIST site to help you think through organizational and cultural best practices.

Box number one on the far left side is Leadership. Everything rises or falls on leadership.[†] Leadership informs or directs box two, Strategic Planning, and gets feedback from them to re-focus goals and decisions. Leadership also informs and directs box number three, Focus on Patients, other Customers, and Markets.

---

[*] NIST Baldrige Site and Publications, http://www.nist.gov/baldrige/
[†] Maxwell, John, *21 Irrefutable Laws of Leadership*, Thomas Nelson, Nashville, 1998.

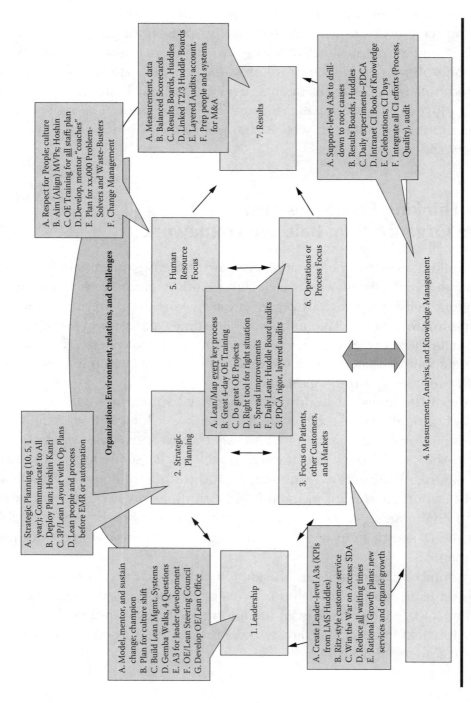

Figure 3.10 **Baldrige framework with major Lean efforts for each box.**

Box number four, underneath the whole model, is Measurement Analysis and Knowledge Management. This is a critical part of the continuous improvement philosophy, but strangely less used as a strategic weapon in most healthcare organizations. Healthcare remains in the DRIP phase on this one: Data Rich, Information (for informed decisions) Poor! All hope their multimillion-dollar investments in electronic medical record (EMR) systems will fix this.

Healthcare providers would never treat a patient without a baseline and goal for certain "vitals." However, at times, staff avoid the required use of data when it comes to managing their processes. True, healthcare does more than its share of financial analyses, but few do process analyses well. These first four boxes focus on the leadership level and roles of the organization.

Box number five is Human Resource (HR) Focus. It organizes and assesses how you are using and developing your Most Valuable Players (MVPs), your people. HR Focus and box number six, Operations or Process Focus, *should* go hand-in-hand, as shown in the framework. Most organizations have as a value: "People are our most valuable resource." However, they are slow to train, reticent to develop leaders from within, and quick to cut. Most leaders do not see all staff as vice presidents in training.

Operations or process focus is where most organizations relegate Lean, process improvement, Six Sigma and other toolkits. However, there is much more to process management as you are learning in this book.

If leadership sets and adjusts great strategy and goals, with a laser focus on customers, and models the use of measurement and analysis, what would happen? And if your people, your MVPs, and your processes are really humming like a finely tuned machine, guess what you are almost certain to get? Box number seven is Results.

The framework keeps the focus on the right things. Now, the authors are not saying go apply for a Baldrige Award. They do recommend using the framework and assessments to check your understanding of the organization as a system.

S&W leaders used this framework in a unique way. They showed how Lean thinking could penetrate every part of the organization. In each framework area, the top six or seven Lean "interventions" needed to improve and sustain are listed. For example, under leadership, an organization desiring deep penetration of Lean thinking might consider these efforts:

A. Model, mentor, and sustain change, communicating to all staff how they fit into Vision and Mission. Learn what it is to be a champion for change.

B. Make plans for this culture shift. What are your plans?

C. Build Lean Management Systems. That is what this book is all about.

D. Use and learn A3 thinking for leadership development, not just one-time problem solving.

E. Move leaders to commit to at least weekly Gemba walks toward building LMS, and also time with their sensei. Ask the Four Questions (detailed in Chapter 4, Step 4, Part 3: Daily Accountable Process).

F. Have an exceptional Lean Steering Council who model and focus the organization on doing the right things (forward-looking) and doing things well (backward-looking). Knock down hurdles.

G. Develop an effective internal Lean Promotions office.

Some of the other initiatives are self-explanatory. The Lean initiatives in lighter color (red in Steve's teaching slides) were the focus areas for FY14 and FY15 at S&W. Note: they did not start Lean efforts in the darker areas shown right away. Continuous improvement means, well, continuous. The "fonts" in their call-out boxes just got redder each year.

It may seem like Scott & White's 40+ Lean initiatives were broad and all over the map. However, it was quite the opposite. Each was focused and carefully deployed. One great tip the authors give is to focus your efforts in one site, in one area, and on a limited number of new things. Make it work in a pilot effort. Then, spread it.

Ratings: At times, leaders rated their progress in each call-out box on a 1 to 10 scale. They did a quick assessment, and then wrote the average score in the small box next to each of the Baldrige areas. However, the leaders eventually gave up scoring the boxes. The more times the leaders went to see Toyota in San Antonio and other mature Lean systems, the **lower** their self-assessed scores became.

If this has happened to you, lower scores as you realize how far you still need to go, welcome to the journey! That is exactly what is supposed to happen. Assessments help leaders define what "good" means, and how far they still need to go.

This methodology, assess and "gap close," can bring forward good action items from your leadership team. However, after a while, the authors feel that score can be a false goal (higher scores by adding superficial "trappings" of Lean), or worse, too critical for good leaders. The process is more important than the score.

Here is a tip: The authors encourage you to add your own efforts and details in the boxes of this hamburger model. Adding your own Call-out Box efforts to this Baldrige framework can help you build your culture of *safety*, *openness* (just culture), *trust*, *quality*, or any other focus area.

S&W's was mainly focused on Lean thinking. Just document your own set of initiatives, get buy-in from your leadership team, and go. The authors encourage you to contact them as you find new and interesting applications for these tools.

You are never done with Lean thinking. S&W is well into the lighter (red) font efforts after about seven years of concerted efforts. They are proud of this. There is so much more. A larger form can be found in Figure 7.1 in the back.

The model is thorough and shows where S&W is headed in building a culture of continuous improvement. The latter half of this book details two key items in the leadership box—items C and D, building Lean management systems, and Gemba walks with the Four Questions. This will be the focus of Chapters 4 and 5.

Tensions Are Natural in Every Transformation

Another critical point to end this section on Lean philosophy is natural tensions. If you feel that some parts of your continuous improvement effort create **tension**, it is probably working, or will work. These tensions are always present. Tensions in the human body are bad. Tensions in the Lean world are usually good. Natural tensions between two opposing forces can keep you moving on a straight path between them. Steve likens it to walking on a high ridge with pits of alligators on both sides of you. Veer too much left or right, and snap!

An example is getting too far ahead of your leaders. Early adopters run fast with the tools. The middle pack does not. So, a tension question is, "When do we start another facet or effort on our Lean journey?" S&W leaders pondered this frequently. If you start it too early and with some mild coercion (Bob and Steve smile), it has a tendency to fizzle, smolder, and die, especially if the leaders do not understand **why** they need to take this next step.

Tension Pulling One Way	Tension Pulling the Other Way
Standardize	Improve
Use standard improvements	Let teams make improvements
Prescribed	Flexible
Mandatory	Voluntary
Detailed	General
Do it this (best) way	Figure out best for you
Rigid project setup checklists	Flexibility in scheduling and doing
SMART goals	Stretch goals
Problem solver	Problem finder, celebrator
No layoff policy	Layoffs when volume drops

Figure 3.11   Natural tensions on the Lean journey.

Yet, if you wait until all leaders (even the laggards) are pulling, a decade will go by. When building a wall or house, it is not wise to lay the next brick too late. The organization loses the benefits of the next concept. In addition, there are parts of the Toyota House that you must deploy sequentially. This pace tension has always been a hard one for Bob and Steve.

There are always natural tensions between seemingly opposing forces when transforming your organization, especially in deploying TPS principles. Figure 3.11 shows a list of what seem to be "choices" that leaders must make on their Lean journey. They are Lean topics where tensions exist. Again, these tensions are not bad. They actually help create better solutions.

Standardize vs. Improve: Defending Standardized Work

With these two principles, there is no tension, really. Note that they are both in the foundation of the Toyota House. Standardized (or just standard) work is a checklist documenting the best way we know how to do a task or a job today. Standard work is one of the most powerful but least used Lean tools in healthcare.

By documenting the current best practice, standard work communicates the change. It can be used for training, and then used again to audit that all staff are using the "best way." As the standard is improved, the new standard becomes the baseline for further improvements, and so on. Improving standard work is a never-ending two-step process.

This principle is very important in the clinical quality improvement world. As stated earlier in this chapter, unintended clinical variation elimination will produce a better chance of a quality clinical outcome. Standard work is the standard!

While that statement may seem to state the obvious, clinical practice using standard work can improve more rapidly. What has been observed is as follows:

> *Clinical leaders develop pathways. These are standard work sets used in the management of patients. As their standard work units are adopted and approved by the clinical teams, the pathways are pushed out to daily practice. It is not unusual for clinicians to want to "make these their own" by modifying the pathway. Now, rather than standardization, we have allowed for unintended clinical variation to occur at many clinical sites.*
>
> *This makes gaining knowledge and improvements difficult. We once asked a Chief Medical Officer if he had standard clinical pathways. His answer was that he had many—one for each physician!*

It is best for the entire clinical team to accept the standard pathway, use it for a while, and then reconvene to discuss small tweaks in the process. There are reasons for intended clinical variation (e.g., leave off aspirin). However, this further reinforces the need for standards, and for a solid EMR that helps error proof the delivery processes.

Imagine each physician doing clinical processes only as he or she were taught, all by different teachers in different health systems in different states!

The higher principle behind standard work is more important than the "form." It states there is one best way to do something. That statement is true whether or not we believe it. Standard work is in the foundation of the Toyota House. If you don't get a start on standard work, the advanced principles will not work.

The tension comes in when people do not understand where standard work fits into improvements. They are not opposites. They work together. You can be both innovative and standardized. People ask, "How can you encourage staff to come up with ideas if the process must always be done the same standardized way?" This is where tensions are quite powerful.

They are actually two sides of the same coin. You cannot improve something until you have standardized it.

One mistake people make is to think of standards as a one-time thing. Sometimes, an engineer or analyst is assigned to write or develop standard work. This is far from the Toyota model. The workers, usually your best workers, always help document and develop standard work. The new standard is then communicated widely to the staff so that all can share in the benefits.

Leaders will then audit that everyone is using the new standard best way. Why? Everyone must do the tasks the same way so the team can get a new set of baseline metrics for the process. Why? So you can compare it to what you were doing before. How will they know if the new way is improved? Leaders audit all staff only for a few days, or until all staff are observed. Then, the new standard best way is once again open for more improvement.

In brief, standardization is a process that encourages further improvement. It boldly states that the standard is just "the best way today." It assumes it will be improved tomorrow. The key process steps are: update standard work, communicate to all, and then audit to ensure all are using the best way. Then, after a few brief days or weeks of audits, encourage the next round of improvements.

Steve likes to say he likes ugly standard work! He means standard work that is handwritten with improvements again and again. He likes when improvements are made faster than the administrative staff can keep up with the "official" digital versions. That is how he knew improvements were happening when he was Production Engineering Manager at Delta Kogyo.

A good graphic to help you understand the interrelationship between the two is shown in Figure 3.12. Standardization is like the wedge that props up the rock (work-process) so it does not roll backward. Then, you make another improvement, which rolls the ball forward.

The standardization process again props or sustains these new improvements. Standardization is a process to ensure your improvements will be sustained. Without standardization, all improvements will eventually roll back. It can actually get worse than before the change. The process of *Stabilize, Standardize,* and then *Sustain* ensures improvements do not slide back.

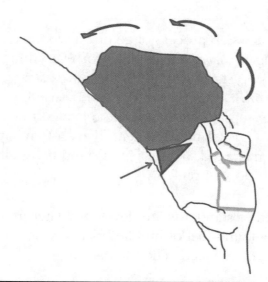

Figure 3.12   Standardize (wedge) before the next big push up.

(Forced) Standard Improvements vs. Team-Based Improvements

Steve gets this question less than the previous one, but still quite a bit. Does one force a standard set of "known" improvements on staff, or do they allow them to go through the thinking process on their own, even if their result is slightly different?

During Steve's ED simulation in their core training course, someone usually notices that each team member applied 5S (visual management) differently. Some suggest that Steve should stop the idea flow and "decree" a standard, usually suggesting their own great labeling scheme be made the standard. These comments are valid, especially for color-coding and safety items. However, Steve usually answers, "Let them keep at it until Round 4 (final round)." Somehow, when teams keep pulling the waste out, they get closer and closer to the same look and operations without taking away the ownership of their own good ideas.

In other words, they will get much closer without forcing them—just keep improving and "own" the changes. Lean thinking says let staff learn themselves; let them try it their way. It says let them feel good about proving the concepts work. Standardization can come later, when the sheer number of improvement ideas starts to slow down.

It becomes simple tweaks. Standards on color-coding are usually developed a few months into a Lean transformation, as are formats for standard

5S Review: 5S is a 5-step process of getting a workplace clean and orga-nized and keeping it that way—a place for everything and everything in its place! Each step starts with an S: *sort/scrap, straighten, scrub, stan-dardize,* and *sustain.* Different S words can be used, but the meaning is similar. These five steps can and must be repeated to move an operation closer to the goal—visual management. Steve often says, "An area can either be visually managed, or you could stand there all day telling staff what to do. Which do you prefer?"

work documents. Other standards are developed later in the improvement process, as in the look and feel of huddle boards, who audits what and when, the managing of elevated action items, etc.

Detailed Standard Work or General

This tension may sound like the opposite of a standard again, but Lean thinking allows for free reign of ideas, especially in healthcare. Processes in automotive, electronics, and other industries are frequently studied. They prescribe what the index finger and the thumb on the right hand are doing in their standard work.

At least to start in healthcare, you need to be flexible. Steve recommends this guideline: if the slight variation does not have a negative impact on key measures (true quality and safety data), then be flexible. However, if there is a measurable difference, you must use the most detailed standard way. The tension between flexibility and prescribed methods is always there. It is not a bad thing.

Do It This One Best Way vs. Figure Out Best for You (Rigid vs. Flexible)

Do not assume that the first statement is negative. The principle of Standard Work declares there is in fact one best way—it is the way that is docu-mented. The second statement sounds more flexible, more people focused. However, what if staff interpret this to mean "everyone does what is right in their own eyes." Tensions. We have mandatory vs. voluntary, rigid vs. flexible.

"Do it the way I tell you, I'm the engineer (or leader)!" TPS says the team should figure out a better way than the current standard, document it, and then make it better tomorrow. There will be constant tension between these extremes. With TPS, you lean toward the workers figuring out how to do any task better. This requires a change in thinking for most leaders. Some do not ask for ideas because they feel they will lose their small amount of control, or they will need to re-train staff.

Toyota adapted parts of TPS from the U.S. military. After WWII, Toyota leaders seized upon *Training within Industry** as a way of cross-training their employees for the myriad of tasks needed for the many products they make.

On rigid vs. flexible, there are some key myths about TPS. One is that their environments are democratic, with associates voting daily whether they should work on tasks. Steve saw little of that. In fact, it was abundantly clear who the leader was, what he or she did, and why.

Rather, there is *shared* respect. When leaders hear respect for people, they often think of it as one-way—that the leader must respect the worker. This is how they will get their ideas flowing, right? However, at Toyota, respect is two-way. The workers must respect the leader as well. The leader must make the final decisions after gathering input from all staff and stake-holders. The workers give input and know that someday they could be the leader. This concept of mutual (two-way) respect helps describe the proper tension between mandatory and voluntary.

TPS is a voluntary system in many ways. Employee ideas are volun-teered freely. However, they all follow a mandatory process, including how their ideas are tried out. But the leader makes the final decision. The teams implement the new change rapidly.

Another wrinkle on this tension is using *rigid* project setup checklists. To keep control of an improvement effort, the Lean coach may say a team must go through a rigid setup process over many months before they can get their desired workshop. Steve heard from many leaders who just walked away because they could not wait for three months before improvements could start.

Steve recommends both a rigid workshop setup checklist and flexibility. How? Most Lean coaches or facilitators start needing structure—a checklist with timelines. As they get more improvement efforts under their belt, they learn to "pull forward" analysis and some (limited) improvements. It is like

---

* Huntzinger, Jim, *The Roots of Lean: Training within Industry and the Origin of Japanese Management and Kaizen*, LEI website, https://www.lean.org/common/display/?o=106, accessed August 2014.

giving "air" to a manager and team that is drowning. An organization learns to be rigid where needed (e.g., no workshops without "baselines"), and flexible where possible.

As Lean thinking matures, an organization will produce more tools and checklists. This is good. Telling a leader he or she must jump through hoops to "earn" a workshop is bad. There must be a balance. This can be learned.

This tension is not bad. The authors suggest that you lean toward flexibility. As you become more mature in the process, you can put more checklists and structures in place. A good Lean coach will help design the workshop with only the amount of time that is useful for teams and adds value.

SMART vs. Stretch Goals

Another natural tension is SMART (Specific, Measurable, Attainable, Realistic, and Time-bound) goals vs. stretch goals. The tension is whether you make the goals realistic or make them stretch. In S&W's case, they always try to lean toward stretch. However, you can have both. Sometimes S&W leaders set a reasonable sub-goal, maybe halfway through a period.

As an example, 97% or more of patients wanting a same-day appointment are accommodated, or recruiting maintains a steady pool of top candidates ready to take jobs at S&W. Why not? These are stretch goals. Now, you need to make them SMART goals. In the next six months, the department is going to improve where they are at by 20%. Even if the eventual goal is zero, they can achieve a six-month goal of 20% improvement from current levels. This tension is natural, but good. One thing you may need to change is an all-or-nothing reward or bonus system. This actually "trains" staff to pick lollipop or soft goals, not stretch.

Problem Solver vs. Problem Finder

Being called a good problem solver is one of the greatest compliments you can get. However, as leaders, what do we think about a problem finder? Some yell at them, or at least roll their eyes. Shoot the messenger, or worse. Some think negatively of those who bring up problems.

Now, what would you do about someone who celebrates finding a problem? S&W trains its staff and leaders to be problem finders and problem solvers! Then, with error proofing and intense variation reduction, S&W teaches them to be problem preventers.

Steve often states, "When faced with choosing either extreme A or extreme B, the Lean choice is usually C—somewhere in the middle, or maybe somewhere off the line and out of the box from the two choices offered."

No Layoff Policy vs. Layoffs for Volume Imbalances

This is the hardest tension for the authors. They feel all healthcare can and must shrink its costs. Our nation cannot afford the ever-increasing costs. At the same time, healthcare organizations will grow in breadth, covered lives, and even beyond local areas through mergers and acquisitions. Again, the authors suggest that you lean toward a No Layoff Policy. You can have both. In the first year of its Lean journey, Bob issued an ironclad promise: No employee would be laid off due to Lean improvements. They have honored that promise.

That said, the healthcare business is changing rapidly. Technology is changing rapidly. For the most part, S&W did not do multiple workshops or heavy idea generation in areas they knew would shrink (e.g., temporary data re-entry, manual billing, contract staff areas for short-term upswings, etc.).

A great example of this policy was when S&W's laundry services closed. The merger with Baylor Health Care System brought with it a good, partner-owned contract laundry service. Knowing this, plans were made to deploy all staff in other areas. One of the key managers even joined the Lean team.

Not Big Enough vs. Too Big

Steve offers one more tension, just to be balanced. Starting around 2005, leaders at S&W asked the question, "How big is big enough?" Big enough to survive the coming waves of changes in healthcare. Big enough to purchase equipment and supplies at the lowest prices in economies of scale. Big enough to haul in capital for buildings to house expanding operations. Maybe big enough to tell a testy payor to take a hike unless they pay a fair reimbursement amount!

However, could a healthcare system become too big? If other industry consolidations are similar, it is possible. The concern of too big is that system-wide change becomes very difficult. Giant healthcare organizations get slow and bureaucratic. Geography prevents much of the economies of scale in middle management because all healthcare is local. Maybe a bigger concern is that very large companies require top leaders to become separate from their operations, and maybe focus too much on external matters while the Titanic chugs along.

It seems that a General Electric company-within-a-company approach might work here. It would need to be systemized enough to yield the financial positives of the first paragraph, without the negatives of the second paragraph.

Chapter 4

How S&W Did It—Applying TPS to Healthcare

The path S&W followed can help nearly any organization. The authors readily admit this flight plan was not perfect. However, it worked. They believe these principles and key learnings can be translated to nearly any type of operation.

This chapter shows how S&W applied TPS to its healthcare system. A few other healthcare systems started their journeys before S&W, but little of what they learned—their pitfalls, fits and starts, and how they specifically adapted TPS or other philosophies—has been published.

It would be great to end with a statement like "S&W did it all." Continuous improvement is in fact continuous. It is a journey without end. S&W accomplished what it has done thus far mainly on its own. It helped to have a sensei in the early parts of its journey. It takes a stubborn, unswerving commitment from the entire group of top leaders to make true transformation happen.

S&W followed a unique path and trajectory over its first six years of intentionally deploying Lean or TPS principles. Figure 4.1 shows its increasing ideas arrow. It was not a perfect journey. It is just what S&W did. There is wisdom in the sequence and continuation of each step. Here is how S&W did it. S&W hit an acceleration or inflection point somewhere between points two and three on the graph.

Fiscal years are shown along the horizontal axis through FY14. Along the vertical axis, it roughly shows the number of implemented and sustained ideas. However, Steve often calls the Y-axis "Lean goodness" because

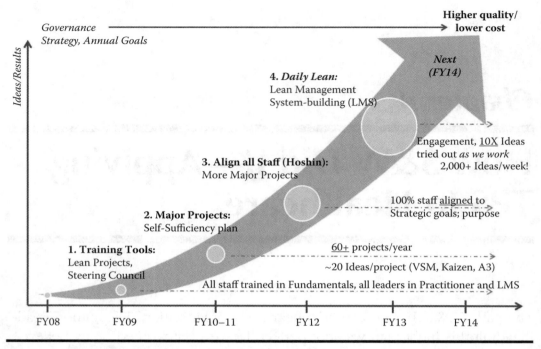

Figure 4.1   Scott & White's Lean flight plan and path.

it includes many effectiveness measures like ideas, engagement, savings, growth, etc. Each numbered effort on the arrow continues forever. Once started, these foundational parts of the effort must continue to "fuel" the focused efforts that follow.

As noted earlier, Bob sought out and then attended a Lean healthcare seminar in December 2007. This course represents the first dot on the timeline. So if Bob's seminar was the zero point, Step Number 1 was *Training* or preparing the minds of key leaders and key project team members. For the first year, there was a lot of focus on training with some initial projects or workshops.

Every organization does Lean training and projects. This did not make S&W unique. However, one unique feature of this early phase of S&W's Lean effort was their tracking and requirement of "deliverables" from every training course. Their stated purpose of the course was to produce people—staff and leaders—that thought differently.

Their deliverable was to apply what they had learned, usually a waste walk for an early orientation course or a project from a multi-day Lean training session. At S&W, Lean training, deliverables from each training course, coaching from a full-time sensei, and projects were crafted and linked together.

Early in Step Number 1, S&W established a Steering Council. This council has been part of and separate from the executive leadership team's main weekly meeting. This has changed over time.

Please notice the arrows to the right of each numbered effort continue infinitely. This is on purpose. Welcome to the continuous part of the continuous improvement journey. S&W keeps on training—more than 6000 through their common core courses. The more they train, the more they train.

Steve jokes if he told Bob the total amount of time that it would take to train the minds of leaders to think differently, he would have run away screaming. Each staff member participates in 8 hours of Lean Fundamentals (Lean 101) training one month after their orientation, followed by a 4-day Lean Practitioner (Lean 201) course, followed by a 3-day Lean leader (Lean 401) course. More information on these courses is in Chapter 4, Common Core Training. Many brief workshops and just-in-time courses are also taught as needed.

Somehow, each step of the Lean journey opens up or releases the energy and the ideas of the next step. Both Bob and Steve believe this continuous training effort was necessary. Almost 90% of all S&W leaders who have at least one direct report have been trained in some multi-day Lean courses to date. More than half of all staff has as well.

Step Number 2 on the arrow was Major Projects. After training, S&W leaders were hungry for some project successes. S&W's first training graduates scoped out a few big projects like operating room (OR) and emergency department (ED) end-to-end flow of patients. They scoped out inpatient flow all the way to their primary care provider. They were huge projects in both scope and known roadblocks. Unafraid, they took them on.

Again, everybody uses Lean tools. Everybody mixes the tools into projects (or workshops or events). However, S&W did not conduct Lean projects like most organizations. They had a push by Steve and some colleagues. However, they learned to do projects using a self-sufficiency philosophy.

Steve and coaches from an outside organization facilitated some demonstration projects or workshops. Their plan required that one or maybe two internal S&W coaches shadow them at all times. Steve's team might fully facilitate one and or maybe two of a particular style of workshop at a site. However, if they ever did three (or more) in the same area, something was wrong! A pace of around 60 projects (big and small) per year has been maintained. Notice that projects do not and cannot stop. They are keys to continued cross-functional transformation.

This self-sufficiency philosophy quickly became a strategic advantage for S&W. It taught Bob's staff rather quickly "how to fish" for themselves. In this phase, major projects with a self-sufficiency approach, S&W invested heavily in staff members who were to be full-time Lean coaches. They also invested deeply in part-time Embedded Coaches who stayed in their departments, working key jobs but still leading continuous improvement efforts.

Not one project was conducted unless an internal Lean coach and supervisors in the area were ready to shadow and learn from the outsiders every step of the way. Leaders created and tracked each project to ensure S&W minimized its outside help and maximized internal staff's learning.

Over the 2-year period shown in Figure 4.1, some 50 key individuals became somewhat self-sufficient with Lean tools and principles. Bob says, by the end of their first year, teams started to produce some very good results, requiring less and less outside help time.

Step Number 3 on the arrow was *Align all Staff.* This was a key step in their Lean journey. Timing was critical. This was originally planned early in S&W's Lean journey. Bob started their Lean journey when he was the Chief Medical Officer and Chief Operating Officer. There was also a huge system-wide building and expansion program going on. S&W held off on goal alignment until Bob became the CEO, new leaders were in place, and the organization was ready. This effort takes time and energy to implement, much like the principles in the foundation of the Toyota House.

In Japanese, this alignment process is called *Hoshin Kanri.* S&W needed to align all of its Most Valuable Players (MVPs), its staff, toward specific, strategic system goals. S&W never had effective and aligned system-wide goals before for all staff. Too many leaders felt that their own departmental success was the goal. Bob and Steve felt they needed alignment so that every individual could see how he or she fit into the over-arching mission, vision, values, and annual goals.

Analogy: When General Bob, the CEO, said, "In order to win the war, we must take those two hills over there," all staff needed to do something different. Going through the same motions will not get them there. All of Bob's direct reports and then their charges all the way up to the direct performers needed to see how their actions link into the bigger battles and goals.

At S&W, this also allowed leaders to align major improvement projects. However, their earliest list of prioritized projects looked more like a jigsaw puzzle than a battle map.

One big difference between goal-alignment and true Hoshin is aligned actions. Another is translating goals to something within a staff member's control. Some organizations say they align all staff by giving the floor sweeper the same margin (profit) goals as the executives. What will the sweeper do, sweep harder? Goals need to be translated from the language of money and roll-up metrics to the language of things. Things that can be seen and counted at the end of the shift! S&W calls these process or input metrics. More on this in Chapter 4, Daily Lean (LMS).

A big question for Bob was whether to align <u>all</u> staff or just the top few layers. Should he try in the very first year of this major effort to get all 13,000 staff members through the process?

Steve remembers his recommendation. He told Bob to do this well for only the top two or three levels in year one. However, Bob said, "No. We can't have two separate systems, just like a person can't be partially pregnant. We're going to do Hoshin for all staff or none!" And, they did. By the end of the year, all 13,000 staff members had some sort of aligned goals and saw how they fit into the bigger picture.*

Steve and Bob used the terms *crawl, walk,* and *run* to describe the first three years of Hoshin deployment. In retrospect, Steve calls it crawl, crawl, change software tools, crawl again, walk, and then jog. Chapter 6 is loaded with tips on how S&W did this.

Step Number 4 on the arrow was *Daily Lean* and Lean Management System-Building. Bob feels this major "people" effort was the most dramatic and yielded the biggest benefits to their patients and S&W as a whole. They call this LMS-building. It is more like Nirvana.

Steve warns that staff do not usually get to this Idea Generator in their first few years of a Lean journey. It is built on a solid foundation where you train the minds of leaders and staff, and then allow them to apply the principles on projects. You should have several years of waste-busting, and even root-cause problem solving (A3 format) before rapid-fire huddles really move the metrics!

Steve outlined the basic idea to leaders and garnered their support. He trained leaders top-down. It is critical that leaders actually lead this part of the journey. As Dr. John Toussaint of ThedaCare states in his book *On the*

---

* In reality, some staff had goals, but not effective two-way conversations. It took S&W at least four years before most staff had good two-way conversations and aligned goals with their supervisor.

Mend, "The *ultimate arrogance* is to change the way people work without changing the way we manage them."* Leaders need to build the daily Lean systems. Therefore, they need to know what and how.

Bob and his team were dedicated to this effort. Having all staff briefly discuss daily Lean improvement in huddles and then try them out while they work was exciting. From their start, most improvement efforts linked in some way to huddles. However, the idea huddle itself was just a small part of the bigger LMS effort.

Bob issued his **CEO Challenge** in 2012: Ten times the number of implemented ideas per year tried out as they work! Within 12 months, S&W staff rose to the challenge. Just for central Texas staff, they are now at a steady pace of about 2000 implemented ideas per week (not a typo, more than previous years' totals)!

S&W still trained staff in Lean basics and their role. They still did many great Lean projects, and they still did Hoshin Kanri every year. These earlier steps never ended.

Where S&W is headed beyond FY15 is a deeper investment into people—especially the supervisors and front-line managers. They must be self-sufficient with the Lean tools in order to lead teams at their huddle boards and in simple projects.

Another model showing how all four parts of the S&W's transformation arrow model comes together is in Figure 4.2. S&W leaders use Hoshin and

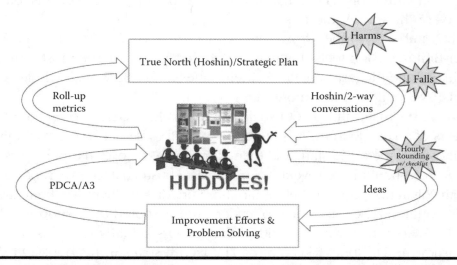

Figure 4.2   Scott & White's linkage of Hoshin, huddles, and A3 problem solving.

---

* Toussaint, John, and Gerard, Roger, *On the Mend*, Lean Enterprise Institute, Cambridge, MA, 2010.

Video: Bob Pryor presenting the President's Award for best Lean project, CLIP Fair, November 3, 2011

About four years ago, Scott & White started on our endeavor to build a system that allows our 13,000 staff to use all of their abilities to make S&W better. As you heard in your training, "Some days a little, some days a lot!" As the journey continues, the little we do every day is compounded by the lots we do on great projects, and this my friends really makes a difference to our patients. What I saw on almost 100 summary boards out there today was the "lots." The major steps you have taken in your projects took S&W from our current state to where we are today! We are achieving our future states!

This work has been done by you. We didn't bring in fancy consultants. We are not chasing the rabbit as the book says. What S&W is known for, and what we are proving, is that S&W leads, and everyone else chases us!

It is clear that you understand the methodology. You applied it. You got your results. And, our patients will now reap the benefit of what you have accomplished and will continue to do.

two-way catchball conversations and then huddles to generate improvement actions and problems to solve. S&W tries the simple huddle method first. If that doesn't work, they start problem solving.

(Left arrows) Through rapid PDCA cycles and good A3 problem solving, these actions improve the metrics at all levels including the roll-up metrics for the entire site or region to ensure efforts are on track. S&W desires these feedback systems be rapid and visual.

Step 1. Lean Training and Tools

Video: Bob Pryor presenting the President's Award for best Lean project, CLIP Fair, November 3, 2011

Four years ago, Paul Dieckert and I went to Michigan in December to learn Lean from the best. We traveled to the icy northlands of another country called the United States. As you know, we live in the Republic of Texas [laughter]. In that frozen tundra, Paul and I would come back from class every day and say, "Aren't these amazing techniques! What if we could really engage all 13,000 employees at Scott & White to come to work every day to make things a little bit better?"

Well, you did. Just think, after four more years, where will we be? Wow! Wow! This is a dream come true.

And this isn't easy work is it? You still have a day job while you are doing all these improvements. But today, you come to work every day, you use your brains, then you go home and tell your family, "I made a difference today. Not just in my job, but for my friends, neighbors, and patients!"

Well, you really do make a difference. Your teams did this!

As the authors said earlier, everyone does training. On the date of this writing, searching "Lean training" on a popular search engine yielded 93.3 million results! So, how does the typical large organization leader make this important decision? Steve offers these tips, straight from author and Lean pioneer Jim Womack:[*]

1. Find a change agent. How about you?
2. Find a sensei (a teacher whose learning curve you can borrow).
3. Seize (or create) a crisis to motivate action across your firm.
4. Map the entire value stream for all of your product families.
5. Pick something important and get started removing waste quickly to surprise yourself with how much you can accomplish in a very short period.

Bob would be the first of many change agents at S&W. Nevertheless, he would be the most important one. Throughout their journey, if you asked anyone at S&W who leads their Lean effort, they would point to Bob, their CEO. Remarkable, isn't it? Not to Steve or any other Lean coaches.

Regarding #2 above, Steve's learning curve would be borrowed. This would include his experience with training, standing up steering councils, roles and responsibilities, projects, setup checklists, and every reasonable tool used at S&W.

---

[*] Womack, James P. and Daniel T. Jones. *Lean Thinking: Banish Waste and Create Wealth in Your Corporation*, 2nd ed. Simon & Schuster, New York, 2003. These steps were also summarized by Womack and Jones in the Foreword of *Learning to See* by John Shook and Mike Rother, LEI, 1999.

Steve started applying Lean to healthcare in early 2006, but he did not have deep healthcare knowledge. Looking back, Bob insists this was actually helpful. Many deeply experienced healthcare "experts" would join S&W and quickly sing, "Tried that. Doesn't work." Bob needed facilitators who would not buckle when the chorus started.

As the authors discussed earlier, their crisis did not need to be created. In addition, because S&W had a much higher government-pay patient mix than other health systems, their revenue curve dipped much earlier. Bob and his team did not see this as a bad thing. It would merely hurry along much-needed changes. Healthcare was just too darned expensive!

Mapping all value streams and getting some quick wins were also planned steps for S&W on its journey. In fact, S&W might have been the leading purchaser of the large rolls of white static cling write-on sheets over the past decade. More on projects in the next section.

Steve had a concern. He had taught company and university-based training courses for decades. He taught over 1000 students per year in one university program in multiple Lean programs. They carefully used the word "certificate" instead of the belt-style "certified," but still Steve fretted.

- Did these "graduating" students apply what they learned?
- Did they ever make an impact by using this stuff?

One thing was certain: pre- and post-tests were not a good indicator of effective usage. Merely counting students who lasted through training courses was not either. Steve called this "sheep dip" training. Sheep were dipped in a new tank. Baaa. Then another. No change. Baaa. Sigh.

Therefore, about three or four years into its Lean journey, S&W started measuring something that made common sense. S&W started measuring deliverables or outcomes from each course. It started with one Lean class and then spread to all of them, at least in principle.

School systems speak of outcomes-based education. But, what does that mean? S&W developed a list of the applications, projects or interventions they wanted participants to use quickly after their courses. They developed a simple tracking spreadsheet to show the actions after the course. They called these after-requirements.

Then, they did something radical. They assigned a Lean coach to *every* participant. The coach would help "walk" them through their after-requirements. Their supervisor would be involved in the selection, execution, and project success.

Before the training class, the instructor/coach would inform, cajole, and assist the participants to bring data and materials to the class. Students would bring and then work on project-scoping tasks in class. The coach would give clear directions about what would be expected after class. The participants would not receive their certificates until they did the after-requirements.

A certificate is not a big deal for a physician. However, you would be surprised. When you track completion, when you make it visible, when you measure the outcomes, they tend to get done. S&W leaders are sure of one thing—if you don't track it, it won't get done!

The way S&W approached Lean training and tools training was different. It wanted to change the thinking of every participant. S&W's focus was on people, from the point that they were on-boarded to the point to where they were self-sufficient leaders. S&W leaders know they are not there yet. They do believe they will eventually accomplish this for all leaders. It has remained in all their written goals.

Orientation and Two Hats

Do you remember your most recent orientation experience? The authors can hear the groans. If Lean thinking was to permeate every process, these principles need to be taught on every new employee's first day—orientation training.

Human Resources staff decided to walk the talk. Their goal was to fix and integrate All-Staff Orientation into the wider culture of continuous improvement effort. With a coach to facilitate, this team rolled up its sleeves and began the hard work of renovating orientation.

Tip: You can use Lean thinking on anything containing a process—even improving staff orientation! This process was a key to developing a well-oriented, flexible, capable, and highly motivated staff member.

Orientation:

We all have two jobs:
  #1: Do your job excellently
  #2: Improve your job processes every day

Figure 4.3   Orientation and executive introduction of "Two Hats."

In the opening session of orientation, a high-level leader challenged each new member with an overarching principle. Steve calls this "two hats." The leader will tell all new staff members that they enter S&W wearing two hats. Their job was to do their job well—hat #1. And, their job was also to make their job better—hat #2.

In Figure 4.3, the new S&W employee has two hats. Some leaders clarified this even more. They used the words that Toyota leaders told S&W leaders.

New employees were not just told to make their jobs "better"—as in a code word for work harder. Rather, they were told to make their jobs *easier.* This is very empowering for a new employee. Make your job add more value for the customer. You own your job. Remove the stuff from your day that you hate to do (if it is waste) and do more of the stuff that you went to school for.

In staff morale surveys, S&W staff were "highly engaged" when they were huddling daily and being asked for their ideas. This added great satisfaction to the employees. They were not told to check their brains at the door, or that they were hired just for their hands. Every day, equally as important as doing their job well, they were to improve their job.

Early on, some staff members returned from this renewed orientation to old-thinking supervisors who told them to keep their ideas to themselves. New staff pushed right back saying a leader like past Chairman of the Physician Board Dr. Andrejs Avots-Avotins or Dr. Pryor told them they wear two hats, and to have any leaders who disagree talk to them directly!

An important part of two hats is how leaders were taught to clarify it. For hat #1, they would say, "Do your job well—follow the standard work posted near your work area." For hat #2, they would say, "Make your job better—we will teach you new tools and then you can find a better way." Another cool wrinkle for hat #2 was to say, "Make your job easier. Slow down and get it right the first time!" There is something very empowering about going slow to go fast.

An orientation story: Bob Pryor was born in Temple. As stated in Bob's background, he worked at Scott & White as a teenager cleaning the morgue! He cleaned up pieces and parts off the floor of the morgue in the basement at the end of each day. He started on the bottom rung of the corporate ladder.

So, imagine Bob speaking to new staff members on their first day of orientation, some hired to sweep floors and clean. He would tell them, "I started where you are. I cleaned the floors. I cleaned the worst areas and dirtiest stuff."

Staff love to connect with their leaders. Imagine the new floor sweeper going home thinking, "Maybe I can be the CEO someday." That is a powerful thought, and very unusual after one's orientation.

S&W leaders sought to develop Lean thinkers, and it started with orientation.

Continuous Improvement Training

Training prepares the minds to fix processes. Training is one of the most important yet misused tools in creating a culture of continuous improvement. Done well, the minds of all staff are prepared for rapid and effective application of Lean principles in a fun way. Done wrong, it is misery with no clear application or purpose. In a series of motivational posters, the one called Tradition says, "Just because you've always done it that way doesn't mean it's not incredibly stupid!" In addition, healthcare staff are just too busy to put up with useless training.

Everybody does training. Everybody does Lean projects. Scott & White did these well, and capitalized on the investment.

One of the most significant differences was that S&W required deliverables from participants and tracked what they do with the training after the course. Some say, "If the learner does not learn, the teacher has not taught." S&W prescribes to this plus another critical factor: Don't teach principles unless there is a plan for the participant to use them. An after-plan of deliverables was the key.

Any lasting change requires patience. Just like a diet, small steps, repeated consistently, create new behaviors. These behaviors can and do create a new way of thinking and eventually a new culture. Training can be the first step toward transforming processes. If your organization only counts "dead bodies" (participants that "survive" a course), the authors strongly recommend something different. Make a plan for each participant to use his or her training—an after deliverable—and then track and assess whether he or she did it.

Within a year of S&W's merger with Baylor Health Care System, it was clear that multiple methodologies for continuous improvement would confuse staff, create an environment where the leaders need to choose a "version," and cause staff to repeat multiple classes of similar yet differently named concepts.

Therefore, three Common Core of Continuous Improvement short-courses for all staff (including revised orientation) were planned. This Core would replace several other versions of competing basic CI training and serve as the language of Baylor Scott & White Health (BSWH) in the future. Like the courses before it, the Common Core would be improved on every delivery.

Figure 4.4 shows the purpose of CI training and development in the stick figures. Staff and leaders arrive, sometimes without many tools or a common language for CI. Since people are an organization's greatest asset, S&W invested heavily in them toward being highly skilled leaders. The goal was not only for them to understand and use all CI tools and Lean thinking, but also to learn them well enough to develop other staff and leaders too!

Each participant/leader would also become teachers. S&W leaders saw this journey as a 5- to 7-year effort. This requires patience and investment. These pathways were to help every individual improve his or her work processes (hat#2), and become the person that he or she really wanted to be at Scott & White Healthcare.

Figure 4.4 also shows the training course lengths ('/' for less than a day and 'X' for each full day). The arrows demonstrate that each course is only the *start* of learning. Note that each arrow has more arrow lengths than black Xs. This is because the Lean journey was not about training at S&W. It was more about the doing. The words below each course represent the deliverable that is tracked and required to achieve their certificate. For several courses, participants are assigned a Lean coach to help them through their project deliverables, applying what they learned.

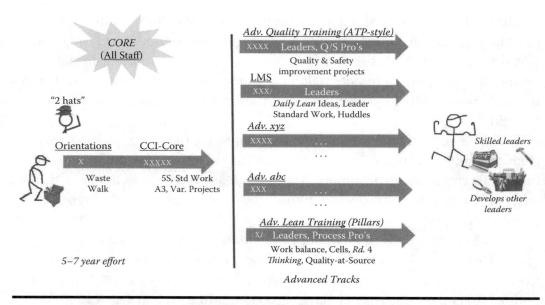

Figure 4.4 Common Core CI training and immediate applications for staff (from draft model).

Common Core Training and Applications for All Staff

The Common Core represents all courses and applications to the left of the vertical line. These are required for all staff, and are a significant step in creating a culture of continuous improvement. To the right are advanced CI courses with course lengths and deliverables.

To date, over a dozen varieties and slices of advanced CI training are being deployed. They represent advanced ways of building a culture of continuous improvement in the areas of:

■ Safety (and Justness)
■ Quality
■ Process
■ Respect and Teaming

The Core represents the start of a journey. Not of continuous improvement because the authors believe that already exists inside of every person—leaders just need to set it free. The start for every new staff member at S&W would be orientation. As stated earlier, a top leader would clarify their two hats.

About 30 days after their 2-day orientation training, all staff are required to take a day-long *Lean Fundamentals* (Lean 101) course. In it, staff fix a simulated ED using Lean principles. By fixing the ED, they teach themselves the concepts of workplace organization, problem solving, flow, and many basic Lean tools. They also learn the basics of waste-ology—the identification and removal of all categories of waste.

Their deliverable to earn a Lean Fundamentals certificate is clarified during their course—a waste walk. They will typically start the deliverable immediately. A simple form is used as shown in Figure 4.5. The eight categories of waste are listed on the left side of the form. Staff document one observable waste in each category while they are walking through their own area (thus waste "walk"). They are encouraged not to over-think solutions. They ask, "How can I reduce or eliminate it?" Then they write their possible solutions to the right of each waste.

Staff are taught to seek ideas to fully eliminate the waste if it is pure non-value-added (NVA). However, if it is NVA but currently required (e.g., by a government entity, risk, etc.), sometimes the only thing they can do is

Waste Walk Checklist		
Waste	**What do you see?**	**How to improve**
Defects, Errors, or Rework		
Overproduction		
Waiting		
Not Utilizing Employee Creativity		
Transportation		
Inventory		
Motion		
Extra Processing		

Figure 4.5   Simple waste walk form.

greatly reduce the time it takes in their day. The staff members review their waste walk with their supervisor, who circles at least one action for the staff member to try. Over the next few weeks, the supervisor ensures staff members have an opportunity to try out their ideas for waste reduction, making them check to see that it worked.

A waste walk is required of all graduates. It is tracked, and they do not get their certificate for the class until they have completed their waste walk. A larger form can be found in Figure 7.2.

They learn the philosophy, methodology, approach, and terminology— the common language for all staff.

The next course required for all staff in the Core is the *Lean Practitioner* Lean 201 course. Building a culture of continuous improvement is continuous. Each staff member is paced by his or her supervisor through these steps, although some take 3 to 4 months, and others take 12 to 18 months through their application—depending on the degree of difficulty. Some go back to pick up concepts they did not apply in earlier training courses.

In the Lean Practitioner course, participants are taught 20 or so Lean tools and principles wrapped around a fun, hands-on simulation. The goal of the practitioner course is for staff members to learn and immediately put into practice the principles of Lean. S&W leaders want to create Lean thinking leaders at all levels. This four-day course was greatly improved over time, adding S&W examples and even tips that fit its culture. S&W has trained over 6000 leaders in its four-day Lean courses.

Five different variants of multi-round simulations are used in the Core and advanced Lean tracks to teach important principles. It is more important to learn deeply and remember than to memorize acronyms and definitions. That is why S&W uses simulations so much.

Students are taught the Toyota House Model.[*] The house is also used to guide deployment and building of their Lean processes and value streams. Staff are taught different ways of thinking.

A key one is *Round 4 Thinking*. Round 4 thinking references the fourth and final round of several S&W simulations. In it, staff solve their remaining problems, balance work, get to one-piece flow, build in quality, and even take time to talk to the patients. Moreover, they do all of this without more staff or floor space! Round 4 thinking requires all these principles in place

---

[*] A basic definition of Toyota House and many other key phrases can be found at: http://www.lean.uky.edu/reference/terminology/

before any additional staff and space are requested. Why? In Round 4, they are not needed.

Probably the most critical principle weaved through all four days is that Lean and TPS are a **system**. You cannot do one part or pick and choose the parts you like. Like a car, you must have key pieces in place before it drives well. Steve saw dozens of large health systems attempt to shortcut their Lean journey, demanding ROI after the first workshops, and impatiently installing work-cells, even though the systems were not built to sustain them.

Students are also taught about value stream mapping (VSM) and A3 problem solving by working on exercises they brought to class in small teams. They learn about leadership in building a culture of CI. They see how the vision, mission, and values of S&W are deployed using Hoshin Kanri to all staff. These cascaded goals become the key Trend Charts on each supervisor's huddle board. In the class, they are given a brief overview of huddling and their key role of bringing forward ideas (second hat).

They bring real-life problems and processes into their A3 problem solving and value stream mapping (VSM) exercises. They work in teams and separately. It is a very hands-on course.

As mentioned earlier, a key differentiator in the journey at S&W was required deliverables from each key course. After their Practitioner course, S&W asks staff members to get involved in some sort of project. It could be an A3 problem-solving project, or a facilitated workshop like a Kaizen project. Others take on cross-functional projects using VSM. Staff are taught by their Lean coach how to select and use the right Lean tools as needed.

After graduates achieve most of the goals documented in their project charter, their coach gives them their *Lean Practitioner* certificate. This is equivalent to a Lean Six Sigma green belt in most organizations. S&W coaches also work with staff enough that they can use the tools on similar problems and processes in the future. Their project is seen as only their start of more improvements.

S&W did not require a project early in its journey. Those first few graduates did not experience a project of their own, and rarely coached other staff to do them. This was a key mistake corrected early on by the S&W leadership team. Later, graduates were also assigned a coach during their course. This was another improvement, as staff could attack a project better with a coach by their side. This did require quite a bit of the full-time Lean coaches' bandwidth.

The authors also strongly recommend tracking the after-requirements of the class, not just attendance.

Advanced Development Tracks for Select Staff

In Figure 4.4, you can see several advanced development tracks. Select staff need advanced training, but more importantly, experiential learning (like workshops) to further develop their CI skills. This was especially true for those in full-time quality, safety, or process improvement roles.

Not everyone will implement advanced Lean tools. S&W's Lean team tailored several advanced tracks for staff that need these experiences to be successful at their current level, and to attain the next level in their careers. For the most part, S&W leaders also saw their staff as "VPs in training."

The first arrow shows an Advanced Quality Training track. To complete this development "track," both the course and an application project (with a coach) are required. This quality and safety improvement track is designed for professionals needing advanced hands-on work to develop their skill sets. The popular Brent James Advanced Training Programs (ATP) and close variants work very well in healthcare. Baylor's STEEEP Advanced Quality course was based on this course.

The next arrow shows S&W's Lean Management Systems-building (LMS) or Lean 401 class. The application was clear—effective huddles and daily ideas flowing. In addition, as great LMS examples cropped up around S&W, they made the Toyota San Antonio tour optional. Today, about half the leaders still go on one of the Toyota guided tours with their sensei to see LMS in action at this world-class facility. Additional go-see tours of mature Lean sites like Medtronic near Fort Worth were also conducted as part of the Lean healthcare leaders' development.

The LMS track was for leaders who have titles of Director and up, but often included key managers at the request of their leader. It was designed for any leader who has staff reporting to him or her. The course was taught to and applied by the top leaders first. It must be learned and then demonstrated by the leader to his or her staff. This was critical to get buy-in for starting up huddles and making them effective.

LMS was one of the more tricky courses to execute because of its leader-first sequencing, as well as its requirement to be run at the same time as the 4-day Lean Practitioner course. LMS students move from their training room to the practitioner course room while they are running and re-capping all four rounds of their fix-the-ED simulation. This way, leaders can practice LMS-building using a fast-changing simulated process.

Staff in the practitioner course also see high-level leaders getting excited about their Lean applications. This further reinforces their learning. They eat lunch together, and then are in the same simulation room together for about two hours of the first two days of their courses.

S&W's Lean team tracks the names of the leaders that take each CI course, and they also assign each a coach, usually their instructor. They schedule and track three guided Gemba walks with them and their coach. This is in addition to the weekly Gemba walks they committed (during the LMS class) to do on their own. They are very purposeful Gemba walks, always in the graduate's own areas.

Some CI efforts are not courses at all. S&W has many interventions that are for everyone. Daily huddles and daily Lean are for everyone. Leaders personally lead the LMS-building effort. All staff are expected to bring forward and try out their ideas in daily huddles.

The fifth arrow shows other advanced Lean tool courses. As staff develop their Lean knowledge through projects, it is possible they only experience a few Lean tools. Thus, the Lean team developed and delivered several tool courses through the Scott & White University (SWU). Several modules can be taken on-demand via the Internet. Others require class interaction and teamwork and thus are taught in a group classroom. These courses cover topics and tools like A3, standard work, pull systems, and error proofing.

A critical part of the continuous improvement track model is the small graphic on the far right. It shows the purpose of the tracks and a key goal for S&W: Developing skilled leaders who learn and apply well enough that they can also develop other leaders. They replicate themselves. They become part of the long line of leader-teachers once they become somewhat self-sufficient. The Lean journey is all about people.

Also understood, but not written in this model, is celebrations. Steve likes to say, "Healthcare organizations do not know how to celebrate!" Change is tough. Celebrate (quick and low cost, of course) every step of the way. Great ideas will flow once leaders unleash them.

A key note on learning models strikes to the core of TPS and the S&W way. It is not enough to train staff on the technical skills to do each task. Organizations that will survive the next century must also teach and model teaming skills and new ways of approaching problems. They must reinforce the ability for leaders and staff to make a small misstep and quickly check their way back on track. Mostly, they must insist that all staff get to the root cause, not just stop at temporary, time-consuming, soul-sucking workarounds prevalent in healthcare today.

Lean Steering Council

In the arrow model in Figure 4.1, the first step in the "swoosh" graphic also included developing, commissioning, and sorting out the duties of a Lean steering council. The authors are careful not to use the word *committee*, from negative connotations of those mind-numbing "standing" meetings where everyone sits.

The first big decision was who would serve on this council, and how others would have input. As you might expect, Bob made the council as wide as possible to achieve greater buy-in. Rather than four or five operations leaders and his Lean expert, he would have as many as 17.

Consensus for 17 leaders takes longer. S&W's leadership team felt quite comfortable pushing back on Bob's ideas, pace, and focus. Some meetings did not yield quick decisions. This is OK. Thick skin is needed to make lasting changes. Bob preferred thinking and innovation to rote obedience. He got it. By the end of S&W's third full year of Lean, a rapid pace of change, a drumbeat, was steady and growing.

A key part of developing the Lean Steering Council was a simple charter. This defined what the teams should do, but not specifically how they would do it. This charter stated goals and a rough timeframe. It clarified what the leaders and team were responsible for.

The next big decision was whether to make Lean or CI part of a current executive steering group meeting or a separate one. This decision is not easy, and usually depends a lot on the culture and how thin the leaders are spread. At S&W, micron or razor-thin spreading was not an exaggeration. S&W's council bounced between being part of another meeting and separate a few times. This is not bad.

As S&W's Lean effort matured, making the Lean steering portion effective was always the focus. Steve recommends that the Lean agenda stop for periods of focus to keep it fresh. Lean became part of the fabric in nearly every planning and leadership group, so there was little risk of it just ending.

By the third year, Bob and his leaders decided to make Lean steering part of his weekly System Executive Committee (SEC) meetings and process. The SEC was the highest-level group of leaders at S&W, outside of its boards. Rather than create another meeting, they made Lean agenda items a key part of the SEC sessions.

The Lean agendas were divided approximately fifty-fifty. Half of it was designed to look *backward* at recent efforts for improvements, to identify which projects were successful and which should be spread or cross-walked to other areas. That was one of their key roles. It was fun if the list of projects to evaluate did not get too long. Even though S&W tried to divide the agenda items evenly, they sometimes spent more time looking backward than forward when there were more projects to review.

The other 50% of the Lean agenda was to look *forward*, scanning the organization for the most important system-level Lean efforts, projects, and interventions to do next. Steve calls this project or opportunity identification. You could summarize their backward and forward looks as *doing things right* and *doing the right things*.

Figure 4.6 shows the "funnel" of projects and efforts that could benefit from Lean analysis and workshops. The Steering Council serves to identify, vet, and group projects so that the system benefits most from the efforts of the teams. It takes organizational time to do projects, so Steering Council leaders ensure this is spent on getting the biggest bang for the buck.

This is important. The authors feel the biggest gap in most black belt or Six Sigma programs is that students are told to pick anything—just pick a project. Therefore, project choices, if left to the individual students, usually degrade to the most basic processes and areas under their direct control. Then, leaders often see these as unimportant. Sort of like straightening the lounge chairs on the Titanic.

The key questions for a steering council are, "Given our goals and current status, what system projects should we be working on, what are the gaps, and who should be leading the projects?" It is the job of the leaders to constantly scan the horizon for the most critical end-to-end interventions. It is an honor to serve on a Lean steering council.

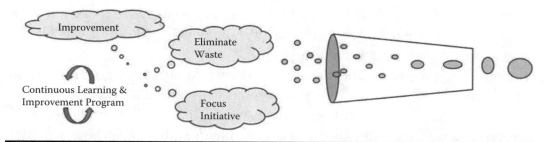

Figure 4.6   Job #1 of Lean Steering Council—funnel and prioritize improvement projects and efforts.

It takes organizational time to do projects, so Steering Council leaders ensure this is spent on getting the biggest bang for the buck.

Sausage Diagram and Project Identification— System-Wide Value Stream Mapping

Before S&W came up with a list of projects, Steve led them through a simple visual exercise called System-wide Value Stream Mapping (SVSM). S&W leaders did not do this exercise in their first Lean steering meeting. This particular graphic in Figure 4.7 was developed about one to two years into S&W's journey. It is rough, but it served to focus leaders on system improvements needed. Here is how they developed and used it.

Steve reserved three separate sessions for the Lean Steering Council to do System-wide Value Stream Mapping. He started with the question, "Why do people come to Scott & White? What do they come here to receive?" The team listed many things like a visit with their physician, emergency department visit, surgery, in-patient stays, prescriptions, second opinions, and more. They listed services that their community valued from Scott & White and then tried to connect them in some logical way.

One logical construct was to show these streams connected in some continuum of care. An example might be when a patient comes in for an ED visit. Sometimes, they are stabilized and then moved to an intensive care unit (ICU). Frequently, they are moved from either ED or ICU into a hospital room. Then, after discharge, attempts are made to reconnect these patients back to their primary care provider (PCP) for follow-up and continued treatment. We hope that they do not need to return.

You can imagine a lengthy, linear continuum of care if it was mapped out in detail. S&W leaders did no "mapping" in this exercise. Rather, they represented each value stream with a long sausage—loosely representing the length of the value stream once it was eventually mapped out. It was like a "value stream map goes here" holder oval.

Connecting the dots: The leaders first drew several sausages in a continuous chain. These were the "reasons" patients came to S&W. They were the big, cross-cutting, cross-functional value streams like the ED, in-patient stays, surgery process, and out-patient visits (e.g., physical therapy). These would be drawn horizontally. Later, the end-to-end sausages were collapsed in parallel, just to simplify the graphic for analysis, rather than in pathways of continuums of care.

Leaders recognized there were also other services that seemed to be in support of some or all of those large value streams like labs, other diagnostic tests, pain management, prescription/medicine, medicine reconciliation,

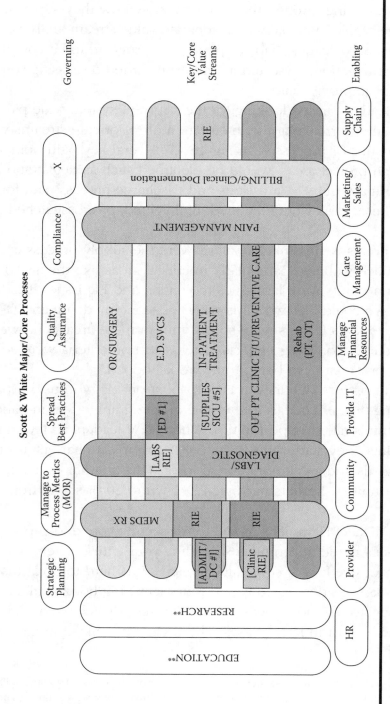

Figure 4.7 Dissection of core S&W processes—called System-wide VSM or the "sausage diagram," with ranked Lean projects at intersections.

and even billing and staff training processes. These sausages would be drawn vertically, cutting through the others to show how they support.

Each sausage would eventually be a separate value stream analysis. In just a few hours, S&W leaders had wrapped their arms around a complex and growing organization, dissected it, and even started discussing some opportunities for improvement.

Next, S&W leaders started looking for their current system-wide pain points. These were normally at the intersection of major care streams with key support streams or processes. In Figure 4.7, several key pain points, or potential Lean project areas, would be identified such as Registration in Family Med (Primary Care), Admissions and Discharge process pain for in-patients, etc. These areas were identified, highlighted, or crosshatched and labeled.

Other pain points in this initial analysis were the supply process (shortages and too much walking, particularly in critical areas like the SICU). Two related pain points were lab issues in general and ED issues. Leaders thought, "Hey, we could kill two birds with one stone by doing an ED-Lab VSM." However, S&W's leaders were spread thin in these areas, and were drained with multiple ongoing projects. Later, selection criteria were added to prevent any one area from being "over-workshopped."

Another Lean project identified was outpatient oncology infusion (patient and staff waiting times). The last one visible on the graphic was in-patient medication administration opportunities. When S&W leaders reviewed these major pain points, they started roughing out Lean project charters, listing at least a few goals and a champion or sponsor. This original list contained 40 or 50 opportunities. Leaders narrowed it down to 20 or so, all from the sausage map.

Steve liked Michael Hammer's model for dissecting core and support processes.* Hammer's model recommends dividing your entire system into no more than four or five key or core value streams. It is hard to do at first, but it made sense. S&W leaders narrowed to four or five big horizontal streams, and then four or five support ones—a total of nine. Areas like education and research waited to start in later phases. These were organized in the center of the graphic.

---

* 77Comply website, 4.1 (b) Determine sequence and interaction of processes—ISO 9001—The right way, May 11, 2014, article referencing Michael Hammer's breakdown with simple graphic: http://77comply.wordpress.com/2014/05/11/4-1-b-determine-sequence-and-interaction-of-processes-iso-9001-the-right-way/, accessed August 2014.

Hammer also recommends identifying a series of governing processes. These were major ones like strategic planning, identifying best practices and spreading them, quality, and compliance. These were drawn and labeled at the top. The lower area of the system map identified enabling processes like supply chain, marketing and sales, IT, decision support systems, Human Resources, etc. Eventually, all of these processes needed to be mapped to reduce waste and greatly improve flow.

When you put it all together, S&W leaders had areas of pain and opportunity in almost every one of their governing, core, and enabling processes. S&W's Lean Steering Council built this original model in just a few days. You can too. Identifying and dissecting your organization for opportunities can be a fulfilling task for a Lean steering council. However, you are not done with just a lengthy list of 20 to 30 opportunity projects. Which one will be first, and then second? That is discussed in the next section.

In summary, a Lean steering council looks forward 50% of the time and looks backward 50% of the time. The model shown here will help you with both views. You can use the sausage map as sort of a heat map showing where you have already applied Lean thinking, as well as to identify improvement projects in the future.

You can also use it to help spread the successes, as most Lean projects focus in one key area at a time. Spreading Lean successes does not happen naturally. S&W waited until its sixth year before they focused a staff member on identifying and spreading best practices from one site and one floor and one clinic to another.

Project Prioritization and Selection Matrix

Steve is an engineer or, as he says, an engi-nerd. He uses spreadsheets to develop most tools. When faced with the next task of a Lean steering council—project selection—he relied on a tried-and-true format from his problem solving training.* The best way to quantify a "decision" type problem and make it repeatable is to use a ***decision matrix***. It also removes any angst leaders have about choosing.

---

* Focus Tools website, Decision Focus Training Reference Card; http://www.focustools.com/pdf/ DFRefCard.pdf.

The project selection process to fill out the matrix is:

1. Step 1: Communicate the goal clearly to all stakeholders, which was to select and prioritize the Lean projects that satisfy all *Musts* and rate among the highest scores on *Wants*.
2. Step 2: Brainstorm and continuously update a list of criteria to be used to prioritize Lean projects (Musts and Wants).
3. Step 3: Apply a weight to each criteria (Want); use a simple nominal group technique (AKA 3-2-1 voting, see next section) to make this more interactive and effective.
4. Step 4: List potential Lean projects (brief: area-event type); start with those identified in the Sausage Diagram mentioned in the previous section; add and combine.
5. Step 5: Answer "Yes" or "No" on each Must for each potential project; only all "Yes" answers will be ranked in the next step.
6. Step 6: Force-rank each Want (row), enter a 1 to 10, multiply by the weight; total each potential project at bottom.

In the decision matrix, leaders choose in advance (key) what criteria would be required for their Lean project candidates. These are the "Musts." If any criteria question answers "No," the project is immediately dropped out of this round of selection.

Next, leaders decide in advance what criteria would be desired to help force-rank each alterative project against each other. These are the "Wants." Steve believes strongly that a selection matrix should be used for selecting at least the first round of end-to-end, cross-functional projects. For S&W's Lean Steering Council, the criteria were developed over several meetings. The project selection matrix in Figure 4.8 was completed after the criteria were developed. A larger sized version of this can be found in Figure 7.3.

There is a sequence to good project prioritization and selection using the project selection matrix. In Figure 4.8, some of the boxes are numbered to help the leaders focus on the steps in order. Step number 1 is the goal: Select and prioritize the Lean events that satisfy all Musts and rate among the highest scores on Wants. This goal statement is meant to lay out the purpose in a single sentence.

Step number 2 is to list the criteria to be used. In a nutshell, the steering council must identify what makes a good Lean project. Some of the criteria will be required (Musts) or else the potential project is thrown out. Other criteria is important (Wants), and will be used to force-rank the potential projects.

Musts are things that must be true of any Lean project. The example given here is there must be improved or maintained patient access, and the second one is increased staff satisfaction. This *Must* was unusual for Steve. However, a negative headcount-focused consulting engagement had damaged the trust for S&W staff in their recent past. Staff satisfaction would be necessary.

The third was increased operational efficiency. There must be some expected impact or staff may not feel the workshop was effective, given all of their time. You will also note this criterion is listed again in the Want section (see next). It is okay to repeat some of the Musts again in the Wants, if leaders want to rank projects on that criterion. Another key Must was no other competing projects. S&W leaders learned from experience that overloading staff and leaders in an area could doom projects.

Wants are also important. Criteria for Wants were also brainstormed. These were used to rank all projects, after they answer all the Musts. Steve recommends minimizing Musts to the top three or four, and the Wants to no more than about seven.

Step number 3 is to weight the Wants. Some will be more important than others. Steve coaches leaders to use a simple nominal group technique called 3-2-1 voting. Once the Wants were written clearly on the whiteboard, each leader came forward and wrote 3 (for 3 points) next to the one they thought was the highest priority, 2 to their next highest, and 1 to the third-highest criteria.

All leaders voted privately by writing on the flipchart list in less than 6 to 7 minutes. Once assembled, Steve gave a weight of 10 to their top vote getter (increases operational efficiencies) and 6 to the lowest (common process, transferrable across system) because the votes were close. The others were weighted according to their votes using simple normalization of the votes.

Step number 4 was to write in the potential Lean projects (brief: area-event type). Most were the 20 or so listed on the sausage diagram, but a few more were added and a few were combined as the leaders wrote them. Please note that leaders should agree on criteria and weighting *before* writing the projects. That way, no leader can write criteria that give undue priority to specific projects (either negatively or positively). The potential projects were written on the selection form in any order.

Setup is now complete; the following steps will now rank the projects.

S&W Lean Steering Council's Project Selection Worksheet

(1) End Result — Select and prioritize the Lean events that satisfy all Musts and rate among the highest scores on Wants.

CRITERIA (2)	(4) LIST ALL POTENTIAL LEAN PROJECTS																	
	1. ED: - Patient in ED room to be discharged or sent to bed (VSM)		2. Temple Lab: From test ordered (ED) to resulted (excl. instrument processing time)		3. EVS-Laundry Delivery (Project on hold at request of Deb S.)		4. Pharmacy: Inpatient medication administration for Adult patients in med/surg		5. Discharge patient from med/surg unit; planning from admit until room is ready for next patient		6. Temple OR: From Consult to Post-Op (increase capacity, schedule?)		7. EVS - OR Turnover (Project on hold at request of Deb S.)		8. Supplies: From SICU Unit re-supply order (std supplies) to avail. for use on Unit	
MUSTS:	INFO	Y/N	INFO	Y/N	INFO	Y/N	INFO	Y/N	INFO	Y/N	INFO	Y/N	INFO	Y/N	INFO	Y/N
Improves or maintains Patient access to healthcare		Y		Y		Y?		Y?		Y		Y				Y?
Increases Staff Satisfaction w/Process		Y		Y		Y?		Y?		Y		Y				Y?
Increases Operational Efficiencies		Y		Y		Y?		Y?		Y		Y				Y?
Aligns w/Vision/Mission/Values		Y		Y		Y?		Y?		Y		Y				Y?
Increases Patient Safety		Y		Y		Y?		Y?		Y		Y				Y?
No competing current projects	roll into one project	Y	re-scope to avoid overlap	Y		Y?		Y?		Y		Y		No		Y?
A Champion exists	Dr. Steve S.	Y	Denise S.	Y	Name?	Y?	J. P.	Y?	A. D.	Y	Bob C.	Y	Name?	Y?	Jon N, IP Clinical Manager	Y?
Goals:																

WANTS:	(3) HOW IMPOR-TANT (1-10)	(5) HOW GOOD (0-10)	INFO	SCORE	HOW GOOD (0-10)	INFO	SCORE	HOW GOOD (0-10)	INFO	SCORE	HOW GOOD (0-10)	INFO	SCORE	HOW GOOD (0-10)	INFO	SCORE	HOW GOOD (0-10)	INFO	SCORE	HOW GOOD (0-10)	INFO	SCORE	HOW GOOD (0-10)	INFO	SCORE
Can be done quickly	8	2		16	6		48				10		80	3		24	1		8				2		16
Capital costs	7	8		56	6		42				9		63	10		70	2	sched	14				1		7
Highly Visible	8	10		80	6		48				5		40	7		56	10		80				10		80
Data easily available	7	10		70	10		70				8		56	4		28	4		28				1		7
Common/translatable across	6	7		42	8		48				9		54	9		54	4		24				10		60
Increase Operational	10	10		100	10		100				6		60	9		90	10		100				8		80
RELATIVE MERIT (Total Score)				364			356			353			322			254						250

RELATIVE THREAT (from Risk Analysis)

Figure 4.8   Project selection worksheet.

Step number 5 was for the leader team to answer "Yes" or "No" on each Must for each potential project. If the leaders were not sure, they used a red font and assigned someone to collect data with a short due date. Notice the ED project and the Temple Lab easily answered "Yes" to all the Must questions. However, the EVS (environmental services) project needed some data.

There were 25 potential projects in S&W leaders' first round, so the spreadsheet continues to the right. Some projects answered "No" and were immediately kicked out to the next year for reconsideration.

A later improvement on this matrix was to add some expected goals and the name of a possible Executive Sponsor for each project. These became Musts as well, or the project would not be commissioned by the Lean Steering Council.

With 14 of the 25 potential projects answering "Yes" for all Musts, it was time to force-rank these 14 in the Want section. Step number 6 is what Steve calls "fun with math!" For each row (criteria), each potential project was force-ranked, giving a value of 10 to the *highest*-ranked project for that specific criteria/row. Usually a 4 or 5 was given to the *lowest*. Notice that all weights and ranks are whole numbers 1 to 10, with 10 being the best.

In the sample matrix for the highest-weighted criteria (increases operational efficiencies), the ED and Temple Lab projects received a 10, but the Inpatient Pharmacy project* only received a 6, and some projects off to the right received less.

Each Want (row) was force-ranked against each other; a 1 to 10 was entered and then multiplied by the weight. Finally, the total points were added up. As the Lean Steering Council reviewed the best potential projects, they can sometimes change the sequence, based on other input and factors (e.g., some projects must be done in sequence, or to avoid overloading support staff in the same area).

This is not just a mechanical exercise by the leaders. It produces a good list of ranked projects. However, it also serves to answer the question, "What characteristics about processes make for a good Lean project?" It identifies the Musts and Wants—the criteria—that will be used to reprioritize and re-sequence all future efforts.

---

* One of the highest financial returns came from Lean efforts and huddles in the Inpatient Pharmacy. This is why Steve knowingly says, "Lean is not a replacement for good leadership. Use any tool with judgment and factor in new input to switch the resulting order when it makes sense to do so. It is just a tool."

Just to keep it simple, a Lean steering council needs to decide as a team what makes a good Lean project. This selection matrix works for any effort—not just Lean or process improvement projects. You could add Six Sigma (or other quality, safety, service or variation reduction effort), and other projects big and small. These could include cross cutting bigger ones like Value Stream Mapping projects, as well as those with quick wins like 5S or smaller problem-solving workshops.

Maintaining the Matrix: How Detailed?

Updating the matrix does not need to be done frequently. As the Lean steering council does its forward-looking scan for new project opportunities, it often *informally* re-ranks the projects. However, it is careful to use the criteria, not crisis-of-the-moment, to re-sequence the projects.

Leaders reviewed the ongoing, ready-to-launch, and new potential Lean projects. They informally did the "math" exercise (quickly) and then re-slotted the new opportunity based on criteria. For the first few years, it was common for S&W leaders to add in new, higher priority projects every few weeks or so.

S&W rarely needed to stop and pull-off an already-started project.

Step 2. Major Lean Projects: Self-Sufficiency Plan

The most common way to apply continuous improvement principles after a learning session is to complete a project. Projects can be fun. They are team-based. As stated earlier, all organizations do projects. S&W leaders were hungry for projects after taking their 4-day certificate course.

In Step 1 of the previous section, S&W's project prioritization and selection matrix was shown. The Lean steering council made sure S&W was doing the right things. On each project, the Lean coaches worked hard at helping teams do things right.

Project checklists, scripts, timelines, and sample presentations and tools all were used to ensure great outcomes. Two key differentiators about projects at S&W were leader roles and self-sufficiency. Both will be discussed briefly.

Video: Bob Pryor presenting the President's Award for best Lean Project, CLIP Fair, November 3, 2011

What amazing work has been done! If we tried to hire consultants to come into Scott & White and do this amount of work, number 1, it couldn't be done. Not the total work you have done.

How does it feel to take a problem that has been around for a long time? Maybe you have even said, "If someone ever gave me the ability — I could fix Scott & White!" I used to say that! {Laughter}

Isn't it a great feeling to spot problems, and have the ability to make meaningful changes! It's not just work. It's meaningful work that affects our patients and their families every day.

Leader Roles

> Everything rises and falls on leadership, but knowing how to lead is only half the battle. Understanding leadership and actually leading are two different activities.[*]
>
> **—John Maxwell in**
> ***The 21 Indispensable Qualities of a Leader***

In *A CEO Checklist for High-Value Health Care,*[†] several health system CEOs report the two foundational elements in transforming processes were:

■ Governance priority (visible and determined leadership by CEO and Board)
■ Building for a culture of continuous improvement (commitment to ongoing, real-time learning)

S&W leaders embraced this challenge.

In his teaching and consulting roles, Steve met with many leaders who were tagged as Sponsors and then "blamed" for CI project failures. In every

---

[*] Maxwell, John, *The 21 Indispensable Qualities of a Leader: Becoming the Person Others Will Want to Follow,* Thomas Nelson, Nashville, 1999.
[†] Cosgrove, Delos et al., A CEO Checklist for High-Value Health Care, IOM Roundtable on Value & Science-Driven Health Care, 2012.

case, the leaders emphatically stated they were never told what they were expected to do nor even asked to do more than attend the team's presentation. When key action items were invariably left on the table un-implemented, team members slowly returned to their old ways, possibly more cynical. Others openly blamed "leadership." There is a better way.

S&W tailored clear-cut roles and responsibilities documents for two key project leader roles—Executive Sponsor (no more than 3) and Process Owner (one and only one). Steve or a Lean coach would read the document with the prospective sponsor and then confirm that he or she chose to do the role. He summarized, "You own the Charter. The scope, goals, and every team member. Please do not second-guess the scope or goals when the team reports out! They are yours. Understand your project and lead behind-the-scenes."

Steve described the setup, workshop, and follow-up process in detail to the sponsors one at a time. He carefully checked their knowledge, ability, and capacity to lead the team. He then prepared them for their big tasks— knocking down hurdles once the team started implementing their major chunks of changes. Change is hard. Thus, sponsors need to be bulldogs.

A sample charter is shown in Figure 4.9. It shows the basic process, scope, team, and goals planned for a VSM-type workshop in fall 2013. A larger-sized version of this can be found in Figure 7.4.

Some key highlights on a charter are:

- Scope (upper left): always listed as "From" and "To"; also clarify areas that are in or out of scope
- Goals (right): numeric, shows baseline and expected improvements (this example blanks out the actual numbers)
- Case for change (upper right): a starter list of the undesirable effects of the current process
- Team (center): Each major area to be mapped is represented; also note that the supervisor of each subject matter area was contacted first allowing them to choose representatives; this gives these areas more input and thus more buy-in
- Dates (lower left): required dates for the team are set; the facilitator will ensure every role from sponsor, process owner, team member and even ad hoc (part-time) members know when they are expected to attend and their roles

SCOTT&WHITE
Healthcare

Inbound Domestic and Global Medical Process

Team Name:	Inbound Domestic and Global Medical Process	**Updated:** 1/14/14
Event Date:	See Schedule	**Created:** 7/22/13

Process Purpose: Define best process for Inbound Domestic and Global Medical Travel. Use existing pricing for physicals with the ultimate goal to create a single process with simple pricing and payment structure.	**Problems/Case for Change:** - History of "1-offs" and independent, quasi-processes - Accepting Insurance and end-to-end coordination
Process Scope: From Patient Intake to Patient Discharge; Final payment by Intake	- **Some partial attempts, and some good work in localized areas?**
In Scope: Interpreter Services, cash paying patients for history and physicals (Initially)	- **No single way for legacy Guests, Walmart, Bundled Patients AND international?**
Out of Scope: All other regions other than Temple; all other visit reasons other than History and Physicals (initially)	- Today, we only accept cash; Future: major global insur (Aetna, Cigna) and Int'l patient's insur (patient pays then reimbursed)

Central Steering Committee:

TEAM

Last Name	First Name	MD Role (RN, IT, etc.)	Manager (Last, First)
F	Miguel	Interpreter Services	Matt B
A	Linda	Business Office	
B	Mark	Strategy/Insur.	
K	Eyal	Hospitality	
W	Barbara	MD Exec Health/Physician	
M	Michael	Guest Services, Transp.	
H	William	Finance	

Executive Sponsor Dr. Andrejs A	Julie	S	Devel. Office
Executive Sponsor Steve S	Tom	M	Specialty Clinics
Executive Sponsor Matt B	Terry	W	Case Manager	Matt B
Process Owner Steven M	Alicia	T	Operations	Scott S
Process Owner	Rose	A	Finance	
O.E. Coach			**AD HOC TEAM**
O.E. Coach Steve Hoeft	Victoria	E	VP Revenue Cycle

PROJECT TIMEFRAME				
	?	?	Legal/Risk	John C
Kickoff/Scoping: 8/2/13 10-noon, Gober	Courtney	B	Scheduling	
Scoping: 8/12/13 noon-2pm, Coates	Robert	P	MD Chairman of Board	
VSM Workshop Half-day sessions > (dates)	Phyllis	R	Clinic Trng	Lorraine B
Followup Meetings:	Patty	C	EPIC Trng	
1 1/15/14 9–10 Conf Ctr	Janda	E	Dir Mgd Care Contracts	
2 End of Feb – TBD 8–10	Dianne	G	VP of Mgd Care/Contracts	
3 3/13/14 8–10				
4 4/10/14 8–10				

Daily or Weekly Huddles(Loc?)

Thursday-reminder for updates; Friday-action plan review by process owner and coach; weekly "wins" post

GOALS/METRICS

ITEM	CURRENT	GOAL
Number of global travelers by month	?	?
Patient satisfaction survey; % responses of "extremely satisfied"	?	?
Per Case: $ received versus cost of services	Partial	?
	?	?
Other metrics: Number of calls for services per month. Conversion rate from number of calls to number of visits. Reasons patients did not receive services from S&W. Time from request for quote to quote.		
1. How to Quote fixed price in advance (process, do we go at risk)?		
2. Can we issue fixed single price Bundled prices? How? To whom?		
3. How much med info can we get in advance? Reliable?		
4. In what conditions can we screen and do procedure in same week?		
5. How to do remote work? 2nd Opinions, Radiology screenings, etc.		
6. If we Quote fixed price "Bundle", can we bill insurance w/o detail?		
7. Do we take international insurance? Best process?		
8. Will fixed rates cause issues with some Insurers?		
9. How do we market this program?		

Figure 4.9   Example Lean project charter for a VSM workshop.

Steve or a Lean coach ensured that the sponsors agreed to all dates they would be needed, and even coached them on questions to ask after the workshop when the teams were implementing actions (like "where are my results?"). He would also jokingly add, "Be glad you are not the Process Owner! They own all the action items!"

For the past decade of applying Lean in healthcare, most Lean projects were consultant-led. The authors do not feel this is helpful. Granted, everyone needs a start. Bob and Steve echo Jim Womack's recommendation regarding a sensei in *Lean Thinking*. He says, "Find a sensei (a teacher whose learning curve you can borrow)."[*]

One difference between a sensei and a consultant is that the sensei will help keep you out of the "bear traps" or deployment missteps while still allowing leaders to learn key lessons on their own.

A sensei asks. A consultant tells. A consultant will attempt to make the leaders more dependent on them (e.g., more follow-on contracts of the same types, showing staff how to use training materials then refusing to allow them to use "their copyrighted materials" after the contract ends, etc.).

To summarize, leaders and leadership look and feel a lot different under Lean thinking. If you notice in Figure 4.10, the leader is depicted as a coach, writing out the plan on a chalkboard and encouraging staff. This was one of the biggest transformation shifts at Scott & White.

A typical supervisor, any person with direct reports, often feels he or she must have all the answers. In Lean thinking, a supervisor becomes the one that helps staff call their own plays. He or she becomes sort of a

Figure 4.10   New: Leader as coach, staff as talented players that need to work together.

---

[*] Womack, James, *Lean Thinking*, Ibid.

player-coach and motivator who is OK cheering from the sidelines when it is more effective. The supervisor needs to have the transparency to say he or she does not have all the answers, but believes the staff members do!

Self-Sufficiency Philosophy

Steve never liked the label consultant. He was taught at Delta Kogyo and JCI using the sensei method, so he passes on this sometimes-painful method to leaders who choose to involve themselves in the contact sport of organization-wide transformation.

The only plan that works for Lean projects is a self-sufficiency philosophy. Steve says, "If the sensei will not give you the date he or she exits the buildings where they worked, you need to get a real sensei." Exit plan. Many leaders see words that sound like self-sufficiency on consultant proposals, but few actually observe a written exit plan that shows how many internal staff become self-sufficient, when, and how they will be developed.

The plan at S&W was for coaches from an outside organization to demonstrate projects or workshops a few times. One or two internal S&W coaches shadowed them at all times. This philosophy became a strategic advantage for S&W and taught Bob's staff "how to fish" for themselves. S&W invested heavily in staff members who were to be full-time central Lean coaches. They also invested deeply in part-time embedded Lean coaches who stayed in their departments, working key jobs but still leading continuous improvement efforts.

Steve and some top-notch senseis quickly taught internal staff at S&W how to run their own workshops and do their own training. They used a three-step development method: see one, do (co-lead) one, and then teach one on their own. The number of times staff members need to see their sensei do each of the three steps was based on their abilities and experiences beforehand, so additional steps were needed at times. Everyone is different. Steve and team allowed the staff members and their supervisors the ability to say when they were ready.

Steve always says, "We pushed them out of their comfortable nests usually a bit before they were ready." Experience and reflection are great teachers on this journey. A person thrown in a pool will try to swim quicker than the one in the classroom.

Another way to describe the train-the-trainer process was similar to the process for learning medicine—practice in chunks. First, they observed or shadowed others—usually their sensei or master coach. Then, they learned to master individual pieces. By stringing some of them together (e.g., co-teaching the first half of a class in one session, then the back half in the next), they learned to master the whole of a course or workshop. Then, S&W took them one step further. They taught the individual how to teach others. This is a unique and very effective approach.

Many, Many Projects

A screen shot of some S&W projects can be seen in Figure 4.11. These represent a few of over 700 tracked projects at S&W since 2009, including smaller "class" projects.

Process improvement projects at S&W can be divided loosely into four major facilitated "workshop" types (from largest to smallest scope):

1. **Effort:** large transformational projects across entire organization, like Same-Day Access, Hospital Patient Flow, etc.
2. **VSM:** larger, cross-functional, end-to-end workshops where the deliverable was an 8- to 12-month action plan; many Lean tool systems are often installed; these were recast every year

	Year	Action Item / Improvement Detail	Clinic or Hospital	Location	Dept	Lean Tool / Project	Type of Improvement	Improvement (free text)	Unit of measure	Per	The Math (free text)
57	2011	5S Hillcrest ER Hallway	Hospital	Hillcrest	ED	5S	Process Time (minutes)	40.00	minutes	Day (24 hours)	
58	2011	Infusion Chemo Supply Kits saved 3 min per patient	Hospital	Memorial	Infusion	VSM	Wait Time - Patient (minutes)	150.00	minutes	Day (24 hours)	
59	2011	H2H File - Dr. Berry	Hospital	Memorial	Med-Surg	VSM					3 mins per patient X 50 patients per day
60	2011	Next Gen File - Chris	Clinic	*All Locations	Family Medicine	VSM					
61	2011	Time to answer customer phone call (PBX)	Hospital	Memorial	PBX	5s	Process time (%)	60.00	percent (%)	Day (24 hours)	60% improvement - average call answered reduced from 30 to 18 seconds
62	2011	Service Level increase (PBX)	Hospital	Memorial	PBX	VSM	Customer Service	19.00	percent	Day (24 hours)	increased from 47 to 66%
63	2011	Decreased abandon rate (PBX)	Hospital	Memorial	PBX	VSM	Customer Service	5.01	percent	Day (24 hours)	decreased from 14.2 to 9.19%
64	2011	RR hospotal 5S	Hospital	UMC - Hospital	Inpatient	5s	Wait Time - Staff (minutes)	500.00	minutes	Day (24 hours)	savings of 5 mins per patient, 20 patients per day 5 doc per day = 500 mins per day
65	2011	RR hospotal 5S	Hospital	UMC - Hospital	Inpatient	5s	roughput - Patient (# of patien	5.00	Patients	Day (24 hours)	5 extra patients seen per day
66	2011	RR hospotal 5S	Hospital	UMC - Hospital	Inpatient	5s	Revenue Enhancement ($)	182,500.00	dollars ($)	Yearly	5 patients day * $100 per pt *365 year
67	2011	BCS lean layout	Clinic	College station	all clinc	Lean Layout	Cost Avoidance ($)	230,000.00	dollars ($)	One time savings	
68	2011	Marble Falls Lean Layout	Clinic	Marble Falls	all clinc	Lean Layout	Cost Avoidance ($)	130,000.00	dollars ($)	One time savings	
69	2011	Marble Falls Lean Layout	Clinic	Marble Falls	all clinc	Lean Layout	Revenue Enhancement ($)	400,000.00	dollars ($)	Yearly	
70	2011	RR OR mesh cart	Hospital	UMC - Hospital	OR	VSM	Inventory ($)	67,000.00	dollars ($)	One time savings	
71	2011	RR OR sutures cart	Hospital	UMC - Hospital	OR	5s	Inventory ($)	16,200.00	dollars ($)	One time savings	108 boxes of sutures returned to supplier
72	2011	pathology lab waste reduction	Hospital	Memorial	Anatomic Pathology	A3	Process Time (minutes)	105.00	minutes	Day (24 hours)	
73	2011	RR 5s Anesthesia cart	Hospital	UMC - Hospital	Anesthesia	5s	Process Time (minutes)	37.50	minutes	Day (24 hours)	2 min/day x 25 cases = 50 min/day of anesthesiologists time before 0.5 min/day x 25 cases = 12.5 min/day of anesthesiologists time after. NET TIME SAVINGS 37.5 minutes
74	2011	RR OR 5s equipment room	Hospital	UMC - Hospital	OR	5s	Process Time (minutes)	630.00	minutes	Day (24 hours)	5min/day x 5 pieces equip per case = 25 min a day x 25 cases per day = 10.5 hours/day saved looking for equipment
75	2011	RR OR 5s surgical trays	Hospital	UMC - Hospital	OR	5s	Process Time (minutes)	50.00	minutes	Week	
76	2011	RR doctor preference cards	Hospital	UMC - Hospital	OR		Process Time (minutes)	630.00	minutes	Week	5 min/case X 25 cases/day = 125 min a day X 5 days a week = 10hr 25 min a week saved
77	2011	pain clinic inventry A3	Clinic	RR UMC 302 Clinic	Pain	A3	Inventory ($)	14,148.00	dollars ($)	One time savings	Top 6 items , Old stocking levels = $22,949, New Stocking levels = $8,801 Savings = $14,149
78	2011	ED charge lag	Hospital	Memorial	ED	A3	Increased collections ($)		dollars ($)	One time savings	pull in charge lag from 7 days to 4 days X $ per day

Figure 4.11   Scott & White Lean project database.

3. **Kaizen:** medium-sized, usually in one department plus support groups, where the deliverable during a brief period was to implement 80% or more of their ideas; a few Lean tool systems are installed
4. **A3 root-cause problem solving:** small to large, focused on a specific problem, where the deliverable is a solved problem with all goals met

Many healthcare Lean leaders and even black belts are surprised when S&W Lean staff relate their work on efforts. Lean thinking became so pervasive at S&W that Lean methods, tools, and even deploying strategy were used in every facet of every effort. If it was big, S&W deployed Lean coaches to support. S&W uses a typical project charter on big efforts, but deploys most of the PDCA cycles in their huddles. More on huddles in Chapter 4, Step 4 Daily Lean (LMS).

S&W also labels projects as "class" or regular. Staff members must complete a Lean project to graduate from their practitioner course. Because of this requirement, "class" projects are not prioritized by a Lean Steering Committee. Rather, the Lean coach assigned to the student will help him or her get started and then coach behind the scenes if needed.

Yet another way to slice S&W's Lean projects is to show how much Lean coach facilitation time was needed. The following list is not exhaustive, but it does show required levels of Lean coach facilitation from most to least:

1. Effort
2. VSM
3. System A3/Kaizen
4. Local A3
5. Lean tool implementation (e.g., pull systems, error proofing, cells, 5S, standard work)
6. "Class" projects (e.g., small A3, 5S, standard work)
7. Just-do-its (little facilitation, except teaching guardrails and ensuring they check to see if it worked)
8. Huddle ideas (no facilitation provided outside of a few demonstrations on how to huddle effectively)

Case for Action	What We Did
• Need to improve transition of care for patient safety & satisfaction • Need to decrease re-hospitalizations → Medicare will no longer pay for Re-Admits w/in 30 days **Goals:** • Reduce readmissions in all DRGs w/in 30 days by 20% • Reduce Fm1 to OBS by 50% • Reduce ED visits w/in 30 days after discharge by 20% • Improved patient satisfaction (Press-Ganey questions related to patient discharge)	• Break HUC and Case Manager/Discharge Planner bottlenecks-NVA Analysis, work level loading • FM1 team reviewing potential discharges at 8 am • Developing dedicated number to call for patients after discharge • Develop standard work for reviewing Rx with patients prior to discharge **Next Steps:** Implement Just Do-Its Review NVA Analysis on Case Mgr. and HUC roles, eliminate/reduce NVA and level load NVA-required items

Expectations/Results	Team
• Reduce Re-Adm in all DRGs w/in 30 days by 20% • Reduce Fm1 to OBS by 50% • Reduce ED visits w/in 30 days after D/C by 20% • Improve Pt Sat (P-G Pt D/C) by mean score of 50% • Schedule all appts. and tests prior to D/C • Decrease no-show rate on D/C follow-ups	**Alma**, MD **Will**, Embedded coach **Julianne**, Quality **Sondra**, 6N Nurse **Allan**, MD **Myra**, 6N HUC **D. Scott**, MD **Terri**, Case Mgmt **Kristy** **Tod**, I. T. Analyst **Craig**, Embedded Coach **Norma**, Resident **Brooke**, Embedded Coach **John**, Resident Dir. **Beth**, RN **Sean**, Home Care **Joy**, PharmD **Paula** **Bryan**, Process Owner **Tiffany**, MD, Process Owner

Figure 4.12 Standard Lean project summary for leaders called a Quad Chart.

A good way to standardize the display of Lean projects to leaders is to require a quad chart summary slide. With dozens of projects ongoing at any point in time in the S&W system, leaders need a standardized and easy way to view results. Figure 4.12 shows a quad chart for S&W's *Hospital-to-Home* VSM Team.

The quad chart is actually four standard slides from every Lean project report-out. The four sections of the quad chart are:

1. **Case for Action:** or case for change; answers why the team worked so hard at changing the process
2. **What they did:** key actions
3. **Results:** or expected results both before and after numbers are shown where possible, and if they met the goal set forth by the sponsors
4. **Team:** it is all about people

Prework Checklist

0
###

	CENTRAL COACH TASKS	PARTICIPANTS (Who else is involved in process step)	TIMELINE (How long before VSM start must item be)	DURATION (Meeting length or calendar block)	EARLIEST DUE (Date)	LATEST DUE (Date)	STATUS ↑ (Date, I, O)	UPDATES / NOTES
				Manual data entry in WHITE boxes only	FIRST day of VSM event (mm/dd/yy) 1/12/2015		(C)omplete (I)n Process (O)verdue	
CHARTER / SCOPING								
1	Identify Executive Sponsor(s)	Leadership, COE Director or Steering	14 weeks	--	Mon 10/06/14	Mon 10/06/14		
2	High-Level scoping meeting with Executive Sponsors	ES, CC	14 weeks	1-2 hours	Mon 10/06/14	Mon 10/06/14		
3	Identify Process Owners	ES, CC	14-12 weeks	--	Mon 10/06/14	Mon 10/20/14		
4	Identify key MDs	ES, PO, CC	14 weeks	--	Mon 10/06/14	Mon 10/06/14		
5	Charter & SIPOC Meeting #1	ES, PO, CC	12-10 weeks	1 hour	Mon 10/20/14	Mon 11/03/14		
5a	Identify team members	ES, PO, CC	12-10 weeks	In Charter meeting	Mon 10/20/14	Mon 11/03/14		
5b	Identify possible VSM dates (or set event date)	ES, PO, CC	14-12 weeks	In Charter meeting	Mon 10/06/14	Mon 10/20/14		
6	Notify Project Manager of VSM Event Date	CC, PM	14-12 weeks	--	Mon 10/06/14	Mon 10/20/14		
7	Give draft Charter to Project Manager	CC	12-10 weeks	--	Mon 10/20/14	Mon 11/03/14		
7a	Update Project Manager on Charter changes	CC, Team Leadership	as needed	as needed	--	--		
TRAINING								
1	High-Level overview with Process Owner(s)	CC, PO	14-12 weeks	1 hour	Mon 10/06/14	Mon 10/20/14		
1a	Scoping Process	CC, PO	--	--	--	--		
1b	Process Owner Expectations	CC, PO	--	--	--	--		
2	Second Training / Huddle with Process Owner(s)	CC, PO	6-4 weeks	1 hour	Mon 12/01/14	Mon 12/15/14		
2a	Create/post project board	CC, PO	--	--	--	--		
2b	Gather metrics	PO	--	--	--	--		
2c	VSM event expectations / schedule	CC, PO	--	--	--	--		
3	Overview Training for team (not been to 4-day)	CC, Team	2-1 weeks	2-4 hours	Mon 12/29/14	Mon 01/05/15		
VSM EVENT PREP								
1	Ensure updated Exec. kickoff presentation on computer	CC, ES	1 day	--	Mon 01/05/15	Sun 01/11/15		
2	Refer to Event Materials Checklist Tab	CC, PM, CLIP Admin	1 day	--	Sun 01/11/15	Sun 01/11/15		

Charter | SIPOC | **Central Coach Prework** | Admin. Assist. Prework | Project Manager Prework | Event Materials Checklist | Postwork Checklist

Figure 4.13 S&W Lean project setup checklist, multi-tab (VSM).

Setup Checklists

The S&W Lean team tailored several project setup checklists, tools, visual systems, and many other great practical helps to get projects going and keep them on track. A Roles & Responsibilities document for two key project leaders was described earlier in Leader Roles.

Figure 4.13 shows a version of a setup checklist. This one is for a VSM workshop. The scope of a VSM workshop is larger. The scope tends to cross multiple departments with many support departments. Moreover, the beginning and end of the process studied is usually wide, sometimes described as end-to-end.

Because of this, VSMs tend to have larger teams (8 to 15 staff) of cross-functional subject matter experts and leaders. This requires enough lead-time to get the right staff in the room. S&W's VSM setup checklist starts at least 17 weeks before the actual mapping begins.

This three-month period allows enough time to "negotiate" for the right staff involvement, and ensures that even providers' schedules can be cleared.

> Up to half of the eventual results are fixed by the time the sponsors and process owners publish the charter (scope, goals, and most importantly the team).

Steve often says up to half of the eventual results are fixed by the time the sponsors and process owners publish the charter (scope, goals, and most importantly the team).

This checklist walks the facilitator and workshop process owner through the setup steps. Once the workshop start date is filled in at the top, the other dates under "earliest due date" are filled in automatically. These dates can be overwritten if the workshop needs to start earlier due to priorities. Codes under "Participants" show who does the task (e.g., ES for Executive Sponsor, CC for Central Lean Coach, etc.).

Note the tabs at the bottom. The first tab is the project charter. This is critical, and is fleshed out by the Lean coach, sponsors, and process owner over time. The facilitator starts filling this out during the very first conversation.

The second tab is labeled SIPOC. This stands for Suppliers, Inputs, Process, Outputs, and Customers. It is very helpful in setting up a large project. First, it bounds the process—shows the scope. And, as process steps are added along with suppliers (of inputs to each step) and customers (outputs of each step), you see that more subject matter experts are needed in order to map the process.

The output of the SIPOC becomes a checklist identifying the types of knowledge that are needed to conduct a successful workshop. It helps flesh out the invite list for the team—who will be required and optional attendees. An example of SIPOC is shown in Figure 4.14.

A larger form is included in Figure 7.5.

The most critical part of a setup checklist is the due dates on the right. The assigned Lean coach and project leaders ensure required project setup tasks are completed on or before these timeframes. As each step is completed, the coach or facilitator documents the date each item is completed and notes on the right. In this way, the setup checklist is a living document used to coach supervisors, process owners, and other Lean facilitators through the process.

About three weeks prior to the VSM workshop, before team training, S&W declared a key decision point. If the sponsor or leader does <u>not</u> complete and send the project charter to team members, clearly stating

Suppliers	Inputs	Process	Outputs	Customers
Patients	Patients	1. Patient checks in, MA prints encounter form	Info into the EMR	Patients
	Med list	2. MA retrieves patient from waiting room and verifies name, DOB	Billing sheets	Providers
		3. MA takes patient's vitals	Rx	Billing staff
Hospitals	Data from hospitals, labs (test results)	4. MA starts a Chart Note. Adds complaint & vitals in note		
Reception	Phone messages	5. MA checks protocol (e.g., is patient due for immunization, foot check); reconciles med list; performs standard tasks (e.g., EKG for chest pain, urine test, or urinary tract infection symptoms) if needed; collects test results. Does depression screening, etc.	Procedures that need to be referred and scheduled	
	Rx Refills requests	6. MA gives gown; starts paperwork for specimen		
Provider	Provider requests	7. Gives immunizations		
		8. MA exits, flips flag, and puts encounter form in bin outside of door		
		9. MA may return (e.g., to draw blood etc.) after provider sees patient		
EMR	EMR data (treatment/ symptom immunizations and tests needed as defined in protocols)	Between Patients, • Rx refills requests • Phone messages for provider • Flowsheet lab reports • Mail normal lab letter • Call patient when needed • Patient visits for just the MA		

Figure 4.14   SIPOC example.

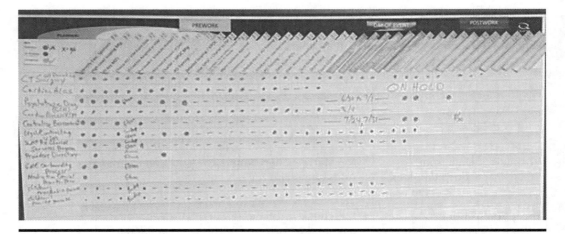

Figure 4.15   Project visual timeline board with setup tasks along top (blurred to obscure proprietary information).

the goals and required meeting times, the workshop will be postponed! Early in S&W's Lean journey, a workshop was postponed at this point. Executives who prioritized and commissioned the workshop, quickly knocked down the roadblocks to get the project going again.

Three other useful tips for projects are: a Visual Timeline (reviewed in huddles), a project pipeline board, and Lean Team Huddles. Figure 4.15 is a visual timeline board in the Lean Team Huddle room showing all projects that have been "kicked off." The setup steps are color-coded and match the project setup checklist from the previous figure. This is a quick way for leaders to see all approved projects and their status.

Another visual board shows the "pipeline" of projects that were requested and "moving toward kickoff." Figure 4.16 tracks the larger projects that go through some vetting and a thorough setup checklist process. The Lean team huddles around this board as well, to funnel and organize projects.

Huddles will be discussed in detail in Chapter 5. It is important to note that S&W's Lean Team also huddles. Whoever is available huddles every Monday to look forward at the workload in the coming weeks. Tasks not covered or overloaded staff will be addressed. They also look back one week in reflection (Hansei). This allows continuous improvement to be made in a systematic way.

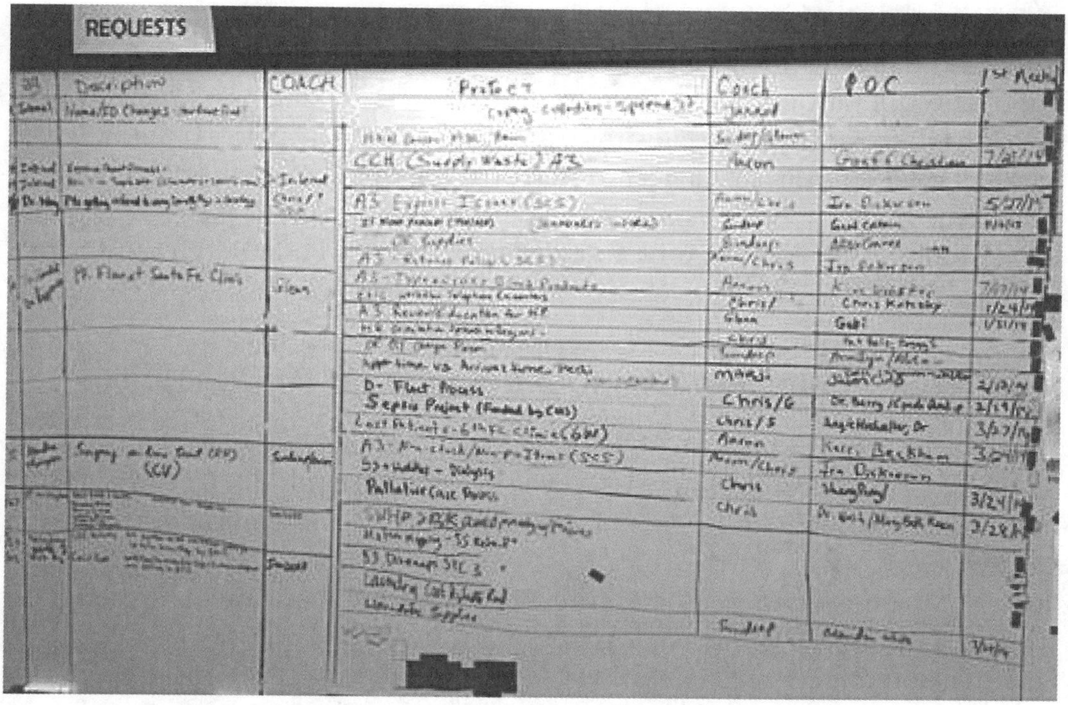

Figure 4.16 Visual board showing pipeline of projects.

Tracking Return-on-Investment (ROI)

As shown earlier in Figure 4.11, S&W tracks each major project in a database. "Process" measures like staff walking, processing and waiting time saved, customer satisfaction, and many others are tracked. In addition, financial measures like revenue gained (same staff), cost reduced, cost avoided, and inventory reduced are tracked. This allows the team to add up process and financial measures for time periods.

As mentioned in the section on results, S&W gets great impact from all staff thinking and doing Lean. However, Bob and Steve insist that it is wrong for the Lean department to say it saved the company money

Key: The authors still insist that the main "product" of the Lean projects and effort is not financial gains or improvements, it is people. People who think differently. Staff who own their processes and improve them daily—on their own! This is more important than short-term ROI.

(by itself or for itself) instead of fully supporting the operations that truly implemented the changes. S&W Lean team does not claim savings—the operational areas do.

In short, Steve happily states the S&W Lean team has never brought forward its own ideas in facilitated workshops, nor has the team single-handedly saved S&W money. Rather, all staff have. In addition, it has added up to a lot. More on this topic can be found in Chapter 6, The ROI Trap and Role of Training.

Lean Project Example—Chemo Infusion (VSM Workshop)

There is no way to choose a single project or even just a few to define S&W's extensive Lean journey. However, one does stand out. In early 2010, the Lean team met with leaders of the outpatient chemotherapy infusion value stream to kick off their first VSM workshop. Figure 4.17 shows a rather large VSM team "walking" the Future State Map (FSM) on Day 2 of their workshop to ensure it meets all goals set forth by the sponsors and Lean Steering Committee.

The process owner and key leader in that area, Theresa, is leading the team with pen in hand at the wall—not a Lean coach! Notice the key process steps on the lighter colored (yellow) Post-its, and the Kaizen bursts in darker color (blue in this case). Kaizen bursts are the changes needed to accomplish the flow and improvements in the process steps closest to them. They make up the core of Action Items to be implemented.

S&W employed several tactics in workshops to radically improve buy-in and engagement like having team members write their own Post-its, walking the map at key "check" periods, allowing supervisors to choose team

Figure 4.17   VSM team vetting the future state.

members to "represent" their area, requiring all team members to present a part of the vision to leaders, requiring team members to bring questions and status to their team huddle, etc.

Executive Sponsor and Chief Medical Officer (CMO), Glen Couchman can be seen to the left, while Dr. Mark Holguin, Process Owner, stands to the right. Other members of the Value Stream team were:

Kevin, Pharmacy (co-Process Owner)
Theresa, Chemo (co-Process Owner)
Mark, M.D.
Alan, D.O.
Jackie, Nurse Manager
Corina, Hall Nurse
Jennifer, Treatment Room Nurse
Valerie, Treatment Room Charge Nurse
Jason, Pharmacist
Julie, PFR
Annett, PSS Treatment Room
Jennifer, Lab
Norma, PSS Hall
Daniel, IVR
Brandi, Clinic Manager

The goals of the VSM effort were a stretch because waiting times had crept up for the past decade as S&W's cancer service line increased visits dramatically. Their goals were to:

■ Reduce average patient waiting time from arrival to chemo start from 68 minutes to a goal of 40 minutes (41% improvement)
■ Hit 95% of first-time starts on the day the ordering physician requested
■ Decrease re-work by reducing the number of patients rescheduled (for non-medical reasons)

Within 10 months after the action plan was created, the Chemo Infusion VSM Team met and exceeded their goals through hard work and good follow-through. Their results were:

■ Reduced patient waiting time to 40 minutes
■ Hit 95% first-time starts on day requested within first 6 months

- Reengineered process to manage schedules to include a Master Scheduler; decreased admin re-schedules to zero
- Reduced 5 to 10 minutes per order by sending orders directly to Blood Bank and receive "ready" call, rather than hand-carrying and waiting on order
- Reduced three copies of order to one (for follow-up orders; saved time and toner/paper)
- Saved 4.2 hours per week by not "signing in" all treatment room patients for the day
- Improved scheduling for patient throughput; now see more patients with fewer staff

Some additional action items implemented were:

- Created flags for uninsured and underinsured to trigger appropriate support in a timely fashion
- Created visual controls for the chemo order process
- Piloted "zone coverage" for chemo order
- Implemented a chemo double-verification (nurse) process
- Reduced chemo batching in pharmacy
- Completed an A3 problem solving analysis on chemo chair availability

Re-Casting a VSM Vision

The reason this project was chosen over hundreds of others is that it was re-casted three separate times. At S&W, once a VSM team reached its goals, or when most actions were completed and results slowed, the sponsors and process owners started the setup process for a *VSM Re-cast* session.

The setup checklist and timeline were shortened, as was the workshop (now one day or less instead of three to four), because the old Future State is now the new Current State. This Re-cast workshop also allowed leaders to involve different staff—a few from the old team plus many new members.

About 12 to 18 months after the original Chemo Infusion workshop, a new team with new aggressive goals was commissioned by leaders. Again, the Chemo Infusion VSM Team exceeded its goals. Its results on this re-cast were:

- Reduced patient waiting time to 18 minutes
- Saved 6 hours per week for PSS = $4,056 annual savings

- Added visual queue for nurses and saved 36,000 steps per week (1.9 million per year) = Annual saving of $9,835 wasted nursing hours
- With more nurse time to care for patients, same-day patient work-ins increased from ~28.5 to ~31.5 per quarter
- Patient per nurse FTE increased: Pre CLIP Ave 5.7/Post CLIP Ave 6.6 patients
- Patient satisfaction improved for likelihood to recommend mean score from 94 to 96
- Improved staff satisfaction from 3.42 to 4.24
- Paper savings (80 copies per day) = $140 annually
- 5S'd chemo room and PSS check-in areas
- Improved patient safety with uninterrupted observation during a drug reaction

After these goals were met, the Chemo Infusion team continued its great Lean journey. The third re-cast was done by the team members themselves, led by a supervisor. This time, the team widened to all Infusion staff, and they used their daily huddle to try out new ideas. Faster and faster PDCA cycles involving more and more team members greatly differentiate S&W's Lean project process from those of other organizations.

Some goals for their latest re-casted future state were:

1. Further reduced patient wait time
2. 60% of all orders turned into the pharmacy the day prior to patient's treatment
3. Late patients will have their IV started within 40 minutes
4. Nursing will beat their CG-CAHPS score hoshin goals

It is important to note that each succeeding VSM re-cast process at S&W required less direct facilitation by Lean coaches. A coach facilitated the first VSM fully. In the first re-cast, the coach kicked off the re-mapping (FSM), and then the process owners took over. The coach was up front only a small percentage of the time. On the next two re-casts, a Lean coach was not up front at all.

This sort of self-sufficiency takes a while, but offers tremendous and lasting improvements. The intact teams, led by their supervisor, can and should eventually lead their own projects. They should only require Lean coach help on advanced Lean tools and with sticky issues.

Spreading Ideas from One Area to Another

Those who cannot remember the past are condemned to repeat it.

—George Santayana

I probably have traveled and walked into more variety stores than anybody in America. I am just trying to get ideas, any kind of ideas that will help our company. Most of us don't invent ideas. We take the best ideas from someone else.

—Sam Walton,
Founder of Walmart

Spreading the gains from one area to another can be difficult. From an outsider's perspective, if major improvements are gained in one floor of a hospital, why don't other floors immediately adopt them? Even within the same building and with similar patient types, this is very difficult. In healthcare, the answer lies in two critical and opposing ideas: change is hard, and people want a "say" in any changes that are thrust on them. You could also add, "not invented here" still rules.

There must be a way to spread the gains from one area to another and from one location to another. Steve often asks, "Are there any benefits, then, of being a system vs. independent facilities?" We must not *withhold the benefits* of a Lean process from an area if we know it could help them.

Getting a department to merely "adopt" what another area succeeded in doing also presses back on a key Lean principle: *There is buy-in through involvement.* S&W allows this buy-in by conducting mini-workshops and by teaching leaders to "walk" ideas to their staff—much in the way the re-cast sessions do.

There are many ways or means to spread good ideas. This book demonstrates the spread concept at the highest level. Some means of spreading the gains (from easy effort to hard):

1. Spread through <u>education</u> (classroom; tools and Lean thinking)
   - Critical mass is developed, a "tipping point," common language evolves; each small success creates a desire for more Lean thinking in a new area
2. Spread through <u>train-the-trainer</u> (leaders and staff: see one, do or co-lead one, and then teach one on their own)

- Copy the actions of a supervisor or co-worker graduates (waste walks, 5S, Kaizens, A3s)
3. Spread through <u>leader meetings</u>: have staff leaders highlight Lean projects in their area (e.g., the System Administrator Huddle)
4. Spread <u>back</u>: A department made improvements, they were spread to another department that improved them further, then these new improvements were spread back
5. Spread a needed idea to local or <u>nearby area</u> (use spread process, PDCA)
6. Spread to <u>system</u> sites
   - Use "mini workshop," spread process and PDCA
   - Incorporate new best practices and standards like order sets for a new EMR, Fast Path ER, or any documented process
7. Spread to <u>partners</u>, to acquired organizations, or even in new construction

Like the list of S&W's Lean project types shown earlier in Results, the above ways to spread move from the least amount of Lean coach facilitation to the most. Spread starts with the training of the minds—especially for front-line supervisors who lead the continuous improvement effort in their areas.

Another principle S&W uses in order to prepare for spread is that it is a three-step process:

1. Stabilize
2. Sustain
3. Spread

A big mistake is to spread an improvement without first stabilizing it. Steve sees this error frequently. In most cases, you do not get a second chance to deploy a good idea from somewhere else. Stabilizing first is also a key principle in the foundation of the Toyota House.

Stabilizing includes ensuring the idea was properly tested in a plan–do–check–act (PDCA) process. In addition, to check assumes that a solid baseline for at least one metric was tracked for a while before trying out the change. Another key part of stabilizing is to write or update standard work for the new processes.

Once these are complete, an idea or change must also be sustained. It is not wise to spread too quickly. Steve has seen many ideas either start out positively only to falter or, more frequently, the change yielded a negative, unintended consequence that was not visible for a few weeks. A good improvement should be tracked (on a huddle board) for a few weeks before spreading.

When an idea is spread, leaders and workers in the new area should be given a chance to improve it further. Steve takes two documents with him when he helps leaders spread an idea into a new area. He brings the list of original problems (UDEs) in the processes that made the change. Team members are asked to check off the ones that apply in this new area. It should be most of them. He also brings a list of the key actions that the original team took to solve or alleviate the problems. If available, he also takes new standard work.

The next part is tricky, and can sound to new staff like they are being forced to use "someone else's idea" if not facilitated well. Steve says to small groups of staff, "Now that you checked many of their same problems, let's review their actions and new process (or standard work). If you have a better way and can prove it, by all means, we will tweak this new process and include yours. But, if you do not have a better way, we would like you to try this way for a brief period."

Staff rarely have tracked metrics showing their different way is better. Moreover, giving them a chance to make their way the best way is respectful and key to Lean thinking. Steve often sees staff come up with an even better way, once they have tried the new way a few times. This is encouraged, and is the basis of Lean.

Spread back: Lean coaches then return to the original area and say, "Do you see these small improvements Area X made? If you have a better way and can prove it, we will tweak this new process and include yours. But, if you do not have a better way, we would like you to try this improved way."

True to TPS-style standard work, one good improvement quickly yields another. Once staff members no longer do what they have always done, they get very creative with new ideas. The key is not to throw water on their early attempts at improvements, nor tell them to "check your brain at the door and just do what I tell you."

Summary of the spread process:

1. Leadership identifies which improvements or chunks of improvements to spread, and best departments that should try them next.

2. A supervisor or Lean coach collects a list of the problems or issues existing before the improvement, a list of the actions they took to solve it, and any new standard work or process flows; also collects copies of any trend charts or data showing baseline and improvement.
3. After meeting with the supervisor in the new area to explain the process, discuss the problems and changes with staff in the new area, showing them the data.
4. Have staff check off the problems that also occur in this new area (should be most of them) and review the actions.
5. State, "Now that you checked many of the same problems, let's review their actions and new standard work. If you have a better way and can prove it, by all means, we will tweak this new process and include yours. But, if you do not have a better way, we would like you to try this way."
6. Work with supervisor to ensure that the new method is followed (audit), and data is being captured on improvements (PDCA).
7. Capture any new improvements made by staff in the new area.
8. If improved, "walk" the new changes and tweaks back to the original area.
9. Continue spreading.

Spread is a critical part of the Lean journey. At S&W, they discovered the power of spread and even focused a staff member on this area. He is the Lean team's "captain of spread" helping leaders through the previous process.

Why Doing Only Lean Projects Will Not Work

What about my ideas?!

—Staff members in every area who were not invited to serve on a Lean project team

S&W spent a full three years doing CI projects and training before they were ready to take the next step. Figure 4.18 repeats S&W's transformation journey. As noted earlier, a big ah-ha moment for Bob was when he saw first-hand the engagement and satisfaction of Toyota associates—all of them!

At the core of this concern about projects is the question, "Do we believe that our staff members have ideas about improving our processes?" If the answer is no, then this book will be of little value to your organization.

However, if the answer is yes, then the new question becomes, "What will be the process or 'vehicle' for tapping these ideas?"

On a typical CI project team, 6 to 15 staff members go on an incredible multi-week journey. However, what about the hundreds of other staff members who were not on the team? How are their good ideas requested and tried out? If an organization does only Lean projects, it fails to tap the daily improvement ideas in everyone's head. If the only way to bring forward an idea is on an occasional Lean project, this limits the flow of ideas. This is not good.

At S&W, leaders desired for their staff to be self-sufficient in most of the foundation (Toyota House) Lean tools. This takes time and is a very lofty goal. S&W wants their Lean coaches to be mentors creating hundreds of expert homebuilders.

The tools and workshops are not the key. They key is to teach leaders to solve problems and create flow the next time *without* needing a Lean coach to facilitate the project.

Video: Bob Pryor presenting the President's Award for best Lean Project, CLIP Fair, November 3, 2011

Marji is making me choose just one project for the President's Award—just one, out of a sea of incredible projects. That is hard! As I walked around, I looked for projects that exemplified our philosophy of continuous improvement with superior outcomes. Drumroll please... The winner of the President's Award for 2011 was the Perioperative Culture Change team! (Cheers)

(Nurse Donna Dew was shoved forward to the microphone.) So, describe your project, how your thinking evolved, and how you felt about it during the project and after it was over. Donna responded, "Yeah, well, it's not over! We're just getting started!" (Bob pumps his fist in the air.) That's why this team won the award for continuous improvement!

(Donna) When we returned from training, we were already scoping out this great project. After the small team setup meeting, the facilitator told us, "Now we want you to understand, you're probably going to have some crying, people are going to be upset..."

I told them, are you kidding us? Crying? C'mon! So, what we did was put a fun spin on it, got everyone engaged, gave out "get out of jail free" cards for our surgeons. We drug around a staff member in handcuffs begging staff for ideas and help to "set her free."

We looked at national benchmarks. Within one month, we were already hitting them! We started with first-time-starts. We even raised the benchmark, which said up to five minutes late was still "on time." The entire OR was on board. We're not done. We go up and down. We need to re-engage staff. We found out that we can make change.

We did not stop there. We started a second project on OR Turnovers. We cut the time for CT and Neuro turnovers in half! We did another effort called 5S. We had some people who hoard stuff (laughter). They were scared to death they would not have something on-hand that the surgeon wants. The first time we 5S'd a room, we found about $8000 of materials that we really did not need. We 5S'd the supply rooms and built trust. In each case, it was the team that did it!

When we did our project, we were constantly looking for three pieces of paperwork: H&Ps, Orders, and Consents. We realized we weren't looking for them only in our 3-day event, we've been looking for them for 15 years (laughter)! A secretary admitted that she batched paperwork, since it took about 20 minutes to scan an item. 20 minutes! One call to IT, and now she does three pieces of paper in less than one minute! No one had ever challenged the many hurdles we faced daily to get each patient into their room on time.

We used to call every patient back, sometimes up to six to seven times apiece, changing their surgery start times. How could they trust us with their lives if we couldn't even get their surgery start-time right? We lock it down now, 48 hours out.

We started our fourth project this month. We took our patient satisfaction up to 96%. You have no idea how difficult these last few percents are! Another person in the OR is starting a project on sutures. I don't think we will ever end because we have a lot of opportunities in the OR. We have a really great team. Change is great. It's how we offer a better product to our community. [Applause]

Step 3. Align All Staff through Hoshin Kanri

After years of success deploying Lean through training and projects, S&W leaders felt there was something missing. Figure 4.18 shows the next major step in S&W's transformative Lean journey—Hoshin Kanri to align all MVPs (most valuable players).

Hoshin means compass or pointing the direction and Kanri means management or control. Putting the two together paints the picture of aligning all staff toward "North Star" goals and then actively managing the compass needles daily to stay on track.

It is a process for pointing the North Stars of all of your MVPs' compasses toward a common vision and goal. Not toward some sub-optimized goal for just their department or, worse yet, just themselves individually, but toward some system or overall good. And when the customer becomes the obsessive focus of all these North Stars, with ever-improving safety and quality, staff see how they fit into the mission, vision, and values of the organization.

Hoshin Kanri is essentially the process for strategic direction setting and alignment. However, it is more. Hoshin starts with the organization's vision/mission/values and the annual strategic goals, and then assures alignment by defining goals, metrics, targets, priority improvement projects, and action

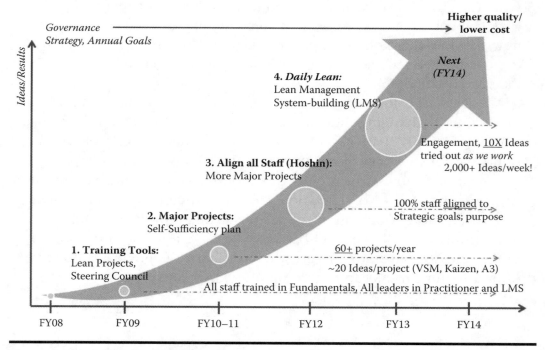

Figure 4.18   Scott & White's Lean journey.

What's in a Name?

Steve remembers coaching Bob in the initial Lean effort at S&W. A few leaders thought it would confuse staff to use Japanese words in their toolkit. Steve quickly tailored most of them. A harder decision was what to name the overall S&W Lean effort. Steve never liked the name "Lean" because it reminds some of headcount cuts. He left the naming to Bob and his leaders. His only recommendation was to avoid calling it something that sounded painful or like headcount cuts.

When he returned for more coaching, he heard the new name. The effort would be called CLIP—Continuous Learning and Improvement Program. Instead of using "leaned" like a painful verb, now staff might jokingly say they have been "clipped!"

When Hoshin Kanri started in earnest, Bob and Steve once again talked about what to call it. Steve suggested something inclusive of the whole CI effort like the S&W Way or something like Strategic Alignment and Deployment. One of the S&W leaders said, "Hey, that spells SAD! I don't like it."

When he left, Steve's only recommendation was to avoid calling it something that sounded painful. When he returned for more coaching, he heard the new name. The Hoshin effort would be called SWAT—the Scott & White Alignment Tool. Instead of using Hoshin, now staff might jokingly say they have been "swatted!"

The effort today is quickly becoming just the "way we think and provide care" at Baylor Scott & White. The overall CI effort is building a culture of continuous improvement. The goal is simple—ever-improving patient care.

plans, which when implemented will achieve the strategic goals. Hoshin Kanri is a process that takes the strategic vision, goals, and plans and then aligns all staff at each tactical level to them.

Hoshin Kanri goes by many other names such as policy deployment, Hoshin planning, and strategic alignment and deployment. At S&W, Bob called it SWAT—the Scott & White Alignment Tool. In a lofty goal, Bob and his leaders directed that all 13,000 full-time staff members at that time align their goals and initiatives using the SWAT process. Because the name changed with the merger of S&W and Baylor Health Care system, Hoshin Kanri will be used throughout this book.

In the buildup of the great space race, the United States was determined to be the first nation to put a man on the moon. About seven years before the Apollo 11 mission, President John Kennedy visited NASA's Cape Canaveral Launch Operations Center. He came across a man sweeping the floor and asked him what his job was. In a statement that shocked the president, the sweeper replied, "I am putting a man on the moon!"

A good story that reinforces the purposes and benefits of Hoshin is about putting a man on the moon. Here is a version told to Steve by an ex-NASA employee.

The floor sweeper saw it. He saw how his job "fit" into the overall mission and vision of the organization. He was not just sweeping the floors. If he did his job well and with high quality, then the technical staff could focus on the hundreds of technical hurdles in their way, the command staff could work their contingency plans, and the astronauts could go to the moon. That is what leaders at S&W wanted as well. This story also demonstrates how every single staff member must improve work processes—starting with their own.

All staff need to somehow see how they fit into a very good mission and plan. All staff need to be mission-minded. Remember, S&W staff are taught from their first day on that they have two hats. Their job is to do their job well and to improve it, starting with their own process. That way of thinking, encouraged throughout the organization, can put a man on the moon. That way of thinking will eliminate falls and infections. That way of thinking is going to produce ever-decreasing costs when the rest of the world is increasing their costs.

All 13,000?

In previous consulting engagements, Steve usually recommended that Hoshin be done well for just a few key leadership levels in the first year. Many prior efforts at S&W also stopped at the director level, including leader balanced scorecard and goal setting. However, Bob said no. He emphatically stated that all 13,000 full-time employees would use the Hoshin process to develop goals in fiscal 2012.

Using the Hoshin (SWAT) tool, S&W leaders cascaded the vision, mission, values, and annual goals one layer at a time throughout the organization all the way up to direct performers. From random acts of improvement to

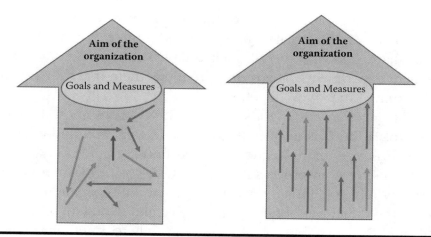

Figure 4.19   Aim of the organization, getting everyone to row in the same direction.

aligned acts of improvement. Not just the goals, but also initiatives or efforts needed to accomplish these goals.

In Figure 4.19, the typical starting condition is shown on the left. Some parts of S&W's very fast growing system were seemingly pulling against each other. Early on, competition was encouraged in regions that were very close to each other. Their goal was aligned, mission-minded staff, capable of putting a "man on the moon."

Many departments and silos charged off in their own directions. Some achieved their own goals, but only at the expense of others. This sub-optimized system performance.

Some pointed up and some pointed down. Some did not point anywhere at all. If each person rowed a boat in the direction of his or her arrow, which way would the boat go? They all needed to row the same way. Right or wrong, they all must row toward a common vision, mission, and goals.

The aim of the organization, the goals, measures, actions, and tasks all need to align in a common direction. The process of aligning all those arrows, which represent goals, efforts, tasks, and projects at the individual site and department levels, was not easy! It means getting all your MVPs to row in the same direction. The Hoshin process requires not some but all your MVPs to do this.

If each person rowed a boat in the direction of his or her arrow, which way would the boat go?

The Hoshin Kanri process focuses the aim of every department and every staff member. It translates the vision and mission into goals over which they have control, which if tracked daily could be used for daily improvement experiments. The process reminds them that they can achieve their goals only if they work together.

The arrow image on the right shows the S&W organization in its third or fourth year of Hoshin, as most staff saw how they fit, and mid-course corrections (Kanri) were more frequent but less frantic.

At S&W, their Hoshin process kicked off with goal setting for the 2012 fiscal year. By July, the annual goals were set, and the process of cascading goals up to the direct performers began. Steve and team taught the leaders and facilitated their first few catchball sessions where an employee respectfully negotiates the specifics of his or her goal with his or her boss and identifies key initiatives needed to accomplish his or her stretch goals. Some sample goal cascades are shown in the coming sections.

At the start of FY12, S&W had no software for documenting all staff goals. Its health system was 13,000 full-time employees strong and growing. Steve tailored a spreadsheet, sometimes called an "X matrix" because of its shape.

Steve also placed a tracking spreadsheet in the second tab, so that staff members could enter a "planned" number where they should end each month for every goal. This one-page *flight plan* gave leaders a great visual tool to track progress. Simple color codes were used and the SWAT forms and trackers were posted outside of many staff members' offices and work areas. This tracker is shown in Figure 4.27, to be discussed in a later section.

Individual spreadsheets created an unintended consequence. Keeping track of the latest version of the spreadsheet, with updates, for all 13,000 files was a challenge! Later, online HR software tools were used. Online tools solved the numerous file issues, but did not support all of the features of Hoshin Kanri.

Figure 4.20 shows the five-step Hoshin process. The first step is to review your boss' goals and then complete a draft of your own aligned goals using the simple Hoshin form or worksheet. Handwritten is fine. Step 2 is to conduct at least one but more likely two or three catchball* sessions where two-way negotiations are made about the specific contributions and actions

---

* Systems2Win website (more complex X-matrix examples), http://www.systems2win.com/c/catchball.htm, accessed August 2014.

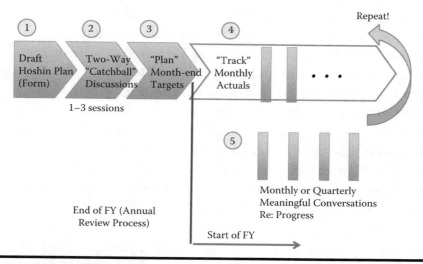

Figure 4.20   Five-step Hoshin process.

for each employee to the department's goals. Sometimes, it requires the first one-hour session just to understand the boss' goals. In the second catchball session, the staff member sometimes does not bring in enough baseline data to set a stretch goal. Thus, it can take three sessions.

After staff members finish aligning their goals, they enter them into a monthly tracker (e.g., for goal 1, staff member will be at 100 by the end of the first month, 250 by the end of the second, and so on). The rate of rise or improvement is not always steady each month. For example, if the improvement is going to be 12%, each month could be increased 1%, or it could go up in bigger chunks after new ideas are implemented. Whatever their

Make Time for Hoshin: Leaders new to Hoshin will require two or three catchball sessions with each staff member. Even if they negotiate easily on each measure, each individual will have four or five key measures. S&W recommends doing these one-on-one if possible. However, there are cases when the initial session can be for a larger group with common goals (like on a nursing unit).

One strong recommendation by the authors is just do it. If not via respectful two-way catchball conversations, then what other method would your organization use to cascade and align goals?

What is it worth to align all your MVPs? How much less time will leaders spend later if they can get staff to row in the same direction at the beginning of each year?

plan was, staff write it down and then track it. Step 3 is complete when the employees are ready to enter their first month's actual data.

The magic of Hoshin is in Steps 4 and 5. In Step 4, staff members update the actual data for each goal and compare it to their plan. If it is way off, actions are taken to correct it (Kanri) back on track.

Note: If staff members huddle around their Hoshin goals daily or weekly, they may not need a separate tracker. Their huddle board will suffice. If goals are not on their huddle board, a tracker is needed.

In Step 5, staff members and their boss conduct monthly or quarterly progress reviews. The words *meaningful conversations* are placed here because early on staff members may not be able to translate goals to those measurable and meaningful to them.

The power of Hoshin is in the word *repeat*. Imagine how good life would be if every boss did quarterly progress reviews with their staff members. If they did a quarterly review recently, how hard would the backward-looking annual employee evaluation be? It may only need a few minutes. Then, the next year's goal setting could take place in the same conversation. Hoshin done right wraps the previous year's goals to the next all in one meeting! There should be no surprises at the end of the year evaluation either.

The more time S&W teams spent on meaningful progress checks, the less time was necessary in their annual review looking backward. If you spend less time looking backward, what could you do with that time? That is correct—doing the forward-looking Hoshin process for next year.

A company that did this very well from the mid-1990s on was Nissan. While at Johnson Controls, Steve learned from Toyota, but he also learned deeply from Honda, Nissan, and others. In Nissan's Hoshin process, leaders would pick their annual goals and literally within two to three weeks, every individual at Nissan had his or her new marching orders. They aligned not only their new goals but also their new efforts. Steve remembers a period when Nissan added stretch quality goals. Within weeks, joint efforts on very small productivity improvements became lower in priority, while Steve and other JCI engineers took on larger and higher priority quality improvement efforts. It seemed strange at first, and then felt very good. The company had spun on a dime to mark good gains in quality for the next few years.

Figure 4.21 shows a grid of results for goal setting that demonstrates the importance of Hoshin. It compares the reaction to results at the end of a period (quarter, year) by a traditional manager to a Lean thinking

Process is:	Result is:	Hoshin Planning says:	Traditional Management says:
Bad	Bad		
Bad	Good		
Good	Bad		
Good	Good		

Figure 4.21 Comparison of results for Hoshin vs. traditional management.

leader who knows the purpose of Hoshin Kanri. There is a huge difference between Hoshin Kanri and traditional management or someone using management by objectives (MBO) only. The chart focuses on the *process* used to develop and roll out structured goals throughout the organization.

The first row reads this way. If the process used to set goals and manage them daily is "bad" and the results are "bad," both would say, "This is bad." Each might fix it in a different way, but it is bad.

In the second row, if the process used to set goals and manage them daily is "bad" but the results for that period are "good," a traditional manager would usually say, "This is good." Moreover, no changes would be made to the goal-setting and execution process.

Do you see possible problems with this? What if the goals were too easy? What if the metrics chosen were not the important ones to compete in the future? In addition, what if leaders that year just got lucky? The process they used is likely not repeatable in future years.

If the process used to set goals and manage them daily is "good" but the results for that period are "bad," a traditional manager would again say, "This is bad." However, a Lean thinking, Hoshin-using leader would say, "This is probably good."

If the leader is course-correcting well, maybe he or she just set a stretch goal too high, or hurdles were only recently removed. The leader should "trust the process." Sometimes the process worked well, but the leader cascaded a goal that was out of their control. If a traditional manager browbeats the supervisor for a missed goal at this point, he or she may just revert to winging it or no process at all.

Lastly, if the process used to set goals and manage them daily is "good" and the results for that period are "good," both would say, "This is good." This is why setting stretch, strategic, and aligned goals at every level of the

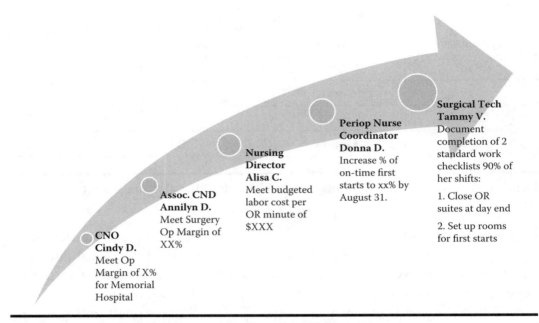

Figure 4.22 Nursing goal cascade for surgery—financial category.

organization is so important. It is not luck! There is a process to cascade and then deploy strategy through goal setting using Hoshin Kanri.

In Figure 4.22, a goal cascade is shown for a single category of metrics. In this case, it is a finance goal cascading from the Chief Nursing Officer (CNO) all the way up* to a Surgical Technician in Memorial Hospital's operating suites. It shows one of the CNO's goals that year—Memorial Hospital-wide operating margin.

Now, if S&W gave that high-level margin goal to a typical technician serving patients on a single floor, what would they do differently? Leaders must help them interpret and translate cascaded goals that meaningfully give them feedback on progress toward higher-level goals.

Once her goals were solidified with her boss, the CNO then cascaded her margin goal to the Associate CNO, Annilyn, using good two-way catchball conversations to "negotiate" a fair-but-stretch surgery department operating margin goal. Then, Annilyn cascaded her surgery margin goal to the Nursing Director, Alisa, using good two-way catchball conversations to get a fair goal of meeting "budgeted labor cost per O.R. minute." Each goal also had a timeframe—usually by the end of the year.

---

* S&W embraces the inverted pyramid idea for levels in its organization to show that the direct employees are the most important. The direct-performer employee is at the top, and is always called Tier-1 or Level-1.

Then, the Nursing Director cascaded her labor cost per O.R. minute goal to the Periop Nurse Coordinator, Donna, using good two-way catchball conversations to get a fair goal of increasing "on-time first starts in O.R." A key financial "lever" Donna and team can push is on-time first starts, to be very intentional in turning and starting these rooms up daily. The actual goals have numbers the authors cannot publish here.

For each cascaded step, staff also discuss ways to achieve these goals, like using variation reduction, Lean projects, or huddles. Thus, Lean is "pulled" into these leaders' areas quite well when they discuss ways to achieve goals at the beginning of the year.

Lastly, the Periop Nurse Coordinator cascaded her goal of on-time first starts in O.R. to the Surgical Tech, Tammy, using good two-way catchball conversations to get a fair goal of completing of two standard work checklists (close OR end-of-day and set up rooms for next day first-starts) 90% of her shifts. Each level toward direct performers gets a little more tactical or practical. Notice that this final goal is something the tech can see and count by shift-end. It is meaningful to her as well as within her control.

So, Tammy and all other techs' goals are going to help Donna meet her goal, which is going to help Alisa meet her goal, which is going to help Annilyn meet her surgery operating margin, which is going to help Cindy meet the margin for Memorial Hospital. That is how goals align and cascade to tactical practical measures in the Hoshin process. It is a series of two-way conversation up and up and up to a direct performer here at Scott & White.

Note that each cascaded goal gets:

- More frequently measured (weekly or daily is better)
- More within their authority and control
- Meaningful to the staff and department leader

Figure 4.23 shows another goal cascade for a single category of metrics. In this case, it is a patient safety goal (hospital-acquired infections or HAIs) cascading from Dean, the VP of Hospitality Services, all the way up to an environmental services (EVS) associate on one of S&W's in-patient floors. It shows one of Dean's goals that year—reduce Memorial Hospital-wide HAIs by 30%—an aggressive and very important goal.

Now, if S&W gave that high-level margin goal to a typical associate cleaning patient rooms, what would they do differently? Would it energize them to sweep any harder or faster? Do they have control over every type of HAI?

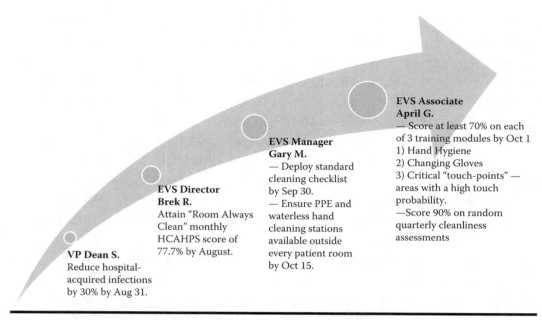

Figure 4.23   Goal cascade for EVS-patient safety category.

Once his goals were solidified with his boss, Dean cascaded his HAI goal to the EVS director, Brek, using good two-way catchball conversations to negotiate a fair-but-stretch overall cleaning team goal of exceeding average HCAHPS goal of 77.7% for the specific patient survey question "room always clean."

Then, the EVS director cascaded his HCAHPS room always clean goal to the EVS manager, Gary, using good two-way catchball conversations to get a fair goal of both deploying standard cleaning checklist (and audits) as well as proper personal protective equipment (PPE) and waterless hand washing stations outside of every patient room within just a few months. Then, the EVS manager cascaded his standard cleaning checklist/hand washing stations goal to the EVS associate, April, to get a fair goal of scoring 70% on

Low? S&W chose to reveal some specific goals for this book, which may sound low to some in the reading audience. To leaders, these goals were personal and challenging, given their various starting points and massive amounts of ongoing construction. The authors encourage all leaders to choose difficult goals that have a big gap between where they are now and where they need to be.

Bob's Man on the Moon Story: Bob wanted his staff members to see how they fit into the vision. On one of his Gemba walks, Bob walked up to an EVS associate who was cleaning a room. He asked, "What are you doing?" Rather than say, "Cleaning," the EVS associate said something like, "I am on the front lines of infection control here at S&W. If I don't clean and turn this room very well, the next patient could suffer—and it could be my relative or neighbor. So, get your germ-laden body out of my sterile room so my next patient can be safe!"

OK, maybe the ending sentence wasn't quite that direct, but you get the picture. Moreover, this EVS associate gets the big picture!

her three training modules and 90% on her random cleanliness assessments, using the standard checklist in Gary's goal.

So, if April does exceptional room cleaning, scoring very high on her audits, and Gary hits his goal of standard checklists and ensuring equipment is available, then Brek hits his goal of "always clean" on the HCAHPS score, and Dean hits his goal of reducing hospital acquired infections. Who wins? The patient! And Dean's great staff members because they see how they fit into the mission.

It is not easy to identify perfect high-leverage measures on the first try. Allow your teams some time to tailor aligned goals. The key is meaningful to them and still aligned with the boss' goals.

Catchball and Contribution to the Leaders' Goals—Different for Everyone

In the previous nursing example, the leader might demand more margin from the surgery department then, say, the mental health department. As an example, the top leader's goal may be an operating margin of 6% overall. However, surgery may be expected to contribute more than an average amount to that goal, like 15%, to cover other departments that are flat. At first, the leader might say to a department leader, "We need 15% margin from you."

Now, here is how catchball works. The department leader may say, "But boss, you have also asked me to start up five new areas, none of which will be profitable as they ramp up." This sort of push back by the staff member is good, and part of catchball. Sometimes, an actual ball is used like a

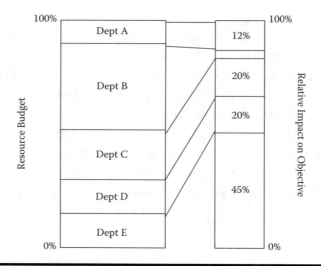

Figure 4.24 Varying contribution levels, based on abilities and expectations, not size.

"talking stick" to encourage the staff member to state reasons for and against a specific number.

Varying contribution levels are shown in Figure 4.24. Some areas might have larger budgets, but are only able to contribute a small amount toward a goal (say margin). Others might be small but they are able to contribute much more than average. If the executive level is to hit its average, it makes sense that some departments must contribute more and some less than the average amounts.

As another example, a leader may say, "My site-wide goal is to reduce salary and benefits expenses by 5%, so your goal is also to reduce these expenses by 5%." Seems fair. However, the staff member may say, "But boss, you asked me to nearly double the volume in my key areas. How in the world can we cut salaries by 5% if we are to grow that fast?"

Good question, and quite common in catchball. During the two-way catchball conversation, boss and staff member will come to a compromise. However, at the end of the day, the boss is still the boss. If they require a certain contribution from the sub-department leader in order to hit the bigger goals, then they ask for it, after hearing them out.

Again, Lean thinking was "pulled" into these leaders' areas as they discuss ways to achieve goals at the beginning of the year. The two-way catchball sessions, done properly, create an environment of continuous improvement and two-way respect with their leaders.

S&W's Hoshin Forms

The S&W Hoshin (or SWAT) form is shown in Figures 4.25a and 4.25b. A larger image is shown in Figure 7.6. This is a simplified version of what is called an X-matrix form in many industries. The process for filling this form out matches the Hoshin 5-step method shown earlier in Figure 4.20.

The associate is given a blank form by their leader, along with their completed one. The boss aligned each pair of Goal/Action Themes to the four system-wide strategic goals along the left-hand side with an X (direct alignment) or an O (indirect alignment) as appropriate. If any of the leader's goals were not aligned with the system, it would "stand out" with just a few Os or blanks.

Next, the employee places his or her blank form under the boss' and fills out a draft Hoshin goals using a "move it up" process. The employee starts at the *bottom* by doing a "mind dump" of all initiatives and tasks that took him or her more than, say, 40 work hours during the previous year. The employee often writes initiatives like "update and send monthly XYZ report." This step is important, and will be referenced with the *TPS Report* story coming up.

Next, the associate fills out draft Hoshin goals using a "one-to-one" alignment process with his or her boss' goals at the top (e.g., if the boss' first goal is for finance, then the employee tries to create an aligned goal to that one first). However, if the boss' goals do not readily apply, it can be replaced with one in the same category (e.g., an associate does not match well with the boss' goal in teaching a safety class, but chooses instead a safety goal of improving hand-washing).

Steve coaches leaders to evaluate their list of goals after the first few, asking, "If I was wildly successful this year, which metrics would improve?" This often yields one to two goals that are "more meaningful" to them and that cascade better to their staffs.

As S&W uses it, the acronym SMART stands for specific, measurable, attainable, realistic, and time-bound. Each goal set must be SMART, stretch and strategic in that it cascades well to the leader's entire team, not just to the leader personally.

After the draft set of goals are completed by the associate, he or she starts to "move up" the initiatives and tasks written below that will help him or her achieve the goal, crossing them off as the associate moves them up.

Scott & White Alignment Tool
How will your team's performance affect our Value and Goals this year?

S&W Mission:
Provide the most personalized comprehensive, and highest quality healthcare, enhanced by medical education and research.

S&W Vision:
Most Trusted and Most Valued name in American Healthcare.

S&W Values:
Teamwork, Patient-Centered, Innovation, Accountability, Excellence, Pride.

Legend:

No Alignment	0
Indirect Alignment	
Direct Alignment	X

Name: _____   Leader: **Steve Hoeft**

OE	Pop Health	Growth	Institutes	Priority	Key Objectives	FY14 — SMART Goals (through "catchball")	(Boss' info goes up here) — Action Themes	Responsible
X	0	0	0	1	1.4 Implement Lean: Standardize and eliminate waste to reduce cost: **Do Great OE Training**	*(1.4.2) 90% of S&W Manager level and above attend 1 or 4-day OE Courses *4 OE Courses at Baylor or non-SW *8 full LMS Courses for S&W staff *3 full LMS Courses Baylor or non SW *(1.4.4) 120 staff attend LMS short courses	*Maintain Master Training Schedules-goal met well before end of FY14 *Track 1+ deliverable after every training session	SH
X	X	X	X	2	1.4 Implement Lean: Standardize and eliminate waste to reduce cost: **Do Great OE Projects**	*(1.4.3) 24 VSM/Kaizen workshops through workshop and results on-line *2 Institute or Pop Health projects *2 Lean Layout (full cycles)	*ID and facilitate workshops *Help develop Population Health processes	SH
X	0	0	0	3	1.4 Implement Lean: Standardize and eliminate waste to reduce cost: **Make Effective Tier-1,2,3+ Huddles**	*(1.4.5) 800+ Huddle Boards with at least 1 new team member idea tried out *50+ T2-3 Boards w/Issue Elevation system *Develop tool & process-do 60 Board audits	*Tailor/accelerate current/new Boards *Support all leaders we teach	SH
X	0	0	0	4	1.4 Implement Lean: Standardize and eliminate waste to reduce cost: **Coach up Huddle Leaders to deploy OE foundation tools**	*180 S&W Leaders thru A3 Wave *200 A3 problems (from Boards) documented on-line	*Guide Huddles to Problem ID/resolution *Deploy A3 Waves with instructor devel.	SH
X	X	X	X	5	1.3 Improve Patient Access: improve customer satisfaction	*Support 4 Access Improvement efforts/projects	Deploy **SDA Effort**! VSM/Kaizen/A3 projects	SH
X		X	0	6	1.7 Financial-maintain Revenue-achieve $50MM Expense reduction	*Lead 6 'Round 4 Thinking' studies	Work Balance, cross-training, studies to support Round 4 Thinking before Additional resources are requested	SH
X	X	X	0	7	1.2 Implement EPIC: Improve efficiency of patient care processes	*Support EPIC Roll-out	Process and Problem Solving Support of EPIC	SH, DS
X		0		8	1.1 Retain high-perf staff: Improve Ee satisfaction: **Retain OE Staff**	*100%	Huddles, Engagement, Communication	SH
				9	*Recommended number of goals is 5			

System Strategies:
1. Operational Excellence*
2. Population Health
3. Growth (Rational and Strategic)
4. Nationally Competitive Institutes
(See FY2014 Strategic Plan Document for Details)

Figure 4.25a Scott & White's Hoshin (SWAT) alignment tool—Boss' form.

Name: _____   Staff Member _____
Sr Lean Coach

Priority	Key Objectives	SMART Goals (through "catchball")	(ALIGNED-Employee's info goes down here) Action Themes	Responsible
1	1.4 Implement Lean: Standardize and eliminate waste to reduce cost: **Do Great OE Training**	*(1.4.2) 90% of S&W Manager level and above attend 1-or 4-day OE Courses *2 OE Courses at Baylor or non-SW *1 full LMS Course for S&W staff *2 full LMS Courses Baylor or non SW *(1.4.4) 30 staff attend LMS short courses	*Teach 25% of all 1-or 4-Day OE Courses (Baylor and S&W combined) *Teach OE Courses at Baylor or non-SW *Track 1+deliverable after every training session	DS
2	1.4 Implement Lean: Standardize and eliminate waste to reduce cost: **Do Great OE Projects**	*(1.4.3) 5 VSM/Kaizen workshops through workshop and results on-line*1 Institute or Pop Health projects*1 Lean Layout (full cycles)	*Work with leaders to ID workshops *Facilitate VSM/Kaizen workshops *Facilitate Pop Health Exemplar project *Help develop Population Health processes	DS
3	1.4 Implement Lean: Standardize and eliminate waste to reduce cost: **Make Effective Tier-1,2,3+ Huddles**	*(1.4.5) 800+ Huddle Boards with at least 1 new team member idea tried out*50+ T2-3 Boards w/Issue Elevation system*Develop tool & process-do 60 Board audits	*Tailor/accelerate current/new Boards *Support all leaders we teach	DS
4	1.4 Implement Lean: Standardize and eliminate waste to reduce cost: **Coach up Huddle Leaders to deploy OE foundation tools**	*5 S&W Leaders thru A3 Wave *8 A3 problems (from Boards) documented on-line	*Guide Huddles to Problem ID/resolution *Deploy A3 Waves with instructor devel.	DS
5	1.3 Improve Patient Access: improve customer satisfaction	*Support 1 Access Improvement effort/project	Deploy **SDA Effort!** VSM/Kaizen/A3 projects	DS
6	1.7 Financial-maintain Revenue-achieve $50MM Expense reduction	*Lead 1 'Round 4 Thinking' study	Work Balance, cross-training, studies to support Round 4 Thinking before Additional resources are requested	DS
7	1.2 Implement EPIC: Improve efficiency of patient care processes	*Support EPIC Roll-out	Process and Problem Solving Support for EPIC *Lessons learned COE session (Sep/Oct '14) *Prepare Temple area Leadership Lean EPIC Go Live *Schedule COE team for Temple/Hillcrest EPIC Go Live	DS
8	1.1 Retain high-perf staff: Improve Ee satisfaction: **Retain OE Staff**	*100%	Huddles, Engagement, Communication	
9	Support Baylor OE Development	2 of every 3 weeks support onsite at Baylor *Map (VSM) key processes. Facilitate future state sharing BSWH processes *Assess OE levels and opportunities for A3 waves	Support OE Development at Baylor Provide Senior OE Coach Leadership	DS

* Recommended number of goals is 5

*Operation Excellence Objectives:

1.1 **Retain engaged & hi-performing staff:** Improve Provider and Employee satisfaction; build strong service culture

1.2 **Implement EPIC:** Improve efficiency of patient care processes

1.3 **Improve Patient Access:** Extended clinic hours and alternate delivery channels to improve customer satisfaction

1.4 **Implement Lean:** Standardize and eliminate waste to reduce cost

1.5 Provide highest levels of **Quality and Safety:** improve outcomes, costs, system revenue

1.6 Improve **Customer Satisfaction:** increase market share and system revenue

1.7 **Financial:** Maintain Revenue-achieve $50 MM Expense reduction

Employee's Major Initiatives: (list)

1) Create course content and deliver training to COE for Demand/Process/Operator Analysis (ACU EVS Room change example)
2) Return to Master's Studies - shift focus from MBA to an emphasis in Medical Informatics - 1st year Goal get accepted to program and finish 1–2 semesters of coursework
3) Write 1 article related to importance of Huddle (metric) boards - publish in medical media
4) Extend reach of Huddle Board learning by beginning a Huddle Board Blog/Twitter/Social Media
5) x
6) x

Figure 4.25b   Scott & White's Hoshin (SWAT) alignment tool—staaff member's form.

The associate adds some additional initiatives as well for the year that would help him or her achieve the goal.

Specific requests for Lean or other help from their leaders are written here. S&W guides all staff to reduce their goals to five or less, if possible. That is why additional goal lines are grey. The Hoshin process teaches focus. Focus is best achieved with fewer goals. Some high-level leaders will have more so they can roll-up all sub-department goals. The staff member reviews his or her draft and sends it to the boss.

It is now time for step 2 of the Hoshin process—two-way catchball sessions. As mentioned earlier, it may take two or three sessions to effectively align goals and ensure they are SMART. Again, the boss will start at the bottom of the form.

The associate moved up many, but likely not all, of his or her major initiatives from the previous fiscal year. This creates the possibility of a TPS Report-type waste, using a reference from the movie *Office Space*.* Near the end of the goal-setting process, the boss and associate discuss whether any of these prior initiatives still at the bottom should be continued (at what priority) or dropped.

Again, Hoshin provides focus. Sometimes focus is achieved by saying "No" to a task that was once required, but no longer adds values. Staff members often applaud this part of the Hoshin process, as it frees them from less value-adding tasks.

The associate and boss will "catchball" all of the goals, paying special attention to the initiatives the associate plans to conduct in order to meet his or her goals. This takes two or three sessions, but gets easier each year the organization uses this methodology.

If the associate is also a leader and has direct reports, he or she will move his or her goals up to the top (boss' info section) and clear the bottom to prepare for sessions with his or her direct reports.

Just like the boss did, the associate will align each pair of Goal/Action Themes to the four system-wide strategic goals along the left-hand side with an X (direct alignment) or an O (indirect alignment). This added crosscheck of having every leader ensure alignment with system goals is crucial. Again, if any of this new leader's goals were not aligned with the system, it would "stand out" with just a few Os or blanks.

---

* *Office Space*, Twentieth Century Fox, 1999. TPS Report: The boss required staff members to spend inordinate amounts of time preparing and editing a weekly TPS Report. However, when checked, no one ever used the report!

The S&W Hoshin Tracker, showing month-ending planned sub-goals in flight plan format, is shown in Figure 4.26. Nearly every S&W leader who used this part of the original spreadsheet kept using it even after online HR database tools were deployed. It quickly shows progress on all goals. The supervisor knows the associate's plan aligns and dovetails into his or hers, and has motivation to help. The associate stands to get a positive or negative review based on progress.

The authors did not include this example because the goals shown were perfect. It just shows one example of how a one-page plan provides valuable visual progress checking in the simplest way. The authors hope that online HR database software firms make true Hoshin part of any goal-setting tool. A larger-sized version of this can be found in Figure 7.7.

The example shows a Senior Lean Coach reporting to Steve and his progress through January. Notice this hard-working employee is nearly all green on his "Actual" rows (shows as light grey) for seven major goals listed. Patient Satisfaction data was woefully delayed and pending.

The first two columns are copied directly from the goals on their Hoshin form. A baseline from the prior year is entered for each goal set. Then, the flight plan for each goal is entered, showing where the metrics should be at the end of each month for every goal (e.g., for the coach's SWAT facilitation goal, he should finish October with 20 sessions and November with another 10, and so on).

Remember, these parts of the spreadsheet are filled out at the start of the year. The staff member knows best and tailors the monthly amounts showing how he or she will fly all the way up the year-end goal.

In steps 4 and 5 of the Hoshin process, the associate updates the actual data for each goal and compares it to his or her plan. During the monthly or quarterly progress reviews, the associate and boss will focus on actions needed if any metric needs mid-course correction (Kanri).

Some other key points from the tracker are worth noting:

■ The associate needs help getting updated HCAHPS scores for his or her specific sites and questions.
■ The updated date is barely into February, so actual data entered for February is only "expected"; the associate will update again at month-end.

Goal Alignment Target Tracker

Staff Member: **Sr. Lean Coach**

Today's Date: 2/12/13

FY12

Today →

LEGEND

| Met Goal |
| Slightly Behind Goal |
| Unable to Meet Goal |

Key Goals	Targets	Responsible	Baseline	Measurement	Objectives	Sep	Oct	Nov	Dec	Jan	Feb	Mar	Apr	May	Jun	Jul	Aug	Totals
[NEW] # LMS Huddle Boards w/at least 1 Idea implemented	80 Boards Stretch goal 125 boards	Mike	Few	# Boards	Plan-Bds	new	new	10	10	10	10			10	10	10	10	100
					Actual	n/a	n/a	20	50	82								152
					Notes					HC-87 Bds, 322 Ideas; RR- 65 Bds, 65 ideas								
Deploy SWAT with aligned input measures	Lead and facilitate 60 2-way SWAT conversations at Hillcrest and Round Rock	Mike		# Facil.	Plan-swat	n/a	20	10	0	0	0	5	5	5	5	5	5	60
					Actual	n/a	20	0	0	0								20
					Note			requests	requests	requests						FY14	FY14	
Inpatient Satisfaction score	Round Rock Hospital (HCAHPS): Pain well controlled - goal 70% Doctor communication - goal 90% Nurse communication - goal 90% Room cleanliness - goal 90% Patient notified of new meds - goal 75% Recovery at home - goal 90%	Mike	50% 80% 72% 66% 62% 70%	% - 7 factors	Plan	61%,88%,6 3%,55%,49 %,71%,71%						progress mtgs	progress mtgs	progress mtgs	FY14	FY14	FY14	
					Actual	61%,88%,6 3%,55%,49 %,71%,71%	61%,88%,6 3%,55%,49 %,71%,71%											
					Note													
Deploy LMS system-wide # trained and # Gemba walks	Co teach LMS 10/2012 Lead/ train LMS 11/2012 Teach LMS 1 class Lead 30 Gemba walks - Hillcrest/ Round Rock	Mike	Few	# trained plan Gembas # Actual Gembas	Plan teach	Shadow	Co-teach	15	15	0	15	0	15	0	15	15	0	90
					actual teach	Shadow	Co-teach	30	28	45	15							118
					plan Gembas	0	0		15	15	15	10		10		10		75
					Actual Gembas	10	17	30	29	20								106
					Note			teach LMS met goal	superv trng	superv trng								
Facilitate Lean Layout workshops	Facilitate/complete 1 Lean Layout Map 1+ future state Patient flow Capture changes in 1+ work flows and create standard work for changed roles	Mike		# w/s or add-ons	Plan	0	0	0	0	0	1	1	0	0	0	0	0	3
					Actual	0	0	0	1	0	1							1
					Note				BJI (work flows)		BJI (work flows)	BJI (implem changes)						
Achieve measurable Quality improvements on 70% of Lean and LMS driven projects	incorporate a quality measurement on 70% of projects facilitated	Mike	NA	5/ month	Plan	70%	70%	70%	70%	70%	70%	70%	70%	70%	70%	70%	70%	70%
					Actual	60%	80%	100%	80%	100%								
					Note													
A3s created (roll into new goal below)	200+ A3s entered into the system	Mike			Plan	0	0	20	20	20	0	goal change	goal change	goal change	goal change	goal change	goal change	60
					Actual	0	0	22	20	0	22	goal change	goal change	goal change	goal change	goal change	goal change	64
					Note													

Figure 4.26 Scott & White's monthly Hoshin tracker—updated monthly and used in one-on-one progress reviews.

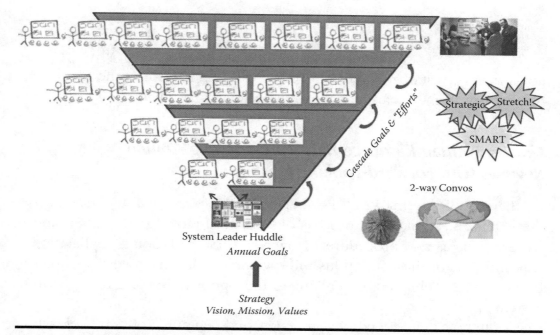

Figure 4.27 Scott & White's goals cascading from executive boardroom up to direct performers, matching Hoshin and huddle goals.

Figure 4.27 shows how S&W cascades aligned goals and key initiatives all the way from the boardroom up to the direct performers serving patients. They do this using the Hoshin process, along with effective two-way catch-ball conversations to develop goals for all staff that are meaningful and more process-focused vs. month-end output measures.

Each leader is to develop goals that are SMART, strategic, and stretch. When done well, all staff can see how they fit into the vision, mission, values, and strategic goals at S&W.

Also shown in this figure are the huddle boards. These will be discussed in more detail in Chapter 4, Step 4 Daily Lean (LMS). Note that the measures on the huddle boards match the Hoshin goals of the supervisors at each level. They should be the same for all team-wide goals. When the goals change, the huddle board is updated and vice versa.

This is another way that Lean thinking infiltrated almost every area at S&W. Leaders say Lean thinking is just the way we deploy our strategy. Once the strategy and goals are set, Hoshin is a great way to roll it out, and huddles are a great way to execute improvements toward aligned

Lean thinking is just the way we deploy our strategy.

goals for every staff member at every level. The ideas and the feedback mechanism from a Lean management system clearly keep you on track.

Linking Human Resource Backward-Looking Annual Reviews with Forward-Looking Hoshin

By the end of the first year, S&W's Hoshin process was integrated into the Human Resources-led process of backward-looking annual employee review policies and procedures. However, forward-looking goal setting was still part of the continuous improvement or Lean process, as noted in Figure 4.20. This led to challenges and opportunities for the growing system.

The authors believe end-of-year review and beginning-of-year goal setting will be reduced to only one meeting—maybe 25% of the session backward-looking because quarterly progress reviews were already completed and 75% forward-looking to set aligned goals and initiatives for the next fiscal year. Think how much time that would save your leaders and staff to do them both in the same meeting!

Another benefit of the Hoshin process is how it highlights the vision, mission, and values of the organization. In the sample Hoshin form in Figure 4.25, this appears on all forms to the far left and shows how every boss' goals and tasks align to them (the Xs and Os). This serves to remind all staff of the vision, mission, and values of S&W and how they fit into it.

Yet another benefit of Hoshin to the annual review process is how it, in addition to numeric goals, aligns behaviors and competencies. These are best "caught" by the supervisor in the monthly or quarterly progress reviews. Hoshin makes the HR annual review and evaluation process much easier.

Strategy

Until about 2010, S&W had no clear strategy. It was a big realization and admission. More accurately, it was merely grow baby grow! There is something both good and bad about a growth "strategy" of *hire 'em and build it...and they will come*. However, it also seemed rather non-strategic.

S&W had goals. However, where did the goals point? Strategy is more about what you will *not* do than do. True strategy says no to some things in order to fully focus on other things that you must do well. It is more about the direction of your excellent care and processes. Therefore, S&W spent a full year discovering where to point its growing organization. Looking back, it was a good thing it did not wait another year!

Strategy is a funny thing. S&W's executive leaders seemed to be effective, young, focused, and fairly unified, given their varied backgrounds. However, to evolve a strategy that **guesses** where reform, reimbursement, population trends, costs, medicine, education, technology, and patient preferences would lead is not easy. However, a strategizing and re-strategizing process must be done.

As stated in the opening section of this book, Bob marveled at his conversations with healthcare leaders around our country—all of them had the same strategies! All were pursuing cost reductions, staying ahead of reforms, and planning for population health. The key will be who will *execute* the best!

S&W had a huge advantage over other health systems—the Scott & White Health Plan. For decades, S&W kept patients out of the hospital and treated them in a common-sense way. Many medical residents remarked at the simplicity of their training at S&W: "do the right thing." Having covered lives in their own health-focused health plan allows an organization to get quick feedback on care processes. S&W was already keeping people out of the hospital and avoiding unnecessary treatments and charges.

Advanced Practice Professionals (APPs)

Another key advantage that worked into S&W's strategy was its use of Advanced Practice Professionals (APPs). It used a growing number of them as actual providers as much as regulations allowed, and even gave them a voice in its physician-led organization. S&W wanted APPs to be only licensed, certified non-physician healthcare providers that rendered direct patient care. They must have delegated prescriptive authority, be credentialed and privileged, and must be billed independently.

Thus, S&W treated Nurse Practitioners (NPS), Physician Assistants (PAs), and Certified Registered Nurse Anesthetists (CRNAs) as APP providers, rejecting the terms mid-levels, allied health providers, or extenders. Like much of their history, S&W made inroads into this area out of need.

For decades, the small market of Temple, Texas struggled to keep up with recruiting and retaining physicians. As it started to focus more on team-based quality care, many S&W physician leaders recognized their duties were well-suited for collaborative practice. With strong financial needs and a few isolated successes within the system, S&W leaders accelerated APPs in practices.

In a smart move, S&W leaders first met with and listened to their *current* APPs. What were their needs? APPs needed a few benefits given to physicians like Continuing Medical Education (CME; time and funding), training, annual evaluations by their physician leader (not an administrator or nurse), improved system communication, committee involvement, and recruitment under a physician model. They wanted to be accepted by physicians as valuable to their overall practice.

It was and still is a lengthy journey, but S&W achieved penetration and better low cost models of care using APPs. In Figure 4.28, the chart on the left shows S&W's increase in operational revenue with dramatic increases in in-patient and out-patient visits, as well as the number of physicians vs. APPs over time. Figure 4.29 shows the breakdown of APPs by type.

In a study of APP usage in S&W's orthopedic department, S&W benefited an average of nearly $100,000 annually per PA. They reduced post-surgery length-of-stay, and yielded a much higher case mix index for the practice. While official data was hard to parse in the orthopedic study, S&W also found that most of its patients liked seeing APPs.

It should be noted that the orthopedic department used its three PAs in different ways in their three sub-specialty practices. It is likely that only one style of usage is not effective. It needs to be tailored to the APPs' abilities as well as the practice's needs.

In addition, the APP acceleration effort was also a key to S&W's Same Day Appointments (SDA) effort, as APPs took on many of these patients.

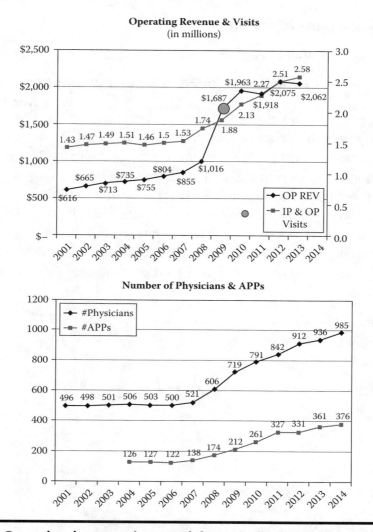

Figure 4.28 Operational revenue increased dramatically with the increase of APPs.

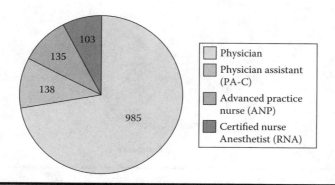

Figure 4.29 Breakdown of APPs by type.

S&W Strategy Development

We are just deploying our strategy!

**—Clinic leader in S&W's most competitive market
leading her huddle**

At S&W, Lean was the process used to deploy strategy. Workshops and projects were aligned to and folded into more strategic efforts. The usefulness of Lean principles in deploying strategies was discovered early at S&W. The authors also feel that its usefulness is yet to be fully exploited.

Figure 4.30 shows what became known as the swirl. The five categories of strategic goals worked together to create operational excellence in the center. If S&W were excellent in achieving these goals, it would be excellent overall. An operationally excellent organization then focused on three high-priority strategic thrusts:

1. Population Health
2. Nationally Competitive Institutes
3. Rational Growth

Figure 4.30 The "swirl"—three strategic efforts or thrusts depending on excellence in all operations.

The five categories of strategic goals were:

1. Quality and excellence in the healthcare experience (quality and safety)
2. Operational excellence (balanced metrics)
3. High-performing staff and teams (developing and retaining)
4. Advanced technologies (temporary: huge Epic EMR implementation that fiscal year)
5. Healthy communities and workplace (completing the Triple Aim)

These five categories guided S&W huddle boards for several months until the merger with BHCS. After, they reduced to four inarguable ones: quality/safety, service, finance, and people.

The top circle of the swirl is Quality and Excellence in Healthcare Experience. It represented quality and safety, as well as patient satisfaction. Several sub-metrics cascaded from this first category. The second circle in the swirl is Operational Effectiveness. Operational Effectiveness included financial goals—basic blocking and tackling for success like beating the budget, productivity, and maintaining cash.

The third circle in the swirl is High-Performing Staff and Teams. S&W measured morale. They also measured retaining high-performing staff in all areas and employee engagement in annual surveys. S&W needed better, more frequent measures. You will see more discussion of this topic in the huddle board section. Turnover costs an organization more than it knows, and more than it can afford.

The fourth circle is not usually a category of metrics, but S&W had to elevate it temporarily because of how critical implementing EPIC was to their success. This category included EPIC as well as using the right technology to add value to the patient experience and to reduce cost.

The fifth circle was one that changed over time. It used to be Growth (or Growing at all Costs). S&W's fifth Operational Excellence goal became Healthy Communities and Workplace. This included the population health movement, keeping people well. This better aligned with the Triple Aim.

Turnover costs an organization more than it knows, and more than it can afford.

S&W leaders attempted many parts of population health early on, more than most other healthcare organizations. Bob and his leadership team wrestled hard with the competing ideals of "right thing to do" vs. "getting paid for what we do."

With the rollout of the strategic plan, the leadership team became laser-focused on being an operationally excellent organization.

Population Health

A lot has been said about population health in the past decade. However, what is it really? A good definition is *improving health for a defined group.* Unfortunately, if you do not clearly define the group you are addressing, population health becomes nebulous.

When focused on specific groups, it takes on meaning and leads to a specific set of strategies that can be used to move targeted groups to healthier lifestyles and outcomes. That sounds easy, but it is not. Different populations require different strategies. Some target groups are:

■ Specific health plan enrollees (covered lives)
■ Shared savings group of patients (e.g., Medicare Accountable Care Organization, or ACO)
■ Specific neighborhood
■ Chronic disease groups
■ Clinic group or provider's panel of patients

Someday, leaders at S&W believe most reimbursements will change to capitated amounts for larger groups of patients—sometimes called risk contracts. It takes years of preparation, hard work, an integrated health delivery system, a robust integrated health record system, and sometimes flexible reimbursement changes to move a large health system toward effective population health management. S&W leaders started preparing early on for a large chunk of their health services market share to support population health.

It is a scary thought that someday most or all healthcare services will get reimbursed with a small, fixed, capitated amount for the year. It is even scarier to imagine being accountable to keep patients healthy and out of the hospital when they sometimes do not want to improve their own health. Like dieting, this concept makes a lot of sense—just eat less, move more.

However, in day-to-day practice, it is very hard because it deals with preferences, motivation, and discipline. It is scary, but it is also the right thing to do.

When reimbursements "flop" to capitated contracts, health systems may for the first time be challenged with true "health" care (e.g., rewards for keeping a population healthy). Until then, today we have only "sick" care (e.g., fee-for-service reimbursements that pay only when a patient is sick enough to need a doctor or hospital visit).

The key for health organization will be carefully transitioning toward population health and capitated payments without going bankrupt. Eventually, the authors see most healthcare moving away from fee-for-service only reimbursement toward paying per "covered life" to keep a population healthy.

S&W also had strategies around developing nationally competitive institutes and service lines, as well as rational and purposeful growth, rather than growth at all cost. A rational, strategic growth plan evolved.

Healthcare is moving rapidly toward service lines, like Cancer and Heart Institutes. The hope of service lines is that the patient becomes primary. Once they arrive, providers come to them or they are escorted through the delivery system. The promise of a patient-focused service line is this: If you can just get to a certain door, we will do everything possible to heal you.

The focus is on the patient. All activities must change. No longer can staff merely point a patient toward a different department or building. Patients today are self-directing and self-advocating—sometimes even self-caring as they self-navigate complicated care streams. It does not need to be this way.

Many patients are scared, sick, and have never walked the rocky path of multi-stop specialty care before. Nor do they want to return—ever! It must change. Service line or value stream leaders should be tasked and empowered to help accomplish this in the near future.

> The promise of a patient-focused service line is this: If you can just get to a certain door, we will do everything possible to heal you.

Step 4. Daily Lean: Lean Management System-Building (LMS)

> LMS significantly changed how I work with my team to improve care and outcomes!
>
> **—Cyndy Dunlap, CNO**

The power of Lean is *Daily Lean* and the enabler of Daily Lean is Lean Management Systems-Building. As this book was being written, more ideas are being implemented each month at S&W than in a full year of Lean projects beforehand. LMS-building changed the pace of ideas as well as the engagement of staff at S&W. It is powerful.

As mentioned in Chapter 2, healthcare leaders need to shift from the simple heuristic thinking that worked in the past to a new way of thinking that is more nimble—one that uses more brainpower. The brainpower of your executive staff is not enough. To survive and thrive, the brainpower of your whole staff can and must be harnessed.

The authors have written this book to help you do just that. When staff huddle together briefly and daily around gaps and problems, this unleashes their pent-up creativity. In addition, these ideas provide a way out of the shifting sands that the healthcare industry now finds itself in toward the next oasis on the horizon.

Unleashing Ideas—The Iceberg

Once it is developed and vetted, S&W deploys its strategy and achieves its goals by building Lean Management Systems. A good analogy for describing the need for Daily Lean systems is an iceberg. As seen in Figure 4.31, an iceberg has some visible peaks above the water level. This is what people normally see. This is true in implementing Lean as well.

Figure 4.31   Iceberg with visible home run projects.

People tend to see the large Lean projects like value stream mapping. They see rolls of paper and Post-its covering walls. They do not tend to see the hard, foundational work of standard work, the learning, missteps, and even the many small, individual ideas.

To add a baseball analogy, the projects are like home runs. Home run hitters knock a few out of the park. However, this does not happen every at-bat in baseball. Neither should an organization rely solely on home runs for its continuous improvement effort. Base hits are small ideas implemented and sustained by team members. So, if there are 10 base hits for every 1 home run, and base hits win the game, shouldn't an organization expect the same ratio in their continuous improvement effort?

Steve's opinion is that organizations, mature in their CI journey, will have 10 times the number of base hits as home runs. It makes sense that an organization would have many more small ideas.

S&W taught staff how to do Waste Walks to uncover waste every day in their jobs. S&W even made a Waste Walk exercise required to earn the Lean Fundamentals course certificate! However, where were all the Daily Lean ideas? Why so slow?

Moreover, who is "playing" in the game if only projects are used to bring forward and try out ideas? A large value stream mapping project has around 15 full-time team members. Therefore, 15 people go on an incredible journey of learning and improvement. But, what about the other 1000 staff members in the building? How do they engage? How many ideas do they bring forward? Do leaders even ask?

Everyone does Lean training and projects. Some even "try" to involve others by putting a flip chart in the hallway to "write any ideas" for the cool Lean team to implement. Other staff members have brains, and ideas, too.

This brings up a fundamental question. Do you remember in Chapter 2, Bob's Bold Statement, where Bob asked this question after seeing and hearing Toyota associates? "How can all our staff try their good ideas out every day?" Bob and his leaders at S&W discovered, unless they were on a Lean project, leaders rarely even asked them for ideas.

S&W wants the full iceberg. Figure 4.32 shows the power of the iceberg analogy. A much larger mass floats below the surface than the visible home run Lean projects.

In an organization building a culture of continuous improvement, 90% of all ideas implemented should come outside of coach-led projects. There just

How are ideas incubated and tried out in your organization? Ask any staff member about one of their goals, and then ask them if they have any ideas to close the gap. Bet they will tell you an idea if you are patient and probe a little.

Ever wonder when and how these ideas are brought forward? Also, if they brought the idea forward to try out, is there a quick way to check feedback data to see if their idea worked? Should ideas be tried out if there is no baseline, nor quick way to check?

are not enough projects, facilitators, or even patience for 100% engagement using only projects.

So, how are ideas incubated and tried out in your organization? It is difficult to solicit staff members' ideas in large communication meetings. If they did, who would try them out? They should flow out of brief, small team discussions around gaps in performance. Teams should bring them forward and try out their own PDCA experiments.

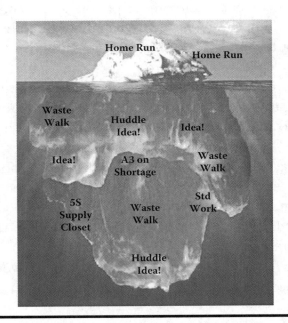

Figure 4.32 Iceberg—much larger below the surface with thousands of less visible base-hit ideas.

The key question then is, "How and when will we gather staff ideas, and how will management provide quick feedback data so they can *check* if their ideas worked?"

The iceberg in Figure 4.32 shows many base hits just below the surface. Many are labeled Idea or Waste Walk. Wastes are not hard to identify. Steve teaches they are daily tasks staff members hate to do (e.g., walking, searching, filling out forms in triplicate, meetings, redoing tasks, etc.).

It is easy to identify waste and think of a way to reduce it. However, what then? Some leaders say, "Just do it!" Do what? When? Who does what? What is the "experiment?" How would they check if it worked? There needs to be some kind of vehicle or format for implementing these many small base-hit ideas.

Other base hits in the iceberg are labeled A3 on Shortage (a supply item), Standard Work, and even Huddle Idea. What if every person every day brought up an idea and was willing to help try it? What if each department tried out a new idea every day or at least once a week? How much further ahead would that organization be?

Once this gap was realized, Bob and his leaders also asked, "Why so slow?" With as much training as S&W did, why aren't these ideas flowing daily? The answer is leadership. Not in a bad way, it is just another gap. It is the absence of a Lean Management System. Leaders will build them.

In David Mann's book *Creating a Lean Culture*, he says probably only about 20% of the actual time and effort in transforming value streams is on the physical Lean changes to a process to make it flow. Eighty percent or more is installing the Lean management system to encourage

Question: How about you? Do you think 80% of the time and effort in transforming processes is building a management system? If not, what percentage is it? What if you did not build an active management system? How would ideas be checked? Who would spread the good ones?

Can employees generate their own "pipeline" of data to check if their ideas worked? When would they do this? Do they have permission to huddle briefly to discuss (plan) ideas? When? Where?

ideas and to help make them stick.[*] The authors have also found this to be true as well.

"Ultimate Arrogance"

S&W leaders started building Lean Management Systems immediately after taking their Lean leadership course. All participants were required to pre-read *On the Mend* by Dr. John Toussaint of ThedaCare. John says, "The *ultimate arrogance* is to change the way people work without changing the way we manage them."[†] S&W leaders found that to be true as well.

(*Here comes Steve's foot stomp.*) It is management's job to build the systems by which employees' ideas can be brought up and tried out. It is management's job to build the feedback systems so that employees can measure whether they worked. It is management's job to help align metrics so that everybody's North Stars are heading in the same system direction. It is management's job to spread good ideas through layered audits. It is management's job to build the system.

That is what John meant by ultimate arrogance. At S&W, the most important work of a leader is to build LMS—the idea collection and feedback systems. This is both a daunting and exhilarating task. Leaders need to ensure their measures are aligned to the system goals and that they drive behaviors that reflect the mission, vision, and values of the system.

Four Parts of Lean Management System (LMS)

There are four related parts to build in a Lean management system. They are:

- Leader standard work
- Visual controls
- Daily accountability process
- Leadership discipline

> It is management's job to build the systems by which employees' ideas can be brought up and tried out.

[*] Mann, David, Ibid.
[†] Toussaint, John, Ibid.

Each part will be covered in detail in Chapter 5, but a brief overview is needed to set the stage for this real difference-maker in S&W's Lean journey.

Something changes inside a staff member when he or she brings forward an idea, his or her team agrees to try it out, it works, and then a leader thanks them and makes it part of standard best practice. It changes in a very positive way when they see a meaningful measure move toward the goal, and when the leader and other team members recognize them in a huddle.

The staff member with the idea goes home that night, gathers his or her family around, and says, "Kids, if I wasn't working at S&W, that place would be going to heck in a hand basket. I am helping achieve all our goals with my ideas. You should have seen how happy the boss was today when my idea worked! I knew it would. I think I'll bring up another idea next week."

No one can take this away from the staff member. He or she earned it. You will not be able to stop the huddle process and team ideas. It doesn't matter if it you call it Lean, CI, operations excellence, or yellow duck. When staff take control of their work processes, solve problems, and please their customers, they will *never* go back to the status quo, even if big bosses try to stop their effort! They will do it anyway. Something changes inside of them.

The most engaging, fulfilling, satisfying thing that happens to an employee can and should happen every day. It starts in their huddle. And, it is very addictive. Others want this recognition and appreciation as well.

Back to the four parts of LMS-building. **_Leader standard work_** provides the structure to shift the focus from solely results to processes <u>and</u> results. In **_visual controls_**, each leader with his or her team translates goals into visual "expected vs. actual" charts (like trend charts). S&W repeats a common mantra for visual controls: <u>Five feet, five minutes</u>. In five minutes or less, any leader standing five feet from the visual board should be able to

---

Something changes inside staff:

> "Kids, if I wasn't working at S&W, that place would be going to heck in a hand basket. I am helping achieve all our goals with my ideas. You should have seen how happy the boss was today when my idea worked! I knew it would. I think I'll bring up another idea next week."

—Typical S&W Staff Member

It (daily accountability process or huddles) is the vehicle, the structure for 100% engagements. It is how all staff wear their "two-hats."

see what is being measured, how they are doing, and if they are improving. Ideas should be visible as well.

The third key part to build is the ***daily accountability process***. The daily accountability process is the format where each leader and his or her team brings up ideas and does experiments to improve work processes. It is the vehicle, the structure for 100% engagements. It is how all staff wear their "two-hats." A final important part of LMS-building is ***discipline***. You must have discipline to follow through consistently, every day, on the first three elements.

The fourth part is leadership discipline. Without it, gains and improvements made in the other parts will quickly backslide. The four parts of LMS are shown in Figure 4.33.

Part 1: Leader Standard Work

Leader standard work documents what leaders do to ensure their processes run as designed, and then improve them. In it, the leader stays

1. Leader Standard Work
- Shows when leader is available for C.I.
- Maintains Visuals and Accountability process
- Monitors recently implemented improvements

4. Leadership Discipline
- Causes daily attention to system
- Promotes and sustains improvements, stability and accountability

2. Visual Controls
- Focuses on the process
- Makes waste, problems, delays stick out

3. Daily Accountability Process
- Converts gaps on Visuals to Ideas/actions
- Eliminates root causes
- Links vision to action to improve processes

Figure 4.33   Four Parts of a Lean Management System (LMS).

process-oriented by spending more and more time in the Gemba. In addition, leader standard work codifies what it takes to move to a *standard day*. They need to spend less time putting out fires and instead focus their team on addressing root causes.

There are many good examples in John Toussaint's book, including leader standard work. S&W tried to use some of those shown in the book, and ended up with a standard work format of its own. If you look at S&W's basic format for leader standard work in Figure 4.34, it shows what the leader is going to be doing daily, weekly and monthly! It shows a blank form and one leader's early example. Leaders continually improved these over time.

It is meant to be handwritten at first. Leaders start documenting this during their Lean leadership course. A larger sized version of this can be found in Figure 7.8.

Leaders have two main responsibilities. They must run their departments and drive improvements every day. Thus, leaders must develop and systematically follow daily standard work; otherwise, they get distracted on the latest crisis-du-jour. If the leader gets distracted, improvements backslide quickly. Leader standard work attempts to communicate their most important job—improvement!

The main users of leader standard work are the leader's staff members. When leaders post and communicate this, staff can see when they will be "interruptible" for continuous improvement, when they will be doing Gemba walks, and when they can be approached with ideas that need encouragement and elevation. It is good to post this on the team huddle board.

S&W does not want their leaders to just publish their packed meeting schedules on leader standard work. A super-packed schedule of standing meetings thwarts continuous improvement. Why are they called standing meetings anyway, when everyone sits with little interaction, problem solving, or idea flow?

Leader standard work also serves to counter schedule-packing meetings. It presses in the opposite direction to free the leader to do the higher-purpose, more-fulfilling work of improvement and problem prevention with his or her staff. In fact, when the leader does more Gemba walks along with more frequent, shorter huddles, other "meetings" normally filling his or her schedule get done before, during, and after Gemba walks and huddles. Steve calls this effect the ***meeting busters***, and sometimes the "mini, impromptu huddles after the big huddle."

Leader standard work demonstrates the commitment S&W wants each leader to put on building improvement systems.

Leader Standard Work

Name:_____ Department:_____

Daily
1.
2.
3.
4.
5.

Weekly
1.
2.
3.
4.
5.

Monthly
1.
2.
3.
4.
5.

Gemba Time
1.
2.
3.
4.
5.

Leader Standard Work

Name: _Regional CEO_ Department:___Admin_____

Daily
1. Review emails — 6 am, noon and 5 pm
2. Review planner, prioritize daily work and develop weekly action plan — 6:30 am and 6 pm
3. Review daily report (clinical actual RVU vs. budget, hospital census, Ed throughput, OR)
4. Lead daily leader huddle
5. Conduct gemba walk-in clinic or hospital department

Weekly
1. Attend executive huddle
2. Prepare for and attend BOD, clinic ops, leadership team, system administrator meetings
3. Prepare for and attend status meetings with COO, CMO and direct reports
4. Time in gemba — hospital or clinic; combine with huddle board layered audit
5. Review minutes from appropriate quality and regulatory meetings

Monthly
1. MORs with clinic and hospital departments
2. Review monthly reports (access, patient sat, core measures, harm score, Hoshin goals, financial, and statistical reports, region dashboard)
3. Prepare and conduct SWMH BOD meeting
4. Tour one central region clinic, and one non-region site of care

Gemba Time
1. Gemba walks daily
2. Audit leader huddle board, collect and review from all other boards
3. Elevate one idea and ensure feedback
4.

Figure 4.34   Scott & White's leader standard work form with example.

Part 2: Visual Controls

Visual controls measure how key processes actually performed vs. expectations. Visual controls answer the question for the leader and his or her team, "How are we doing, right now?" on meaningful goals. It needs to provide quick feedback to the team, as in the next day or at least by the end of the week. How can staff members do experiments without the ability to check quickly if their ideas worked (PDCA)?

Figure 4.35 shows S&W's typical format for a Visual Control Board. It is so closely associated with the daily accountable meeting called the Huddle, that

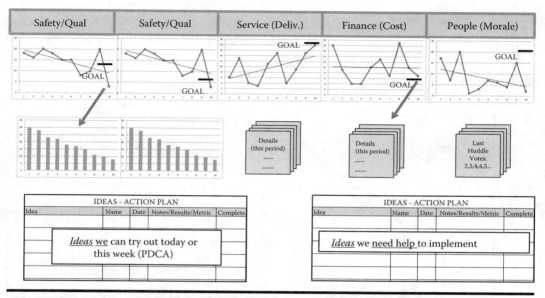

Figure 4.35   S&W's typical three-section format for a huddle board (visual controls).

it is most frequently called a Huddle Board. The board is divided into three important vertical sections:

1. (Top) <u>Visual control charts</u>, usually four to five trend charts showing progress on the team's key process indicators (KPIs). They always have the goal on them. S&W strongly recommends handwritten charts using simple, blank, lined graphs (daily or weekly marks) where staff members put an "X" or dot on the chart by hand in pen or marker. The simplicity of handwritten charts makes them quick to update by anyone, and staff seem to better understand and own the data when they handwrite them. Be sure to note the reasons for misses on all charts in the Why section (below).

2. (Middle) The <u>"Why" section</u> is usually a Pareto chart[*] tallying up various reasons for misses. Or, it could also display a detailed report allowing drill-down for the very latest data point on the trend chart above it (e.g., if the dot above shows average turnover time of all operating rooms for the day or week, the "Why" section report could show detail time by room or crew). Remember, we do not blame individuals in TPS. The process is the problem; people have the solutions.

3. <u>Idea lists</u> and temporary project charts are in the bottom layer. S&W uses two different idea lists. The one on the left is for ideas team

---

[*] The Free Dictionary, *Pareto Chart*, http://encyclopedia.thefreedictionary.com/pareto+chart.

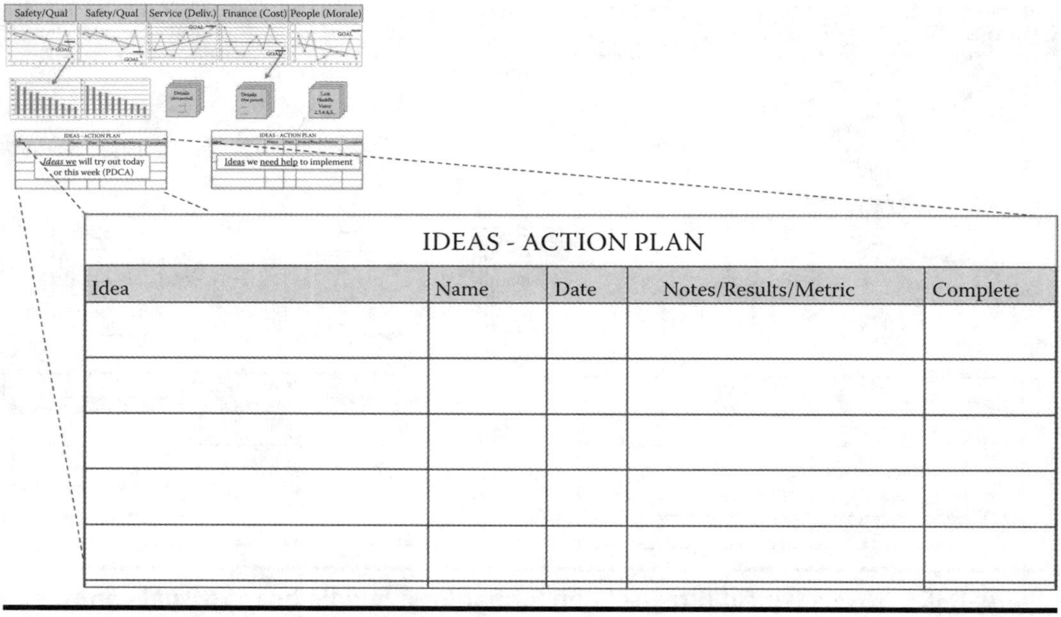

IDEAS - ACTION PLAN				
Idea	Name	Date	Notes/Results/Metric	Complete

Figure 4.36   Close-up of an action plan.

members will try out themselves while they work. They are usually brainstormed in the huddle or brought by problem solving teams. The list looks like a standard action plan as shown in the close-up of Figure 4.36. The idea list also shows the metric that the team is trying to impact. This sets up their PDCA experiment better. The list to the right contains ideas from the team that they need help on (e.g., cross-functional changes out of the team's span of control).

What Do You Put on a Huddle Board?

The obvious answer is cascaded, aligned goals, charted so all staff can easily see actual vs. expected. More accurately, the goals align to the same categories of metrics cascaded from top leaders—the strategic goal categories. Many authors have written about developing balanced sets or scorecards of measures. Steve recommends an oldie but goodie called Measure Up.* The authors' pyramid model shows a better way to develop a balanced set of measures than other methods that yield too many.

S&W liked the categories Toyota put on its boards. When the S&W leadership teams visited Toyota facilities in Kentucky and San Antonio, they

---

* Lynch, Richard and Kelvin Cross, *Measure Up: Yardsticks for Continuous Improvement*, 2nd ed., Wiley, New York, 1995.

> Coming up with a balanced set of metrics is very important. If you elevate one metric, you often get it at the expense of other things.

consistently saw five simple letters for all huddle board categories—S, Q, D, C, and M:

1. Safety
2. Quality
3. Delivery
4. Cost
5. Morale (Toyota also uses HRD here for human resource development)

Coming up with a balanced set of metrics is very important. If you elevate one metric, you often get it at the expense of other things. Like speed at the expense of quality. You can't do that; not in healthcare. Employee morale is number five. That does not mean employees or morale is the lowest of all metrics. It is in the top five out of hundreds of metrics.

Workers Need Input or In-Process Measures to Do Experiments

Workers need a balanced set of process or input metrics. They need measures with data that can be easily tracked—daily. Process and input metrics are shown to the center and left side of the typical process model shown in Figure 4.37. Process and input metrics are ones where staff can typically see and count them at the end of their shift.

Soon after leaders saw SQDCM at Toyota, top leaders started using them. Within a few months, S&W developed a specific set of five strategic goals. (S&W swirl categories from Chapter 4, Step 3 Hoshin Kanri). Most S&W huddles immediately adopted these categories to match the strategy used in

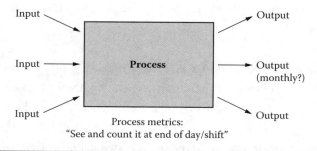

Figure 4.37   Workers need in-process and input metrics.

Hoshin goal setting. Bob continued to use SQDCM on his executive huddle for a long while. He felt if it was good enough for Toyota, it was good enough for his board.

Another name for cascaded, aligned goals is Hoshin goals. These are the goals cascaded up from the top leader to the supervisor and front-line staff. Supervisors and team leaders should track input or process metrics on their boards. They should match their Hoshin goals set at the beginning of the year. They should be tracked in the form of a trend chart, showing where they are now and where they are trending.

Other things to track on your boards are issues or problems. Just ask staff what issues are important to them, and need to be solved. If you are going to do experiments to solve them, you need to track the number and impact of those issues.

Rather than create more and more trend charts at the top, sometimes a team needs to make a temporary chart to track specific interventions on problems. For example, if an inpatient unit team is solving an accuracy problem, they may need to temporarily track the number of times they call the pharmacy (or the MD's office) to clarify something using a simple "tick mark" sheet. The team will see this measure come down rapidly as they try out ideas to solve the root cause of the problem. Once the root is addressed and several weeks of "zero defects" are tracked, this temporary chart can be pulled from the lower section of the huddle board.

To summarize what should be on your huddle board:

■ Categories of metrics
■ Balanced, aligned, high priority set of measures
■ Team leader's Hoshin goals—important metrics, meaningful to the team, shown in trend charts with goals on them
■ Metrics over which the team has control; updated frequently
■ Issues or problems, sometimes with temporary "tick" charts for experiments

In order to do effective PDCA experiments daily, staff need to see trend charts updated daily. They need help from management to develop a pipeline of metrics they can see and count by the end of the day. Then they can update them daily by hand, and do experiments to change them daily. You want metrics within their control that move quickly. Not ones like annual employee satisfaction surveys.

> In order to do effective PDCA experiments daily, staff need to see trend charts updated daily.

Therefore, what do you put on a huddle board? Definitely not pictures of grandkids and cats—not that there is anything wrong with that. Keep those boards in another area of the break room. There should be no more than four or five meaningful, fast-moving trend charts with ideas below to try out.

One time Steve asked his sensei how many metrics an individual or team should measure. Like all good sensei, he answered with another question. He said, "Steve-san, how many fingers are on your hand?" No more than four or five. Even an airplane pilot, with all those bells and whistles on his or her aircraft, flies from moment to moment with adjustments based on just four or five indicators. Experiment with your board to find those four or five fast-moving leverage metrics and you will see success.

Note: It is not easy at first to develop a balanced set of four or five fast-moving input or process measures. Sometimes you guess a metric that is hard to measure or not well correlated with the higher-level measure (not a "leverage" metric). Sometimes, other factors "wash out" a metric that should move quickly when teams try out their ideas, but does not.

The authors suggest that all staff do Hoshin Kanri well at the beginning of the year to cascade goals. In the first years of Hoshin, teams may need to start by just picking one meaningful measure from each of the strategic categories, or SQDCM if you do not have them. Keep asking your staff what is important to them because, early on, you will need to change some of the metrics during the year. You do not change the aligned category of metric, just the specific fast-moving process measure.

Steve recommends reevaluating what a team measures and huddles around at least every three months or so. It is good to totally tear down all charts every so often and recreate the board. It keeps the team focused. Some leaders even move the huddle to another wall, with just a flip chart for a while to keep the data and ideas fresh. You never throw out the process of goal setting or veer from the system goals. However, you sometimes need an empty board in order to choose better, aligned leverage measures. Make sure that you are tracking measures that the team can improve.

Some items must be on the huddle boards. Some are optional, based on the level and type of team gathering at the boards. The following chart shows the general direction given to leaders for their visual controls (huddle boards):

Must-Haves

- Trending data (at least one metric)
- Goals on each chart
- Ideas (action plan)
- A way to escalate ideas (cross-functional/cutting ideas that need more help)

Could-Haves/Should-Haves

- Trending data (up to five metrics)
- Analysis under each trend chart where there is a miss ("Why" charts)
- Fishbone/Five Why's section (for doing quick analysis on each miss)
- A common way to solve problems (use A3 form and process; teams meet outside of huddle)
- Leader standard work
- (Leader huddles) Hoshin forms arranged in line-of-sight to system goals (necessary for at least the first few months of each year)

Close-Up of a Hand-Tracked Measure

Nursing units love to huddle at S&W. They get it. Figure 4.38 shows an early trend chart for reducing overtime. Since cost was one of their categories of

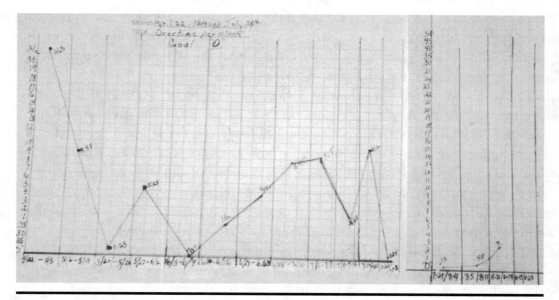

Figure 4.38 Nursing unit trend chart.

metrics, leaders in this unit cascaded down overtime per week in this unit. Their goal was zero.

In the initial four to five weeks, they made good progress. Then, turnover and required EMR training hit and it started to rise again. However, they analyzed why, and brought it back down again. Today, this team maintains very low overtime costs.

Close-Up of All Three Sections of Huddle Board

Figure 4.39 shows a typical blank "daily" chart at S&W. This one is for the Human Resources Recruiting team, and was posted on their huddle board. It shows the number of times screening questions (from checklist) were used for newly posted jobs in their department.

The next figure shows a typical Why graph directly beneath the trend chart in the middle section of their huddle board. For every miss, staff would write the reason and put an "X" in one of the columns next to it. If the reason was already written, they would add another "X." This becomes a type of Pareto chart on its side.

Steve and the Lean team found that staff really like the simplicity of hand-written trend and why charts. There are often multiple pages of why (or any) graphs for a few reasons:

- Multiple page document: Usually a drill-down report showing detail for a data point on the above trend chart
- Past history: It is good to show the breakdown of causes from past weeks or months
- Different chart: Sometimes multiple why graphs are posted this way under multiple trend charts to take up less space on the board

Figure 4.40 shows the third or bottom section of the huddle board. In this case, the HR Recruiting team had two Post-it ideas that day in huddle that they "need help on." Because of different learning and participation styles, leaders are encouraged to hand out Idea Cards or just Post-its for staff to write and "turn an idea in tomorrow," if few good ideas are flowing.

Even if staff are bold, sometimes they do not want to be hasty about saying out loud an idea for improvement. The "Idea Card" allows them to cogitate, discuss with others, and maybe even visualize it better as they work through the day. Steve suggests that leaders try a multitude of

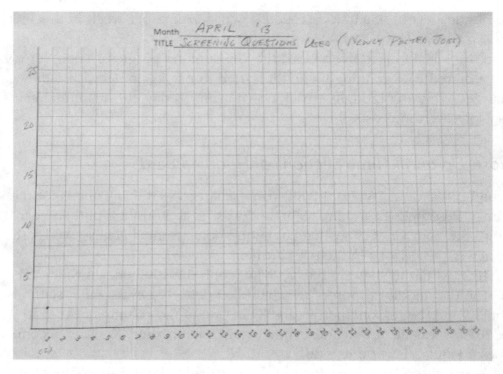

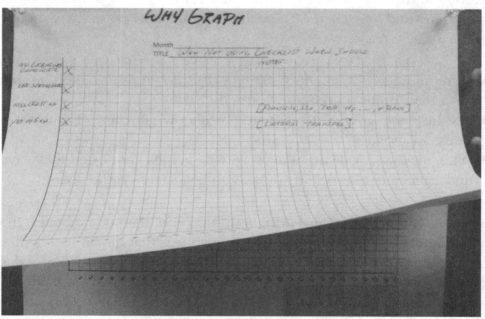

Figure 4.39 Typical blank "daily" trend chart and Why graph directly beneath it to document misses.

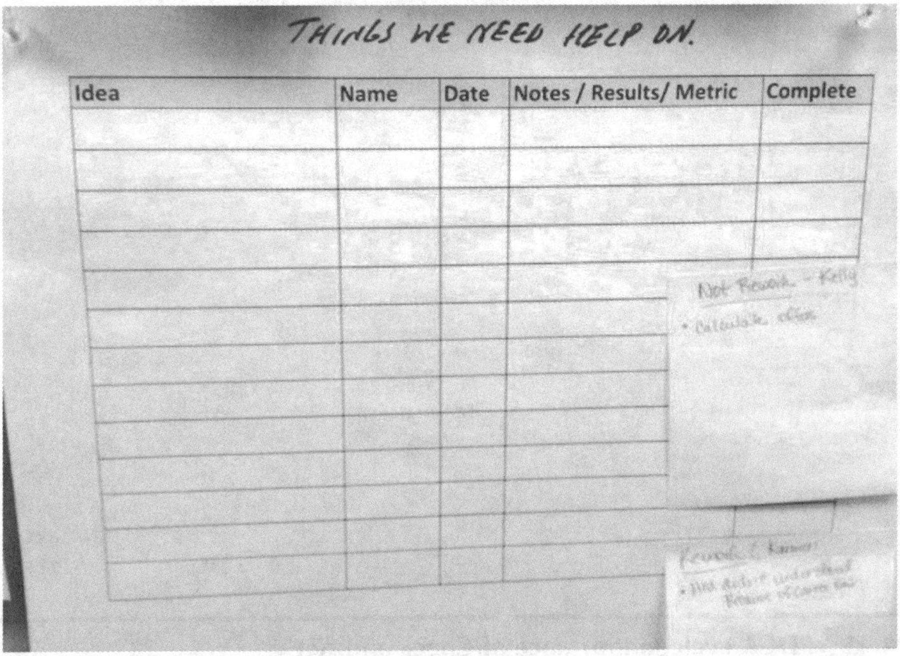

Figure 4.40   Idea list the HR team needs help on, with two idea Post-it notes from huddle.

brainstorming, cards, locations, timing, and even small rewards to encourage more ideas. In fact, a leader could have his or her own huddle experiment—how to generate more ideas—by trying different ways of requesting and collecting ideas.

Part 3: Daily Accountable Process

There will be three main items discussed here in this very important third part of LMS:

1. Daily accountable meetings or huddles
2. Gemba walks by leaders
3. Systemizing: Tracking and layered audits by leaders to sustain and improve

Huddles

The first topic will be the most visible—the huddle. A huddle is a daily team meeting, but it is much more engaging. It is typically stand up, which keeps

Figure 4.41   PDCA cycle; importance of Check and Act.

them brief. They are always located at a huddle board so the team can see its visual controls up close—expected vs. actual.

In the huddle process, team members learn to fly. Team members are given the keys to their own processes. They make decisions, learn, make improvements, make suggestions, and then get "instant gratification" when their charts show improvement toward goals. They use their visual controls to improve processes and implement changes.

It is important that leaders help design the data pipeline by which their staff will experiment on their own processes with guidance from their supervisor. Leaders encourage ideas and build ways to check, as shown in the PDCA cycle in Figure 4.41. Check and Act are shown larger in this figure. Why? It demonstrates the importance of checking that the idea worked and acting (adjusting or adapting) to update the charts, standard work, and training manuals to hard-code the improvement as the new standard.

As discussed in the previous section, team members need input and process measures that can be evaluated by the end of the shift or week. Imagine doing a medical treatment on a patient such as adjusting his or her prescription. Would you check the patient only after a month and a half passes? No! The patient could be harmed by then.

To properly check their experiments, it must be today's data or last week's data at the very least. When staff see the gap between actual vs.

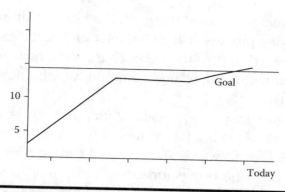

Figure 4.42   Trend chart with a goal line clearly marked on it.

expected on meaningful measures they track daily (input and process measures), then their interventions can be started before month-end result measures can even be collected.

In a typical huddle, a leader picks the topic or goal of the day and reviews the current gap (expected vs. actual). Given the gap, the leader recaps some things the team tried in the recent past. Then, the leader says, "I don't know what to do, but I believe you do! What can we try today, while we work, to make it better? What can we try as a team today to get closer to the goal?"

There is always a gap of some kind. A trend chart is shown in Figure 4.42 with the goal on it. You can see the gap, especially when they first started to track it that month. This team is well on its way to beating the current goal, then resetting an even better goal to help their patients. S&W leaders believe their staff will rise to the occasion with ideas to close the gap. Leaders trust their staff and vice versa. This is scary at first. After making solid progress on every goal, it gets easy and fun for the leader.

In addition to asking how teams can make it better and close the gap, S&W leaders also encourage staff to bring up problems and issues. Start by writing out the problem for all to see. Remember, big problems brought up at the huddles often need to be spun off to a small A3 team. When appropriate, the team will spend a few minutes writing possible causes on a fishbone diagram, usually adding the Five Whys to the most likely "branch."

Checking: In huddles, the team leader will ask if the metric changed from yesterday or this week's experiment. What went well? Quantify it. It is not enough to say, "It felt better." What didn't go well? Again, quantify it.

Another reason to quantify it is to spread the best practice. What would happen if you try to spread a success to another area with the words "Well, it kind of feels better"? Staff naturally resist outside ideas. It is harder to resist with a clear before-and-after improvement story.

If it moves the metrics toward the goal, the leader will make the change part of their everyday process (which is to act or adjust). As stated previously, leaders help staff update the trend charts with new goals, update standard work and training manuals, and communicate the new best practice to all staff on all shifts.

Staff also need to take part in checking that their ideas worked. Staff are usually excited about checking the results of their experiments, especially if they brought the idea forward. As discussed earlier, something changes inside a staff member who brings forward an idea that works.

Big note: Try to keep your huddles to 15 minutes or less. Make it a standing huddle, with staff very close to the visual controls. Keep it brief. The only way to do that is to focus on one of those categories of metrics each huddle. If a viable idea is brought forward, the team and leader will clarify the experiment that will be tried that day (who does what). Then, the leader may say, "Hands in everyone. Ready, Break!" It's a huddle!

Gemba Walks

Another key part of the daily accountability process is leader Gemba walks. In a Lean thinking organization, leaders and staff walk to the Gemba for many purposes:

- To identify and eliminate waste
- To observe, search for data, and speak to staff related to problem solving
- To audit that best methods are being used
- To check for the absence or presence of Lean management system in an area

The last purpose will be the focus of Gemba walks for the remainder of this book. They can be referred to as LMS-building Gemba walks. Leaders must do Gemba walks to reveal the absence or presence of LMS in any area.

Gemba is a Japanese phrase, commonly used in manufacturing organizations. The phrase *genchi genbutsu*, *genba* or *gemba* for short, means actual place.* All problem solving happens in the Gemba, looking at the actual thing in the actual place of work. Problems cannot be solved in a

---

* Lean Enterprise Institute Online Lean Lexicon, *Gemba*, Lean Enterprise Institute, Cambridge, MA, http://www.lean.org/Common/LexiconTerm.cfm?TermId=219 accessed August 2014.

Question: What do you think? Do you believe it takes six months of weekly Gemba walks before they feel natural or become a habit? Would it take six months before you really get used to patiently asking the four questions and helping build LMS? How frequently do you jump in to solve the immediate problems yourself? Shouldn't that change too?

The authors believe it takes that long or more. Good Gemba walks are an acquired thing. Every person taking S&W's Lean leadership or LMS-building course must commit to do a Gemba walk every week for the next six months, at minimum. Few participants thought it could become an engrained habit in less time!

conference room. Gemba for S&W means going to the place where value is added, looking at the process and talking with the people who do the work daily.

In a typical Gemba walk, a leader will go, then look, and then talk. They go to the Gemba, look at the operation, flow, and staff from a few yards away. Then, they start their questions of staff. It also reminds leaders to listen to staff. Gemba walks are performed on a routine, regular basis—usually weekly. Gemba walks are the method S&W uses for setting and following up on expectations for all leaders to build LMS in their areas.

In S&W's Lean leadership course, each participant makes a commitment. David Mann's book says it takes about six months of weekly Gemba walks before they become a habit and you develop a Lean approach to managing in the Gemba.[*]

Each Gemba walk reveals the absence or presence of key parts of a Lean management system when they ask the Four Questions. The four questions reveal how well they are building LMS. These four questions are listed in Figure 4.43.

Surprisingly, this will also answer your question, "What should be tracked on a team huddle board?" When asked what charts, Steve asks a different question of leaders, "Are you doing weekly Gemba walks and asking all four questions?" If they are, team members will tell them what is meaningful. That is question number one. As leaders do more and more Gemba walks, they hear what staff feel should be measured. So, go ask your staff what is important to them.

---

[*] Mann, David, Ibid.

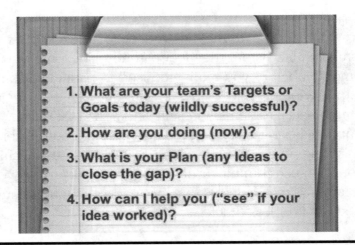

Figure 4.43   Four questions in an LMS-building Gemba walk.

Let's review the four questions in order. Question one, you ask, "What is your team's target or goal today?" Note: the question is *team's* goal not personal goal (like get out of here on time, retire, raise kids well, get over this cold, get promoted, etc.). At the direct performer level, it usually boils down to a quality, a quantity, and a morale goal.

Warning: Staff will sometimes freeze up when a leader asks this question. They either believe that the leader wants a specific answer, so they mumble, "Motherhood, apple pie, oh I forgot our mission statement…" Or, if they have not been asked that question before, they are truly pondering how specific of a goal the leader wants to know (e.g., profit in a hospital, length of stay, etc.).

S&W leaders sometimes need to clarify question one with, "If you and your team were wildly successful today, and you went home bragging to your kids, what would you brag about? How would you measure that?" If the leader is patient, the staff member will reveal a goal he or she feels is important in his or her area.

Question two, you ask how are you doing, *right now* (for a specific goal in question one)? Steve coaches leaders to add, "right now." Otherwise, you get, "It's going great!" (Probe deeper.) How do you know it is going great? "Well, my boss told me." When did your boss tell you? "At our last meeting." When was your last meeting? "Six months ago." Head thump.

Another problem that arises on question two is feelings vs. frequently tracked measures. LMS does not run on feelings. It runs on fact and data. If a staff member says he or she is doing well on the goal, clarify with "Can you show me?" Many times, you will hear the person say, "No. I don't think we track this measure." Do not blame. The four questions are working perfectly to reveal the absence or presence of LMS.

Warning: Sometimes the staff member mentions two or three goals when answering the first question. The second Gemba question must be specific to *one* of them to be effective. The leader doing the LMS-building Gemba walk should pick one. Ask, "You said you need to get hand-washing up to 100%, break in new staff in less time, and reduce falls. For falls, how is your floor doing now? If they say, "I don't know," remember, it is management's (main) job to build these feedback systems.

Question three, you ask, "What are your plans?" Adding, "Any ideas to close the gap?" There is almost always a gap between expected and actual. Maybe they are beating their goals. Thank them. Usually, they are less than the goal. There is a gap. If this team member is huddling, his or her leader should have prompted a similar question during huddle. Remember, the supervisor says in huddle, "I don't know what else we can try, but I believe you know. What can we try as a team today to get closer to the goal?"

If the team member is *not* huddling, question three may be very new to him or her. Question three is the key to Gemba walks (and huddles). If you ask it and listen deeply, encouraging them, you will get ideas! Sometimes huge ones, sometimes out-of-the-box stuff, but almost always an idea. Staff think more about improvement and solving daily problems than leaders know. Good staff members coach little league teams, they run local parent-teacher organizations, and even local churches. They have ideas!

Staff are taught in their Lean courses at S&W to focus on their processes. Thus, many of their ideas are process improvements. However, do not limit the ideas to process improvements. The authors strongly believe that small ideas, thousands of them, will change healthcare delivery systems permanently for the good!

S&W always guides what is tried out daily with two guardrails for just-do-it ideas: It has to be low or no cost, and it must not have even the possibility of a negative impact on patient safety or quality (forgive the double negative). If both are true, then just try the idea. Clarify what the experiment will be, who will do what, and what measure will be checked and when (usually the next day). More on two guardrails in Chapter 5, Two Guardrails.

Daily experiments are always guided by the supervisors. They determine when it starts. They clarify who does what. An experiment is not done in a chaotic way. They are designed experiments brought forward and run by the staff who do the actual work.

Even better, staff will enthusiastically try out their own ideas. There is a Lean axiom full of truth: There is **buy-in through involvement**. Employees do not argue with their own ideas. Can it get any better than total involvement of all staff? Just huddle!

For question four, you ask a typical question, but with an untypical purpose. You ask, "How can I help you?" The leader is not attempting to help them implement their idea. Rather, they are asking, "How can I help you see, with data, that your idea worked?" They are seeking to build LMS.

Do you see the important difference? Leaders ask how they can help staff build the feedback systems by which ideas can be brought forward and then **checked** to see if they worked. If the leader intervened to help the employee implement an idea, it *might* cut the legs out from under the supervisor, especially if he or she already decided not to do it for some reason.

Leaders at all levels must do Gemba walks. They do them with staff at all levels. It is an honor to be the leader observing and the employee being asked.

The focus of Gemba walks is for leaders to "see" the absence or presence of LMS. Leaders want their four questions to reveal weaknesses or gaps in LMS. It is management's (main) job to build Lean management systems so staff can try out their ideas. Therefore, Gemba walks must be hard-coded into every leader's standard work. They may do Gemba walks because they "have to" at first. However, eventually, they see them as *the* work not *new* work.

The most important part of LMS-building revolves around questions two and three. The staff member just told the leader a good idea that could close the gap on a goal. However, think about this question. What if the employee and team tried out their idea today? Would they be able to "see" tomorrow if their idea worked? What metrics do they currently have? Are they measured daily? If they cannot check if it worked, why even try it out? It is management's job to build these systems before requesting ideas. Or, you will have chaos and staff will only be able to say "it feels better." It is management's job.

Two more important questions for Gemba walkers are: With whom, and where? Always ask the four questions of individuals, not a board. This seems obvious, but many leaders just starting out want to show off their fancy new

> What if the employee and team tried out their idea today? Would they be able to "see" tomorrow if their idea worked?

board to their coach, rather than "test out" the absence/presence of LMS. The four questions must be asked first of an actual staff member.

Steve coaches leaders to Gemba walk with a person in their workplace. They are to choose someone who is working, but not too busy.

Their huddle board will eventually have data and charts answering, "How are we doing?" Eventually, staff take the Gemba walking leader to their huddle board. It should have the answers for question two on it!

A Gemba walk may end up at their board. However, you must allow the staff member to take you there. Staff need to know how they are doing on key measures right now—while working. Thus, the questions are asked only where they work. Maybe the board and information need to be closer.

Absence of LMS is not a bad thing for a leader. It only shows there is more to build and learn. Steve coaches leaders to only ask questions on a Gemba walk and not point to their huddle board. Sometimes, when they want the staff member to go to the new huddle board, a leader will say, "You know (vigorously pointing their head toward the huddle board in the background) what we talked about yesterday in the huuuuuuddle…" Either staff members know their goals and how they are doing now or they don't. Either they understand what is on their huddle board or they don't. It is management's job.

Another key principle is that Gemba walks are used at S&W to teach leaders how to build systems for daily process improvement. Leaders are not to wait for someone else to make changes or a Lean coach to conduct a workshop. They are masters of their process, within the two guardrails, and can even elevate ideas that are bigger. Accountability is taught and caught. The LMS toolkit is engaging and simple.

More Gemba Walks, More Time

Gemba walks, huddles, and encouraging the flow ideas is not *new* work, it is *the* work. One early graduate from a Lean leadership course was Shahin Motakef, President of Temple and Central Region. Like others in the class, he committed to personal weekly Gemba walks immediately following the course. He and Cyndy Dunlap, CNO, quickly realized that Gemba walks helped them get their daily work done. Somehow, they had more time, not less.

So, they went "all in," committing to daily Gemba walks in the first full year as they built LMS in their region. Cyndy said of the full Lean management systems-building effort, "Lean Management Systems significantly changed how I work with my team to improve care and outcomes. The skill of creating daily accountability within the organization tied quality and Lean tools together to create real time improvements!"

S&W also assigns each leader a personal sensei for his or her LMS journey. It is usually the instructor of their Lean leadership course. They are required to do three guided Gemba walks with their sensei before they earn their *Lean Leadership* certificate. They do a sensei-guided walk about every four weeks after the course. This allows them to do some Gemba walks on their own in between. See Chapter 5 Building LMS for more detail on guided Gemba walks.

S&W learned a lot about Lean management system building from Toyota. Over decades, TPS founder and collector, Taiichi Ohno, tested and documented principles that worked. Fujio Cho studied under Ohno and later became the longest serving president of Toyota's American division. While at Johnson Controls, Steve was influenced by the consistent TPS visionary, Cho-san.

Toyota leaders influenced S&W in many other ways as well. A long-time friend and fellow Lean consultant for S&W, Dennis Raymer, studied under Cho-san for over a decade. Bob wanted every possible part of TPS adapted at S&W for healthcare.

Cho-san would often say, "Go see, ask why, and show respect." S&W made that a key part of its Lean Leadership course and Gemba walks. Go see. Go to the Gemba. Look deeply at the department from afar for a few moments. Can you see flow? Does there appear to be a bottleneck? Are all employees actively adding value, or appearing to?

Now, it is time to step forward and address an individual staff member. Ask why. Understood between Gemba questions two (revealing a gap) and

"Lean Management Systems significantly changed how I work with my team to improve care and outcomes. The skill of creating daily accountability within the organization tied quality and Lean tools together to create real time improvements!"

—Cyndy Dunlap, RN, MPA, NEA-BC, FACHE
System Chief Nursing Executive, Scott & White Healthcare and Chief Nursing Officer, Scott & White Memorial Hospital

three (any ideas) is basic problem analysis. Ask, "Why is the team off its target?" This question is never asked in a negative way, but in a curious, probing way with the purpose of bringing out staff's ideas and building feedback systems. This shows great respect.

S&W teaches that respect is always two-way. It is not just a boss showing his or her employees respect by listening to their ideas. The employees also show their boss respect by trusting their ideas will be considered without any sort of bias or punishment. They trust that leaders will allow them to try out their own ideas.

Some ideas will not work perfectly. However, two-way respect also means the boss has the right to decide which ideas are tried out and when. If one staff member wants to try one way and another wants to try something different, the boss must make the decision. And, sometimes two *sequential* experiments are better than one.

> Respect people's feelings. Even if it doesn't mean anything to you, it could mean everything to them.
>
> **—Unknown**

Daily Experiments

Steven J. Spear says Toyota enables "a series of nested, ongoing experiments, whether the work is as routine as installing seats in cars or as complex, idiosyncratic, and large-scale as designing and launching a new model or factory."* The result: Every worker every day constantly looks for opportunities for improvements in his or her own work processes. Toyota teaches all staff how to use the scientific method and PDCA cycles to experiment on work, making all workers investigators. From that simple method, Toyota gets ever-improving results.

At S&W, leaders want every worker experimenting, using supervisor-led PDCA cycles, every day on their daily work. Remember the picture of the

> Toyota teaches all staff how to use the scientific method and PDCA cycles to experiment on work, making all workers investigators. From that simple method, Toyota gets ever-improving results. Do you?

---

* Spear, Stephen, Learning to lead at Toyota, *Harvard Business Review*, May 2004.

> The beauty of LMS is that workers do not spend extra time away from work doing this. They try out their own ideas *while they work*!

iceberg? Only 10% or so of all ideas are going to come out of facilitated projects. Where will the other 90% of ideas come from? When staff huddle just 15 minutes each day, focusing on a single metric/gap and identifying ideas to try out, they are becoming *process doctors*. Just 15 minutes each day. The benefit is success and survival.

Of the implemented ideas now at S&W, 90% come out of huddles. As this is being written, S&W is averaging about 2000 implemented ideas per week from its 16,000 full-time employees. This is more than it had in a whole year prior!

The beauty of LMS is that workers do not spend extra time away from work doing this. They try out their own ideas *while they work*! Daily experiments are now part of their daily work. Imagine, if you have not built Lean management systems yet, 90% of all possible improvement ideas are being withheld from your bottom line. Worse, 90% of the benefits of waste busting are being withheld from your staff! They hate waste!

So, what is *Daily Lean*? Brief, focused, daily huddles by teams at their boards to bring up and try out ideas, combined with leaders in the Gemba daily, asking the four questions, auditing, and encouraging progress.

Simple. Staff huddle. They come up with improvement ideas and use PDCA for each experiment under the guidance of their supervisor. Leaders help ensure that staff track ideas and results. Leaders audit and elevate ideas that are out of the team's control. After an early Gemba walk, Bob exclaimed, "This is the most fun I had in many months!" Don't miss this fact—leaders have always wanted to unleash the power of ideas. LMS just creates the vehicle and format to do so.

> After an early Gemba walk, Bob exclaimed, "This is the most fun I had in many months!" Don't miss this fact—leaders have always wanted to unleash the power of ideas. LMS just creates the vehicle and format to do so.

LMS Examples

While it would be nearly impossible to describe all huddle boards and teams at S&W, a few LMS examples will help your understanding. The following examples give the reader a taste for huddles, huddle boards, and the teams that accelerate their engagement and ideas because of them.

The following examples were not chosen because of large results. As you will read, some were very rough initial attempts. Rather, they show the breadth and depth of LMS at S&W.

Nursing—Labor and Delivery (L&D)

One huddle team that embraced LMS early on was the Labor and Delivery nursing unit at Memorial Hospital. Figure 4.44 shows their board around February 2013. This team was energized by huddling.

At the very top, L&D had annualized goal trend charts and some temporary project metrics. They had five strategic goal categories on the second row down in the picture.

Under each category is at least one trend chart measuring the best levers of success—their key process indicators.

At the beginning of the month, blank trend charts with 31 "day" marks across the bottom were placed under the five categories. The nurses updated

Figure 4.44   Labor and Delivery huddle board—year 1.

these charts themselves by putting a dot where they ended the day. Best practice: Rather than cover up the previous month with another daily chart, they moved the "average" dot for the whole month up to the annual charts on top. This allowed the team to "see" the great improvements they made in earlier months, even when additional gains got tough later!

Underneath each trend chart is the Why section for analysis and drill-down detail for the most recent data point on the trend chart above. The bottom section is for ideas. The L&D team came up with quite a few good ideas. A key focus was on patient satisfaction. The team presented its story to many inside and outside leaders.

L&D probably tore their board down fully four to five times in the first year. This is encouraged at S&W. Choosing meaningful, cascaded goals linked to overall goals is not easy in the first few years.

One category where L&D initially struggled was their quality or safety goal. The suggested goal in this category, cascaded from hospital leadership, was falls. However, not many 20-something women fall in general. This team could have "mailed it in" that year and achieved their goal. However, that would have been too easy for them. They asked themselves, "Is there a better quality goal that forces us to get better?" They chose quality goals that were much harder to reach.

Here is a brief summary of ideas that helped them hit their goals:

- Call lights: Patients hit their call light signaling for some assistance. L&D nurses felt they could reduce this to near-zero by doing hourly rounding. If they were in the room, on time, checking their pain/position/potty (the three Ps), then call lights could be greatly reduced.
- Meaningful hourly rounding: Not just checking the box, but tending to patients' needs while in the room and discussing in the huddles what else to check.
- Noise level: Especially at night.
- Timeliness of pain meds: Timeliness, along with a lot of education on the pain meds.
- Answering their phones: This may seem simple to those outside of inpatient nursing units, but, depending on staffing, it is not. The hospital unit clerk ensured patient calls roll over to them if not answered in 30 seconds.
- Discharge: Improved the timeliness and quality of discharge through improved education and handouts.

- (Important) Nurse manager rounding: They focused on opportunities for improvement rather than check-box auditing.

The engagement and energy of the L&D staff could be seen and felt after the first few weeks of huddling. The ideas they implemented worked. They hit many of their initial goals early in the year. So, what do you think they did? The team raised the bar on key goals, and came up with even more ideas!

There is value in every idea. Something visible changes within them when employees bring up ideas, the team tries it out, it works, and their leaders and peers recognize them. When this happens, they do not care what the effort is called. They go home bragging to their kids. They feel like their brains, their ideas, their professional selves are being fully engaged— maybe for the first time! S&W leaders are very proud of the L&D unit at Memorial.

Figure 4.45 shows the L&D huddle board around July 2014. Nursing Manager Kayla Skala, to the right of the board, is leading this huddle. Their five to six key trend charts changed a bit, but the basic look is similar. Different from other boards and not mentioned thus far, L&D also added:

- Vertical "Kudos card" holder to the right
- Temporary projects to the far right (C-section problem solving)
- Physician involvement (several attend the huddle on rotation)
- Supervisors from L&D and related areas (Tier 2) also huddle at this board because their metrics were similar (overlapping in some cases)

Figure 4.45   Labor and Delivery huddle—year 2.

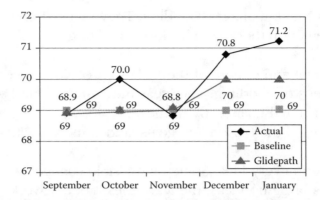

Figure 4.46   Overall patient satisfaction improvement.

Temple Memorial—Overall Patient Satisfaction Effort Using Huddles

How do you link a system-wide effort like patient satisfaction improvement to every level from the chief to the direct performers? At S&W, staff and leaders would say huddles!

Temple Memorial tried this over a three- to four-month period in early FY12. Figure 4.46 shows overall patient satisfaction improvement for their first three months after using patient satisfaction drill-down scores for each specific unit as well as a list of "Top 10" ways to improve (from the survey vendor) to each huddle.

They improved the top box score for Memorial campus as a whole. Even though it was small at first, this improvement was meaningful because progress lagged earlier for many reasons. Units like L&D and others were critical in moving the entire campus toward their goal.

Quotes from Nursing Leaders

You heard the quotes from CNO Cyndy Dunlap earlier. It would be good at this point to hear a few comments from other nursing leaders as well.

One said, "Huddling is the best tool we have ever implemented." To her and her team, it did not matter what it was called. Interestingly, this nursing unit said they "huddled a lot" prior to LMS building, but somehow huddling for ideas and quickly trying them out was different—it just changes things.

Another leader said, "It is exciting to see my direct reports looking for and finding ways to make process improvements. They no longer say, 'That's the way we've always done it.' Now, they confidently say, 'Find 'em and fix 'em' to problems and opportunities."

Another higher-level nurse leader's comment was even more impactful. She said, "The way we use huddle boards has made me more aware of current issues and how to prioritize work. I am now able to display core measure data on departmental huddle boards for discussion of opportunities and celebrations."

Can you imagine one lone nurse leader trying to push the quality effort forward at his or her facility? Now, they have an army of aligned staff seeking improvements and, for the first time, seeing both the gaps and the immediate impact of their improvements. Steve calls idea huddles with daily updated trend charts "instant gratification" for staff. Staff can now help achieve system-wide goals starting in their own areas.

Monthly LMS Huddle Success Stories

Both Bob and Steve love stories. S&W documented many of the hard-fought successes early on. Specific ways to promote and spread wins and best practices will be discussed in Chapter 6.

The following list is a small window into one good month at S&W. In February 2013, Steve published the following Huddle Board Wins, just a subset of the overall successes that month:

Hillcrest Baptist Hospital Wins:

- Access: Appointment with specialty clinic from 5 to 2 days.
- Reduced re-collected lab samples from 5.4% to 3.4%.
- Increased referrals to cardiac rehab clinic from 17% 1QFY13 to 28% in December and 33% in January.
- Reduced No Call/No Shows in outpatient therapy from 13% to 3.2%.

Round Rock Region Wins:

- Improved patient satisfaction scores for EVS "clean" questions by over 17%.
- Nurse Triage Line calls answered by person (not machine) from 20% to 50%.
- Sun City clinic improved patient satisfaction scores on *Likelihood to Recommend* from 44% to 90%.

Brenham Hospital Wins:

- EVS had no standard or expectation for stocking cleaning carts; end-of-shift standard work was created whereby the cart was always ready for next user.
- Observations of hand hygiene compliance were lower than expected; volunteers were recruited and hand hygiene compliance increased to 99%.

College Station Hospital and Clinic Wins:

- Medical Records saved one hour per day; trained all staff to benefit from this improvement.
- Hand hygiene compliance improved from 93% to 100%.
- Contact isolation compliance tripled from Q2 to Q3.

Temple Wins:

- Reduced GI backlog from 59 to less than 30 in three weeks.
- Reduced <30-day reschedules in GI department from 27 to 4.
- Labor & Delivery: Nurse Call Light response time and on-time C-sections both beat their annual goals (by mid-year).

Llano Hospital Wins:

- Nutrition Services Patient Satisfaction improved from 4.0 to 4.4 by piloting a new tray and cart to keep food warm.
- Reduced ED length of stay to goal of 2 hours or less; tracked physician average cycle time.

By February 2013, S&W had almost half of its director-level and higher leaders trained in its full Lean leadership course, with training-the-eyes tours of Toyota and other mature LMS facilities. Even better, S&W was investing heavily in front-line supervisors and managers with a fun, 3-hour LMS Quickstart workshop. This critical mass of leaders not only continues to build LMS daily at S&W, these graduates also teach other leaders!

In addition, by February 2013, the Lean team was tracking about 650 huddle boards with maybe 3000 total ideas visible on all boards. This was all within the first six to eight months of the effort. It is possible to move quickly if leaders commit.

Figure 4.47 Sharyl Rogers demonstrating EVS mobile huddle board (left); storage of all four mobile huddle boards (right).

Temple Environmental Services (EVS)

Leader Sharyl Rogers and team developed mobile huddle boards to bring the huddles to her mobile EVS staff. This was a very innovative solution for staff that do not have offices and need to move fast. She is shown demonstrating the boards at Bob's executive huddle in Figure 4.47. EVS team members continue to try out good ideas to help S&W patients.

In Figure 4.47 on the right, each of the four main teams or "pods" stores their mobile boards using Velcro on the leader's huddle wall. When a pod team is ready to huddle, the leader grabs the smaller board and runs to the designated hallway to huddle.

The front of the small board has two to three main metrics (see Figure 4.48). Trend or Why charts are on the back. A topic of the day is brought up, teams see the gap, and they brainstorm ideas to try out that day. Ideas are recorded and brought to the leader huddle (Tier-2) for controlled experiments and to quickly spread them.

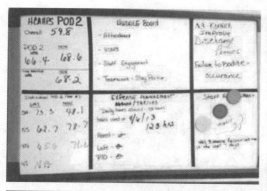

Figure 4.48 Close-up of mobile huddle board with Why charts located on the back of each section to document misses.

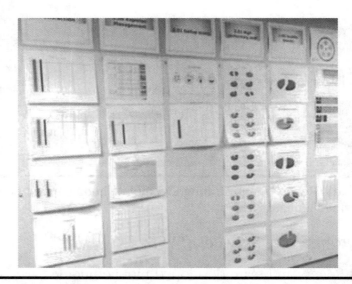

Figure 4.49   EVS Tier 3 huddle board; more metrics due to the differences between areas, elevated ideas at bottom.

Finally, the EVS leaders met with other leaders on the Hospitality Team (Tier-3) huddle. They elevate and spread ideas, along with implementing their own ideas (see Figure 4.49).

Everyone at Every Level Huddles—A Tier-3 Leader Huddle

Everyone at S&W huddles, especially the leaders as seen in Figure 4.50. The leaders from Temple Region are huddling: Cyndy Dunlap, CNO; Dr. Steve Sibbitt, CMO; Alita Prosser, Finance; and Shahin Motakef, President of Temple

Figure 4.50   Scott & White leaders huddling.

and Central Region. In Shahin's Tier-3 huddle today, over 20 leaders report on key metrics. They used simple red, yellow, and green magnets and color-coding. If a leader's category is red, he or she needs to bring an action plan.

This is important. The tendency is to avoid specific questions like "Why?" if leaders are not used to it. However, "Why?" is the question that all leaders must ask when their team has missed a mark. Shahin worked out a process to deal with his question "Why" using a single category first. If a leader's metric is red for a few days in a row, then what? What will be their response? The authors believe that leaders must answer this before their first huddle.

In manufacturing, good statistical process control (SPC) on key metrics calls for an Out-of-Control Action Plan—the specific set of actions taken to get back on track. Shahin wanted to define and codify the process of uncovering gaps, and then quickly moving toward resolution. His constant question "Why" related to soft volumes or missed key metrics was eventually answered with data and action plans. If you are red, bring the reasons why and your actions to the leader huddle!

Figure 4.51 shows Waco Region President Glenn Robinson huddling with his executive staff in early 2013. Staff members shown are Richard Perkins, Will Turner, and Marcy Weber. Glenn's wall opened up to show different areas of metrics on the "wings." This same wall now houses visual controls for two different daily huddles. It also contains the innovative elevation card system shown later.

Figure 4.51   Glenn Robinson huddling with staff.

Figure 4.52   Kevin Smith and Betsy Patterson huddling.

Figure 4.52 shows Taylor leader Kevin Smith with CNO Betsy Patterson at their huddle board in early 2013. LMS has proliferated to most if not all of S&W operations today. There are still some holdouts in support areas, but a common operating system is prevalent. It leans heavily on LMS and huddles for engagement, buy-in, and idea generation.

It is the leader's job to build systems that allow ideas to be brought up, tried out, and checked for success. If everything rises and falls on leadership, then how can any organization delegate the work of transformation to low-level team members without changing the way they manage and build first?

S&W invested in its leaders. They are taught: Build Lean Management Systems, make it work, help your team make improvements, set a new standard, and make it sustain through layered audits. Then, help spread these benefits to another area.

S&W's Employee Engagement "Outlier"

In spring 2013, S&W's "Highly Engaged" scores on its annual employee survey indicated it was doing something right! Scores were higher than previous surveys. But to keep with the times, there were many organizational benefit package reductions and even pay changes that had occurred. Experts would have expected the percentage of highly engaged staff to go *down* in these circumstances. S&W leadership dissected the scores.

S&W leaders knew huddles would be game-changers. At the very core, they spur engagement and ownership—at least of the teams' work processes. Therefore, S&W added a specific question to the standard survey. It was:

CQ13.   How often do you participate in a huddle with others from your
   work group to discuss issues and propose solutions to those issues?
   1. Daily
   2. Not daily, but more than once per week
   3. Weekly
   4. Monthly
   5. Rarely/Never

This question was added for all staff and again in a separate list of questions for all physicians.

The results were astounding. A survey company staff member called it a "statistical outlier" because it correlated so closely with "highly engaged." No single question was even close to determining highly engaged employees than this question. Early in the LMS-building process, 70% of all S&W staff were huddling daily or weekly! In addition, a whopping 80% of all nurses were huddling daily or weekly! Bob and his leaders were ecstatic.

Even better, the survey revealed something S&W leaders felt would be true. Of all staff that huddled daily, 59% were in the highly engaged category vs. only 22% of those who rarely or never huddled! This was nearly a 3-to-1 swing and a significant indicator of engagement.

Even if the staff huddled more than once per week or weekly, but still huddled, they were "highly engaged." Something changes for staff when their ideas are heard and tried out. They feel respected and, well, engaged. The LMS process gives staff control over their processes. It helps them feel like they are part of a success story where patients get better and employees' voices are heard.

Huddles work. People have ideas. It is management's job to build these systems. If you have not considered any other reasons to build LMS, consider the impact S&W saw in staff engagement alone—even in a down period!

Summary of S&W's Idea Generators

To summarize all the ways S&W staff generate ideas, please see Figure 4.53. It is much more than Lean. As you can see, staff and teams attack problems

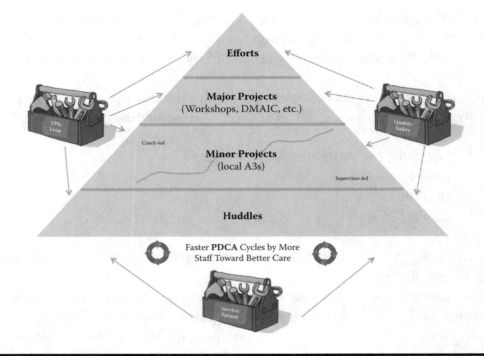

Figure 4.53 Idea Generators or Formats at all levels from Multiple Toolkits for faster PDCA Cycles by More Staff.

and waste at all levels of the organization. They also do so in many "formats" shown on the pyramid.

The bottom is widest because they happen more frequently—even daily. There are more of them. *Huddles* draw from even more than the three "toolkits" shown here—TPS/Lean, Quality/Safety (sometime six sigma), and Service/Patient-focused.

But, ideas in huddles are constrained to simple changes within the two guardrails. These small changes are sometimes called ***Just-Do-Its*** (JDIs). A decent definition of a JDI is small change that can be accomplished using the *Rule of 3s*:

- with 3 or less people
- in 3 or less days
- with 3 or less steps

This type of definition was helpful at S&W as they defined the types of ideas that can be tried out at huddle boards versus in larger projects. Note: Large variation reduction efforts sometimes require longer "check" periods.

Care should be taken to avoid negating longer-term variation reduction experiments with daily experiments in huddles. As always, "experiments" are checked and approved by the supervisor before conducting. S&W also started limiting the number of experiments to *two per week* at each board, to avoid having one bad effect negate three or four other great ideas.

S&W generated ideas in *Minor Project* teams, like smaller problems to be solved (local A3s). The squiggly line shows S&W's desire that their supervisors be self-sufficient to facilitate small problem solving on their own. Coaches were available for others.

Above this are *Major Projects*, like Value Stream Mapping and Sepsis reduction in particular departments or even crossing departments. Some of these projects required advanced expertise in the quality or Lean toolkits and used the right tools for the right situation.

The top of the pyramid is, hopefully, the smallest in number, but likely the largest in impact. These are system or division-wide *Efforts*. Examples of efforts would be EMR implementation, Magnet Nursing certification, Same Day Appointment, "infectious disease" process, prevention and practice drills, etc.

All of these opportunities for ideas draw from an ever-widening toolkit. But, they are all based on faster and faster PDCA cycles, by more and more staff, toward better care for patients. They all come down to PDCA. So, stop fighting internally about which form or detailed step you are on. Get busy building systems that draw out ideas—before it is too late!

A JDI is small change that can be accomplished using the Rule of 3s: with: 3 or less people, in 3 or less days, with 3 or less steps.

Chapter 5

The Huddle System (LMS)—In Detail

Quarterback: "484 Pump Curl on two, on two. Ready? Break!" "Set! Red 80, Red 80, Hut-Hut!"

Offensive Coach: "That didn't work! What do you see sky cam?"

"No one covered Tim?!"

"Great! Tell Tom to call it again to Tim next third and long."

One theme that threads this book together is *ideas*. Another is *effective huddles*. Huddles are not new. Just watch American football. Employee huddles are not new either. They are not new in healthcare or in many other industries.

However, very few of these huddles produced ideas for improvement daily that were discussed, tried out, checked, and then made part of the improved standard so everyone can benefit (PDCA). Few employees were asked for their ideas in huddles. Even fewer created systems by which ideas were all aligned to the organization's North Star goals, with tougher ideas elevated to leader teams who also huddled frequently for this purpose.

Try this simple experiment. Walk to the nearest staff member in your workplace. Ask him or her three questions:

1. What is the biggest goal for the day for you or your department?
2. How are you doing on that goal right now?
3. Do you have any ideas on how to make it better?

If it has been a while since a leader asked them for their opinion or ideas, you may need to press them a bit. When they give you one, ask yourself, "If they tried out that idea, would they be able to tell tomorrow if it worked?"

Do you see where this book is leading? The most significant concept in this book is not huddles. It is who builds the systems around them and why!

The next two full sections are referred to as LMS-building because each part must be built and leaders must do the building! The authors chose not to repeat many of the basic LMS ideas from Chapter 4. A few concepts do repeat enough to bridge the readers to the next level of detail, and to connect them to building a wider culture of continuous improvement.

Keep It Simple: Two Guardrails to Guide All Daily Lean Ideas

Kaizen means ongoing improvement involving everybody, without spending much money.

—Masaaki Imai, Founder of the Kaizen Institute Consulting Group and author; helped popularize Kaizen methodologies in the western hemisphere

Steve remembers his and other companies deploying Total Quality Management (TQM) efforts in the 1980s. They used a good team-based framework, but did not provide a toolkit for staff. He believes the effort meant well. However, it was extremely unfocused. Steve's first "huddle" with a well-trained TQM team went something like the following:

Leader: "Who has any ideas?" [silence]
Leader: "C'mon team. I know you have one."
Carl: "Well, I've been thinking…"
Leader: "Yes, yes."
Carl: "I think it's too hot in here most days." [Note: it was a float glass factory that melted silica sand]
Team: "Yeah. Yes. That's right."

The next few meetings offered up other "biggies" such as the need for a basketball hoop, more comfortable chairs for their TQM Circle meetings, that it was now too cold [Note: it was now winter], and the coup de gras, the need for a juice machine for better health.

After adding up the costs of all these "improvements," the Plant Manager quickly stopped the TQM Circle meetings. Again, the facilitator and team meant well. However, where is the improvement toolkit? In addition, shouldn't the ideas be focused on improving something more specific than just quality-of-work-life issues? Shouldn't ideas move forward the common mission and vision of the team and organization? And, are all ideas good ideas?

Like most of their daily improvement systems, S&W's guardrails were very simple. Ideas were to be focused mainly around closing known "gaps," made visual on a large board in the area where teams huddle. And like a road, there were only two guardrails. Staff were not just allowed, they were encouraged to bring up and then try out ideas that:

1. Were low or no cost
2. Did not have even the possibility of negative impact on patient safety or quality (really, the ideas should improve both)

So, with guardrails clearly communicated, the teams charged off. The authors offer one more tip here: Ideas are easy for teams to generate. Having fast-moving, aligned measures, and getting teams to feel secure enough to focus their problem solving and ideas around these gaps takes some time. However, they are always thinking.

How about you? What guardrails would you put in place to keep your teams from veering off into the ditch, but with enough leeway to encourage innovation?

The good news is this gets easier. Just stick with it. The hardest part of the above tip is actually choosing the proper "levers" or fast-moving aligned measures—and then getting a daily (or weekly) pipeline of data to better display progress on this measure to the teams.

Leadership, Gemba, and PDCA Cycles

As stated earlier, everything rises and falls on leadership. Moreover, LMS-building is a full-contact sport for leaders. They go first. They build their huddles first. They show their staff how to lead huddles, and then they are available for CI in the workplace (leader standard work).

So, how do new leaders learn to lead in a Lean way? Steve offers a different sensei question. "Can we learn how to be a Lean leader in the Gemba?" Because of the nature of this book, you know it will be a resounding "Yes!" In fact, you can only learn to be a Lean leader in the Gemba.

In Figure 5.1, you see CNO Cyndy Dunlap on a Gemba walk. She stopped to ask the four questions to a nurse. She pulled the leaders to their huddle board in the Surgical/Trauma Intensive Care Unit (STICU) area. Cyndy is learning with the team members present, and she is setting up question four, "How can I help?"

The STICU team members had learned a great deal on their most recent experiments. They showed Cyndy their last few PDCA cycles—most worked

Figure 5.1 Cyndy Dunlap on a Gemba walk.

How about your organization? What do your CNOs do? Do they do daily Gemba walks to draw out ideas, help build quick feedback systems, elevate ideas, and encourage staff?

They may not all experience the idea flow and engagement that Cyndy's teams did after starting LMS-building. However, why not try?

very well and moved their metrics forward. Some did not fare as well, but leaders still encouraged staff to keep trying. It is never one solution that turns around a department because it is never only one problem that plagues it. Many PDCA cycles on many gaps are needed.

The team members shown are also receiving some good feedback as well. Cyndy checks the idea list to the right—the ones they need help to try out. She will help elevate them up to the next level's board. She will also encourage them.

Cyndy developed eyes for waste. However, she did not keep this to herself. All nurses experience waste in their work tasks every day. Leaders are learners. Then, leaders are teachers. You must develop eyes for waste as well. A big waste for leaders is not maximizing the ideas flowing for all teams to hit their goals. Don't leave any idea "on the table" or floor. Help staff pick up that low-hanging fruit! The faster the better.

Another important benefit of daily Gemba walks is what Cyndy avoids. She avoids "filtering" of staff and process issues. Leaders get filtered information, especially about problems. It is considered a weakness in some healthcare circles not to be able to do something by themselves or immediately solve problems themselves!

It is hard to know when information is being filtered. However, when the leader goes to the Gemba, speaks with staff members about their ideas, and sees dozens of ideas in process on their huddle boards, it is very hard to filter what is truly going on! If a staff member's ideas were being squelched, Cyndy would hear it. If true roadblocks (or road blockers) are stopping progress, she hears about it, and can delicately respond.

Small "l" Leadership First

Another critical principle at S&W is learning to repeat small "l" before working on big "L" leadership. Small "l" leadership is doing one PDCA cycle with a staff member as shown in Figure 5.2 again. Can the leader help execute one PDCA experiment with his or her employee?

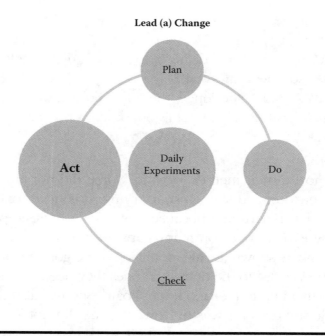

Figure 5.2 Leading a small change through one PDCA cycle before mastering Big "L" leadership.

Let's take an example. A staff member has an idea. He wants to try those little rubber-bottom socks so his patients do not fall. Plan, Do, Check, and Act (or adjust). A leader's job is to help the team member work through one cycle. The leader makes sure all staff know the experiment that will be conducted that day or week. They make assignments, careful to involve the employee who brought up the idea. They help make sure the right sizes of socks are available and identify the fall-risk patients that need them. Then, they do it!

In their next huddles, they help the team "check" to see if the idea worked. In advance, they identified the specific chart that will be used to check, and when it will be checked. If it worked, then they Act to adjust the standard—ensuring that everyone gets the benefit of the improved process. This will include communication, training, and then audits (simple, visual checks) to ensure all staff are using the new waste-reducing idea. Standard work and training documents will be updated as well.

Until a leader can lead one small change through a PDCA cycle and sustain it, he or she is not ready for big "L" leadership. Leadership at S&W starts with building LMS focused around a single change. Books are written about big "L" leadership, including authoritative books by impressive leaders who ooze charisma and somehow keep all staff happy. Since S&W cannot hire

Jack Welch as a nursing supervisor, it teaches all leaders to start by repeating many PDCA cycles with and for their teams. By the way, S&W has many great leaders now!

S&W boils leadership down to something simple. *It is management's job to build the systems* by which workers' ideas can be brought forward, tried out, checked, and then adopted into the new standards. The leader is a chief servant, but still fully accountable to meet all goals. When ideas flow, everyone receives the benefit of reduced waste and solved problems. Imagine a day like that! Now, make it happen.

New Ways of Thinking

John Shook has been one of Steve's friends and mentors for over a decade. John is President of the Lean Enterprise Institute, and author of *Managing to Learn*[*] along with many other great books. John likes to say, "Sometimes you have to act your way to a new way of thinking." Several new ways of thinking are described here.

Certain parts of LMS-building will feel unfamiliar as you initiate them. Some feel downright foreign at first. It is hard for a supervisor in a huddle to tell his or her staff, "We've tried X, Y, and Z and we're still not at the goal. *I don't know* what to do, but I believe you do! What can we try today to improve this goal?"

What are the new ways of thinking and acting? S&W leaders teach a Lean adage to reinforce John's statement: *Trust the process*. This is hard when some leaders succeeded in the past using different means. A different way of understanding John's statement is, "Sometimes you have to fake it until you make it (a habit)." It is not "faking it" in a negative way, like when you do not believe it. However, trust that your staff—doing many PDCA cycles faster and faster—will help lead your team to needed improvements.

Some things will be very different for the Lean leaders as they build Lean management systems. They will not only develop leader standard work for themselves, they will also post it and communicate to their teams when they will be "available for CI" and in the Gemba. They will strongly support employee standard work through visibly auditing that everyone uses the best practices. There is one best way—the way that is documented. And, teams can make it better.

---

[*] Shook, John, *Managing to Learn: Using the A3 Management Process to Solve Problems, Gain Agreement, Mentor and Lead*, Lean Enterprise Institute, Cambridge, MA, 2008.

In addition, everything is made visual. This principle is called Visual Management. Leaders can delegate more authority to frontline staff. They help build feedback systems and watch them fly. There is also a focused daily accountability process where the leaders physically lead their huddle, with follow-up Gemba walks.

Another "new" way of acting relates to problem solving. A Lean adage is: "No problem" is a problem. In other words, there are always problems. Hiding or working around them just makes them reappear tomorrow. *Find it-fix it* is the new mentality and process.

S&W uses structured A3 problem solving. No more sweeping it under the rug. No more time-consuming workarounds. All ideas outside the huddle (and some problems within) must be presented in a standard A3 format. In addition, the A3 process is a very good leadership development process and toolkit.

Jim Womack stated in his book, *Gemba Walks*, "The life of Lean is experiments. In short, Lean is not a religion but a daily practice of conducting experiments and accumulating knowledge."* Note: the life or purpose of deploying Lean thinking is not immediate cost savings or headcount cuts. The goal is improvement experiments. Experimenting daily and accumulating the knowledge. That worked, this didn't. That worked, let's spread it. Leaders and staff must go through these learning cycles themselves, very rapid-learning PDCA cycles.

In summary, the goal is faster and faster PDCA cycles by more and more staff. More Plan, Do, Check, Act daily experiments.

Think about this question, "How many problems are present in your system?" Every problem will require at least one PDCA loop to resolve it. So, how are we going to fix healthcare? The answer may be easier than you first thought. How are we going to transform healthcare? One problem at a time. Whose ideas will solve them? Good. That is Lean thinking.

If there are 100 problems, you can and will work your staff through 100 PDCA loops. So, let's get busy. There is no silver bullet. There is no one single change. There is no new computer system that fixes all of your broken processes and meddlesome problems. There is no single leader that is going to move you out of this long-term but workable set of solutions. What will work is a philosophy, a mind-set, of constant PDCA cycles involving every staff member every day. This is a key to transformation.

As mentioned earlier, David Mann has an interesting use of the 80/20 rule. He writes, "Do not wait for the 'real work,' the physical changes of Lean implementation to be done before turning your attention to implementing the

---

* Womack, James, *Gemba Walks*, Lean Enterprise Institute, Cambridge, MA, 2011.

Do you think this is true? Do you think that it takes 80% or more of the time and effort to build the management system to encourage and sustain the physical changes? Do you feel it is management's job? Discuss this with your staff and team.

management system. Your Lean implementation depends on it to survive!" He continues, "In a successful mass-to-Lean conversion, no more than 20 percent of the effort involves the typical 'what you see is what you get' physical changes"[*] (e.g., layouts, changes to achieve flow, pull signals, etc.).

He writes, "The remaining 80 percent of the required time and effort is made up of tasks less obvious and more demanding."[†] It is building the Lean management systems. What will your leaders do different to encourage and sustain this?

Another crucial part of Lean management system building is to focus on process. David writes, "The Lean management system consists of the discipline, daily practices, and tools you need to establish and maintain a persistent, intensive focus on process. It is the *process focus* that sustains and extends Lean implementations."[‡]

Here is a summary of what David calls the *virtuous cycle*.[§] The team tracks meaningful data on their visual controls (trend charts) and displays it in their daily accountability meeting (huddle). Focusing on the current gap results in brainstorming (and sometimes problem solving) for process changes. The team walks the idea through a PDCA cycle. Then, the leader follows up (written in their leader standard work) to sustain the change. This

A Big *Virtuous Cycle* for S&W as a whole Health System: S&W started with training of the minds, and then did facilitated cross-functional projects. They used a simplified Hoshin process to align all the MVPs to common North Star goals, and then built Lean management systems so ideas of all staff could be released for the benefit of patients and staff. Each step was co-dependent on the other steps, especially knowing and sustaining the earlier steps.

---

[*] Mann, David, *Creating a Lean Culture: Tools to Sustain Lean Conversions*, 2nd ed., Productivity Press, 2010.
[†] Mann, David, Ibid.
[‡] Mann, David, Ibid.
[§] Mann, David, Ibid.

prevents the improvement from backsliding. "As Lean management, with its closed-loop focus on process, becomes habitual, little by little, almost unnoticeably at first, a Lean culture begins to grow."[*]

S&W is building a culture of continuous improvement by encouraging ideas and getting them through faster and faster PDCA loops by building daily Lean management systems.

Slow Data Feedback to Team Means Slow PDCA Experiments

When S&W subtly shifted from managing in a results-only focused system, process focus started to flourish. They still got results, too. Process focus requires frequent feedback, earlier called *input* or *process* measures, in order for staff to provide interventions before the month end results are added up. The authors believe an accurate and frequent pipeline of decision data is still one of the greatest weaknesses in healthcare.

Healthcare prides itself in using empirical data on patients to make them well. Providers and staff do experiments on patients. Nobody would prescribe a drug and wait for a month and a half to check the outcomes on the patient! They would demand daily or even more frequent feedback. Why would work processes in healthcare require anything different?

Think of every staff member being a provider—a *process* doctor. They need to do daily experiments on work processes to make them better. The processes are sick. Your staff can help, if you let them. Staff must have daily or at least weekly feedback data, or it will be very difficult for them to check if their changes worked.

Figure 5.3 is a very important graphic. Direct performers, first line supervisors, and managers cannot do experiments with month-ending results data. They must use process or input data. The box represents every work

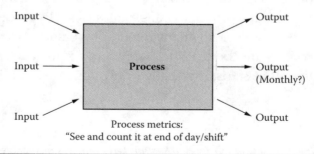

Figure 5.3 Staff and supervisors need process and input metrics for experiments.

---

[*] Mann, David, Ibid.

process in your system. It uses inputs and processes to make outputs. It all can be measured.

On the far right, there are output measures. These are your system-wide, (some) required-by-law, month-end measures like profit, total system costs, quality, etc. This is the most typical type of data in healthcare, although it is often available only at a very high level and woefully late. This output data is most often "scrubbed" in a slow, complicated who-gets-credit-for-what process, and pops out of the finance department about a month and a half after the period starts. How in the world could a department or team do an experiment without getting feedback for 1.5 months?

Think about steering a car. Imagine driving and needing to turn left. However, you have no windshield! This car has no windows at all. You get some feedback data, but it comes out of a little ticker tape printer by your dashboard, and gives you a "picture" of what is outside using only numbers. One more problem—it prints 1.5 months after you should have turned! Crash!

Moving from right to left is not easy. Employees need help translating the language of *dollars* (month-end results measures) to the language of *things* that they can see and count at end of shift. This is the purpose of the Hoshin Kanri process. It starts with your annual goals (results and output focused) and translates them to each level of the organization in a cascading manner into daily process and input measures using catchball. Catchball is a series (usually two to three at the start of the year) of two-way conversations between boss and employee.

Process measures in healthcare or service processes are things you can see and count at the end of the shift. It is useful to have computerized reports for time-stamped data (like those coming out of EMR systems), but you cannot wait a month and a half to see what worked!

If staff can see it and count it, then they can track meaningful measures by putting a dot on their own blank trend chart. Staff have control over it. Input measures are even easier because, even before the shift starts, you know how many staff, patients scheduled, available slots, etc. Staff need input and process measures in order to do daily and weekly experiments. This is a critical part of the PDCA cycle and effective LMS.

Building LMS

The authors did something crazy. They picked up David Mann's book, *Creating a Lean Culture,* and tried to implement the principles page-by-page in their healthcare and support processes. Do you know what? It worked. In the same manner, you and your staff can pick up this book and implement these principles in your work processes.

There is something bigger than Lean, Six Sigma, or any focused toolkit. It is building a culture of continuous improvement. It includes Continuous [fill in the blank] Improvement:

- Safety
- Quality
- Process
- Patient satisfaction
- Justness
- Risk
- Employee engagement
- Any other focused area or metric

Continuous *everything* improvement. A culture of improving every important measure every day by every staff member. Not only is it the right thing to do, it is fun. Let it change your career like it did for some S&W leaders! Every one of the above areas can be improved through effective huddles and LMS.

Building LMS is a full-contact sport. It is not for the faint of heart, nor for those who will not walk to their Gemba to go-see. Any middle level leader can easily break the chain of escalation up to direct performers and down to leaders.

At S&W, it did not take long for roadblock behaviors to surface. S&W had some middle level leaders with the nickname "Can't find the Gemba." Some are not leaders today. Repeating Dr. John Toussaint's statement from earlier, "The ultimate arrogance is to change the way people work without changing the way we manage them."* At S&W, that meant building LMS, starting with making small PDCA cycles work in their huddles, then auditing, tracking, sustaining, and ultimately teaching other staff members how to do this as well.

Lean Leadership (LMS) Course

Here is more detail on S&W's Lean Leadership, or Lean Management Systems-building (LMS), course. After some time, leaders just called the

---

* Toussaint, John, Ibid.

course and effort LMS. Maybe the most important facet was that S&W **leaders** learned and applied LMS-building first. Leaders must physically, verbally, and mentally lead this effort. It only works top-down. They learn to build their own huddle process, and then bigger LMS processes. They tell their staff, "Come and see mine, then do the same."

Two key textbooks for this course, to be read by participants in advance and discussed throughout the course, were David Mann's *Creating a Lean Culture* and Dr. John Toussaint's *On the Mend*. Steve and team then worked with participants to tailor ideas and principles into S&W's healthcare and support processes, along with hands-on exercises and best practice observations.

In the LMS course, leaders are taught that it is their responsibility, their job, to build Lean management systems for their staff. It is easy to apply Lean tools, remove waste, and start to transform processes. It is harder to build systems by which the tools and changes can "stick" and even get better daily. The natural tendency is for changes to revert to the way they were.

As mentioned earlier, David's book states 80% or more of the work of transforming and sustaining changes is to build the Lean management systems.[*] These idea-generating, daily Lean systems are the starting point of Lean Leadership at S&W.

However, what does this mean? What exactly do Lean thinking leaders need to do that is different? Sometimes, it is easier to see the pieces of the system in someone else's area. Even better, what if they could watch an area being transformed using Lean principles in just two days (the study period of the leader course)?

In addition to John Toussaint and David Mann's books, S&W also used physical, small-scale simulations and a unique overlap of courses. S&W conducts the first two days of Lean Leadership (Lean 401) on top of its basic Lean Practitioner (Lean 201) course. S&W uses multiple simulations in all Lean courses. Could Lean 401 leaders learn to build LMS by observing other staff transforming an ED in their Lean 201 simulation?

In four half-hour periods spread out over two days, Lean Practitioner course participants conducted four rounds of the "fix the ED" stick-person simulation. During these sessions, Lean leaders swoop into the room to watch the transformation rounds and listen to their recaps. Steve and other instructors then return with leaders to their separate classrooms. In this way, the two classes sit on top of each other, or overlap.

---

[*] Mann, David, Ibid.

As the leaders excitedly remember their own Lean Practitioner course experience and even the role they played, the LMS instructor pulls the class together. The instructor asks, "What did the ED teams do after that first round?"

Someone eventually offers, "The facilitator asked them to list the problems they saw on the flipchart." Sensei asks, "Then what?" A leader offers, "They discussed what things could be done quickly, even the next day, to fix some of these problems."

Here it comes. The sensei presses, "So, you are the leaders. Pretend that was your area. *When do we do that*—what you just saw? When do we list problems and ask for actions?" Silence. "If someone tried out one of those improvement ideas in our area, would they be able to tell by looking at some chart the *next day* if it worked?" Silence.

Steve bangs his hand into the other for effect, "It is management's job to build the systems by which their team's ideas are brought forward and tried out. It is management's job!" Thus begins a journey of increasing ability by leaders to identify the absence and presence of LMS. It starts just minutes into the leader course!

LMS has been a very impactful course. Many S&W leaders have stated that deploying LMS changed their careers. Most would say it changed the way they managed. Most CI courses teach the importance of leadership, but they stop short of demonstrating what that entails. A few describe the leader's role, but only in general. Very few explain what a leader needs to **do** to make continuous improvement happen and then "stick" in their areas.

The key question for a S&W leader becomes: How does my job change in a Lean management system? LMS answers this with specifics about where, when, and how. It demonstrates with scripts and tips how they will build boards, huddle, Gemba walk, ask questions, and maximize engagement.

S&W not only tracks the names of leaders that take each CI course, it also assigns them a sensei—usually their LMS instructor—and then schedules and tracks three Guided Gemba Walks with them, always in the graduate's own areas. This is in addition to the weekly Gemba walks they committed to do on their own during class. The leader typically does three or four on his or her own first. This way, their guided walk with a sensei will be more helpful.

The first Guided Gemba Walk is with a direct performer in the leader's area. This level is referred to as Tier-1 because it is the most important level. It only takes about 15 minutes, but the sensei schedules a full hour so that Hansei (reflection) can happen immediately after. It also allows time to coach the leader on his or her huddle board. The leader is taught how to "see" the absence or presence of LMS by asking four very specific questions.

Sometimes the manager over the area is informed in advance by the leader doing his or her guided Gemba walk. However, the authors found it far better for the supervisor *not* to be present during the Gemba walk. This allows staff members to be very honest about what is and is not known about their idea-building systems.

After trying three to four more Gemba walks on their own, the leaders schedule a second Guided Gemba Walk with their sensei, usually focusing on the immediate supervisor of the individual from their first walk (Tier-2). This allows the graduate to ask the four questions again, but also to check if there is a way for ideas from direct performers to be *elevated* to their superiors. Supervisors must actively huddle and offer their support. You will see more details of an elevation system in Chapter 5, Elevation System.

Briefly, an elevation system brings an idea to a higher level to be implemented. That way, leaders do not lose the benefits of the idea. Direct performers often have great ideas, but sometimes they are unable, at their level, to get them done. The elevation system starts with a second list of Ideas/Actions on every huddle board where they can write crosscutting ideas and issues. Other ways to document elevated ideas also work, like Post-its or a 3 × 5-inch card system.

For example, a team of direct performers improving on-time starts in the OR may bring up a need for anesthesia to arrive five minutes after a "pull" signal. They typically cannot get this idea done on their own, so they elevate it to the next level, who discuss the idea in their huddle. The leaders must follow through and respond back to the teams on elevated ideas, even if to say they cannot do the idea this year.

After trying three to four more Gemba walks on their own, the leaders again schedule a third Guided Gemba Walk with their sensei. This time, the focus will be to develop the leaders' own huddle and board (Tier-3), the elevation system, and some powerful tools for making huddles more effective like the layered audit.

Let's recap LMS education. The leaders have completed their pre-reads (two books), taken the Lean leader course, and made some impact on at least one huddle board for direct performers, transforming it into an idea incubator with aligned daily and weekly metrics.

They also made some impact on metrics on their own huddle board, along with weekly Gemba walks to uncover the absence and presence of a Lean management system in their areas. After the third Guided Gemba Walk

"But, if you don't use the tools, and you don't hit your goals, then God help you, because I won't!"

following their class, the graduates receive their certificate. They are desig-nated a ***home run*** leader, having been through all four parts. They are now expected to be both an LMS-builder and a teacher themselves.

Required Courses?

S&W does not require their leaders to take Lean Leadership or Lean Management Systems-building, but it is strongly encouraged for them. Leaders are often told, "You might meet your goals without using Lean thinking and LMS. "But, if you don't use the tools, and you don't hit your goals, then God help you, because I won't!"

In other words, use all of the resources and tools provided, and then lead your teams well. It is not a threat. It is just a strong offer to use all tools provided. That is what they are for. It is hard to watch a supervisor pound a screw in with a hammer, or work around the clock without tapping ideas from all of his or her staff!

It seems less respectful to require leaders to come to a class. Most of what they need can be learned in the Gemba. However, it is very difficult for the sensei or instructor to do this one on one when a single leader is ready to take another step. There needs to be some balance. For S&W, lead-ers are strongly encouraged to take the Lean leadership course and apply it immediately. Without this common language, leaders will not be able to speak across their departments with the same impact.

More on Gemba Walks in the LMS Class

Lean leaders do an exercise in the class called the Gemba walk exercise. This is also practice for what they committed to do weekly following the course. After reviewing a slide to remind the participants about the four questions and tips on how to respond when faced with tough situations, the class is divided into groups of two to three.

Each group is assigned a coach and a related area in the building where the course is being conducted. They will each do a practice LMS-building Gemba walk. Course leaders try to match them up in somewhat similar areas (e.g., administrative staff go to administrative areas, clinical to a some-what similar area).

Steve likes to have physicians practice with another physician, but it is not always possible in the unscheduled practice Gembas. The groups are given 45 minutes to complete a Gemba walk by each participant. They briefly reflect with the coach between each one to maximize their learning.

The first Lean leader goes to the target area, stops to look at what is happening, and chooses a staff member. They tell them they are "just doing a class exercise," and ask if they can take 10 minutes of their time. These staff members are usually not their direct reports. They ask the four questions while the coach and two to three participants listen in.

The coach or sensei asks two main questions in each reflection immediately after the practice, and away from the staff member. He or she asks, "How did you do?" The Lean leader usually says, "Terrible" or something like that. The sensei and others will encourage him or her. They usually did fine.

Then the sensei asks, "What was the idea your practice person gave?" Silence (the other listeners note this and are more ready). In the rush to complete the questions, the Lean leader rarely remembers their ideas. Senseis don't miss them. They are the jewels of LMS. The sensei reminds them of an idea, usually receiving, "Oh yeah! That was a pretty good idea!"

Now for the kicker. The sensei asks, "If the team member tried out that idea today, does he or she have the feedback data or chart to see if the idea worked by tomorrow or the end of the week?" The Lean leaders often say there is not. Sometimes it is close. As S&W conducted these exercises many times and LMS was built in most operational areas, it got better.

Steve reinforces that the LMS-building Gemba walk just worked. They briefly discuss what parts of LMS need to be built or buttoned up in this area. They discuss what the Lean leaders would do if this were their area. The sensei demands that they write down what is needed to build LMS and emphatically states this will need follow-up.

Steve also points out some tips for all, usually how to focus and clarify their questions. They share tips on how to handle multiple goals, listen deeply, and press respectfully for an idea. The leaders are ready to see absence and presence of LMS in their own areas now.

By this point, the Lean leader has seen absence and presence of LMS in a simulated ED environment, then in case studies in the class, then in a best practice area at S&W, sometimes at Toyota (optional for later groups), and now in a practice Gemba walk with their sensei. They are ready!

Over the next two months, leaders will create and update their own huddle boards. They will also sponsor and create a supervisor/direct performer

How about you? What do your CI class participants need to do to graduate? Do you know if they applied any of their past training? What deliverables are they expected to produce for the organization after a typical course? Do you feel the rigor of all these deliverables is too high? Discuss this with your staff. Please include your training director.

team's huddle board in their area. They will write and post their leader standard work. They will become more interruptible for continuous improvement and spend more time in the Gemba. They will likely need to do a waste reduction exercise in their own day to free up time to do all of this. They will do weekly Gemba walks. In addition, a sensei will coach them on three Guided Gemba Walks spaced apart about one month each.

Once these steps are completed, they receive their certificate as a home run graduate of S&W's Lean leadership course. Wow. It is worth the effort.

Now, they will spend even more time in their Gemba. Why? They need to build LMS, do Gemba walks, and then audit and track all huddle boards in their area. Daily crises cool down as they follow their leader standard work. Staff and internal leaders develop rapidly as they lead huddles and become effective at PDCA cycles and problem solving. Staff engagement goes up. Way up!

Idea Lists

As discussed earlier, huddle boards at S&W contain two idea lists. While this may not seem novel to you, think about the expectation represented by posting two idea lists—one for the many ideas teams will try out themselves while they work (their experiments) and the second for ideas they need help on (e.g., cross-functional changes out of the team's control). The expectation is that *all* ideas will be considered, evaluated within the guardrails, and tried out.

As S&W Lean coaches help leaders build their initial boards, they often post three or more team idea pages on the left side to demonstrate that their ideas will soon fill multiple pages. One page on the right is enough to start. Leaders need to come to these boards, elevate ideas, and respond back. The right-side list should stay short. Higher-level leaders will often have a large area for tracking their elevated ideas, usually on cards.

Ideas are usually brainstormed by the team in the huddle, but sometimes they come out of problem-solving teams. They may also be ideas that worked elsewhere and are being spread to another area.

Audits and best practice sharing will help drive the team toward consistency later. Just get the leader up-front, get a pen in his or her hand, and focus the team on ideas—within the guardrails—to close the gaps.

One important point on idea list formats: be flexible. It may seem odd that Steve-the-standard-guy suggests this. However, early on, you want leaders to own their boards. This sometimes means they use flip charts, Post-its, cards, or even just handwriting on a white board. Audits and best practice sharing will help drive the team toward consistency later. Just get the leader up-front, get a pen in his or her hand, and focus the team on ideas—within the guardrails—to close the gaps.

Leader Standard Work

Here is a case where brevity is better. Leader Standard Work is just a checklist. The main user of this is the leader and her staff. It documents when the leader is interruptible for CI by her team.

Every process and person in a Lean system should have standard work. Top leaders may have less "daily" structure, but they still should have times when they are available for CI. A top leader may only have a quarter of his or her typical week defined in leader standard work. Key vice presidents and directors may have up to half. However, front-line supervisors really need to have most of their day and week somewhat scripted.

Granted, stuff happens and they veer into firefighter mode. However, this is what leader standard work is trying to prevent! It is trying to prevent them from going into firefighter mode for days or weeks. It teaches them to fix problems, train staff, huddle, and stick to what they do best—fire prevention through building LMS.

Once a leader commits to following leader standard work, something happens. At first, it gets worse. Problems seem to come up from everywhere. Do not panic. Delegate, ask staff reporting to you to bring data and ideas for solutions (maybe bring a rough A3), and commit to following your standard work!

You may be shocked at how many times staff "dump" problems on their superiors, without even attempting to solve them. Problems go up the chain of command—unless you don't let them. A parody of this is in the following quote. Teach your staff to solve problems. Teach them to take 15 minutes today to solve a problem they face daily.

I don't gripe to you, Reiben. I'm a captain. There's a chain of command. Gripes go up, not down. Always up. You gripe to me, I gripe to my superior officer, so on, so on, and so on. I don't gripe to you. I don't gripe in front of you. You should know that as a Ranger.

—Tom Hanks as Captain John Miller, *Saving Private Ryan* *

After following leader standard work for a few weeks, a subtle shift will occur. You will get your day back. Crisis after crisis will be replaced with a more steady flow. Less time will be diverted by problems outside of your control. And, most important, you will have time to lead continuous improvement in your areas. This is the most important job of a leader. No one else can or will do it.

Visual Controls

Many examples of visual controls and huddle boards are shown in the next section. Some key points are needed to reinforce what has already been written about Chapter 4, Visual Controls. They are "chaining" all huddles from the CEO up to the direct performers and back, three tiers, and keep it simple!

Chaining All Huddle Boards Together—No Weak or Missing Links

In LMS, there needs to be a chain of accountability, some overlapping points of connection, so that ideas can be elevated up to the next level. There

---

* *Saving Private Ryan*, DreamWorks Pictures and Paramount Pictures, 1998.

must also be quick way to communicate priorities and changes from the top through the huddles to all staff.

As noted earlier, S&W uses Hoshin Kanri to cascade all goals up to the direct performers. This provides two-way communication of goals during initial catchball and progress meetings. In addition, there is another key communication, from staff to leaders through elevation. If staff come up with ideas outside of their control, a leader elevates them. Who? When? Moreover, is there a team that huddles at the level above staff that elevated it? If the chain is broken, two-way communication is also broken.

This is why it is so important for leaders to go to the Gemba, ask how they can help, and look at the idea list on the right-hand side of the boards. The elevation system is also described in Chapter 5, Layered Audits.

Each huddle board must be "linked" to something higher, like a chain. David Mann likes to say, "If you don't link all these layered huddle boards together (Tier-1 direct performers linked to Tier-2 supervisors to Tier-3, etc.), good ideas start to slide into the ***pit of instability, backsliding, and despair.***"[*]

If you don't have these huddles connected all the way to the top, if one is missing, improvement ideas cannot be shared or elevated. When there is no one to elevate to, if no one cares, teams will stop bringing up good crosscutting ideas. It is often the best ideas that are just outside of the team's direct control. They need help from leaders to get these ideas done. And the employees who came up with the idea still want to assist, if leaders help them get traction.

Three Tiers

S&W differentiates three tiers of huddle boards. Tier-1 is the team leader and direct performers. This is where the rubber meets the road. This group must be huddling and tracking daily metrics. They should have three to five trend charts on their board. They do a stand-up huddle, pick one metric, and move toward solutions. They should be doing experiments frequently, and bragging to any leader that walks into their area. This is the Tier-1 huddle.

Tier-2 is where supervisors or managers meet. Remember, they are running the business, but they are also improving the business, too. Their job as leader is unique. They need to build the systems and drive improvements.

Improving work processes while managing them feels like making a sharp left turn while driving 60 miles an hour. Tier-2 huddles have similar agendas

---

[*] Mann, David, Ibid.

as Tier-1s, but they also spend time discussing ideas that have elevated from their Tier-1 huddles. Updates are brought back to their teams. This group also has a huddle board. Their metrics should also roll-up from the Tier-1 boards. They should have asked their teams why before attending this Tier-2 huddle. The categories should match fairly well. The goals should match the Hoshin goal of the director or leader over all these supervisors who leads the huddle.

Tier-3 is where the directors, vice presidents, and up meet. Any level above the Tier 2 supervisors huddle is referred to as Tier-3, all the way to the CEO. In Lean parlance, this is the value stream (or service line) manager's huddle on up to the CEO. All of these tiers must link to one another. Leaders must go to the huddles at all levels to see, understand, learn, and elevate ideas.

Tier-3s have a huddle board and discuss elevated ideas. However, they tend not to have a lot of small just-do-its. Teams below them should be taking on more and more of these. Rather, they commission system-wide A3 problems, value stream mapping improvements, and even large efforts like length of stay and patient satisfaction improvement. These are managed out of the Tier-3 huddles and cascaded back to Tier-1s.

Keep It Simple

Huddle boards should be handwritten. Anyone can walk up and put a dot on a chart. However, they do need data. Sometimes the best way to display data is for a person to view the report online, and then place a dot on his or her trend chart for today or yesterday. Key pages of the detail report or data should be printed and placed in the Analysis section of the huddle board under the chart and refreshed each period. This allows leader and staff to drill-down for possible causes of any misses.

Have fun with feedback, data, and ideas. Always make them visual. In addition, ensure that ideas are not dropped. Building a tracking system that gives feedback to the teams that brought them forward. Treasure ideas. Make them a priority. Seek to say yes to them and try them out, teaching staff to follow the PDCA process.

Treasure ideas. Make them a priority. Seek to say yes to them and try them out, teaching staff to follow the PDCA process.

Execute!

Bob likes to say, "All healthcare systems have the same strategies. The only difference will be who can execute!" It is true. Healthcare leaders do not lack improvement initiatives. In the near future, what will differentiate the survivors from the dinosaurs will be the ability to execute on all levels—leadership up to the frontline staff.

S&W does not differentiate much between ideas to be worked through a PDCA cycle that came from a huddle board vs. a Lean or quality project. Figure 5.4 shows two different strategies for tracking execution of an action item. Both rely heavily on a Lean principle—make it visual.

You can see a type of "moving card" system on the bottom of Figure 5.4a. This is used mainly for elevated ideas at huddle boards, but it is also used in some Lean projects. The typical way of tracking and making "overdue" items more visual on Lean projects is in Figure 5.4b. This shows a type of Project Action Plan, with "weekly checks" on the right-hand side.

The important part of this tracking form is that it is large, updated, and posted weekly on the project board in the area being transformed. You can see a few items highlighted darker gray (red on the spreadsheet) with an "X" in it to show the item was late. You can see two of the three items turned light gray (green) again after the items were completed.

Daily Accountability Process (Huddles)

A daily accountability process starts with leaders helping to build simple, visual controls to identify gaps, and then collect ideas daily that staff can

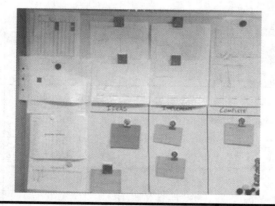

Figure 5.4a To execute, make actions, progress, and lack of progress visible.
(Continued)

ED VSM - Action Item List / Process Owners: Lesley B, Tim S	Last Updated = 6/30													
VSM Process Step	From Kaizen Bursts = 121	Actions	Owners	Comments/Issues	Type (Just Do Its = 28, Intermediate = 60, Long Term = 21)	Recovery Plan (if behind)	Due Date	Weekly Checks						
								5/11	5/18	5/25	6/1	6/8	6/15	6/22
1) Pt drives up to ED		Communicating and educating about VSM to ED department	Lesley B, Dr. S	Develop training matrix; track	Just Do It		6/15							
	Approval From C-Suite	Develop Business Plan and Case Study for New Courier	C-Suite	Executive Support	Intermediate		6/30							
	New signage for registration entrance in ED.	Work orders for better signage for registration desk that is not registration. Decide what the signage should say and what size.	Jessica R, Sue B, Gwen D	6/15 - A. All signage should be written in English and Spanish B. Place a hanging sign above Lobby Tech that reads, Information and visitor passes C. Change out ER registration sign above the desk to read "Emergency Room Check-In" D. Designate a 5 ft. check-in line, on the floor, in white, for both Emergency Room check-in as well as Registration E. Change standing sign to read "Please respect others' privacy and remain behind the white line until called and turn off all cell phones"; both E.R. and Registration. F. Place a directory sign to the left of the check-in desk G. Place a sign for elevators on the back wall of E.R. waiting area with a big arrow pointing to direction of elevators. Signs ordered, Sue will put in work order through plant ops for floor markings and Arrows. 7/20 - Sherry will do Mock up. 8/17 Jess will follow up with Sherry about MockUp	Intermediate		5/30				X	X	X	X
	New Valet position 24/7	Build case for Dr. S Dr. S to approve	**Glory R,** Rita S, Dr. S, Tony W	6/15 Glory & Rita putting together presentation for Dr. S. Setting up time to meet with him in the next week or so. 7/20 - Meeting with Dr. S and Dean S scheduled for end of August	Intermediate		7/6							
	Valet need medical training on basics on patient transport.	refer to new valet position above (SOP)	**Glory R,** Rita S, Dr. S, Tony W		Intermediate		7/14							
	Lobby tech out front with a wheel chair 24/7 (see clinic setup). Sort patient vs. non-patient	Redefining role of lobby tech. Build case for Dr. S. (Pilot) Dr. S to approve	Ruben P, **Donna C,** Dr. S	Body mechanics, getting patient out of car. 6/15 - Ruben reported that the techs are scheduled to attend BLS in the next couple of weeks. Ready to pilot them being out front to be proactive in helping get pt out of car. Need to have body mechanics training. 7/20 - Getting staff hired & trained. Working on	Intermediate Pilot JDI		6/4					X	X	
	Police department coverage 24/7 in the ED.	Build case for Dr. S and Dean S (Exec Team) Dr. S to approve	Dr. M, **Tammy B,** Exec Team	Contracts with other companies already in place 6/15 - Benchmarking other hospitals to see their process. Meeting coming up with group and Security. Tammy to check on contract with police and amounts.	Long Term		7/14							
2) Pt arrives	Greeter role re-defined.	Standard processes for greeter role.	Robyn F, Hope L	Ongoing, developing role as new technologies emerge (kiosks vs op-center) 6/15 Moved computer and desk closer to front door. Pilot upcoming 7/20 - Write out SOP/Educate on doing it the same all the time. Need to revise the standing order for Non Contrast CT to be with permission of the staff 8/17 - Working with Registration to get them next to greeter. Need to get Registration help since Gwen is gone.	Just Do It		6/11						X	

Figure 5.4b (Continued)   To execute, make actions, progress, and lack of progress visible.

However, it is not enough to slap up some key process indicators (KPIs) and tell a team to huddle. It will fail—every time—without the management system supporting it.

do to improve them. That was a mouthful. Sometimes it is just easier to say huddle and do Gemba walks, but those are only parts of the management process needed to sustain.

The daily accountability process requires at least three key parts:

A. The huddle
B. Leader Gemba walks
C. Increased floor time for leaders

The actual huddle is located at the visual control board, usually called the huddle board. However, it is not enough to slap up some key process indicators (KPIs) and tell a team to huddle. It will fail—every time—without the management system supporting it. The authors have seen this happen repeatedly.

Maybe for the first time in an organization's Lean journey, something solid will be required from leaders. For LMS, they actively and personally build these systems. It is the leader's job to help build the data pipeline for the team huddle board, to ensure their goals are aligned, to give them permission and encouragement, to help the team bring ideas forward and try them out. Plan, Do, Check, Act—daily in the huddle. This will require more floor time for leaders.

Part A: The Huddle

The first part of the daily accountability process is the huddle itself. Healthcare staff, especially nurses, have been huddling for many years. However, there is a very important difference in LMS. LMS huddles yield ideas, ideas that are tried out daily and improve meaningful measures for the team.

Standard Work for the Huddle: All processes and staff should adhere to standard work. Thus, there should be standard work for the huddle.

Question: If your teams have been huddling for years, go attend one. How many metrics can you see in 5:5 (five feet away in five minutes)? Can you see trend charts? Are they up-to-date? Do they have goals on them? What is the gap between expected and actual (today) for each goal? How about ideas? Count the number of ideas you can see. If there is an idea, is there a clear metric where staff can look to see if it worked by the next day or week? If not, you do not have a Lean management system-type huddle.

Here is an agenda for a typical first-level (Tier-1) huddle:

- (3 min) General communication. Already typical for many huddles in healthcare, but it was the only topic.
- (10 min) The leader or assigned leader-in-training introduces the one topic-of-the-day. This is the power of focus in brief, daily huddles.
  - Different team members "own" each metric category. This is a great leader development strategy. The owner displays the updated trend chart. They point to actual (right now) vs. expected (the goal). That highlights the gap. Use your hands to show the gap. They repeat what has been done thus far. Then, they brainstorm ideas that could be tried today to close the gap.
  - [Decision point] If there is a problem without a known root cause, brainstorming actions may not help. The team might start the Five Whys and then kick it out to an A3 team to solve.
- (2 min) The team quickly comes to consensus on the one to two ideas or actions they will try today or this week—the "experiment." The leader then clarifies who does what, and when the team will check to see if it worked.
  - If there is no consensus, or more data is needed, the potential action and issue is written on the Idea List for follow-up, with the name of the person responsible for gathering information and due date.
- If needed, the leaders end with brief questions and answers. Sometimes leaders introduce a second metric if there is time.
- For teams comfortable with fun, the leader says, "Everybody, hands in. Let's say 'Just Do it' on three. 1, 2, 3, 'Just Do It!'" Just like a football team. It's a huddle for goodness' sake.

S&W provided all staff with two video examples of early S&W huddles. One was an executive huddle led by CEO Bob Pryor, and the second was a nursing huddle on 5-North in Temple. These huddles were early and rough but they demonstrated some good tips. You can do this. Just start.

As LMS and huddles matured at S&W, leaders realized that many issues have unknown and "sticky" root causes. It is not likely the team will "guess" their way to success. The team will need to kick it out to an A3 problem-solving team. The team may start a fishbone diagram analysis, or do some Five Whys. If a very likely root cause pops out, the team members and leaders might start brainstorming ideas to close the gap.

Huddle Tips

S&W leaders learned many ways how-to and how-not-to huddle. The following lessons learned can help you in your journey.

The first is to huddle standing up! If the posture of the staff is standing, then the huddle must be brief. Brief, daily huddles are better than long, drawn out monthly meetings.

If you want to keep the meeting short, don't provide any chairs. In addition, if staff stand up, blood flows to their brains. They remain engaged, at least while the huddle focuses on problem solving and their own ideas! It also takes less space, and allows huddling in a hallway, break room, or nearly anywhere.

Before seeing them, leaders sometimes say daily huddles by all teams will take too much time away from work. Maybe you can start with a compromise. If staff already do a 1-hour meeting once a week, try 15-minute huddles four days per week. It is the same amount of time. You just need to focus staff on one topic for brainstorming ideas.

You will be surprised by the idea power this yields. Fifteen minutes is a good amount of time. Tier 2 and 3 leader huddles sometimes last 30 minutes, and thus are conducted only two or three times per week. However, they really need to be shorter if you are going to stand up.

Use daily or weekly input and process data. If you are going to build systems by which staff try out ideas, you need to give them the ability to check if it worked by at least the next day or the end of the week. You may need to come up with a "proxy" or faster-moving measure than the perfect one you first brainstormed. Get help from a data analyst. Remember, it is

OK to update progress on trend charts by hand. Almost every huddle board at S&W started with simple blank charts where staff added their own "X" or dot daily or weekly.

Focus on one metric in the huddle. This is the power of focus.

Also, have a captain or owner for each category of measure on your board. Write his or her name visibly under each section or category so that everyone knows who will update the charts and lead the brainstorming for that topic-of-the-day. This will really develop leaders' skills fast and bench strength on your team.

Part B: Leader Gemba Walks

S&W has been building a culture of continuous improvement for the past seven years. Leader Gemba walks, used to build LMS, have accelerated this journey in a big way. These Gemba walks done with the purpose of building Lean management systems use four simple questions to unveil the absence or presence of Lean management systems in any area.

Leader Gemba walks are Part B of the daily accountability process. Gemba walks are an acquired thing. It is not natural for leaders to accomplish their work tasks this way—but it works!

Tip: It is best not to have the staff member's manager nearby while leaders are doing a Gemba walk. It is OK to warn them, but staff members in departments that are new or feel less secure may not tell the full story under the steady stare of their supervisor.

In the past at S&W, bosses rarely went down two or more levels to "see what staff were doing." Some felt they were cutting the legs out from under the supervisor in the area. In reality, quite the opposite was true.

If the big boss comes to the team and asks, "Are you making progress toward your goals, and how can I help you?" it motivates and energizes the team. In fact, when they say, "Show me your best stuff," or, "Show me some results," it shows interest, gives creativity a boost, and demonstrates that their ideas are a priority. It can energize the troops more than anything the supervisor could do.

Gemba walks and constant Gemba presence are better than any "change management" newsletter or email. A sensei can help walk you through some of the natural questions to ask. S&W sensei taught leaders how to ask the four big questions that unveil the absence or presence of the Lean management systems. In addition, they coached them to build elevation, layered audits, and other systems to sustain and spread the gains.

Regarding Gemba walking, David Mann writes, "As Lean management novices become more skilled through Gemba walks with their sensei, they gradually develop their own expertise as Gemba walkers, teachers, and auditors of Lean management. It then becomes their turn to Gemba walk with their subordinates; teaching and helping them develop their own mastery of Lean production and Lean management."

This "requires patience and tolerance for frustration. It is not fast... There is no good alternative to Gemba walks as the method to learn Lean management. That is because Lean management is a mindset." Mindsets don't change overnight, it comes through experiential learning, not just reading a book. The next statement is very powerful. It says, "Six months of weekly Gemba walks is on the low end of the period necessary to develop a Lean approach to managing."*

At S&W, they teach leaders to *Go, Look, Talk* in Gemba walks. Go to the Gemba, where the work is occurring. Look; don't just start talking. Look for flow-stoppers, imbalanced work, and problems from afar for a moment. Find someone who is working, but not too busy for five or six minutes of questions. Then, talk. Ask the four questions.

Fujio Cho, President of Toyota, spent a lot of time on the shop floor. So much so that people probably thought he was a production worker. He dressed like all other assembly workers, too. His mantra was, "Go see, ask why, show respect."

Go see. He said, "Senior Management must spend time on the floor," in the Gemba. Ask why. He instructs others in the sensei method to "use the (5) 'Why?' technique daily." Keep digging deeper. "Why" is not a bad question. Just like an audit is not a bad thing, either. Then, show respect. Always respect your people. Respect their ideas. Respect their input. You hired them for more than just their hands.

Figure 5.5 again shows the big four questions with a few clarifying statements, warnings, and tips. The first question is, "What are your team's targets or goals today?" Because some staff do not really know what you are digging for, it is good to clarify this with another question, "If you were *wildly successful* today, and went home bragging to your family, how would that be measured? What would that look like?" Staff typically name one or more team goals after this.

---

* Mann, David, Ibid, p. 123.

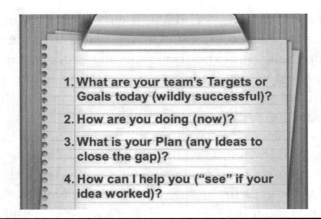

Figure 5.5   The Four Questions asked of staff in every LMS-building Gemba walk.

The second question is, "How are you doing *right now*?" Does the staff know the gap? For each meaningful metric, do they know actual vs. expected (right now), and can they "see" the gaps?

Maybe the staff member just mentioned a quality, quantity goal, or multiple goals. So, choose one and clarify, "How are you doing on that quality goal right now?" They start to say, "Yes, we're doing well." Then they hear "right now" and might say, "Well, I'm not sure."

In most cases, there is no quick feedback to them. At this point, the Lean management system-building questions have revealed an opportunity, something the leader needs to do. The purpose of the four questions is to reveal some gaps. The staff member may have been chosen at random, so do not be disturbed that all or even most of them will not know what is on the new huddle board that was recently put up. They will eventually. You need to be consistent, persistent, and demonstrate its usefulness.

If the staff member says, "Fine" or "Good" to question two, respond with, "Show me." Some leaders are hesitant to ask this at first because they feel it is intrusive. However, it is not. If it is asked respectfully, desiring to see if their management system is working, then the workers can sense the motive of the leader is to help them.

If the worker cannot get quick feedback, it is management's job to help, starting with the leader doing the Gemba walk. This is a great demonstration of servant-leadership because it is the boss who usually receives an

The purpose of the four questions is to reveal some gaps.

action, not the employee. See if the worker can show you what his or her key measure is right now.

The third question is, "What is your plan?" S&W leaders add, "Do you have any ideas to close that gap?" If they do not produce an idea, ask in different ways like, "Have you ever thought about how to make this better?"

Most of the time, they start by listing ideas that have been tried thus far. Listen and keep pressing. A key purpose of the Gemba walk is to surface an idea to check the effectiveness of LMS built thus far. If you are patient, you will hear some real jewels from the employees. Steve marvels at the simple good ideas heard on Gemba walks.

The employee will typically tell you something like, "You know I have been thinking about this. What if we help the front-end staff in the mornings or what if we..." Good ones.

The fourth question is, "How can I help you (see if your idea worked)?" It is not "How can I help you implement that idea?" You are trying to build a Lean management system, so the question is, "How can I help you see if your idea worked?"

At this point, stop and reflect for a moment. If the employees implemented the idea they just told you, would they be able to tell if it worked tomorrow or by the end of the week? If the answer is no, remember, it is management's job to build these systems. Steve guesses that 70 to 90% of the Gemba walks at S&W in their first two years ended with no on the question above. Sometimes, an employee cannot even state a target or goal (question one).

The leaders must help their staff answer these questions:

- What are our team's key targets and goals?
- Did leaders make a board displaying quick-moving input or process measure charts with goals?
- How are we doing right now? Is today's gap visible?
- Where will we write our ideas?
- How will we know it worked?
- Where will we look to check to see if they worked?
- What then? How do we let everyone know and benefit from the waste-busting, problem-solving idea that just appeared to work?

It is management's job to build the systems by which the workers' ideas can be brought forward and checked to see if they worked. This is quickly

> Even in the huddles, leaders ask the four questions of each chart at their huddle board.

revealed by asking the big four questions in just one area. However, it also reveals itself system-wide through dozens of Gemba walks in all areas, not just one or two. Listen. Your staff will tell what they feel is meaningful.

To summarize, the four questions are used in a Gemba walk to reveal the absence or presence of LMS. Imagine all of your leaders doing these weekly for six months. After a while, it becomes natural. At S&W, a sensei goes with them about once a month for at least three guided Gemba walks, guides them in Hansei (reflection), and then offers more technical tips on their huddle boards after the walks.

Go see and ask why. This is a great opportunity for leadership development. Even in the huddles, leaders ask the four questions of each chart at their huddle board, although the key goals should already be posted (the trend charts). In Gemba walks, they see if the goals posted are effective and motivating staff to try out targeted actions. Normally, they find some absence of LMS and write down actions to build it stronger.

Go see, ask why, and show respect. Recognition of positive effort is powerful. Today at S&W, if a high-level leader shows up in a department, it does not scare staff. In fact, areas that huddle consistently want this! They are just as vocal and passionate about closing the gaps on their key goals with or without top leaders. If the president shows up, team members are no more or less excited than if the janitor wanted to know.

Part C: Increased Floor Time for Leaders

One important requirement for daily accountability process is increased floor time for leaders. However, working against this is *a big shift*. In David Mann's book, he recognizes a huge shift for leaders in general. The authors concur that it is happening in healthcare as well.

The authors believe much of what nurse, technician, research, emergency department, surgery, and other area leaders do now was once the responsibility of support groups like human resources, recruiting, staff management, finance, quality, marketing, and maintenance. In effect, other functional groups in service and support areas over time have *shifted* parts of what used to be their work to these value-adding care process leaders.

In effect, other functional groups in service and support areas over time have shifted parts of what used to be their work to these value-adding care process leaders.

At your organization, do you think this is true? Have support functions shifted what used to be their administrative duties to care process leaders? Must they now do their own recruiting, staff management, Family Medical Leave Act (FMLA) tracking, IT, data entry, and data "digging?" What other duties have been shifted? What can be done about this?

Let's get personal. Is it difficult for you to spend time in the Gemba because of activities shifted to you? Which ones? Ask this question of 10 or so frontline supervisors. Write down their input. Then, do the exercise with your leadership team in the pie chart in Figure 5.6. And, challenge who should do these shifted support tasks.

Some examples are payroll, attendance, tracking Family Medical Leave Act (FMLA), inspections, prep for audits, quality data collections, and other metrics. Staff leaders often are required to do these themselves in their spare time. They do their own customer relations. They do all kinds of record keeping, inventory counts, clinical trial forms, documentation, and staff evaluations. Then, there are "must attend" meetings called by these same support groups wanting feedback on tasks they shifted!

Gradually, this work comes to occupy the majority of the leader's time. The cumulative effect of transferring or adding all of these tasks is time away from the actual work processes. Time in the Gemba for continuous improvement is the first to be affected. The CI process is put on hold, or worse, non-standard practices creep in. The most important person needed on the floor in value-adding areas has been buried in paperwork in his or her office! Leaders must help reverse this.

We want our day back! S&W always does a useful exercise in its Lean leader course. Individually and then in teams, they attempt to list every task, meeting, and requirement in their day that is non-value added. In Lean terms, list all wastes.

If you remember from Lean training, only a small sliver of your day is truly value-adding. Consider Figure 5.6. If you did a pie chart of your day, maybe it averages 10 hours total. There may be just a small amount of time adding value, shown in the lower right corner. This is the stuff staff went to school for. The question is, how do they do more of this without

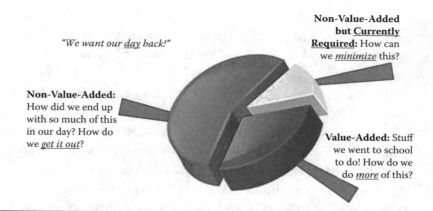

"We want our _day_ back!"

Non-Value-Added but Currently Required: How can we _minimize_ this?

Non-Value-Added: How did we end up with so much of this in our day? How do we _get it out_?

Value-Added: Stuff we went to school to do! How do we do _more_ of this?

Figure 5.6 Value-added and non-value-added time in a leader's day, pie chart.

just increasing the pie (length of workday)? Lean provides tools to do this! Leaders can apply Lean to their day as well as work processes.

The rest of the pie is non-value-added (NVA), or waste. Part of this NVA may in fact be a large slice (upper right), but it is currently required—usually by law. Healthcare has a lot of this. Maybe it is publicly reported information gathering, certifying that nurses have done required training, maybe general communication with staff, etc. There are also some tasks that are NVA pure waste. Re-doing something again, retyping, rework, walking, checking data that should have come to you accurately, and maybe some meetings are pure NVA.

In Lean thinking, the reason staff are taught to divide NVA into two categories is that something different is done to them. If the task identified is NVA pure waste, the goal should be to completely **eliminate it**. If it is NVA currently required, the only thing you can try to do today is greatly **reduce the time** it takes to do them. You still need to do them—for now.

The Lean leader class is challenged to do this quick exercise individually. It is fun for most. Then, in teams, they identify ways to reduce and eliminate each waste.

In a 10-minute exercise, the class finds a way to reduce 30 to 60 minutes of waste per week quite easily, sometimes more. Imagine what a nurse manager could do with 60 minutes freed up. What could they do? We must help them get their day back!

You have probably made the connection already that this exercise immediately applies to every leader's day, not just those in class. If it works in *their* world, why wouldn't you find even *more* in the typical leader's day or week? What would a typical leader do with 60 freed-up minutes this week?

What about you? Why not stop and do a waste walk of your day. List NVA activities and tasks, and then try to reduce and eliminate them. Make meetings briefer with agendas. Eliminate some. At the end of your exercise, how many minutes per week can you free up? What will you do with that time?

We hope increased floor time. Increased time for CI. They must build LMS and do Gemba walks. They must audit the boards in their area. They must be available for continuous improvement. That is a lot of musts.

In class, each leader is encouraged to take a few of the actions from this quick exercise back to his or her workplace and truly eliminate some waste. It is not an exercise —it really works. In that freed-up time, they find time to do CI with staff and increase Gemba time. They document this freed-up time in their leader standard work, starting in the class. Brains are humming after this exercise. Eliminate 30 to 60 minutes, then and only then, add Gemba time and LMS building. That is the Lean way!

Let's summarize the daily accountability process. There are three key parts to it. There is the daily huddle, leader Gemba walks, and increased floor time (through waste elimination). Tracking, audits, and elevation will be covered in Chapter 5, Elevation System.

Leaders Must Keep Teams Moving up the Stairs

So, why are rapid PDCA cycles so important? Why daily Lean? Figure 5.7 shows an improvement pathway for a typical healthcare team. The gap between where they are and where they need to be can be large. If you asked the leader of the team to close this big gap, their shoulders will sag (more) and most will say, "I'll work harder." But, there is a better way!

How do you eat an elephant? One bite at a time! Sometimes, you cannot close a big gap in one change. If you are on the bottom right of the picture, sometimes you need to take one small step up before you can even see the next opportunity for improvement. In the CI process, a good change yields even more good changes. Imagine a person stepping up on the first stair. Now they can see better what is on the stairs above them.

Sometimes you can't see the forest for the trees. However, if you clear a few "trees," or make another small step up, now you can see even further. After a few steps, more improvement opportunities and real issues will be

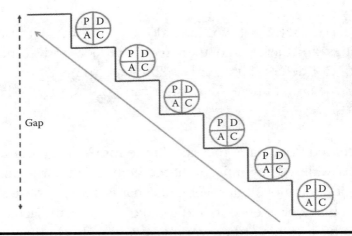

Figure 5.7 Stair-step model: Why leaders need daily small PDCA steps upward.

clear. The leader must step in at key times to keep the team headed up the stairway.

As a leader, your job is to make sure every step of the way the team members are going through the proper cycle. Plan, Do, Check, Act. It is the leader's job to build systems so they can keep trying out their ideas and quickly checking. In addition, it is the leader's responsibility to make sure it does not backslide.

The leaders must commit to root-cause problem solving and prevent staff from just doing work-arounds every day. In addition, they need to help staff overcome bottlenecks and constraints, like lack of equipment or missing signatures.

Leaders also need to help their team remove barriers like non-supportive support groups; or feedback that is too slow. If leaders do this, team members naturally will continue moving toward their target. Healthcare staff make good problem solvers, if taught and allowed to get to the real root causes and try out possible solutions.

A very simple huddle board is shown in Figure 5.8. Steve helped staff in this department "commandeer" the board, which previously had pictures of dogs, cats, and grandkids on it.

You can see four trend charts representing goals in their strategic categories. Steve helped the supervisor hand-draw the trend charts showing only "dummy" data on blank paper to demonstrate the concept. Choosing the measures was easy for this team, since they already had good goals. They just needed daily data, not monthly. They committed to collecting it daily.

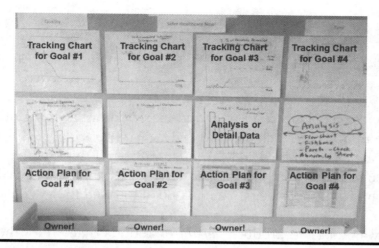

Figure 5.8   Simple huddle board.

The analysis "row" was explained and sample Pareto charts and analysis detail reports were hand-drawn. Four idea lists were shown because the leader wanted to make it easy for staff to see the impact of each idea by just "looking up" at the trend chart above it to check.

Notice that there is an owner listed under each category of measure. The leader was pleased that she did not need to both collect all current data and lead every huddle. This was a good leadership development opportunity for staff members assigned. Four different staff members were assigned—each in the area he or she knew best. The leader committed to spend time with each one to ramp them up and explain the simple huddle process.

Then, something magical happened. The leader and Steve walked to the unit, as Steve explained Gemba walks. A key staff member was asked the four questions. Without even seeing it, she listed at least two of the huddle board goals as meaningful to her, and she had data! Data for that day was available for the third chart (Safety—percentage reconciled within two hours). The leader returned to the board and put a real dot on the chart. Then she drew a line showing their goal. Steve asked the leader if she was ready to huddle. She said, "Why not?"

It was not perfect. But, within 60 minutes of placing the first hand-drawn dot on a chart, the team huddled, and staff immediately came up with a great base-hit idea to close the gap. It was implemented and checked the next day. The percentage reconciled within two hours nearly doubled within a week! How do you think the staff members with the ideas felt when they went home?

Every root problem requires at least one PDCA loop. How are we going to fix healthcare? One idea and PDCA loop at a time.

LMS reveals gaps between actual and expected on meaningful measures for staff, on trend charts that are updated daily if possible. Seeing these gaps, team members immediately and naturally start thinking of ways to close the gaps. They usually don't start with costly things. They can and will close the gaps with their ideas. You just need to build the systems and let them!

Do not wait for IT to produce *ker-thunk* reports (named for the sound produced when a large stack of paper hits the table, never to be opened). Do not wait for fancy spreadsheets. Make it visual. Do not let formal experiments scare you. Just help get the data flowing and allow staff to put a dot on their own chart. They know there is a gap. Let them start doing experiments with their ideas as quickly as possible.

Each individual step in LMS-building is easier than you think. In addition, it is more satisfying than other transformation efforts, as you will soon understand. It stirs up emotions and fulfillment in staff like no other initiative. It is real. And, it sticks.

Examples of Huddle Boards (Old and Newer)

Many examples of huddles board and tips have been presented already throughout this book. The following examples focus a bit more on the teams and their many small, base-hit ideas. The teams and their ideas fueled the improvement engine at S&W. Again, these examples were not chosen for their large results. Some of these teams were very early in their LMS-building.

Memorial ICUs

The Intensive Care Unit (ICU) departments stepped up to the challenge of huddling and even expanded the number of metrics they were tracking daily. Nursing teams generated numerous ideas to improve key metrics. Huddles are daily and most metric charts are updated daily. This is the norm in the entire department. The main three areas can be seen in Figure 5.9.

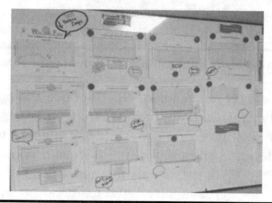

Figure 5.9   MICU, STICU, and CTICU huddle boards.

ICU physicians also began huddling (on rotation) after the ICU Nurse Director started huddling in all ICU areas.

Medical Intensive Care Unit (MICU)

A key huddle board goal in the MICU was reducing Catheter-Associated Urinary Tract Infection (CAUTI) incidents. The team identified key contributing factors to achieving zero CAUTIs. These were inputs measured daily, rather than waiting for the few incidents to occur. They are now tracking four key input factors: Red seal broken, Peri-care completed, drainage bag positioned below bladder, and drainage bag not over 2/3 full in all audits.

The first chart in Figure 5.10 shows the monthly CAUTI results. The team also tracked key input measures, where each line was color-coded to represent one of the four input factors mentioned earlier. Controlling these four inputs helped them stabilize and then reduce the number of CAUTIs.

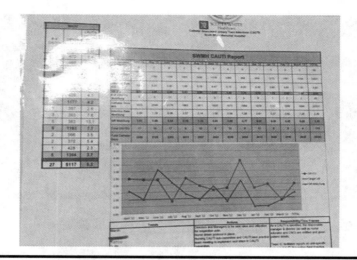

Figure 5.10   CAUTI monthly results and weekly input factor charts.

In Figure 5.11, catheter audits also helped reduce the number of CAUTIs. The audit used a checklist of daily proper care techniques of the catheters. You can see their audits increased toward the goal at the top rapidly, then fell the following Monday. They solved the new staff communication issue and returned to 100%. What gets measured gets done.

As these key factors were stabilized, the team closed in on their aggressive goal of no CAUTIs. They experimented with the input measures to determine which best predict and directly impact the key output metric of CAUTI incidents.

The team also attacked Central Line-Associated Bloodstream Infection (CLABSI) rates using the same process, identifying key input measures. The

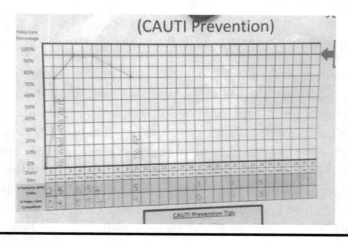

Figure 5.11   CAUTI daily care audits.

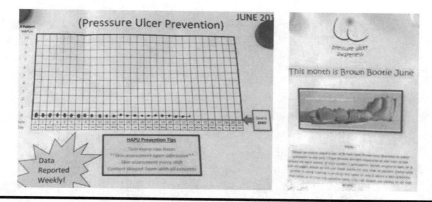

Figure 5.12 Pressure ulcer trend chart and proper equipment usage job aids from the STICU huddle board.

MICU continues to reduce their overall hospital acquired infections (HAIs) using huddles.

Surgical/Trauma Intensive Care Unit (STICU)

A key huddle board measure in the STICU was reducing pressure ulcers. The STICU team also identified key input metrics and then generated ideas to keep these at the goal (zero). Ensuring use of key equipment was part of their input metric, so pictures like those shown in Figure 5.12 were used on the boards.

Cardiothoracic Intensive Care Unit (CTICU)

A key huddle board measure in the CTICU was reducing the number of patients that are extubated after 24 hours as seen in Figure 5.13. Achieving consistency and stabilizing at zero has been nearly achieved. Key ideas from the staff on their board resulted in big improvements.

One key idea was to make the times visible for every patient on the team whiteboard (noting allergies) as seen in Figure 5.14.

The picture in Figure 5.15 was taken on a Gemba walk with Shahin at the ICU physicians huddle board. The physician, Dr. Chris Spradley, answered the four questions well, and took Shahin to his team's huddle board.

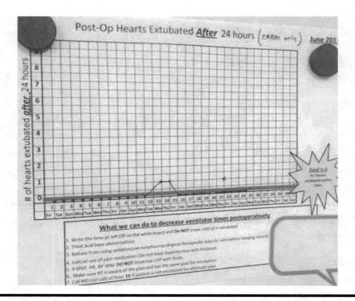

Figure 5.13   CTICU huddle board trend chart.

Gemba key metrics on this board were:

■ Hospital Acquired Infections (HAIs): Ventilator-associated pneumonia (VAP) was reduced near zero and CLABSI trended down within a year
■ Fellow teaching
■ Patient flow
■ Mortality tracking

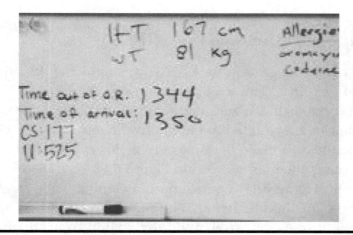

Figure 5.14   CTICU time observations.

Figure 5.15   Shahin Motakef on a Gemba walk with Dr. Chris Spradley at the ICU physician's huddle board.

Some other features of this physician huddle board at the bottom were that they tracked ideas using the categories: Complete, Standard, Rethink, and Implement. The far right side of their board had other category boxes needing huddle visibility like:

■ Equipment issues and needs
■ Idea lists
■ Wish list

Temple HR Recruiting

HR recruiting team began using the screening questions portion of their new HR software to prescreen candidates. On the board in Figure 5.16, their key metrics were:

■ Recruiting screening questions used
■ Recruiting checklist used

The recruiters wrote their ideas on the two idea lists to the left at the bottom of the board. They used Post-its on the ideas they needed help to implement—the idea list to the right. It is imperative that top leaders visit these boards often and look for ideas that need to be elevated.

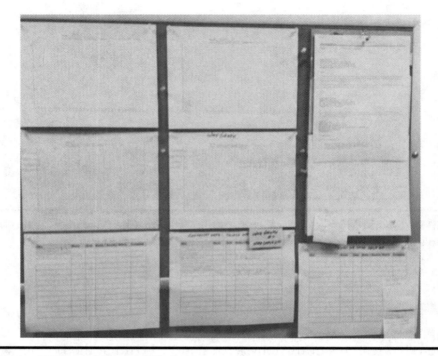

Figure 5.16 HR recruiting huddle board.

Taylor POS Collections

Back in 2013, clerks in this small ED had a historic average of collecting only small amounts per year. The team began tracking ED collections, summarizing totals on all leader boards. Taylor increased collections by 250% in the first three months alone!

Figure 5.17 shows their board, with a close-up of collections by area and then by the three individuals. Note there was no blaming these good staff members. The process was broken. Staff helped fix it. Also, notice these charts were hand-drawn. This daily look at data gave staff quick feedback on their ideas and progress.

Temple Orthopedic Clinic

In the large Temple Orthopedic Clinic, leaders wanted to engage more staff. Given their staggered start times, they scheduled two different huddles.

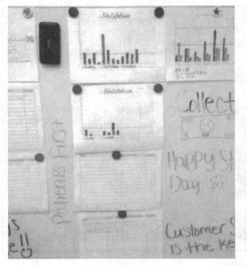
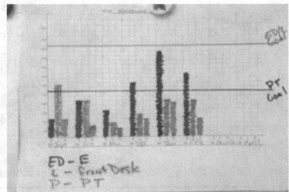
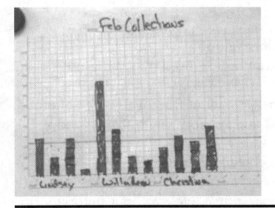

Figure 5.17   Taylor Hospital tracking ED collections.

Note: Leaders may need to try out different huddle times during the day and possibly do two huddles to accommodate staff, sometimes straddling lunch. Two brief mid-morning huddles worked for Ortho at 8:15 and 8:30 am, with half of the staff in each to avoid disrupting patient flow.

Figure 5.18 shows their huddle board at the back of a very busy clinic hallway. They started with four initial trend charts. They met their EMR preparation goal early and took it down. Two new metrics were added, both focusing on improving the patient's experience. They were:

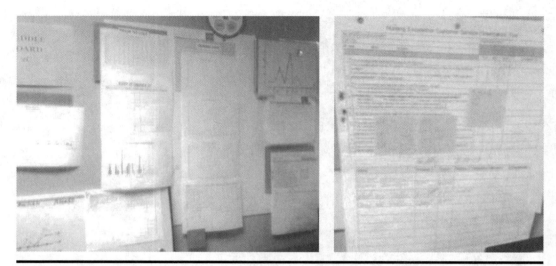

Figure 5.18   Temple Ortho Clinic 2C huddle board.

- X-rays not entered before the appointment time
- Personal touch-base with patients waiting for more than 15 minutes

Ortho leaders are trying to achieve better patient flow. They tell patients the reasons why the doctors are delayed and by how much. Data is now being tracked daily with ideas.

The Ortho team's early idea list can be seen at the bottom of their board. The close-up in Figure 5.19 states they need a "hook by (the) scales" for patients to hold their personal effects (coat, purse, etc.) without putting it on the floor or handing to staff when they take vitals. Their idea was to install a simple hook. It was implemented the next day. Patients noticed this and

Idea	Name	Date
Do not encourage Remove Duulp~	Ker	2-1F-13
Hook by Scales	Ken ff	2-1t-13
Come out farther	Cheryl	2-8-13

Figure 5.19   Action plan close-up from Ortho clinic huddle board.

were pleased. The simplicity of hundreds of ideas that flow from huddles is the power of LMS.

Temple GI Procedures

The Gastrointestinal (GI) Clinic and Endoscopy Procedure Rooms had a big backlog. They were persistently high—as high as 500+ and as low as 350. This example shows how a key metric was displayed in three different ways.

At first, the team just wrote the current backlog numbers on a whiteboard (see Figure 5.20). It was erased after each meeting. Not much was accomplished because they could not see their backlog trend.

The next step was to leave the previous numbers on the board for a while. This provided some visibility of trend, but still yielded few actions. After GI started huddling, they used a simple trend chart of the backlog (see Figure 5.21). The combination of visibility, priority, and ideas for improvement worked.

The GI team started huddling around the backlog measures weekly. They engaged the entire staff to help reduce backlogs. From the start, the improvement was dramatic and rapid. After just three weeks, they reduced the backlog numbers to the low 20s. From 500+ down to the low 20s!

In addition, patient reschedules (patient and doctor-initiated) were originally very frequent, so the team started tracking reschedules. Once this became visible, it got the focus of the team. Within four weeks, the numbers improved by 62% and less-than-30-day reschedules reduced 85% (27 down to 4).

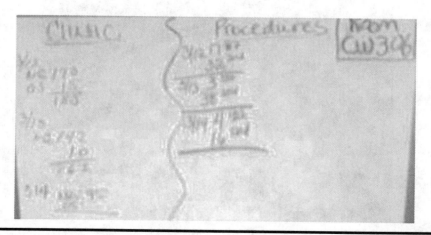

Figure 5.20 Old Temple GI backlog board.

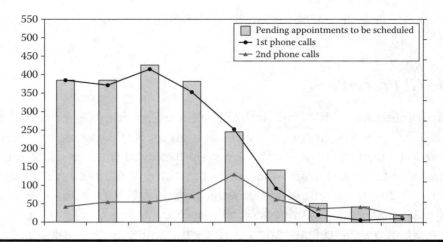

Figure 5.21   New Temple GI backlog trend chart.

Staff will start and continue to generate ideas if the gap between actual and expected and their ideas are made visible. The huddle board and process are the key drivers in making these conditions happen.

Taylor Lab

In Figure 5.22, you can see lab tech hands on their board while brainstorming. You can see their Hoshin (SWAT) goal-setting section first on the extra-wide board. Then, you can see the five strategic categories with key metrics

Figure 5.22   Taylor Lab huddle boards—multiple levels.

under each. Based on their gaps, team members came up with ideas to run their improvement experiments.

As an example of a major cost-saver, the Lab team wanted to reduce ABG reagent cost. The original contract was set up through the vendor when Taylor was an independent hospital. This was prior to becoming part of S&W. Their experiment was to move the ABG reagents to Central Lab and get staff access to order the product. The system-negotiated pricing resulted in a 50% cost savings.

McLane Children's Hospital Physical Therapy/ Occupational Therapy (PT/OT)

A key difference on this board (Figure 5.23) was part of the culture of McLane Children's. They wanted to have a fun-looking board, so they used the department's artistic creativity. They also had children get involved in labeling the metric categories.

Key metrics on this board were:

- PT/OT outpatient visits
- Outpatient missed appointments
- Physician turnover
- Average insurance turnover trends

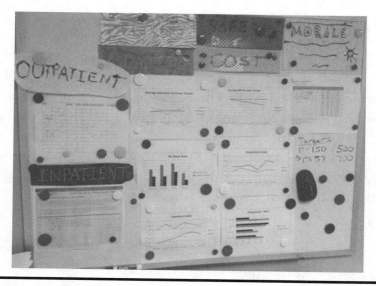

Figure 5.23 McLane Children's Hospital PT/OT huddle board, children helped make it.

Figure 5.24   McLane Children's Hospital Imaging huddle boards.

McLane Children's Hospital Imaging

A key component of this huddle board was the way that it ensures staff recognition. They built a "High Five" board right next to the main huddle board as seen in Figure 5.24.

Key metrics on this board were:

- MRI with and without sedation ratio
- Second shift exam count

McLane Children's Hospital Lab

McLane Children's Hospital had some of the most creative boards. The lab was very visual (Figure 5.25). They choose a different theme every quarter. A common element for this board was to put up pictures of patients. A lab department typically does not interact directly with patients. It reminds them of whom they serve.

Key metrics on this board were:

- Overtime (cost)
- Lab exceptions (quality)
- Clotted specimens (quality)
- Delivery of completed lab results (service)
- Morale (people)

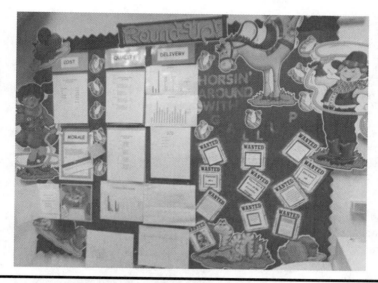

Figure 5.25 McLane Children's Hospital Lab huddle board.

Llano Nutrition Services

Patient satisfaction in the kitchen at Llano is all about food quality, delivery, and temperature. Two challenges they have are preparing and then delivering great food at the right temperature to patients who might have restrictive diets. Within just weeks, the leader and her team improved their specific patient satisfaction question (food quality and food temperature) scores from 4.3 and 4.0 respectively, to 4.5 and 4.4.

Some ideas implemented were a new tray (see after and before at the bottom right of Figure 5.26), and new menu items that stay within patient dietary restrictions. The leader also acquired a closed cart system from Temple to keep food temperature consistent. One action at a time, this team is hoping to reach their stretch goal of a perfect 5.0!

Hillcrest Baptist Physical Therapy (Re-Evaluations)

Sometimes, teams addressed simple problems in their huddles. Hillcrest Baptist's Physical Therapy unit needed to schedule re-evaluations of patients. A staff member wrote a problem on a Post-it note to be discussed and then added to the idea lists. In Figure 5.27 it says, "Problem: difficulty with tracking when re-evals are due. Is there some way to track this? Very difficult when a physical therapist goes back and forth between patients."

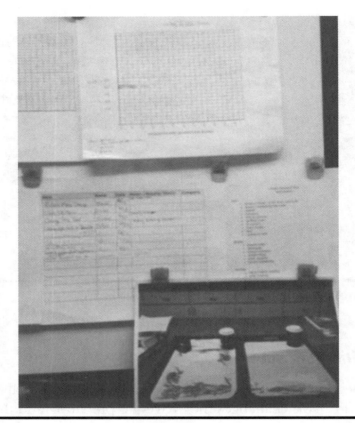

Figure 5.26   Llano Nutrition Services huddle board.

Scheduling re-evaluations and tracking them was important. In their first draft (at the bottom), they created a hand-drawn form. Someone quickly put it into a spreadsheet and tried this second draft the next day. You can see the third draft chart, still in use today. It is a simple checklist. In just three days, the team went from hand-drawn to rough draft spreadsheet, to finalized check sheet.

Temple Pulmonary Lab

Temple Pulmonary Lab used their huddle board and process to deploy their "Back to Budget" action items (in Figure 5.28). One effort was to track staff overtime each pay period. The team also uses a simple "Why" bar graph that categorizes the main reasons "why" staff had the overtime (right). Ideas to stay on track are flowing from this hard-working team (bottom).

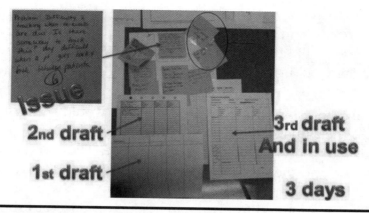

Figure 5.27   Hillcrest Baptist Physical Therapy huddle board.

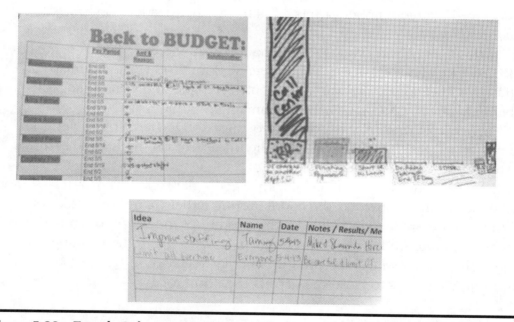

Figure 5.28   Temple Pulmonary Lab back to budget action items, Why graph for overtime, and the team's idea list.

Entering a Huddle: Senior Executives

Steve taught the first Lean leadership course at S&W for Bob and his top leaders. Bob started his executive team huddle the next workday. They have been huddling ever since. The executive huddle room served as an incubator for ideas, tracking, Hoshin Kanri, and demonstration of the four parts of LMS to all other staff including trend charts.

How about your organization? Would the top leaders be willing to do first what they ask of all other staff? If it became a showcase, a best practice example, how would that motivate your staff?

Every Lean leadership group after Bob's class would come see the leaders huddle on their final day of class before they did their Gemba walk exercise. This was a critical factor driving change. They would see their leaders huddling and then create their own. Many would try to make theirs even better.

Figure 5.29 was captured from an early video produced to show all staff how S&W leaders huddle. It was edited lightly and posted on the intranet. It received a large number of hits as staff saw their leaders demonstrate huddles.

In this split picture, you can see about half of the exec huddlers including Chief Quality Officer Dr. Tiffany Berry, Bob, CNO Cyndy Dunlap, Chief Strategy Officer Steve Sullivan, President of Temple and Central Region Shahin Motakef, CMO Dr. Glen Couchman, and COO Pat Currie.

The topic of this daily huddle was quality, so Dr. Berry presented the expected vs. actual for a few key quality measures on the huddle board behind her, under the Quality heading.

You can notice a few things quickly as you glance at this room. First, it is small. It became known as the cuddle room, rather than the huddle room. If the room is small, what must be the posture of the dozen or so huddlers? Right, standing. And, if they are standing, how long can the meeting last? Right, short. Frequent, brief stand-up huddles focused on one or two metrics and soliciting ideas to close the gaps is the norm for S&W huddles.

Figure 5.29   Scott & White's executive huddle.

Bob helped recruit and develop a seasoned group of leaders, all attracted to the challenge of transforming healthcare. They wanted to be on the cutting edge of transformation. To use a surfing analogy, the team could see a big wave forming. It would be a fun ride, but it was also scary at the same time.

Something strategic was in the air and playing out in real time. Achieving population health, rational growth, and world-class institutes, all while maintaining financial balance would be a challenge. If you invest too much in different finance models too soon, you crash. If you delay, you could crash even harder later.

Step into Bob's executive huddle room for a moment. Here is an example of how Bob's huddle tackled an issue. One strategic goal was "Retain 90% of all high-performing staff." However, when S&W started huddling, this was extremely challenging—all healthcare organizations were cutting expenses and staff! Many structural and benefit costs were cut. Many departments could not replace staff that left. Keeping morale high was a challenge.

This measure was tracked by the HR Chief in the huddle. If there were gaps, the team came up with ideas. However, at this high level, there would be few easy just-do-it ideas. Most required deeper, slow-brain, root-cause problem solving for each reason staff left. This required a strong knowledge of A3 problem solving by all leaders. They needed to be able to do and lead A3s in their sleep!

The exec team did not solve specific problems in their huddles. However, they started the analysis, and often kicked off A3 teams. Turnover of physicians and APPs was analyzed. Sometimes, they reviewed turnover by other positions as well.

As an example, the team dissected data and prioritized why high performers in the centralized call center were quitting. A fact kept surfacing that S&W changed the shift start and end times. Somehow, this change caused all sorts of childcare issues for high performers in the Call Center.

The team dissected another job function— transporters. They also had too many high performers leaving. Again, data showed there was a shift time change. Many of these good workers' families owned only one vehicle and their spouse worked a different shift. The car was needed earlier than their new exit time.

When the team focused on why (analysis), small changes were made that reduced turnover of good employees. This can be done with every key measure. Just huddle.

Note: Sometimes a change can bring about an unintended consequence. This is why it is so important to develop a PDCA culture, not just a do, do, do (or a plan, plan, not-do) culture.

When staff huddle around frequently updated metrics, it elevates the "Check" and the system-wide North Star goals. Huddling helps people make positive changes and then sustain them.

Elevation System—The Strong Chain

Briefly, an elevation system is a way to bring an idea to a higher level to be implemented and then give feedback to the originator. That way, staff and organization do not lose the benefits of the idea. Direct performers often have great ideas, but sometimes they are unable to get them done at their level. The elevation system starts with a second list of Ideas/Actions on their huddle boards where they can elevate crosscutting changes.

This is why S&W leaders are taught to go to the Gemba and look at the idea list on the right-hand side of the boards. This list contains ideas that the team needs help to implement. These ideas need to be "linked" to higher-level boards with feedback coming back to them—like a chain.

If ideas are not elevated, teams will stop bringing up these valuable cross-cutting ideas. They need help from leaders to get these ideas done. Huddle leaders need to continue tracking all ideas, even those elevated to and from their huddle.

As leaders start working on the elevated ideas, they often move the card or Post-it to the *in-process* column. Once completed, they move the card to the *completed* column, and bring feedback to the team that elevated the idea. This elevation system links multiple levels of boards into a strong chain so that all good ideas can be tried out. It is another demonstration of how important leadership is in creating a culture of continuous improvement.

Colored-Card System to Track Elevated Ideas

A tweak of the idea lists worked well and is gaining momentum at S&W. It solved a particular problem with elevated ideas. How do you keep them visual on the board of the original team and the leader (two boards)? Leaders often wrote the ideas needing elevation on a scrap piece of paper or Post-it. You guessed it. Sometimes they got misplaced or fell off.

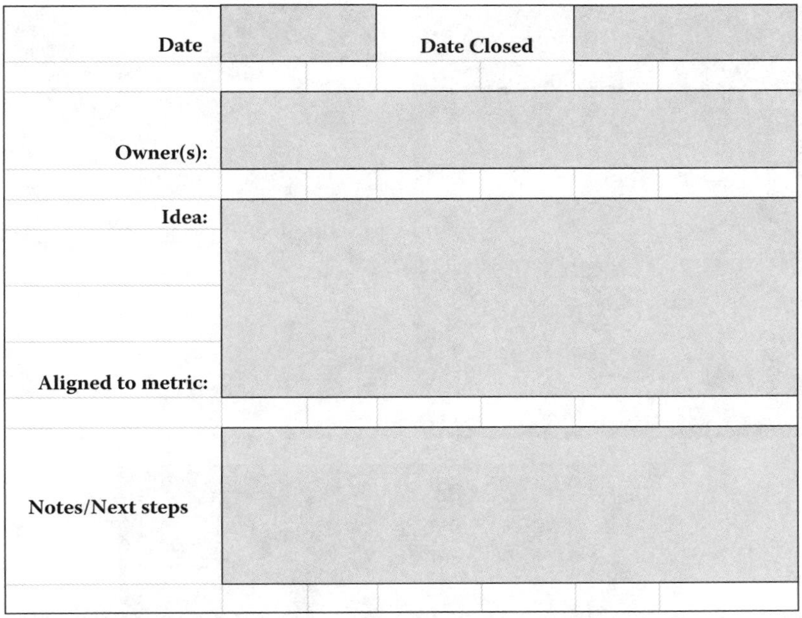

Date		Date Closed	
Owner(s):			
Idea:			
Aligned to metric:			
Notes/Next steps			

Figure 5.30   Color-card system used for documenting and elevating an idea to a leader board.

For leader boards especially, a better elevated idea tracking system was needed. A S&W innovator* used colored cards to visually track ideas through a 3-step implementation process (evaluation, in-process, complete). Since leaders could not remove and carry the whole idea list to their board to elevate, they needed to write it down. If they write it down, why not on a standard pre-printed card (see Figure 5.30)?

The leaders posted the elevated idea card in the *under evaluation* column on their board until their team agreed it had merit and could be worked. As they started working on it, they moved the card to the *in-process* column, and sent input to the originating team that the idea had started. Once completed, they moved the card to the *completed* column, and gave feedback to the originating team, thanking them and stating the results. This provided *visual control* of the progress of all ideas, including those elevated, and reminded leaders to "keep them moving."

This visual elevation colored-card system caught on in many regions because of its simplicity. It was recommended and built-in for many new boards.

---

* Credit to George Brown, Director Clinic Operations-Round Rock Region, his boss, Colleen Sundquist, VP of Clinics, and Michael Baratz, Senior Lean Coach.

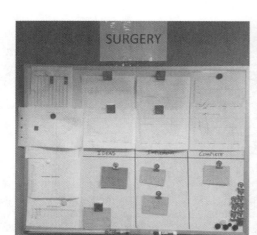
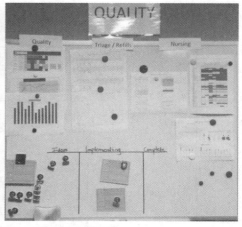

Figure 5.31   Colored-card system examples tracked in three status areas along the bottom of huddle boards.

The color codes S&W used on cards were:

■ Red cards: Ideas that have been elevated ***from*** a direct report's board up to the leader's board (there would be no red cards on a Tier-1 direct performer huddle board)
■ Orange cards: Ideas from the leader's own team
■ Green cards: a copy of ideas that have been elevated ***to*** the boss' board.

Since colored paper was not always handy, an improvement on colored cards happened within the first month of use. Single-color, pre-printed cards were made where staff circle "elevated from direct report board," "our team," or "elevated to big boss board." Figure 5.31 shows what the colored-card system looks like at the bottom of three different huddle boards—a Tier-2 (Surgery) and Tier-1's for a support group (Quality) and a clinic.

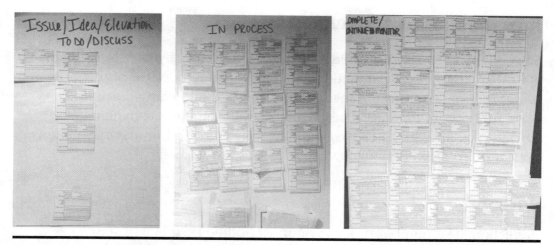

Figure 5.32 Idea card system for elevated and team ideas on flipcharts next to Waco region leadership huddle board.

Be flexible on the formats. It is more important for new LMS leaders to "own" their boards than it is for them to have a perfectly standardized board early on.

Another example of visual elevation is this flipchart/card elevation system on President Glenn Robinson's (Tier-3) board at Hillcrest Baptist. Figure 5.32 shows pages that contain both team and elevated ideas. This solved the typical problem with Action Plan lists, where many elevated ideas ended up "buried" under other pages of ideas as the letter-sized idea lists stacked on top of each other on active huddle boards. Note: It is exciting to think that "too many" ideas create small concerns like "get buried."

The leader team held each other accountable not only to get these elevated ideas completed, but also to give frequent feedback to the originating teams that first brought them up. Many ideas elevated from direct-performer teams were real jewels that helped patient care and created better flow.

Notice in Figure 5.32 the blank cards in the pocket below the "In Process" chart of ideas. Also notice the "self-tracking" huddle attendance log in the pocket next to the blank cards. Staff at all levels check themselves in at each huddle by placing an X next to their name under each huddle date. All huddles were tracked with a goal of conducting 90% of all scheduled huddles.

Interventions to Accelerate Ideas

Steve knew early on that huddle ideas would eventually start to slow down after many months of daily huddles. This is mainly because of the *low-hanging fruit* factor. In the initial stages of huddling, many quick and easy fixes are brought forward. These early ideas resemble low-hanging fruit—easy to pick and do. Later ideas are fewer in number, but may have bigger impact on metrics. Be patient. These phases are necessary.

Analysis

Prediction: The number of ideas on most huddle boards will start to decrease every 6 to 12 months, unless some type of intervention is taken to accelerate ideas again.

Analysis: After early "giddy" brainstorming phases, most low-hanging fruit will be picked. What remains are tough, sticky problems with no obvious root cause, or big projects.

Solution: Lean coaches must prepare supervisors and leaders at all levels with interventions to accelerate more innovative ideas. **A3 *waves*** and one-on-one coaching will be used to equip them to lead A3s and basic foundation tools on their own. Help with major projects will be needed soon after the effects of top problems are reduced.

Figure 5.33 shows an expectation Steve had about three known huddle idea "erosion" periods or stages. He saw these happen in transformations in

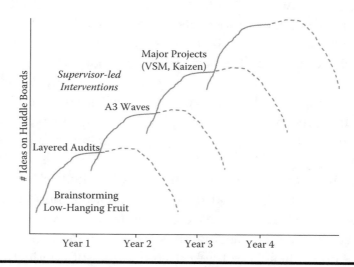

Figure 5.33 Chart showing "erosion" of ideas in stages with interventions to prevent.

other industries. This allowed S&W to plan interventions before the erosions. The Y-axis shows the number of ideas on huddle boards. The X-axis shows time.

In the earliest two stages, teams used mainly brainstorming to generate ideas to close gaps. Let's call these the brainstorming stages.

After 6 to 12 months in any phase, the weekly number of ideas will start to reduce; that is, unless you expected this and are ready with interventions to prevent erosion. The following table shows the stage, what leaders might hear from staff and supervisors near the end of the phase, and the intervention needed to accelerate ideas again.

Stage	Heard from Staff and Supervisors Near End of Phase	Intervention to Accelerate
1. Brainstorming (low-hanging fruit)	"We huddle, but it's just a meeting." "No. No one ever asked me for an idea. Why?"	Layered Audits and 2-Deep Tracking
2. More brainstorming (higher-hanging fruit)	(Supervisor) "We haven't got many ideas lately. Maybe our huddles aren't working." "I'm not giving another idea until someone works on the good (tough) one I gave last month!" "Boss, you keep saying 'show me your A3', but I haven't done one. Can you show me a good one that you completed?" "I can't think of any other ideas to increase our current measure on the chart."	A3 waves or cohorts Change cascaded metric (to one the team can impact)
3. Sticky problems	"I could use some help." "Most of the problems are outside of our area."	Major projects (VSM or Kaizen workshops)
4. Major projects	[Boss smiles a lot; gets promoted]	Systemize

In the first stage, Brainstorming (low-hanging fruit), the number of ideas on most huddle boards will start to erode about after 6 to 12 months of daily brainstorming. What leaders might hear from team members near the end of this stage is, "We huddle, but it's just a meeting." And, "No. No one ever asked me for an idea. Why?"

Many teams were probably told they "had to huddle" and some leaders may not have been fully trained —especially on why they must huddle. Huddles that are not "effective" peter out first.

The very best way to energize a huddle and make it more effective near the end of this stage is with layered audits. Layered huddle board audits will be discussed in detail in Chapter 5, Huddle Board Audit System.

In the second stage, More Brainstorming (higher-hanging fruit), a team will again start to see the number of weekly ideas decrease after 6 to 12 months of brainstorming. What leaders might hear from a supervisor is, "Hmm. We haven't got many ideas lately. Maybe our huddles aren't working." Also, a staff member says, "I'm not giving another idea until someone works on the good (tough) one I gave last month!" And, "Boss, you keep saying 'show me your A3', but I haven't done one. Can you show me a good one that *you* completed?" [Boss walks away.]

Discussions with team members and review of the ideas and metrics will likely show brainstorming-only picked off many low-hanging fruit. However, what remains are tough, sticky problems with no obvious root cause.

The very best way to energize a huddle and make it more effective near the end of this phase is with **A3 *waves***. A3 waves will be discussed next (Figure 5.34).

In the first comment above (not many ideas), this is likely due to an underlying problem that cannot be solved by just guessing. They may not have learned to analyze well and seek root causes. This is OK at first. The huddles are working as expected. Moreover, it is worth doing straight brainstorming for a while as the low-hanging fruit stage brings engagement and

Concern	Why?	Leader Response
Ideas not flowing at huddle	1. Leaders not trained	1. Train leaders including after-coaching
	2. Ineffective huddle or board	2. Ensure layered audits
	3. No action on tough issues	3. Escalation process with feedback
	4. Mainly problems remain	4. Start leader through A3 wave

Figure 5.34 Responses from a leader when ideas slow down.

moves metrics. However, this is more of a shotgun approach. You will need more as the "pile" of opportunities in front of a team becomes mainly problems that have no obvious root cause.

S&W taught its teams early how to do A3 problem solving in several classes. But, the case study exercises in class did not prepare supervisors to lead real problems in their teams. It seems the best way to train problem solving to supervisors and managers is to *not* train them (classroom). Best is to challenge them to write up their biggest problem on an A3 form and bring it into a small group led by a Lean coach where they actually work on their own problem!

In the second comment above (no more ideas until we work on my good/tough one), it is likely that the supervisor realizes a sticky problem is lurking beneath the idea or suggestion. An example of this was an idea to send out more reminder emails to ensure staff show up for training courses. Will this work? Probably just as "well" as the four to five emails sent earlier. A team-based A3 problem solving exercise will unearth deeper root causes and lead to better solutions.

The third comment (show me your A3) reveals that supervisors do not always know how to do deep root cause analysis either. Again, it is management's job to build these systems to generate and try out ideas. A key part of that is A3 root cause problem solving. The best way to do this is *non-training*—an A3 wave on actual, large problems.

The fourth comment (can't think of any more ideas) is common around this stage. You may notice it in the second stage as well. It is a sign that the team has tried many ideas but could not move the metric. It could be that the root cause is still not clear.

Or more likely, the metric the team is trying to improve may be too high-level, or not fast-moving enough for the team to improve it at their level. The team needs to change their cascaded metric to one they can impact better. An example might be OR surgeries. The cleaning crew measured the number of surgeries, which is out of their control. It may be best for them to measure a cost metric like room turnover time or rooms cleaned per person.

> The fourth comment (can't think of any more ideas to improve metric) is common… Likely, the metric the team is trying to improve may be too high-level or not fast moving enough for the team to improve it at their level. The team needs to change their cascaded metric to one they can impact better.

In the third stage, Sticky Problems, the number of weekly ideas on most huddle boards will start to decrease again after about 6 to 12 months of daily brainstorming. What leaders might hear from team members near the end of this stage is, "I could use some help," and, "Most of the problems are outside of our area."

The very best way to energize a huddle and make it more effective near the end of this phase is to provide them with help and facilitation on major improvement projects (VSM, Six Sigma, or Kaizen workshops). Projects were discussed in detail earlier. Members of the team that gave the idea should serve as representatives and bring back data, gather input, and prepare the team for changes in their huddles.

Interventions

A solution to each of these erosions is to prepare supervisors and leaders at all levels (even the CEO) with interventions to accelerate more innovative ideas. The first intervention was basic layered auditing of huddle boards. This serves to ensure the huddles are effective. The simple questions S&W used on the audit were not the key. The key was to have multiple leaders in a chain-of-command all looking at boards. This makes huddles effective.

After some low-hanging fruit, the second intervention was A3 waves or cohorts. A3 waves utilize small group (other supervisors who have taken a big problem into the group working sessions) and one-on-one coaching to equip them to lead A3s. There are not enough facilitators in the company to facilitate all problems every day. Supervisors can and should lead these for their teams at their own huddles.

A3 Waves

S&W found that leaders from frontline to the C-suite were not equipped to lead problem solving on their own. So, waves were successfully piloted. In a typical wave, 15 or so frontline leaders bring an important problem from their area to the hands-on sessions and work on it for just a few hours once each week with a coach until they got traction.

A "wave" is a good word for the A3 hands-on learning process. When one wave hits the shore, another is forming right behind it. This is true of problem-solving waves as well. Each wave that finishes helps the next wave as well, building your internal ability to solve even more problems. The new wave would see the previous wave report out on their successes. This made them even more determined to "do better" than their predecessors. It helped them see the finished product and hear great lessons learned.

At S&W, as the number of ideas started to peter out, they challenged leaders to identify the top or toughest 2 to 3 problems in their area, identify a frontline supervisor who would be best to solve it, and send him or her to the seven-week wave. Leaders prioritized the best process problems, served as sponsors, and chose the supervisors for the wave.

Problems were selected in advance by leaders with help from finance. Then, participants were chosen who best fit the project and requirements. The 15 or so projects would be represented by a single leader in the wave, but they would be expected to work on it with their boss and bring the analysis to their huddles as well to get more ideas and buy-in. Each student had his or her own project, which he or she owned and was accountable for. They were commissioned by their bosses to go to the wave and solve this important problem that was impacting their team.

The two-hour sessions held each of the seven weeks cover one section of the A3 form. The session agendas were roughly:

- 30 minutes—reflection on last week's lesson
- 45 minutes—new instruction
- 45 minutes—individual coaching on their projects and "homework" assignments

Each wave ended in an eighth and final session, at a heavily attended graduation celebration. In order to get progress on their problems, this report-out was sometimes delayed two to three weeks after their seventh session. This also gave the finance department time to approximate their gains to-date and expected at completion. True to the idea of a wave, the next wave or cohort participants attended graduation. They saw great problem analysis and heard leaders encouraging staff. It greased the skids for a good wave for them as well.

Results

Some waves of 15 or so problems produced savings of over $400,000. However, they also produced a greater product than cash—leaders. Leaders who could solve future problems, lead their staff through the process, and even teach others. The participant's manager and senior leaders were integrated throughout the entire wave and process. The focus was on problem solving, but A3 waves were also a terrific leader development tool. Cost, quality, and safety improvements were secondary.

Interactive exercises in the waves helped translate academic concepts into applied, tangible concepts. Both the results from their class projects and the process itself became sustainable for S&W. Future instructors were developed in a "See one, Do one, Teach one" structure. Moreover, Lean instructors and high-performing students provide layered mentorship for new cohorts.

One wave, touching another wave, touching another wave, until every single supervisor and manager has mastered good, root-cause problem solving. This is the plan.

Major Projects

The second intervention was projects using tools like value stream mapping (VSM) or Kaizen workshops. These were described in detail in Chapter 4, Step 2-Major Lean Projects. Some measures can be improved best by getting a subset of the team together in a workshop. If two to three departments needed to cooperate to get traction, it normally required a facilitated workshop.

These three interventions—layered audits, A3 waves, and commissioning cross-functional projects—are necessary to prevent the natural erosion of ideas. As the number of ideas starts to reduce, you can kick them back up again by investing in the supervisor and manager's ability to do these tasks. Idea elevation systems were also used to bubble up the need for crosscutting projects.

Figure 5.35 shows the Toyota House again. S&W desires that their frontline leaders be capable of conducting any foundation tool with their staff in huddles. Today, many of them still receive active support from a Lean coach. However, eventually S&W leaders want supervisors at all levels to be able to lead their own change efforts with *any* foundation tool! They realize this is a huge task, and will likely take seven years or more.

S&W desires that their frontline leaders be capable of conducting any foundation tool with their staff in huddles. They realize this is a huge task, and will likely take seven years or more.

Developing The Toyota *House* Model:
Foundation First!

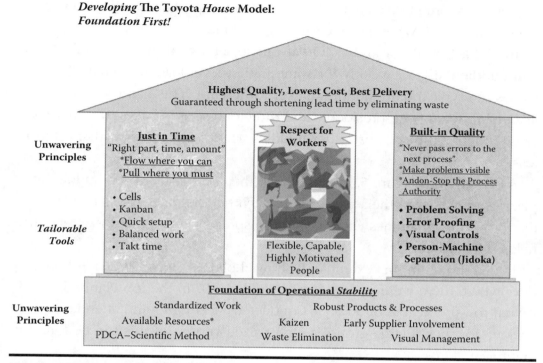

Figure 5.35 Toyota House Model.

The foundation includes standard work, waste elimination, PDCA cycles, and visual management. Even A3 problem solving was added because this foundation stabilizer must be understood and led by supervisors. All of these tools were taught to supervisors who owned the foundation at their team level.

Huddle Tracking System

What gets measured gets done. So, be careful what you measure.

—Steve's sensei, and many others

The next three sections go together. First, S&W leaders started tracking huddles. Then, they started individually auditing huddle boards. Then, they started doing layered audits of huddle boards with monthly presentations to the site leadership team. This first section starts with the basics—tracking and ensuring that all huddles scheduled actually took place.

If it is important, leaders track it. If it is not important, leaders do not track it. It is true. What gets measured gets done.

In FY14, Bob Pryor and COO Pat Currie set a goal that "90% of all staff will huddle daily (or weekly for some higher-level leaders)." Figure 5.36 shows the typical daily huddle tracker for a team. This is for a regional leadership team (vice presidents and directors) so it is larger and more cross-functional than most other huddles. Huddles are best with 15 staff or less.

As stated after Figure 5.32, staff check themselves in at each huddle by placing an X next to their name under each huddle date. These handwritten forms are sometimes entered into the spreadsheet so that the attendance fields self-calculate.

July is shown in this example. It shows holidays (July 4 is shaded out), days where there were no huddles scheduled ("0" in the top Planned and Actual rows), the goal of 90% "% Conducted" (top-right) and attendance (below) for such a large group. A larger-sized version of this can be found in Figure 7.9.

Figure 5.37 shows the same leader's ***two-deep tracker*** for July. Managing two-deep will be discussed in the next section. The actual huddles conducted row from Figure 5.36 is merely cut and pasted into this new tab for each leader (direct reports of Shahin M. in this case) by the end of each month.

Top leaders can pick up this single two-deep page and see if their leaders are huddling consistently. In Figure 5.37, consistent huddling is shown for all leaders except for one near the top. You cannot see how many huddles they "planned" to conduct, but S&W leaders have the full attendance sheet for every one of their direct reports.

One other optional tracking sheet S&W leaders use to track their huddles is called the *Huddle Notes*. A leader can scan this and send to all invitees weekly, in case they miss a huddle or need to check progress on action items assigned.

Figure 5.38 is an example note page from the highest-level huddle at S&W (blurred to cover certain info). The date, attendance, discussion items, and decisions are shown. The line at the bottom of each of the five boxes records action items and follow-up.

Huddle Tracking-FY14																															
Week ending	7/1	7/2	7/3	7/4	7/5	7/6	7/7	7/8	7/9	7/10	7/11	7/12	7/13	7/14	7/15	7/16	7/17	7/18	7/19	7/20	7/21	7/22	7/23	7/24	7/25	7/26	7/27	7/28	7/29	7/30	7/31
VP/Admins	2014																														
Huddles (Planned)	19	1	1	1			1	1	1	0	1	1			1	1	1	1			1	1	1	0			1	1	1	1	1
Huddles (ACTUAL)	19	1	1	1			1	1	1	0	1	1			1	1	1	1			1	1	0	1			1	1	1	1	1
Goal: 90% of scheduled Daily Huddles conducted																														Goal: 90% of scheduled Daily Huddles conducted	100%

Attendance: % of actual | July 2014

	% of actual	7/1	7/2	7/3	7/6	7/7	7/8	7/9	7/10	7/13	7/14	7/15	7/16	7/17	7/18	7/21	7/22	7/23	7/24	7/27	7/28	7/29	7/30	7/31
Ldr: Shahin M	68%	X				X	X										X		X		X	X	X	X
Matt B	58%	X	X		X	X	X	X	X			X	X				X		X		X	X	X	X
Mark C	95%	X	X	X	X	X	X	X	X	X	X	X	X	X	X	X	X	X	X	X	X	X	X	X
Marshall C	68%	X	X	X		X	X	X				X	X	X	X		X		X		X	X	X	X
Michael D	84%	X	X			X	X	X	X	X	X	X	X	X	X	X	X		X		X	X	X	X
Cyndy D	37%	X	X	X		X					X						X		X					
Betti G	63%	X			X	X			X		X	X	X				X				X	X	X	X
Candice G	79%			X	X	X	X	X	X	P	X	X	X	X			X		X		X	X	X	X
Ron H	58%	X	X		X	X	X	X	X			X	X		X		X		X		X	X	X	X
Jacki L	58%	X	X		X	X	X	X	X			X	X	X	X		X		X		X	X	X	X
Susan M	95%	X	X		X	X	X	X	X	X	P	P	X	X	X	X	X		X		X	X	X	X
Thom M	95%	X	X		X	X	X	X	X	P	X	P	P	X	P	X	X		P		X	X	X	X
Tricia M	84%	X	X	P	X	X	X	X	X	X	X	X	X	X	X	X	X		P		X	X	X	P
Richard N	58%		X	P		X	X	P	X			X	P	X	X		X		P		X	X	P	X
Brian O	53%	X	X	X		X	X	X	X		X				X		P		P			P	P	P
Sherry P	58%	X	X		X	X	X	X	X			X	X	X			X		X					
Alita P	42%					X	X	X	X								X		X					
Karen S	74%				P	P	P	X	X	P	P	X	X			P	X		P		X	X	P	X
Stephen S	47%	X	X	X	X	X	X	X	X				X			X	X		X		X	X	P	P
Scott S	79%	X	X	X	X	X	X	X	X			X	X	X	X	X	X		X		X	X		
Denise S	89%	X	X	X	X	X	X	X	X	P	P	X	X	X	P	X	X		X		X	X	X	X
McKinley T	100%	X	X	X	X	X	X	X	X	P	X	X	X	X	X	P	X		X		X	X	P	X

Invited guests

	% of actual																							
Mike A	11%	X			X	X							X				X							
ALA	95%	X	X	X	X	X	X	X	X	X	X	X	X	X	X	X	X		X		X	X	X	X
Tim B	11%	X				X																		
Cheryl B	68%					P	X	P	X	P	P	P	P	P	P	P	P		P		P	P	P	P
Vince C	37%																				X	X		P
Annilyn D	84%	X	X		X	X	X	X	X	P	X	X	X	X	X	X	X		X		X	X	P	X
Nifty G	68%	X	X		X	X	X	X	X			X	X	X	X	X	X		X		X	X	X	X
Tom G	63%	X			X	X	X	X	X			P	P	P	P		X				P	X	X	X
Brian J	74%	X	X	X	X	X	X	X	X			X	X	X		X	X		X		X	X	X	X
Theresa K	5%																							
Ron K	11%											X	X											
Nancy M	37%	X			X	X	X	X	X	X	X	X	X	X	X	X	X		X		X	X	X	X
Jennifer N	32%				X	X					X	X	X				X		X					X
Kelsey O	37%				X						X	X							X					X
Harry P	16%				X							X					X							
Debby S	74%	P	P		X	X	X	X	X	P	P	P	P	P	P	P	P		P		P	P	P	P
Dave S (Lean Coach)	79%	X	X		X	X	X	X	X	X	X	X	X	X	X	X	X		X		X	X	X	X
Lonnie S	16%	P			P																			
Travis S	42%		P		X	X		X	X			P	P	P	X	X	X		X		X	X	X	X
Alex T	5%																							
Chuck V	84%	X	X		X	X	X	X	X	P	X	X	X	X	P	X	X		X		X	X	X	P

TOTAL:	43	17	25	27	30	26	26	25	27	21	22	25	21	19		26	30	28		27	27	24	26	26
		40%	58%	63%	70%	60%	60%	58%	63%	49%	51%	58%	49%	44%		60%	70%	65%		63%	63%	56%	60%	

X = present
P = on phone

Appropriate huddles include: Cascaded Huddle, Daily Temple, and Central Clinic Huddle

Figure 5.36   Daily huddle tracker form with attendance; monthly percentage of huddles conducted is at the top right.

Huddle Tracking- FY14 Week ending	7/1	7/2	7/3	7/4	7/5	7/6	7/7	7/8	7/9	7/10	7/11	7/12	7/13	7/14	7/15	7/16	7/17	7/18	7/19	7/20	7/21	7/22	7/23	7/24	7/25	7/26	7/27	7/28	7/29	7/30	7/31
Shahin M. Team																															
Matt B		1						1							1							1						1	1	1	1
Marshall C	1	1	1				1	1	1	1	1			1	1	1		1			1	1		1				1	1	1	1
Cyndy D	1	1	1				1	1	1	1					1	1	1	1			1	1			1			1	1	1	1
Candice G																					2	1	4	4				5	2		
Ron H		1					2							2	1	1	1	1			1		1	1				1			
Susan M	1	1					1	1		1				1	1			1			1	1	1		1						
Thom M									1		1					1														1	
Tricia M		1								1							1					1		1						1	1
Richard N			1											1							1		2					1			
Brian O	2								2							2					1	1	2							2	
Denise S	1														1							1	1	1				1	1	1	1
McKinley T	1	1	1				1	1		1	1																		1	1	

Each Dept. Leader must define appropriate huddles and track them

Figure 5.37   Two-deep huddle tracker for the leader from Figure 5.36 and all his direct reports.

Figure 5.38   S&W executive huddle attendance tracking and notes (blurred to obscure proprietary information).

Handwritten Trackers

During actual huddles, attendance is taken by hand as in Figure 5.39. In fact, S&W Lean Management Systems almost all started with handwritten, hand-updated, pen-to-paper charts and lists. This ensures rapid updates during the stand-up huddles—not after.

The authors strongly believe in the KISS principles—Keep It Simple, Steve. Most huddles require staff to "sign in" by either placing an X or their initials next to their name and under the huddle date as they enter the room. Sometimes a team will assign a recorder to take attendance. A goal for both percentage of scheduled huddles conducted and attendance was set by leaders.

Managing Two-Deep

Bob had an ah-ha moment in early 2012. Steve repeated the phrase "Leaders must manage two-deep" several times related to layered audits. Leaders need to ensure all staff were huddling and that they were

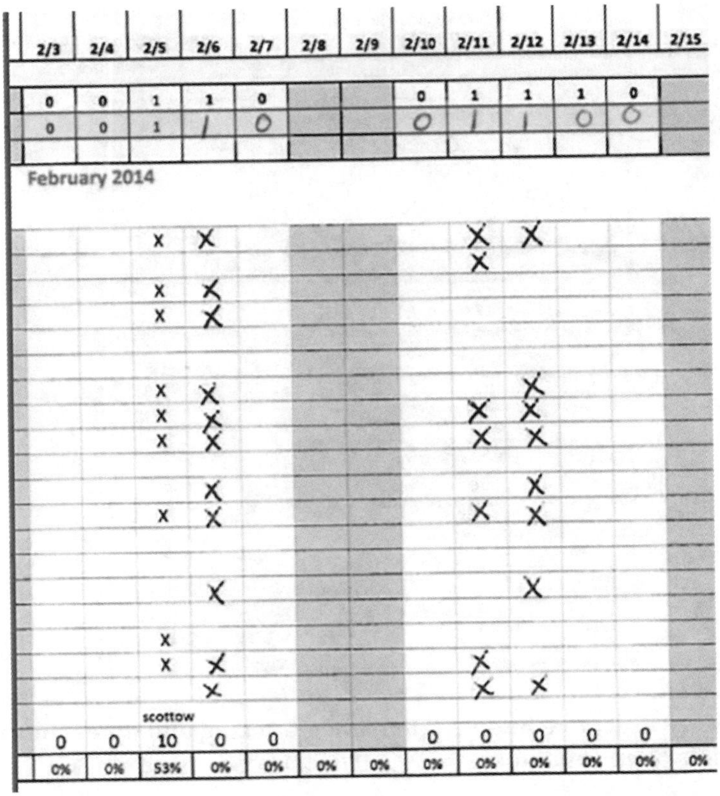

Figure 5.39 Huddle tracker; handwritten on the huddle board.

becoming more effective. Leaders help teams maintain momentum and spread good ideas. They also check and audit to ensure their direct reports, and their direct reports (two-deep) know and lead in a Lean way. Here is Bob's story.

As I learned huddle boards and how to track and audit them two-deep, one day it just struck me. This is the magic of building Lean Management Systems. When you create and lead your own daily huddle and then ensure your reports are aligned and huddling effectively, you teach them both what is important and how to apply Lean thinking to solve problems.

But, when you tell all leaders to track two-deep, they do this at all levels all the way up to the direct performer huddles. All huddle boards are tracked by not one but two or more leaders. This cascading demonstration of what is important and how to improve connects top to bottom in a simple direct-feedback system that is no longer dependent on a single leader. It links them all together. It becomes self-sustaining. However, getting our leaders to do this the first few times was difficult.

Therefore, as magic as huddles are, you cannot maximize their effectiveness without managing two-deep. It is a process. It is how S&W leaders communicated important opportunities and deployed strategy rapidly.

Spread

Two-deep is also how S&W *spread* good ideas and gains across its growing system. There were other methods for spreading successes, but it was easy for leaders to "walk" good ideas up and down their own chain of command. For instance, when leaders or staff saw ideas on someone else's huddle boards that worked, they helped spread it to other huddles. Leaders were required to check on the progress of idea spread. This is all part of managing two-deep. More detail on spread methods can be found coming up in Huddle Board Audit System: Layered Audits.

Communication

Another key part of two-deep was communication. Leaders must communicate important new imperatives to all levels of the organization throughout the year. This is a key role of leaders. However, how do leaders usually accomplish this? Probably in some form that is not read very well (email).

An example of how S&W communicated two-deep was when a region experienced a major change in expected revenue. The leaders needed actions to counteract the drop. As leaders walked this new information to every huddle, they identified issues and ideas, and cascaded the metrics and ideas rapidly to the other groups. Communicating two-deep closed the revenue gap within a few months as ideas flowed.

Then, leaders ensured feedback through Gemba walks and aligned metrics to check if all actions were working. If this is done right, in as little as two to three weeks you can completely change the way the organization is working through this quick communication cascading and feedback mechanism.

Speed is important in today's healthcare. Only through layered huddles can you change an organization 180 degrees in just weeks. S&W leaders

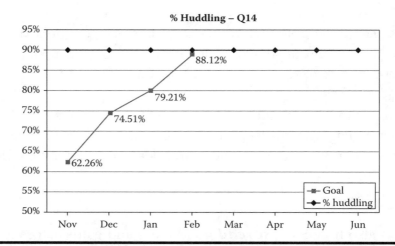

Figure 5.40 Percentage of all staff huddling daily or weekly; first you need a list of all huddle boards.

have seen this happen. Nothing moves the metrics faster than rapid PDCA cycles by all staff in their effective huddles.

Tracking Huddles Two-Deep

Regional senior leadership teams also tracked the percentage of all staff, from top-to-bottom, who huddle daily or weekly. Figure 5.40 shows the first four data points on a chart showing the percentage of all staff who huddle at least weekly.

Round Rock leaders did this first. They took ownership of all 105 huddle boards in their region and ensured they tracked all huddles. They assigned an administrator to collect all individual huddle-tracking spreadsheets at month-end. They set a goal of 90% and quickly met it! An administrator updated and posted this chart at the CEO's first leadership huddle every month.

Managing new changes two-deep and layered audits are similar. Layered audits will be explained in the next section.

Huddle Board Audit System

The authors would like to reveal some early weaknesses in their LMS-building adventure. It happens to also reveal the strength of it as well. Nearly every tool continues to improve! Sometimes staff charge off with an early version of a tool, only to have it change and improve a dozen times before they can complete a cycle of testing. This happened with the Huddle Board Audit Tool.

The earliest versions of huddle board audits were very lengthy! Impossibly so. They paralleled some of the multi-page "walking assessment" forms popularized in the early Lean manufacturing movement. Walking assessments with "radar charts" will be discussed in more detail in Chapter 6, Tip 10: Using Assessments. Steve first saw one of these in Hiroyuki Hirano's game-changing manual called *The JIT Implementation Guide.*[*] He had a multi-page walking assessment in the back of the manual.

Hirano divided a Lean transformation effort into 10 to 12 categories, loosely around each of the main TPS tools. He created audit sheets for each tool with a series of questions that guided the user to "score" the tool's maturity on a 1 to 5 scale. The auditor was to handwrite reasons for the score in each box. Staff would combine scores and then create action items to score higher in the next audit.

In S&W's earliest huddle board audits, the audit was divided into the parts of a Lean Management System (Visual Controls, Daily Accountability Process, and Leader Standard Work). Open-ended questions were used for each category, and then a general 1 to 5 scoring was added. Finally, on each page, the leader was to handwrite the rationale or reasons for the score. In practice, Steve's initial estimate of 10 minutes per huddle board was more like 45 to 50 minutes. Leaders revolted!

Figure 5.41 shows the next version of the LMS audit. What a difference one year makes! True to continuous improvement, Senior Lean Coach Michael Baratz and Round Rock senior leaders changed the audit in a major way.

Figure 5.41 shows an audit that was re-entered into the spreadsheet (from the paper form) so that the score was calculated. Since this was the leader's very first month huddling, their score was low—only 58% scored Yes (7 of 12 questions). A larger-sized version of this can be found in Figure 7.10.

Seeing the need to track and audit huddle boards, Round Rock leaders established a regional goal not only to track and audit, but also to move every board over a target score of 75%! Many new boards scored very low to start. This was both a great goal and a great challenge. Steve's staff needed to coach the leaders that the goal was not just to *score higher.* It was to make their huddles more *effective.*

---

[*] Hirano, Hiroyuki, *JIT Implementation Manual: The Complete Guide to Just-in-Time Manufacturing,* 2nd ed. (6-Volume Set), Productivity Press, 2009.

LMS Huddle Board Audit: *"Measuring the Journey"*					
Leader: **Rachel C**					**Year 1 Form**
Department: **Inpatient XYZ**		Audit Month:	5/1/14		
Board Location: **ABC Region - Pharmacy**					

Go see the Huddle Board; <u>Key Elements</u>: Trend Charts, Analysis. and Implemented Ideas!				
	Goals	**Yes**	**No**	**Notes & Ideas to improve**
Q1. Are there metrics posted?	3–5 Metrics	☑ Yes	☐ No	
Q2 . Are the metrics getting better over time? (Yes or No)	moving toward the Goal?			☑ Yes ☐ No (not scored yet for 'Year 1')
Q3. Are there Trend Charts?		☑ Yes	☐ No	
Q4. An there clear Goals?		☑ Yes	☐ No	
Q5. Are the metrics tracked daily or weekly?	some monthly for T3 and T2 are OK	☑ Yes	☐ No	Some are monthly
Q6. Do the Charts align with their Leader's or System Goals?	show evidence of alignment	☐ Yes	☑ No	Area for improvement
Q7. Are the Charts *current* today or the most recent period?	daily or weekly	☑ Yes	☐ No	
Q8. Is there *evidence* of analysis of Metrics?	evidence = fishbone, 5 Whys, Why chart, list of reasons	☑ Yes	☐ No	
Q9. Is there a place to Capture Ideas?		☐ Yes	☑ No	Area for improvement
Q10. Have Ideas been captured in the last 2 months?		☐ Yes	☑ No	Yes, but not on huddle boards
Q11. Have Ideas been Implemented?	New: please list implemented ideas as of current audit mouth	☐ Yes	☑ No	in progress
Q12. Is there follow-up by leaders (an elevation system) for leaders to take up crosscutting Ideas and issues?		☑ Yes	☐ No	
Q13. Does feedback come back to the team on elevated Ideas or issues? (Yes or No)				☐ Yes ☑ No (not scored yet for 'Year 1')
Q14. Is there *evidence* the team is huddling at least weekly per huddle schedule?	evidence = huddle tracking log, attendance sheet	☐ Yes	☑ No	Meet daily, but not recording: attendance is mandatory if on duty
		7	5	
Monthly Audit Score:		58%	42%	

Figure 5.41 "First Year" huddle board audit form.

The first step in all tracking was a key—a spreadsheet of all huddle boards and locations needed to be maintained. Round Rock started with over 100 boards across its region. If a huddle board audit score was not sent to the "collector," a zero was entered. This quickly encouraged leaders to get their scores in!

Scores increased rapidly after their leader set an aggressive goal. However, this improvement would not sustain unless leaders stayed active in the audit process while creating new habits.

Figure 5.42 shows what became known as the leader monthly huddle audit Quad Chart. The top left chart shows percentage of all teams huddling daily or weekly. The top right chart shows the percentage of all teams that submitted a monthly huddle score (if two or three scores were submitted when layered auditing, the lowest score was used). The bottom left chart shows the percentage of all huddle boards with scores greater than 75%. The final chart shows average audit scores of those that were turned in.

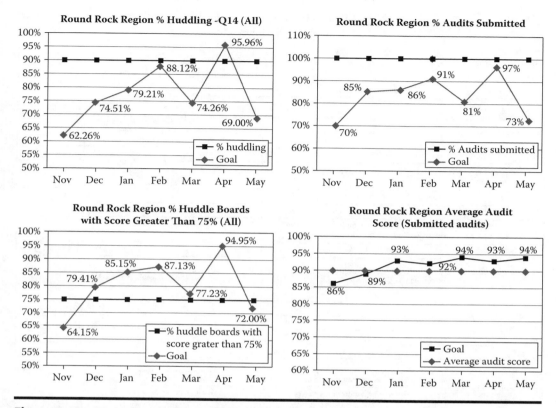

Figure 5.42 Year 1—Leader monthly huddle audit Quad Chart summary.

A single audit collection spreadsheet produced all four trend charts with minimal entry. In May, a leadership change in this region created a small drop. They closed the fiscal year strong, above all goals.

The S&W Lean team was learning just as much or more as the leaders and staff. They needed to reduce the time it took for leaders to audit. A new set of audit questions was needed. It needed to be quicker than the current list. However, S&W also needed to ensure that the huddles were actually moving all metric charts toward their goals!

Figure 5.43 shows the new "second year" huddle board audit form. This was used after the basic one was in place for more than one year. Notice the number of questions reduced from 14 down to just seven. However, the leader must now document (briefly) a few ideas implemented and any metrics that improved during that month. Metric improvement was a focus in the second year. A larger-sized version of this can be found in Figure 7.11.

LMS HUDDLE BOARD AUDIT TOOL
"Measuring the Journey"

Huddle Leader:		Audit Month:		
Audit submitted by:		Scheduled Huddle Days and Times:		
Department:		**Submit audit to XXXX by last day of the month**		
Board Location:				

Question	Notes	Yes	No
Q1. Are huddle board metrics getting better over time (Trending data)?	**IF YES** - List metric that improved during the current audit month. Include details (i.e. Pt. Sat improved from 51% to 73%)	☐ Yes	☐ No
Q2. Are there clear Goals on the Trend Charts?		☐ Yes	☐ No
Q3. Are the Charts tracked daily/weekly and *current today* or the most recent period?	Daily or weekly (Some monthly for T3 and T2 are OK)	☐ Yes	☐ No
Q4. How many Ideas were documented on your huddle board this month?		QTY:	
Q5. Have Ideas been Implemented in the <u>current</u> audit month?	**IF YES** - List implemented ideas	☐ Yes	☐ No
Q6. Is there follow-up by leaders (an elevation system) for leaders to take up crosscutting Ideas and issues and is feedback provided?		☐ Yes	☐ No
Q7. Is huddle leader communicating regularly about system integration?		☐ Yes	☐ No

Ideas *Implemented* - Current Month	Ideas needed feedback from elevation
1)	1)
2)	2)
3)	3) Year 2 Form
4)	4)
5)	5)

Metric Improvements - Current Month		
Metric	Metric at beginning of the month	Metric at end of the month

Figure 5.43   New "second year" huddle board audit form.

The average time to audit a board remained about the same. However, documenting these new ideas and metrics each month took longer for the administrators. It was worth it!

Layered Audits

Another critical management responsibility in building LMS is layered audits. All audits must be layered to be effective. Steve learned this concept early in his career, but had difficulty installing it in healthcare. A foundation tool like standard work requires layered audits. The same was true for huddle tracking and huddle board audits.

A layered audit is both simple and difficult at the same time. Concept: A leader does an audit and then another higher-level leader also checks it,

One of Steve's mentors at Johnson Controls (JCI) Automotive was Georgetown General Manager Phil Beckwith. As Steve wrote in *Stories*, multiple university case studies were written about how Phil, as he tells it, was pulled, kicking and screaming, into the Toyota way.

Steve learned many forms of layered audits from Phil and Toyota. One was how Phil audited all problem-solving teams weekly! There were about 50 problem-solving teams active when Steve first saw Phil's system. Toyota wisely required JCI and all vendors to maintain six straight weeks of zero defects before their teams could stop and celebrate.

Problem-solving teams met either daily for serious problems or weekly for others. They were required to fax their updated A3 forms to Phil. As General Manager, Phil insisted his teams must find and eliminate the root of all problems. Here was Phil's problem-solving audit system.

Phil showed Steve a fax machine in his room. It was placed directly over a large box. Phil reached into the box, grabbed a random handful every day, and then hit the Gemba. He would find a leader or worker listed on a form, thank them for their hard work, and then ask how he could help them move forward on their problems. Every problem-solving team was touched by Phil at least once each month! Don't make it complicated.

and coaches the supervisor who filled it out. Sometimes the supervisor will leave his or her audit form on their board or in a labeled folder. A director then audits by writing on top of the posted audit, coaching the huddle board leader if incorrect. An executive team member would also do the same.

At S&W, Huddle Leaders must self-audit their boards every month. A manager or director audits all their direct report boards bi-monthly (half one month and half the next month). However, the key is for the executive team to audit all huddle boards quarterly (e.g., the seven Round Rock executives audit their own boards, and then all 105 boards in the region quarterly,

A manager or director audits all their direct reports bi-monthly (half one month and half the next month). However, they key is for the executive team to audit all huddle boards quarterly.

As audit scores went up, the percentage of staff saying their huddles were effective went up as well.

which is about one board per week). All audits are collected by a point-of-contact in each region and improvements are rolled up.

Round Rock's first-year audit scores demonstrated something Steve and others on the Lean team expected. As audit scores went up, the percentage of staff saying their huddles were effective went up as well. The audits were working. There is no other intervention a leader can do to move toward effective huddles than installing a layered audit of all huddle boards with a clear, visual goal. Leaders set an initial goal of 75% of all huddle boards above a minimum acceptable score (75%). They did—within just a few months.

However, Round Rock's second-year audit results were even more significant. Since the second year form in Figure 5.43 asked for total ideas, implemented and elevated, they rolled up and presented these at the first leadership meeting of every month. They also tracked ideas elevated and percentage of all audits submitted. This monthly summary allowed good ideas to spread quickly to other areas. They also listed all elevated ideas.

Figure 5.44 shows the Year 2–Leader monthly summary huddle audit Tri Chart. The top left and right charts were the same as previous (percentage of all teams huddling daily or weekly, and percentage of all teams that submitted a monthly huddle score).

The bottom left chart shows the cumulative number of all ideas that were generated and the number implemented on the same graph. Some ideas took more than one month to fully check out, so implemented lags those generated. Again, a single audit collection spreadsheet produced all three trend charts with minimal entry.

The most significant items captured in the second year audit form were metric improvements. When auditing, leaders would write down which metric moved toward their goals in the past period, and by how much. These improvements were put into a simple list in the monthly audit slide set with the Tri-Charts each month. They were then ready to be rolled up into financial and other measures.

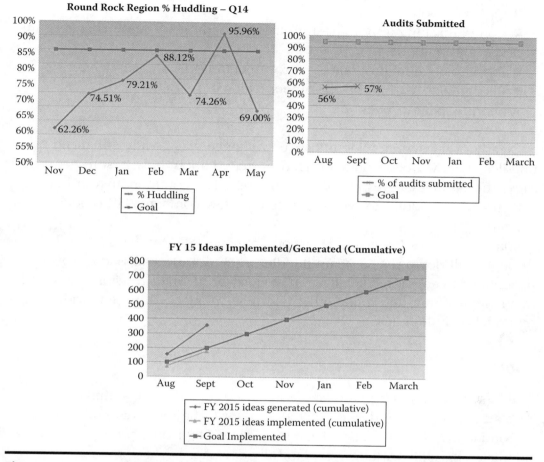

Figure 5.44   Year 2—Leader monthly summary huddle audit Tri-Chart.

Note: Why audit something if nothing is done with them? ***A bias for action*** is taught to S&W leaders in their LMS-building course. Why? If a supervisor or team just "pencil-whipped" their Huddle board audit form, it likely means their huddle is not effective either.

Lean Tools S&W Uses in Huddles

This is where the power of LMS and huddles grows. Before listing specific Lean tools mastered and used by huddle leaders, it would be good to list other general good things accomplished in huddles:

■ Casting vision
■ Communicating important stuff, like HR and organization changes, timing, and reminders
■ Introducing new programs, improvement efforts, and service lines
■ Recognizing staff and peer-to-peer (Kudos)
■ Sharing, peer-to-peer

Nearly every system-wide initiative or change was greatly enhanced by huddles at S&W. Before huddles, leaders fretted about how best to get messages through to staff, especially urgent ones. The common answer became, "Just use your huddles to communicate that new computer/HR/other change."

Major initiatives like Same Day Appointments (SDA) were managed through drill-down data at team huddles in clinics. Back-to-budget, overall patient flow, geographic localization of hospitalists, inter-disciplinary rounding, length-of-stay, and many other efforts were attacked by staff with progress tracked in huddles.

Tools

The best way to describe the Lean tools used in huddles is foundational. As stated earlier, S&W desired that all of their frontline leaders be capable of conducting any foundation Lean tool in the TPS House with their staff in huddles. This skill set takes years to fully develop.

As you can see in Figure 5.45, foundation tools and principles include standard work, waste elimination, PDCA cycles, visual management, and even A3 problem solving (a key part of robust processes and stabilization in general). All of these must be understood and led by supervisors, and thus taught intentionally to them. The slower process was to "transfer the ownership" of the foundation principles from Lean department-facilitated efforts to supervisors and their teams.

One misstep. Like many organizations, S&W taught supervisors Lean tools in a thorough four-day Lean Practitioner course (Lean 201). This course also taught them 100 other principles. All leaders were classroom-trained in A3 problem solving, twice. It did not work well. What worked well was A3 Waves, discussed earlier.

Supervisors learned other foundation principles and tools by participating and leading VSM and Kaizen workshops, and through one-on-one coaching by their Lean coaches.

Developing The Toyota *House* Model:
Foundation First!

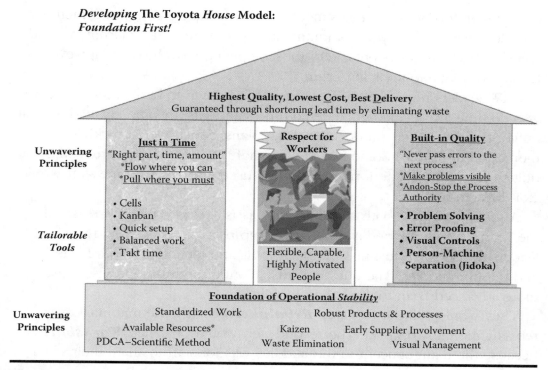

Figure 5.45   Toyota House Model.

In the Toyota House model in Figure 5.45, the authors changed one phrase typically seen in the TPS House foundation because it is different for healthcare than it is for manufacturing. Basic "Preventive Maintenance" was changed to "Available Resources." S&W leaders ensured they have available resources in general. However, they also used huddle boards to track turnover and cross-training needs for their teams.

What they do next is unique in healthcare, and probably any industry. Supervisors can use huddles to rebalance and workshare. More detail on this is shown in Chapter 6, Tip 18: Kaizen or Kaikaku, but a general description of what happens is summarized next.

Rebalance and Workshare in Huddles

Steve taught S&W leaders to use simple, visual work balance tools as they entered another tough budget preparation period. There was a great need, and Lean thinking would be part of the solution again. Losses mounted to end the previous year in some sectors, mainly due to continued revenue erosions on top of heavy investments in new facilities. You may remember that Bob made a no-layoff commitment. There were non-replacements and some cutbacks in areas outside of those applying Lean heavily. However, no layoffs were due to applying Lean.

S&W leaders needed to bring their staffing down to budget levels. There was no time for detailed engineered time standards. Income just had to beat outgo. Budget models produced staffing plans, which were quickly communicated to leaders. Some had just a handful to float downward, some had quite a few. All high performers could be used elsewhere. Some staff would exit through turnover.

After a small pilot with administrative assistants at Children's Hospital, the Lean team developed a simple two-step process. They would teach S&W leaders to use some Just-in-Time pillar tools and techniques with leaders, and then in huddles. The question was, "Could frontline supervisors use more advanced Lean tools in their huddles?"

They would call the first step ***Rebalance*** because the main task was rebalancing the workload. The second step would be called ***Workshare*** because the main concept in the huddles was for staff to share their workload.

Rebalance exercises were led by a Lean coach with a department supervisor and sometimes a lead staff member. It was possible that some departments might need cuts, so it was sensitive. The starting point was not weeks of time observations. There was no time for this, and the budget was clear in most cases. Each department was given its expected staffing level. They were to start the fiscal year at these levels. Most had just a few weeks to get there. Not all departments needed cuts. Some grew. The exercises were done equally on those needing cuts and those growing.

Figures 5.46 through 5.49 show Steve's actual flipcharts used to roll out Rebalance and Workshare. Using four simple flipchart pages, you can learn how to Rebalance workloads initially with a leader and then Workshare daily in huddles.

Please note that the Post-it notes in the figures below are not to scale (e.g., the amount of time needed for each task on a Post-it was not equal, nor is the height of the Post-it equal to an exact amount of time). In addition, the Lean coach often spent a few hours just listening to the supervisor before starting Rebalance. Cuts were never easy at S&W. After listening deeply, the coach would say, "OK, the budget stinks, but it's not changing. Now, let's see if we can get the work done by the ones remaining."

Rebalance Process

Figure 5.46 (left): <u>Before</u> staffing and load. The supervisor and a lead clinical staff member write the top 10 or so tasks for each general job type (e.g., Patient Service Specialist-PSS, Medical Assistant-MA, etc.) on Post-its. Work tasks (brief: noun-verb) were documented along with rough task times if possible. The Post-its do not need to be in sequential order, and the goal is to capture 80% or more of tasks done daily or weekly. This allows leaders to capture most work time quickly.

If they were uncertain about any task time, they would observe a few staff members and update the Post-its. Then, they marked mainly Non-Value Added (NVA) tasks with a red dot. Note: Sometimes jobs are similar and tasks for multiple staff of the same type can be grouped together.

Figure 5.46 (right): <u>After</u> staffing and load (blank). Supervisor and lead staff member will move Post-its one at a time from the Before to the After Chart, asking, "Can this task be done by someone else easily or with some cross-training?" (Mark with "X" for cross-training.) Write cross-training tasks needed for each staff member on the cross-training chart (Figure 5.47).

On the After chart, if the PSS headcount budgeted needs to reduce from six to four, in the first "pass," Post-its would be moved off staff five and six to staff one through four. In the second pass, leaders remove NVA work and then keep moving the Post-its until the work is fairly balanced. The Lean coach may enter the data into his or her spreadsheet to ensure balance (see Figure 5.48). Do not move Post-its marked with a red dot (NVA).

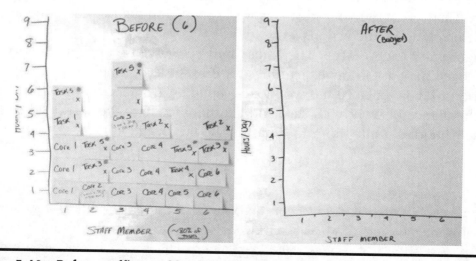

Figure 5.46   Before staffing and load (left); After staffing and load chart (right) is ready for Post-it moves to rebalance.

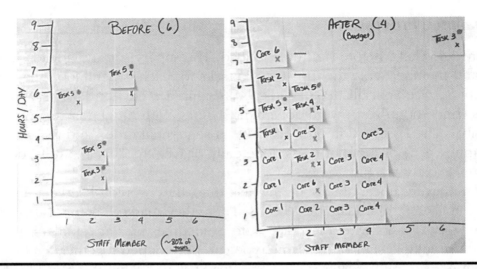

Figure 5.47 Before—NVA tasks remain (left); After—staff member 1 could be over-loaded (right).

Figure 5.47 (left): Before. The Non-Value-Added (NVA with red dots) Post-its remain on the Before Chart. Only move them to the After Chart *after* you use Lean tools to reduce or eliminate waste in these tasks. Even though they are not to scale, Steve encourages leaders to cut the bottom of the Post-it off, to represent that some wasted time was removed before it was shared some-where else.

Just shifting the waste is like playing whack-a-mole with tasks no one wants to do! Rewrite the task on another Post-it and move it to the Actions Chart (Chart 3). Write your ideas for waste reduction next to each one and immediately work the actions.

Figure 5.47 (right): After. The After Chart is now close enough. Supervisor and coach may not know exact times for each task, but they have a secret weapon to daily balance the workload—huddles. Leaders will now try this rough balance of work with staff and get them to share the workload daily in their huddles. Only the After Chart is shown to staff.

Steve encourages leaders to cut the bottom of the Post-it off, to represent that some wasted time was removed before it was shared somewhere else. Just shifting the waste is like playing whack-a-mole with tasks no one wants to do!

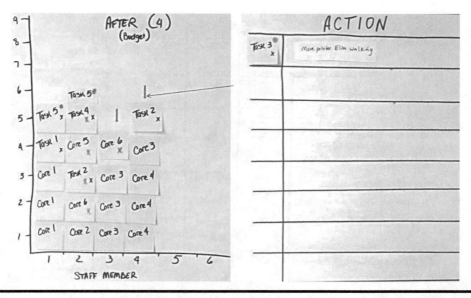

Figure 5.48   After chart (left); ideas to reduce waste and improve balance (right).

Workshare in the Huddle

The After Chart is taken to the huddle to Workshare with staff. With assistance from a Lean coach, the team leader says, "The budget stinks, but it's not changing. Our Lean coach and lead clinical team member helped me get it close, but we need your help. We think the workload is almost balanced for the four staff that remain. So, we need you to try this out today. We will check it daily and share the work fairly if someone is overloaded. If you see waste, let's reduce it on the spot. I will be in the Gemba all week as we work this out."

In the next daily huddle, staff move some work around. They reduce a few wastes. They try some more until the work is fairly well balanced.

Figure 5.48 (left): After. This technique has another benefit. Once staff realize Workshare is a great way to give and receive help, they start using it daily to balance the normal variation in their days (which can be quite a bit in healthcare). For example, in the morning huddle "Staff 1" says she expects to be overloaded (for proper reasons). "Staff 3" and "Staff 4" pick up two tasks they have been cross-trained to do (see downward arrows showing moved Post-its).

Figure 5.48 (right): Rebalance Ideas. Supervisor and staff write ideas for waste reduction next to each Post-it that was moved or changed and immediately work the actions.

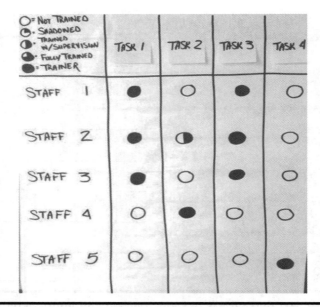

Figure 5.49   Cross-training matrix; updated with every shift of work tasks.

Figure 5.49: Cross-Training Matrix. Key: Most Rebalance and Workshare will require cross-training staff to do the "shifted" tasks. Do not shift tasks to a staff member that is not trained to do the task. Supervisor and lead trainer ensure enough cross-training so that both the supervisor and staff member feel the team member can do the new task. This chart was posted on the huddle board. Staff and leader started closing the gaps immediately to get most staff to fully trained (at least three pieces of the pie).

Figure 5.50: Rebalance Spreadsheet. Data were entered into a simple spreadsheet. Job categories that were "light" stuck out like a sore thumb. S&W leaders marveled that these were often the areas that demanded staff be replaced immediately when they turned over. Some needed it, some did not.

Again, these tasks were not in sequence, and it only represented about 80% of the tasks. In addition, task times were just estimated. However, the analysis yielded a good starting point for good team members and their leader to do daily adjustments. In fact, after the initial shock of not replacing a staff member or two, nearly every team said the resulting work was easier with the ones that remained after Worksharing in huddles for a few weeks.

	PSS CI/CO	PSS REC/CI	PSS SEC	PSS II OR Sched	PSS I INS	PS Blank
Task / Qty / Time	Task	Task				
Calling No Shows	30 / 5 / 150	0 / 0				
Cashing In/Out	6 / 21 / 126	3 / 44 / 132	Template (Mnth) 0.4 / 60 / 24			
Forms	8 / 5 / 40	0 / 0	Pre Cert 15 / 60 / 900			Drs. Signature on Consent Forms 0 / 0
Instructions	100 / 2 / 200	0 / 0	Pat. Issues 1 / 15 / 15			Faxing 0 / 0
Work Qs	0 / 5 / 0	0 / 0	Forms 4 / 10 / 40	PRN Consults 6 / 40 / 240	PreCert Ver. 5 / 60 / 300	OB Packets 0 / 0
Sched Appt Cmplx	45 / 30 / 1350	6 / 30 / 180	Sched Surg 10 / 20 / 200	Work Qs 0 / 0 / 0	Phone Calls Ins. Co. 0 / 0	Puts up Supplies 0 / 0
Sched Appt Quick	0 / 5 / 0	0 / 5 / 0	ReSched 12 / 10 / 120		Contact Pts about Pmnts 0 / 0	Scan Forms 0 / 0
Check In (Late)	0 / 5 / 0	75 / 10 / 750	Letters 6 / 1 / 6	Pre Cert 10 / 60 / 600	Research Issues 0 / 0	Get Clipboard Ready 0 / 0
Check In	75 / 5 / 375	250 / 1 / 250	Templates (Daily) 8 / 60 / 480	Consent Forms 10 / 1 / 10	Infertility 0 / 0	Move Patients 0 / 0
Ins. Ver.	75 / 10 / 750	70 / 10 / 700	Work Qs 0 / 0 / 0	Monitor Snap Board 0 / 0	Monthly Medicaid 0 / 0	Greets Patients 0 / 0
Orders / Assign Pager	400 / 1 / 400	40 / 1 / 40	Phone Calls 128 / 5 / 640	Sched Surg 10 / 5 / 50	PreCert Ver Ins 250 / 0.5 / 125	

Staff	PSS CI/CO	PSS Rec/CI	PSS Clerical (Sec)	PSS II OR Schedule	PSS I INS	PS Service Rep.
Key Task	CI/CO	Rec/CI	Clerical (Sec)	OR Schedule	INS	Service Rep.
Total Task Time (min)	3391	2052	2425	900	425	0
# Staff Req'd by Budget	6	4	8	1	1	1
Total Staff Time	2700	1800	3600	450	450	450
# FTE Current Staff	7.5	4.6	5.4	2.0	0.9	0.0
Over/Under Staff	(1.5)	(0.6)	2.6	(1.0)	0.1	1.0

Figure 5.50 Rebalance spreadsheet (Over/Under used with judgment due to the rapid data analysis method).

Same Day Appointments (SDA) Effort—Using Huddles

S&W deployed a major effort to change access forever for patients in central Texas. Many leaders tried in the past to get an SDA effort going. It is difficult. For decades, S&W on its main campus was known (tongue in cheek) as "Sitting & Waiting." Patients loved the high level of care they received. They loved their S&W doctors and nurses. They just could not get an appointment when they wanted one! Many stated they waited 20 weeks or more to see a specialist. This was not right.

One competitor helped S&W. A competitor put up a billboard right outside S&W's Memorial complex. It was a proverbial finger in the eye. In the Executive Huddle, leaders were livid. Figure 5.51 shows a picture of the billboard. S&W internal staff could joke about the nickname Sit & Wait, but not a competitor!

The SDA Task Force met within a week and the effort was started within a month. Today, if you call S&W for most appointment types, you will hear the friendly person on the phone ask, "Would you like to be seen today?" Many patients were speechless when they heard this offer. As of this writing, over 96% of all patients desiring same-day appointments that fit the rules get one!

The key to deploying this so rapidly was huddles. A simple report showing the percentage of all SDA requests that were accommodated by each clinic was pulled by clinic leaders weekly. They posted it on their huddle boards, and discussed ways to accommodate these good patients with urgent or pressing needs to be seen. It worked.

Figure 5.51   Competitor's billboard outside S&W's main hospital.

Chapter 6

Tips and Techniques

Tips and techniques learned while transforming operations are useful. They can keep you out of the bear traps that trip up others on a similar path. Change is hard. Therefore, leaders need to learn, try, prepare, and learn some more. Borrow the learning curve of a sensei, someone you trust who has a similar philosophy as you. Some general tips are offered here, followed by detailed ones that are numbered.

The first general tip will be for internal change agents—for all the Lean coaches reading this and actively facilitating improvements. The tip is this: you are doing something very good. It is an honor to be chosen to help build a culture of continuous improvement—sometimes one process and leader at a time. If you are applying Lean in your "spare" time or full-time, find other change agents to help you. Tell everyone what can be done and why. Be mission-focused. Your energy will be contagious. Also, widen your toolkit. Attack all gaps, even quality. Partner with your Quality team.

Another good one for Lean coaches is to network and buddy-up with other Lean coaches, even those outside your industry. In fact, make sure you are sharing with others outside your industry. As the authors write this book, they are sharing with another local industry partner further along their Lean journey. If your boss complains about visiting "non-healthcare sites," tell them your sensei, Steve-san, said you need to do this.

Another important tip in general for leaders and coaches is to never, never stop learning. The body of knowledge of TPS applied to non-manufacturing is growing rapidly. Some blogs and websites have suspect "knowledge," but remember, you must work through learn-apply cycles yourself. Give yourself some grace to make mistakes—just learn from them.

Steve asks every coach he meets, "Who is your sensei?" Many consultants now throw that title around, so please be careful. To be a good sensei, you must have learned under a good sensei. Even those who have implemented Lean for a while should go back under a sensei. Their methodology sticks better and can move you along your journey slower (yes, slower).

Now for some general tips for leaders. The authors would like to prepare you for some things they wished others had told them early in their journeys. One is that things will sometimes appear *worse* before they get better. The reason for this is simple. A Lean management system highlights and exposes problems and waste. Leaders who are not prepared for the onslaught of issues, embarrassing data, and waste often "turtle up" and back away from Lean system building. It is hard to see and hear so many exceptions to what they thought was their finely tuned system. It will take more time and presence in the Gemba to accept the good in problem finding.

Another tip is to prepare for some specific pushbacks, now that you know they are coming. One is "It will never work here." Steve recommends that you use the power of focus. Focus your transformation work in a pilot area for enough time to demonstrate Lean tools and build Lean management systems. Move fast. Then, when the naysayers pipe up, just say, "It can and it does. Come and see!"

Another pushback you must prepare for is the "laggards." Many middle and top leaders will not accept the people-focused, servant-leader principles necessary in Lean transformation. It is said that 10% of staff will be leaders adopting changes, 80% will be followers, and another 10% will be laggards actually fighting the changes. They often give lip service when the big boss is around.

Steve recommends discussing in advance which behaviors will be acceptable and which ones need to be dealt with immediately, including moving the naysayer out of the Lean areas or even letting them go. Steve has seen many organizations get wind under their sails and take off with Lean after just one naysayer is quickly dealt with. Steve saw staff thank their bosses who finally moved the knuckle-draggers out!

That said, allow some grace for leaders and middle managers until they have tasted and seen that Lean is good. Often, top leaders are trained and see the "magic," but then impatiently expect all other staff to see and know what they just learned. The learning and adapting will be slow for most middle managers.

A final general tip is on change. As you build LMS, every job will change. Every one. From the floor sweeper to the President. Every job must change. For workers, there will be huddles and thousands of successful PDCA cycles around their ideas. For leaders, there is a new way and a new "day." They will experience full-blown LMS-building, leader standard work, layered audits, and increased Gemba time. What they get in return is nothing short of career or even life changing.

Tip 1: To All Leaders: Have Patience!

The biggest tip the authors offer you is to have patience! Rome wasn't built in a day. You need to **go *slow* to go *fast***. The battle is for the minds and hearts of all staff. Edicts, consultants, emails, and rah-rah speeches do not transform. The Lean philosophy and tools must be understood and used by all staff, not just by a few colored belt or experts in your organization. This will take time.

Steve and Bob have a running joke. Bob often states, "If I knew how long building a culture of continuous improvement would take, I probably would not have started!" We hope that you see both the humor as well as the truthfulness of Bob's statement. His humility shows as well. He didn't know what he didn't know.

Bob would often ask, "How long will this phase or effort take?" Steve answered, "We can get quite far in the next year or two." He wasn't lying. He just wasn't telling Bob that it would take much longer to standardize,

Video: Bob Pryor presenting the *President's Award* for best Lean project, CLIP Fair, November 3, 2011

We've only just started on this journey. Toyota has been at this for a long time; much longer than four years. When we talk to people at Toyota, do you know what they say about themselves? They say, "We are just scratching the surface." So, if Toyota is just scratching the surface, maybe we are just starting to make a dent too. I truly believe, if everyone works together continuing to improve, some days a little bit and some days a lot, we will lead the healthcare industry through the tough decades approaching. They will say, "We wish we were more like Scott & White!" This is how we are going to get there!

Let's take a breath, and all give each other a hand. You are all winners!

sustain, and then spread these principles. Many of S&W's early models and drawings for LMS showed 5 to 7 years before supervisors "owned" the foundation. This is a reasonable timeframe to turn all staff into waste-busters and problem solvers.

Was it worth it? This is a valid question. Bob's short answer is, emphatically, "Yes!" Today, he is very glad for every step of his journey, and considers himself just starting.

The question in Bob's mind was not, "What is the ROI?" or "Should we ask all staff for ideas?" For Bob, the questions were, "Why would we not engage them fully—mind and body?" and then "How best do we do this?" As stated earlier, Bob's philosophy was grounded in his belief in people.

There was great wisdom in doing this when Bob and his leaders did. As more and more healthcare revenue "capitates" (fixed reimbursement for every "covered life"), this will become much harder! No matter which way healthcare turns, a big part of the solution will include turning on the idea power latent in the minds of your Most Valuable Players—your people.

Steve developed a good timeline that best demonstrates the need for patience. Figure 6.1 shows a continuum from –10 progressing all the way to +4. Most consultants and even "early adopter" leaders feel that they can do an intervention to move staff members from –10 all the way to 0 (decision point, sometimes referred to as "drinking the Kool-Aid"). This should never be an instant goal.

Those who have spent time under a sensei set a different goal: Move one-leader-at-a-time through a *Thinking Change* continuum one-step-at-a-time. It is very rare for someone to "leap" from –10 to 0. Also, don't miss the fact that you could be the "messenger" on early steps of this pathway.

Steve would like to thank his friend and itinerant preacher, Tom Harmon, for the idea behind this model. Tom sent this to attendees of a conference at Camp Barakel around 2002. It was printed in a *Faithful Men of Michigan* newsletter around this same time.

Here is another great tip: If you see a good format or model, use it. Don't reinvent the wheel. That is waste. Wasteful tasks usually start with "re-" as in re-do, re-draw, or re-invent.

Patience. Remember Lean is like a diet. It makes sense—just eat less and move more. Dang is it tough to make it happen every moment of every day! The tools in this book should give you both the confidence to try and the courage to keep trying in the face of obstacles, real and created. Keep moving. Keep trying.

Actively resisting change	−10
Going his/her own way; busy firefighting	−9
Aware of something different in messenger	−8
Has positive attitude toward messenger	−7
Aware of difference in areas shown by messenger; still skeptical	−6
Learns key principles	−5
Has positive attitude toward principles	−4
Sees initial trials of lean thinking (by others)	−3
Sees some success in his or her own area with principles	−2
First trials on their own with lean tools; heavily involved	−1
Decision: Lean Thinking works for me!	0
Tries/spreads lean to more areas under their control	1
Recognition by leaders and others of success	2
Teaching others how to think lean, apply tools	3
Lean thinking zealot	4

Figure 6.1   Change continuum; staff move through one box at a time, be patient.

Tip 2: Make It Visual!

A key Lean principle is to "make it visual." As in, make all problems visual, make the "bad" condition "stick out like a sore thumb," or display an important metric large and visible so all can see. There are hundreds of applications of this principle. Making important stuff visual is also the key to more effective huddles.

Four ways to use huddle boards to make it visual (and to make it happen) are:

1. Post trend charts with goals clearly marked on them.
2. Post leader audits on the huddle board.
3. Post a cross-training matrix showing every staff member's progress (or lack thereof) and readiness to help share workload.
4. Post elevated ideas and track them through completion.

Steve and Bob have seen example after example of this phenomenon. The simple act of posting meaningful trend chart measures on a good team's board causes them to suggest immediate improvements to close the gaps. This is not merely a Hawthorne effect.

Here is what happens. When leaders choose four to five meaningful, aligned measures for staff and then update with handwritten dots on the charts showing today's progress, it declares to all staff that these metrics are important! They can rally around a few focused measures of team success. When something is important and there is a visible gap (between actual and expected), if allowed, staff will think of ways to improve it! Now, what if every team member thought of a small way to close every gap—every day?

Another visual "win" is to post all leader huddle board audits. This helps in two ways. Staff see the audit and gaps. This gives them a chance to make changes. Next, other high-level leaders also come to the board, see the gap, and use these audits as part of their layered audit system. For example, they can see, discuss, mentor, correct, and improve the local leaders' board and process together.

"Correct" is too strong of a word. Coach is better. If the supervisor says their board has only the latest updated charts, and each chart is over two months old, it creates a teachable moment. The score is not the key—a quick way to "check" ideas is the key. A layered audit levels the expectations about what huddles and visuals should be like.

Another visual "win" is to post a cross-training matrix. Figure 6.11 later in this chapter shows another example of a cross-training matrix. Cross-training is a difficult task in the busy world of healthcare. Even initial job training is difficult! However, it is essential to building high quality and safe care processes. In addition, it allows workload balancing of processes, which makes them fair for all staff.

The authors have found that posting important "sharable" tasks with each staff member's current status causes a very consistent reaction. Staff members immediately want cross-training. They want their circles filled in! There is a desire to learn all necessary tasks—even ones that help other team members. In addition, making this visual also applies positive pressure on the leaders, who need to make sure the training happens.

A fourth "win" for visuals is to post elevated ideas and track them through completion. As discussed earlier, this helps the teams and leaders. The teams see their ideas are valuable. They like to hear, "Your idea is going up to the big boss' board. She will be here with a progress report of all elevated items soon."

Once visual, leaders are accountable (and reminded) to move their teams' elevated ideas through to completion. Most leaders are very proud that their "Done" section is filled with completed ideas. Their good teams are counting on them! Remember what Bob said earlier, "This is the most fun I had in many months!"

Healthcare leaders and teams do not lack problems to work on. They lack the ability to execute daily, and especially on longer-term improvements. The very busy healthcare leaders and staff require this sort of visible accountability.

Tip 3: Be Flexible

Change is hard. Leaders need to be flexible regarding training, projects, and building LMS. It is more important that a team leader "own" his or her system than to force a standard format, especially as they are getting started. In addition, if a leader is drowning in problems, he or she may not be able to work through a detailed 17-week setup checklist for a project! Sometimes, relief must come quickly—as in today! A good sensei can help you determine when to be rigid and when to be flexible.

Regarding training, some staff are so busy they only have evenings and weekends. That said, these same staff are always counted on to give up said evenings and weekends. Steve and Bob do not believe any of their training offerings should be microwaved down to just hours. However, some tailoring is needed for busy staff.

A good example is S&W's *Nurse-Provider Lean* course. In just two short days, they learn the basics of Lean and LMS. This is not for nurse and physician leaders. Rather, it helps very busy staff. Courses can be split up over several mornings or evenings.

Another good example is the *LMS Quickstart* course. This three-hour *non-course* starts with a few slides, then works a group of supervisors through the process of building their own huddle board, and then practices with them how to lead a huddle. It is an effective use of their time, and leaves them with the ability to huddle immediately at the end of the session. S&W supervisors preferred to call this course *Build-a-Board* because that is what they were doing.

For projects, S&W started out using a rigid setup checklist and timing system. By the end of their sixth year of Lean, they realized many leaders could not even start a project due to rigid setup tasks and timelines. When they experienced crunch time, they ended up trying non-Lean "fixes" instead for many important efforts. They needed immediate relief from problems—temporary countermeasures.

Today, S&W Lean coaches work with the leaders they serve. They review key metrics needing improvement, as well as the leader's list of projects and efforts they are already working. The Lean coaches do not add a series of "Lean" projects to a leader's plate. Rather, they bring Lean thinking to the leader's already bulging list of current change efforts.

True, some overarching and cross-functional flow projects still need to be assigned by a system steering council. However, the Lean coaches jump into the projects already planned by top leaders. Even on traditional Lean interventions like VSM, Lean coaches now "walk" leaders through a flexible setup cycle. The same amount of setup may be needed, but they may only have two hours available tomorrow. So, they start with two hours, and "pull forward" some quick wins.

For LMS and huddle boards, Steve also found that ownership is critical. Early on, an HR leader emailed all staff, stating they must post a certain huddle idea on their boards and discuss it. It was not the employees' idea, and they let Bob and Steve know they felt manipulated being asked to post an idea that would not apply well in most areas.

Another required flexibility is with the boards themselves. You may have noticed in several pictures how different each board "looks." Supervisors need to feel that the huddle boards are their own— actually, their team's. Steve says, "Let them 'own' their boards." It is not good to be too prescriptive regarding which charts go where. True, S&W requires three vertical sections of any board—metric charts, analysis (Why charts), and ideas with elevation. Trend charts should be balanced in the four categories of metrics. But beyond that, teams are free to try many alternatives. Problem solving and project boards are often built on either side of the team's main huddle board.

Leaders owned their boards. They used the general guidelines and constantly evaluated whether they were working on measures important and meaningful to their staff. And, they used layered audits to continuously improve and standardize.

Tear 'em Down

S&W also encouraged staff to "tear down" the charts on their boards every three months or so. This allowed leaders to challenge what they were measuring, whether they were really impacting the bigger goals, and in general, to keep it fresh. Ideas can get stagnant unless leaders try multiple ways to keep it fresh.

Some areas even shifted the team to another wall, posting a blank flip chart, just to brainstorm the team's biggest issues and challenges. This usually started another acceleration of team ideas.

Tip 4: Understand How Change Affects People

Change is hard. The only ones that like change are babies with dirty diapers! Thus, the key job of leaders is to lead people through the change process. Many great books and articles have been written about change management.

BusinessWeek published an article that included five key questions that determine the likelihood that a major change will succeed or fail.[*] They are:

1. How is the vision (or change) different, better, and more compelling?
2. Are the leaders personally committed to the change?
3. Does the organization have the capacity to make the change?
4. How ingrained is the current culture?
5. Will the change actually deliver the identified outcomes?

The author highlighted Cisco Systems, Citrix Systems, and eBay as being able to adapt quickly to constantly changing environments. They have "fast-paced cultures driven by personal accountability for results."

---

[*] Buckley, Phil, The key to managing change, BusinessWeek.com, May 01, 2013.

Sounds slow, doesn't it? Too slow? When moving your entire organization through a big change, how well is your fast process working?

The author also highlighted how an international airline failed to adapt quickly. They announced details of a new aggressive cost-cutting program. But since then, the airline did not demonstrate the skill or culture to execute its plan effectively. Alienated employees staged ongoing strikes that have hurt customers and only *increased* costs.

In a recent leadership lesson, Stuart Briscoe* used the following, simple 3-step method to help people along the change process:

1. Start with where they are, not where you feel they should be.
2. Move in the direction they are willing to go (as long as it is in the general vicinity of our North Star).
3. Move at their speed, not yours.

Tip 5: What You Measure Is What You Get; So, Be Careful What You Measure

No one can serve two masters, for either he will hate the one and love the other, or he will be devoted to the one and despise the other. You cannot serve God and money.

—Matthew 6:24, Holy Bible (ESV)

Tip 6: Put Some "Teeth" into Hoshin Goals

You need to reward good behavior and challenge bad behaviors. Make sure your rewards do not reward *bad* behaviors! Seriously. Assemble your staff, and discuss each current goal asking, "Is there any way to 'game' this goal, to achieve it at the expense of other important things?' You will be surprised. Or shocked.

---

* Briscoe, Stuart, Disciples Behaving Badly, sermon at Temple Bible Church, Temple, TX on February 23, 2014.

Here is a rare older story that Steve did not publish in *Stories From My Sensei*.

Steve was greeted by the Plant Manager as he entered the auto seat assembly facility south of Detroit. The young Plant Manager told Steve, "I'll bet you can't find any waste in my world-class factory!" A challenge.

Steve walked alone to the receiving dock. He observed a forklift driver pull a rack of foam parts out of the trailer parked at the unloading dock. The driver jumped off his lift, walked to the side of the rack, looked closely at the label, and then climbed back on his lift. He proceeded to pull another rack out of the trailer, jump off, and stare at the label. Repeat 15 more times. He pulled the last rack out, jumped off, stared, and then scanned the label with his hand scanner.

It was what he did *next* that puzzled Steve. The young man proceeded to reload all the racks back into the trailer! Double handling (or triple). Steve walked forward saying, "Excuse me, sir, why are you putting the racks back into the trailer?" The forklift driver let out a string of cuss words, stating he hated the practice and was forced to do this.

The Plant Manager appeared around the corner, saw the interchange, and whirled away. Steve chased him down saying, "Why do your forklift drivers reload all the foam racks back into trailers?" The Plant Manager made a comment about forklift drivers always saying dumb things. Hmmm.

Steve walked back to the forklift driver. He asked, "Who told you to reload all the racks back into the trailers?" The forklift driver pointed his finger at the Plant Manager and said, "Him. He did."

The Plant Manager led Steve to the receiving office area. He said sheepishly, "My bonus measure this year is solely based on inventory turns." He continued, "My plant does not need to 'officially' receive the trailer full of foam until the last rack is scanned. It doesn't hit my books until the last rack is received."

Steve walked with the Plant Manager outside and then alongside the trailer. Steve asked, "What is the name on the side of the trailer?" The manager read off the company's name. Steve's company made all of its own foam, frames, seat covers—everything. Steve blurted, "You are screwing our own company! It's not some outside supplier, it's us!"

When Steve returned to his office, he took down a bulleted list called *Rules to Live By*. He read: **Rule #1: What you measure is what you get—so be careful what you measure**. He frowned. He crossed out the word *measure* and wrote the word *reward* over it. He pinned it back up on his wall.

It also really helps to align *behaviors* for all staff. Frequently communicate and publicly demonstrate commitment to your organization's values. One other thing S&W did in the second year of Hoshin Kanri was to place a large end-year evaluation value on accomplishing Hoshin goals.

S&W gave a 50% weighting on Hoshin goal performance. Another 25% was related to living out the organization's core values like teamwork, accountability, excellence, and innovation. Lastly, for leaders, they had 25% for key behaviors appropriate to their leadership level like execution, passion for results, influence, and leading teams. Giving Hoshin goals "teeth" in initial years was important.

The linkage between Hoshin goals and the annual review for the employee is both delicate and important. It is delicate because the minute you associate dollars to any goal, the natural tendency is for staff and leaders to create goals that are neither stretch nor strategic. It is also important to reward good behavior, as well as meeting goals. Bob says he met many physicians who were exceptional surgeons, but total jerks to staff and patients. Somehow, balance is needed as well when locking in goals.

The authors believe it is very important not to have any sort of all-or-nothing gamble on reward goals. You really need to encourage the process of goal setting with progress checks and balanced measures. Remember, good process, good results; bad process, eventually bad results.

The Hoshin process must tightly align with the mission and goals of the system. This is delicate because it has to do with money, but it is also strategic because when a person sees that he or she actually has a say—during catchball and progress reviews—it is empowering. There is a lot of discussion and planning up front to do Hoshin well. It differentiates this approach from most other one-way goal-setting approaches.

One small confession. Many leaders did not schedule enough time to do catchball properly with their staff at S&W. In fact, in the first year, some staff got to the end of the year, and said, "What are SWAT (Hoshin) goals?" It is difficult to move an entire organization overnight. Stay with it!

Tip 7: Partner with a Lean Leader— Even in Another Industry

The first leadership team from S&W was able to see Toyota in Kentucky. However, over 500 more leaders viewed TPS and LMS in action at Toyota in San Antonio, Texas. In addition, several S&W leaders had colleagues in other healthcare organizations, where additional benchmarking and best practice sharing could take place. Virginia Mason learned from Boeing. ThedaCare learned from Ariens, a snow blower company in Wisconsin.

Rather than absorb the view of only one consulting company, the authors strongly recommend partnering with local organizations who are farther along on their Lean journeys. This sharing helps leaders in particular. They rarely borrow ideas intact, but they like to hear different ways other leaders approached a similar situation.

Figure 6.2 shows a panel of leaders that learned to see the presence of LMS at Toyota in San Antonio. Free tours are offered three times per day, five days per week at most Toyota assembly facilities for those who register.

As Steve and his Lean team spread their efforts north, they partnered with other very Lean facilities like Medtronic Powered Surgical Solutions near Fort Worth, Texas.

Figure 6.2   Some of the Lean Leader (LMS) course graduates visiting Toyota in San Antonio (first group to Kentucky).

Tip 8: Steve's Sensei Folder

The role of a sensei is not to do all the work. That would rob the leader of a learning cycle. It is much bigger than that. The role of a sensei is to guide staff members, especially other leaders, into a new way of thinking. If the sensei independently does his or her own projects, or tells staff exactly what to do, the sensei interferes with organizational learning. This reduces the chances of sustaining the transformation and changes.

The sensei must walk the delicate balance between doing and coaching, between serving and leading. The main role of the sensei is to model and coach well enough that he or she creates other Lean thinkers as quickly as the multi-year process allows.

As Steve sent email tips-of-the-week, leadership coaching, and major changes in the Lean toolkit, he dropped them into a sensei folder. This created a pathway of sorts for starting up additional sites and spreading beyond the borders of S&W.

There were no individual standout emails or forms. However, the process of "carving a wide path" for others to follow and to learn from was unique. The staff felt they were accomplishing something significant—something that would last. Like a trail guide, they left breadcrumbs where path choices worked well. Like every other area of the Lean journey, they continuously improved the continuous improvement team and processes.

Tip 9: Using Assessments or "Scores" to Grade One's Progress

Steve is only lukewarm on this type of tool for transformation, but he has used and encouraged it a few times in his past consulting. Sometimes it makes sense to use a framework or list of "ideal" questions both to teach leaders and to keep them realistic on how much further there is to go.

That said, Steve has seen Lean efforts using assessments grind down into a hypocritical mess, once staff see that the "real goal" is to score higher by dressing things up externally. Then, they avoid the hard work of real transformation. When it becomes a game to see who can put the most "lipstick on a pig," we have lost the leaders!

Here are some frameworks or assessments, with the authors' tips.

Overall Lean Maturity Score

This is probably the most dangerous because every area in your organization is at different places in their journeys. The tendency by leaders is to give themselves an "overall" grade earned only by the most advanced areas. This causes two bad consequences. First, most departments feel they can "rest" a bit because they have come from 0 to 7 so quickly. Worse, it actually takes pressure off the laggards for more progress because they have also been painted as a 7 or an 8 with the wide brush of overall Lean score.

Another issue is that leaders have severe reactions when their overall score decreases. Earlier, the *Law of Entropy* was revealed stating things always go from an orderly to disorderly state unless energy is put in to restore it to ideal. Backsliding happens the moment leaders divert the eyes of their managers

Funny Story: Early in S&W's journey, the leaders took a trip to Toyota. A few months before the Toyota trip, some leaders, confident with their Lean projects and progress, declared they were an 8 (of 10) overall on a Lean scale. After viewing Toyota's processes close-up and hearing answers in a detailed Q&A session, one of them asked the Toyota Public Affairs leader what overall grade he would give their plant. He did not want to answer, but when pressed, he said they were a solid 7, and had lost some ground with turnover and "brain drain" to help start up other Toyota facilities in America.

Dejected but also more accurate, S&W leaders once confidently at an 8 in their minds, stated their new "score"—a solid 5. Nothing changed in their own processes. Their eyes just became more trained to look for ideal Lean and TPS principles.

The authors strongly recommend that leaders tour world-class or super-Lean facilities, even outside of your industry, at least annually. It helps train the eyes. It gives leaders a new target of excellence to shoot for. ThedaCare paired with a snow blower company, Virginia Mason with an aircraft manufacturer.

S&W was close enough to Toyota-San Antonio, so over 500 leaders to date toured their well-done TPS museum, took their free tram tour, and then received tremendous and transparent answers in Q&A sessions. Steve and his team taught them what to look for and helped them maximize their time at Toyota. Find someone further down their Lean journey and share your learning.

and staff to another crisis or program. As much as Bob and Steve tried to maintain focus, this happened several times on S&W's journey as well.

In summary, if you use some sort of assessment, grade yourself against yourself! Do not compare yourself with the self-score of another department or organization. It is better to avoid an overall score, and just "grade" a list of value streams and processes that still need to flow with perfect quality.

Most important, do not believe for a moment that you are done or can rest. There are fast running competitors all around you. Some of them are non-traditional competitors, who will disrupt the sleepy giants very soon—unless they unleash the power of ideas!

Lean Assessment by Tool or Principle with Radar Chart

Steve first saw a detailed Lean assessment using a radar or "spider web" chart for scores in Hiroyuki Hirano's game-changing manual called *The JIT Implementation Guide.* For the first time, Steve and leaders at Johnson Controls Automotive division could guide their rapid adoption of TPS principles using some proven questions. Granted, leaders needed to define many of the terms as they walked their plant floors when grading, but this is a good exercise early on to do—one that Steve repeated in many of his early Lean deployments.

Steve calls the leader question lists either "Facility Doctor" or "Walking" assessments because of their purpose. It provides a way for the leaders to diagnose and quickly prescribe a get-well plan, *if* the questions are understood and are ideal for the processes being walked.

"Walking" gives the idea of how the assessments are done—usually in small teams of two to three, assigned to certain pages of the assessment, and always in the Gemba (not a conference room). The assessments are usually done for a single facility or key value streams within a larger facility to provide focus and to allow leaders to physically put their eyes on every area within scope.

The typical Lean assessment has several pages, each TPS principle or tool has its own page. An assessment adapted for healthcare can be seen in Figure 6.3. Steve finds these exercises to be good early in the transformation process, but less valuable later because the focus needs to shift from "scoring higher" to transforming every key process and value stream. The

---

* Hirano, Hiroyuki, *JIT Implementation Manual: The Complete Guide to Just-in-Time Manufacturing*, 2nd ed. (6-Volume Set), Productivity Press, 2009.

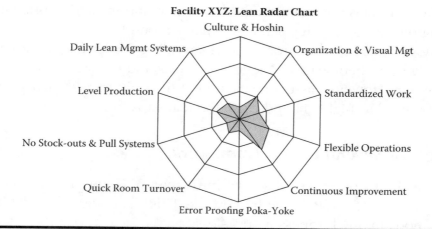

Figure 6.3 Lean radar chart, simple visual summary of all scores.

assessments do help leaders quickly see the bigger picture of Lean, and teach that it is a system, rather than individual tools or parts.

Figure 6.4 shows the summary scores added up on each page of the assessment. You can see that the "Culture & Hoshin" category score from this facility was very low—only 14% of the total score. This is common early on and is likely a fair score by the three or four leaders assigned to this page. Remember, you do not want to compare to another area. Rather, you set an improvement goal for your own area and try to exceed it six months later. You compare only with yourself.

Once these scores are reviewed by the leaders together, they would set a target score six months from that date on each spoke of the radar or spider chart (e.g., improve from 14% to 50% on the Culture & Hoshin category). Sometimes expected scores within 6 or 12 months would be marked by top leaders right on the radar chart. Bigger gaps needed more actions and effort.

Attribute	Score
Culture & Hoshin	0.14
Organization & Visual Mgt	0.35
Standardized Work	0.24
Flexible Operations	0.36
Continuous Improvement	0.45
Error Proofing Poka-Yoke	0.14
Quick Room Turnover	0.21
No Stock-outs & Pull Systems	0.15
Level Production	0.28
Daily Lean Mgmt Systems	0.24

Figure 6.4 Lean radar chart summary scores.

Action items to close the gaps would be written and tracked until complete, checking the score by doing self-assessments monthly.

Today, Steve *leans* away from assessments. The reader may try an assessment early on to help leaders understand ideals and to teach them parts of a larger system. However, assessments are not the only transformative tool that should be used to highlight and close the real gaps in healthcare processes.

Baldrige (or Several Other) Framework

Another is the Baldrige model shown in Chapter 3. Figure 6.5 shows the seven key areas of the Baldrige framework. This "hamburger" model dissects key functions in any business model.

Lean thinking needs to penetrate every part of the organization. One way to show this is to use the Baldrige framework model. The framework helps you see your organizations as a system. It is also useful for focusing improvements. The authors added some of S&W's "efforts" in the call-out boxes, where they felt Lean thinking could help.

The Baldrige and other assessment models (like SAE's J4000,* Shingo Prize,† etc.) can be used in multiple ways. For the Baldridge framework, Steve added important efforts related to his area (Lean, CI) to be done in each category. Other initiatives like quality and safety could lay their efforts over the top of the hamburger model to help align and prioritize efforts. This "visual" look at aligning efforts can be powerful for your C-suite.

A second way of using the Baldrige model is to do self-assessments against Baldrige scoring criteria. NIST writes on their website, "A self-assessment using the Baldrige Criteria for Performance Excellence can help your organization achieve high performance and move toward performance excellence. Even if your organization isn't ready to apply for the Malcolm Baldrige National Quality Award, the Baldrige Criteria are a framework for evaluating your organization's processes, their impact on results, and your progress toward your goals and objectives."‡

At least early on, Steve does not encourage applying for awards in order to "win." That may sound strange, but there is both a *distraction* factor and a *wrong goal* factor that sometimes works its way into play with these

---

* SAE Lean Assessment, http://standards.sae.org/j4000_199908/, accessed September 2014.
† Shingo Prize Model and Assessment, http://www.shingoprize.org/model/, accessed September 2014.
‡ NIST website for Baldrige Performance Excellence Program, http://www.nist.gov/baldrige/enter/self.cfm, accessed September 2014.

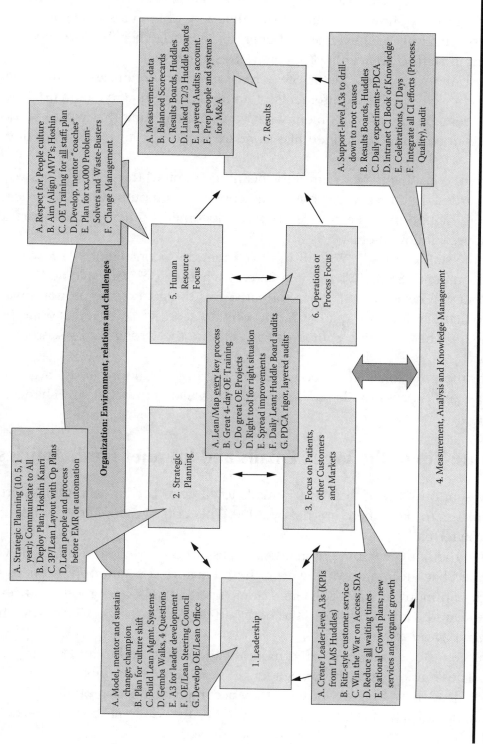

Figure 6.5 Baldrige framework with major Lean efforts for each box.

awards. First, the distraction factor. A quick Internet search with Baldrige and bankruptcy shows too many firms that win, only to lose the game that counts—survival. It takes time and energy to put together the "package," and then train staff to answer appropriately. Too much time.

Next, the wrong goal factor. Steve remembers an organization attempting to rapidly achieve the requirements of an automotive quality standard. The rules seemed simple—document what you do, then audit that what you do what is documented. Sounded like standard work. So, Steve and team dug in.

Then, consultants were hired to "nearly guarantee" the certification would be awarded. The first words out of the consultant's mouth were, "In order to score high, don't ever produce process documents unless you are sure all employee's follow them."

Some staff clarified, "What if most of them do?" Consultant, "Throw out the document!" Staff, "What if it is core to what we do?" Consultant, "The auditors will never know!" Therefore, it seems the goal of the program was not to actually improve quality. It was only to score well on audits done by outsiders. These quality "standards" can elevate the wrong goal—score, not quality!

For these reasons, Steve recommends that organizations choose a good quality and process model, and use self-assessments to help drive change.

Tip 10: Tip of the Week Emails and Intranet Fresh Articles

Steve sent out "Tip of the Week" emails to all Lean Leaders and Quickstart graduates. To date, there are nearly 2000. This critical mass keeps building LMS better daily!

When other corporate communications started to overload leaders, Steve dropped back to monthly. However, these became constant opportunities to coach and motivate LMS-builders. Forms, tips, job aids, and good practices were shared. However, by far, the best part of the Tip-of-the-Weeks was the ***Success Stories***.

Success stories were gathered monthly and distributed to all LMS graduates. These graduates were the leaders of S&W. But, it was not easy to get huddle leaders to brag about what they accomplished. A log of all of them was kept, at least through the first year. It became difficult to track, as ideas implemented went over the 1000-per-week mark.

Two other great ways to communicate to staff were emailed *S&W News* stories and the intranet itself. The Corporate Communications department at S&W was a big help in getting the word out about LMS and huddles. They also helped with the annual Lean Fair, where dozens of awards for Lean projects were presented, including the prestigious President's Award.

S&W News was a weekly or so email blast with tightly written articles about things important to all staff. LMS became a consistent part of *S&W News* in its first two years. The articles were summarized on the email blast, but linked to full articles on the intranet. The intranet then made it easy for staff to see all past articles. Steve was provided with the hit counts, which remained high throughout the effort. Staff loved to see their team highlighted.

One tip for the intranet is freshness. It is not good for important content to be stagnant. Staff today want to see important information in multiple ways. They also want to keep the content brief, with links to longer articles so they can get more if they wish.

Top Five Lists for Huddles

When asked for a series of content for the intranet, a Lean coach wrote up a series of *Top Five* lists regarding huddles. Only minor edits were made in the content of the first two. Some additional formatting was made on the Internet to make them stand out and be remembered. Each was done in the style of late-night TV hosts, who counted them down from the fifth best to the number one best.

Top Five Reasons to Huddle

We always start with *why*. As leaders, we need to know what and how to huddle. However, we also need to know why. This list shows the five key reasons why we huddle. The *Top Five* in reverse order are:

5. When we huddle, we communicate with our peers about work processes and challenges. Good communication up-down and peer-to-peer makes our departments run more smoothly.
4. When we huddle, we uncover problems and then generate ideas to try to solve them.
3. When we huddle, we bring up issues, we share ideas, and collaborate with our peers. This improves employee engagement. Generating and respecting each other's ideas is the very definition of engagement.

2. When we huddle, we often find duplications of efforts. This decreases our workloads and improves care.

1. When we huddle, we get fewer emails and fewer meetings. You can grab the people you need just before and after. Question to leaders: Have you ever had somebody set up a meeting for a full hour with you only to realize it would have only taken ten minutes? Moreover, you quickly realize you need two or three other leaders to make the decision. And, the two or three other people all huddle with you daily!

   This is what you often see after our huddles. In one demonstration video we filmed, at least six "hallway huddles" continued for 10 minutes after the leader huddle. Could huddles be the "meeting busters" we have been looking for? This is one reason why we huddle. We recommend that you start small, but just get started.

Top Five Things We Huddle About (Focus Topics)

We often hear people say, "I don't have time to huddle." This list shows the five brief things we huddle about. The *Top Five* in reverse order are:

5. The thing you are all too busy doing! Example: Staff say they do not have time to huddle because they are deploying a new electronic health record system. Well, isn't that a great reason to huddle? You could focus your brief huddles on solving the issues as they are raised.

4. Patient satisfaction. Patient satisfaction scores can be improved. Most leaders do not have time to address the daily flow of comments from patients themselves. But, you can do this in huddles. These are jewels and can prevent further erosion of trust we build with the patients we serve.

3. Problems. These can be any pains or frustrations in our department. Ask leaders to brainstorm key problems with their teams, and rank them on which ones took the most time and attention away from their patients. Once problems were vetted by leaders, we will initiate A3 waves to address them.

2. Goals. All of us set goals at the beginning of the year. S&W used a Hoshin Kanri process to align and cascade goals for every direct performer. Coaching was provided to leaders at all levels to ensure that huddle board "trend chart" goals aligned and were measures staff could control, and matched their Hoshin goals.

1. Waste. Every S&W employee was taught to identify and eliminate waste in his or her own processes. Huddles were the ideal place to bring up ideas to reduce and eliminate waste daily! Sometimes, leaders would write the acronym showing the eight categories of waste on their huddle board or a flip chart: DOWNTIME. Then, staff would brainstorm specific areas of waste, and quickly come up with ways to reduce it.

To keep it brief, just the bullet points are given for the next 10 *Top Five* lists. These were written to be published monthly for a year.

1. *Top Five* ways to huddle effectively: (January)
   - Keep them short! 15 minutes or less.
   - Focus on just one metric/issue per huddle.
   - Follow and refine your huddle standard work, and hold each other accountable to it.
   - Don't forget to do *Analysis* and generate team *Ideas.*
   - Make just one or two changes at a time (your PDCA experiment), not too many.
2. *Top Five* ways to improve your huddles: (February)
   - Pick a new goal if you hit your first goal.
   - Take static or old information off the board.
   - Pick a topic about which your staff feels strongly. Reduce their pain or frustration.
   - Keep the huddles short and focused.
   - Celebrate your successes.
3. *Top Five* ways to keep your huddles fresh: (March)
   - Streamline your board: If you can't "move the metric toward the goal" after many attempts, it is either a "sticky" problem or maybe staff have no control over it.
   - Make sure you do not have more than 10 to 15 people huddling at a time.
   - Have different staff members "own" different sections of the board (not the manager).
   - Use the Morale/People section to brainstorm fun activities.
   - Gather data with pictures (in the Gemba) and use this for *Analysis.*
4. *Top Five* ways to take your huddle to the next level: (April)
   - Ask staff how high each goal should be, become world-class.
   - Strengthen the middle *Analysis* section; get help from Quality and Analytics groups.

    – Huddle more frequently.

    – Track your huddle attendance and frequency.

    – Make your data more visual (font size, color coding, colored magnets, flags, etc.).

5. *Top Five* ways to restart a stalled huddle: (May)

    – Focus on just one topic about which the staff feels the most strongly; put everything else on hold.

    – Create a Top Ten list of problems, gather data, and focus on the most common or severe problem.

    – Gather problems on slips of paper (some staff do exercises called 5-Minute Frustrations where they document as many as they can in five minutes or less); then divide the board into 3 sections: (1) Evaluate, (2) In-progress, and (3) Completed.

    – Ask for a Lean coach to attend one of your huddles to give helpful suggestions.

    – Change the time or location of the huddle (even to the other side of the room or hallway) to make it easier for staff to participate.

6. *Top Five* things to avoid with huddling: (June)

    – Tracking metrics that your department cannot affect.

    – Using your huddle to convey only one-way information (i.e., announcements).

    – Allowing your huddle to take too long.

    – Just tracking data and not analyzing it or coming up with ideas.

    – Tracking and reviewing metrics where you are always meeting or exceeding your goal.

7. *Top Five* huddle bad habits: (July)

    – Allowing one person to dominate the huddle.

    – Using "blamestorming" vs. brainstorming, or using blame-and-shame vs. problem solving. Focus on process issues, not people.

    – Allowing the huddles to take too long.

    – Focusing on problems that are too large.

    – Focusing on fixing another department.

8. *Top Five* ways to make your huddle board shine: (August)

    – Use visual management/color coding to make the board "tell a story."

    – Streamline your board into 3 "medical" layers: (1) Run Chart (symptom), (2) Analysis (diagnosis), and (3) Ideas (Treatment Plan).

    – Highlight your successes and accomplishments.

    – Clearly link your huddle board to Hoshin goals.

- Integrate patient satisfaction or patient feedback to your huddle board; respond with ideas.
9. *Top Five* ways to increase the number of ideas: (September)
   - Use cards or Post-its.
   - Have an entire huddle focused on brainstorming for a stalled huddle board metric.
   - Emphasize the two guardrails: Ideas that require little or no cost can be implemented and experimented on today.
   - Call it "try-storming": there are no dumb ideas.
   - Integrate "ideas implemented" into leaders' Hoshin goals.
10. *Top Five* ways to link your huddle board to system goals so staff can see how they fit into the mission: (October)
    - Show how your huddle board categories link to Hoshin (System Goal) categories.
    - Visit the bosses' boards to create or strengthen linkages on goals.
    - Focus on tangible "process" measures that support the output measures on senior leaders' huddle boards.
    - Make a visual display of the boss and staff's Hoshin goals; (org chart-style); use string to tie together common goals and efforts.
    - Have your leaders attend your huddles, and attend their huddles as well!

Tip 11: Building the Internal Lean and LMS Toolkit

Version control problems create rework. Rework is a waste. Lean teams hate waste. However, in general, Lean teams seem to be the slowest to standardize their own information and tools! Version control hurts two ways: staff members do not use the latest version or edit an older version; or staff members use a non-standard, untested version which confuses staff.

The phases S&W went through in making their Lean toolkit available to coaches and staff went something like this:

1. "Every man did that which was right in his own eyes."* No standard. Lots of searching. But when the Lean team was small, discrepancies could be caught and consensus quickly reached.

---

* Holy Bible, Judges chapter 17 verse 6, King James Version.

2. Files on computer network: Staff stored things where it made sense to them. Sometimes, files were named in a way that only the coach knew! The network directories truly needed 5S. This was accomplished a few times. Next, discipline was established so that all staff used proper naming and filing conventions (like Memorial Hospital working files in the "Memorial" folder, and pictures in each "pics" folder). The Lean team was taught to display files in detail view, newest on top.

3. Sharepoint, intranet: In this method, only the newest files were stored on Sharepoint. They were maintained by a central person. Again, discipline was needed to check out, get input, and then store the best stuff in intuitively named folders. This also created a different issue. Some staff did not have constant access to the intranet at some locations, so they stored files in advance on their laptop hard drive. This again created version control problems, negating the benefit of the intranet. Discipline by individuals prevented this from becoming a big issue.

Did you know that you can 5S digital information? Emails can be 5S'd. Network directories can be 5S'd. Small warning: digital storage is cheap, so maintaining a few older versions online is not bad. However, don't make users sort through them.

Here is another of Steve's common stories that did not make it into *Stories From My Sensei*.

You know that company intranet? That thing with all the useless information. Why don't we make it useful? Now that you know the 20 or so Lean tools, how do you want to access these tools, examples, and forms? [Class members state the obvious.]

Yes! On the top page, in the corner, make it say *Lean Toolkit*. Maybe list the 20 or so tools. One click! If you click on Error Proofing, what is the first thing you should see? [Student says a good example and the form.] Right! And, if you click on VSM workshop, what do you want to see? [Student says good examples and the forms.] Right, again!

Is there an IT person in the room? [Sheepish hand goes up.] Ma'am, would this be hard to build? [Definitely not.] Lean leaders, please add this to your lengthy list of tips for when you return to the ranch! Let's retake our intranets putting up only organized, useful tools and links.

4. All divisions, intranet accessible by all staff: Many individuals now think and do Lean. They need tools. This is the same as above, but adds user searches for similar projects, tools, and problems. This allows all staff to "steal" good ideas, examples, and download the latest training, tools, tips, and forms.

Tip 12: Using Videos to "Get the Message Out"

A picture is worth a thousand words. Better: a great short video (vine) is worth ten thousand!

Marketing wizards say that a target audience must be told seven times in seven different ways before they even hear the message. Well, even for rolling out something as positive as LMS, seven is not enough. You could send emails, intranet articles, newsletters, and more emails until you are blue in the face, but these seem to bounce off the key users.

Steve likes to say, "anything black and white, printed with 12-point font is invisible or ignored." Maybe that is why S&W adapted so quickly to hand-drawn colored dots on the trend charts. LMS-building is a contact sport. Leaders learn by doing. The closest online format for this is a brief video.

S&W videotaped and lightly edited two good huddle videos very early in the process. The first was Bob Pryor leading his executive huddle. Staff like to see their leaders leading. The second was a very good nursing huddle.

They were outlined but not scripted. Staff was alerted, but no one acted differently. Maybe a smile or two. Steve also wore a small, mobile camera to huddles because it was less distracting.

Tip 13: Have a Bias for Action

Steve's two main sensei both used this phrase and practiced this phrase daily. You must have a bias for action to transform organizations.

Here are two stories from *Stories From My Sensei* that reinforce a ***Bias for Action***. This story was sandwiched in between other similar ones.

(Story 1) Must Cut Inventory in Half—A Bias for Action

[Note: Koji, an alias, was a renowned consultant from a group of ex-Toyota leaders. He had just walked into a rubber-molding factory where he declared it a warehouse in the previous story. Steve was participating on a Kaizen team there. Please see *Stories* for the lead-in and follow-up stories.]

When last we left Koji, he was standing at the door to the factory, brief-case in hand, saying, "Where is factory?" He walked quickly to the back of the factory, as if he did not believe that any value-adding machines or pro-cesses existed here. After seeing the molding machines, he relaxed a bit and then looked at the rows of 4-high pallet racks filled with tons of molded WIP inventory. Joe (Plant Manager) said one of the dumbest things I ever heard. He said, "I see you are admiring my well-labeled WIP racks. We 5S'd our entire inventory!"

The manager had dedicated space for each WIP part number in these racks and labeled them very well. When you dedicate space, you need enough space for the maximum number of parts that would ever be stored in a one-year period. All inventory is waste and should be reduced, not labeled.

Joe proudly narrated as he walked down the aisle, "Work in process inventory from the molding machines is stored in all of these racks. We keep all WIP for Part Number 123 here; all Part Number 125 is here…"

Koji was not following him. He was staring up at the first rack.

He asked, "All Part Number 123 is here?"

Joe said, "Yes. We keep all WIP for Part Number 123 here."

Koji said loudly, "Must cut inventory in half."

The Plant Manager might have been thinking to himself, "That's what we are paying you to teach us."

Joe said slowly, "Yes. That's a good idea."

Koji seemed to be waiting for a different response.

He repeated, "Must cut inventory in half!"

Joe looked perplexed and said, "I heard you the first time."

The only way to describe what happened next is the word "sumo." Skinny Koji slapped one foot down, then the other, saying, "Must cut inven-tory in half!" The Plant Manager, already embarrassed earlier, was not about to be embarrassed again by this skinny man. He slapped his feet down one after the other and screamed, "I said that I heard you the first time."

Koji smiled. It was clear he was enjoying this. Then, Koji screamed as he stamped his feet and repeated several times, "Must cut inventory in half!" The Plant Manager said as he pulled a note card out of his pocket, "OK, OK, Koji. Calm down. I'll write it down."

Koji threw his briefcase on the floor, pulled out a saws-all (metal cutting reciprocating saw), plugged it into the column next to the inventory rack, reached up as high as he could, and started to cut the support post of the storage rack filled with tons of loaded pallets. Joe turned in circles as if he were going to grab Koji, then call for help, then grab Koji. It was a surreal scene. I backed up thinking, "That rack will fall; that guy's going to die; this is called Kaizen—this is crazy!"

Joe tried to pull Koji away, but Koji just growled back and kept cutting. Eventually, Joe eased Koji away from the full racks and then called a fork truck driver to empty the top two rows of pallets from the inventory rack. Koji stood aside, still revving the motor of the saws-all. When the last pallet was moved aside, Koji smiled and then continued to cut through all four posts of the rack.

We all watched as the fork truck driver carefully moved the top of a well-labeled Part 123 inventory rack outside of the plant. When he was finished, Koji pronounced, "Inventory in half! We may now begin the Kaizen event!"

Later that night, after the squint test, I said to Koji, "You could have died out there."

He said, "No, Steve-san, I trusted that he would stop me."

I joked, "You embarrassed him twice in just 10 minutes. I think he would rather see you dead!"

Koji said, "Steve-san, I do this *every time* I enter a factory! It is my *signature*!"

[Note: If you see one of these consultants, check his or her briefcase!]

Koji asked me again, "Do you really want to be a TPS facilitator?"

I told him, "Yes. Yes, I do."

He told me, "Then you must be crazy man! Americans get 'glue in seat' during Kaizen activities. Always sit and eat the donut; eat the donut. You must lead them out of their seats to the shop floor where the work really occurs."

He continued, "You must have a ***Bias for Action***, or nothing will get done."

He was right.

Wait until you hear what Koji did at his next workshop!

■ Application and reflection: Can you cut some of your inventory storage racks or areas in half? Why or why not? Why not do it today?

■ If you physically constrain the only locations where you store inventory, how would your production systems react? Would you need to audit these areas frequently to prevent overproduction?

- Do you have plans to reduce all inventory levels? How are they progressing?
- Is it true that participants in a Kaizen event prefer to stay in a conference room? Why? What can you do to lead them to the place where work occurs?
- Remember, safety first.

(Story 2) Door Here!

About four weeks after the infamous rack-cutting incident, I received a call from the TPS coordinator at the Indiana factory. She said, "He's back!"

I said, "Who?"

She said, "Koji."

I said, "Did you check his briefcase?"

She said, "Yes, nothing but papers this time."

I said, "What happened?"

She said, "Do you remember how the molded rubber parts are moved from the press to the de-flashing cells all the way around the wall to the old extension?"

I said, "Yes."

She said, "Koji was doing a 'Jeffy Walk' from Press #1, around the wall, back to Deflash Cell #1…"

[Note: Every TPS tool attempts to make waste stick out, so that team members must reduce it. One TPS tool is to graph the walking steps that a person or materials take through the plant with dashed lines on a layout of the plant. Some TPS facilitators call this a "spaghetti diagram" because all the overlapping lines look like spaghetti on a plate. Others call it a "Jeffy Walk" after a repeated theme in the cartoon "Family Circus" (copyright King Syndicate). Wherever Jeffy walks, they leave a trail of dashed lines across the cartoon strip. I challenge you to draw worker and material movements for every key process in your factory. Jeffy is in your factory! We must find him and get rid of him, because excess part travel and worker motion represent great wastes in a Lean production system!]

Koji was doing a "Jeffy Walk" between the rubber and deflashing machines. He walked from the rubber molding press all the way around the wall to about the same spot behind the wall, counting in Japanese this time as he returned, "Ichi, ni, san, shi, go, roku, shichi…" He stopped and then retraced his steps.

He stopped at the opening along the far wall, looked back to the second set of machines, and then started counting again along the wall all the way back to the first machine. His count ended on just about the same number. He stared at the wall. The operations were only a few meters apart, but separated by that wall.

Koji said, "Door here."

The Plant Manager said, "You're right Koji. We should put a door here."

Koji paused, and then repeated, "Door here!"

The Plant Manager looked perplexed again, and said, "That is a good idea Koji. We plan to do just that."

Sumo!

Koji repeated for a third time stomping his feet, "Door here!"

The Plant Manager made the mistake again of repeating that he heard him, then said as he pulled out a note card in his pocket again, "OK, OK. I'll write that idea down."

Koji jumped on a fork truck. He threw it in gear, built up some speed, and then rammed the large forks right through the single brick wall! He bounced in his seat, shook his head, and then got down from the fork truck while brushing dust off his pants.

Seeing the hole the forks made through the wall, he smiled proudly and said, "Door here! We may now begin the Kaizen event."

This was a crazy thing to do. There could have been 440 volts of electricity surging through that wall, there could have been a water line, or more importantly, there could have been a person on the other side of that wall! Again, please don't do anything dangerous in your factory. But, do have a ***Bias for Action***.

- OK, that was crazy. But, how can you develop a Bias for Action in your leaders, in all of your workers?
- When was the last time a worker brought up an idea for improvement? How quickly was it implemented? Why?
- The next time you get an opportunity, help the worker implement his/her idea immediately. How might that encourage more ideas?
- Hint: Toyota will often make a change even for morale reasons alone. They attempt to implement 90% or more of their employees' ideas.

Tip 14: Stop Lean and Huddles during New or EMR Rollout?

Heck no! When S&W deployed Epic, Lean thinking and tools were used widely. Lean coaches were heavily involved in everything from (rapid) process mapping to team facilitation. This was especially true in the Go-Live periods. Several coaches carried a pad of flipchart pages and markers around the buildings during the first few weeks after Go-Live. Many processes were mapped and streamlined on the spot.

Another major use of Lean during Epic rollout came with huddles. Some leaders asked if staff would be too burned out with all the Epic training and tasks to huddle. Steve encouraged them to keep huddling—just huddle around Epic tasks and training in advance and then problems as they went live. It worked well. They huddled around Epic issues, which relieved stress, focused them visually on cross-training, and even allowed them to communicate better with IT staff.

Tip 15: Stop Lean and Huddles during a Merger or Acquisition?

Again, heck no! Healthcare is undergoing massive changes to remain affordable. Mergers will be part of this needed change. However, it is not easy to merge effectively. Differing cultures destroyed two large mergers in the north around the time Baylor Health Care System and Scott & White Health were merging.

Because a new operating philosophy and a common language are so critical to building a culture of continuous improvement, the Baylor Scott & White Health organization put a hold on system-wide integration of continuous improvement efforts, while they sorted out the bigger building blocks. TPS takes years to build. However, it can be delayed in just days! Legacy S&W continued its Lean and LMS efforts, gaining momentum and results.

The authors recommend that the merger partners start with a new, common operating philosophy across all operations first. This is counterintuitive, as small departments would be easier. The top-level leaders need to get behind a common approach effort and stay with it. This and an increased amount of time in the Gemba can avoid any backsliding in critical operating units.

Tip 16: Get Flow

When doing Lean projects, a chief purpose should be to get the process to flow. This means no or few stops, and greatly reduced waiting for patients and staff. One of the biggest mistakes Steve sees in Lean projects is a weak future state, or worse, no future state with a total focus on fixing current state problems.

In a value stream mapping workshop, a facilitator or trained leader will map out the current state process. They spend some time brainstorming problems or undesirable effects (UDEs) in the current process. This is good. However, many less-trained coaches and facilitators will try to assign actions to solve those UDEs right away. This is bad! Steve estimates that 75 to 80% of the UDEs will go away—once you achieve flow!

Here is an example. A healthcare team showed Steve a current state with UDEs, but no future state. Steve asked how they were progressing. They said their team started solving problems next. Steve asked which ones they solved. Proudly, they picked up the first one and said, "Here is one." It read, "Not Enough Chairs in Waiting Room." Dumbfounded, Steve asked, "What did you do to solve it?" They replied, "We bought more chairs." (If you are Lean-trained, your jaw should have just hit the floor.)

Again, if you get flow, 75 to 80% of the UDEs go away. Especially ones like chairs in waiting rooms! If you stop to solve them before visioning a good future state with flow, it is like straightening the lounge chairs on the Titanic! It would be better to learn to swim than straighten the lounge chairs, or solve all UDEs.

Steve does recommend coming back to the UDEs. After the future state map is built and vetted out, and the action plans for the next 6 to 9 months are documented, then go back and use the list of UDEs as a checklist. Ask, "Do we have an action planned to address this UDE?" If yes, move on to the next one, or if not add an action item. Repeat until all UDEs are addressed.

Granted, the team will not be able to solve all of them. The team's response to a few might be, "Let's wait until the next year to address this one." The team will tell you which ones they feel will give you the biggest bang for the buck. However, show respect for the issues uncovered in mapping by check-listing them at the end. Just don't straighten the lounge chairs.

Tip 17: The ROI Trap and Role of Training

It is a trap. A leader once asked Steve, "It sounds like you recommend a lot of training to roll out Lean in healthcare. What is the return on investment (ROI) of a typical training course?" To clarify, Steve asked, "Do you mean eventually or right away?" The finance-savvy leader laughed and looked around the room to see if others were catching Steve's "rookie" clarification question. He replied, "The only thing that matters to me is right away."

Steve said, "Negative. Negative ROI." The man looked startled. He asked Steve to explain. Steve said, "At the end of four days of training, you will have proven and applied only one thing—that you can eat donuts and lunches. Right?" Several in the class smiled. "So, your answer is negative." But, we need to prepare the minds before transforming processes!

Another tip is to avoid adding up ROI from each action item of a transformation. Comparing before-after gains on chunks of actions or quarter-by-quarter KPIs add more value, and keep leaders from reacting to the saw-toothing that occurs early on.

Another trap is avoiding the tough tasks in the foundation (Toyota House) due to immediate ROI concerns. Better is to track the longer-term deliverable or outcome you desire. Moreover, be careful to add the change in people, their thinking processes, to your deliverables. This is actually more important in the long run than an immediate project success. Because people will repeat these gains if they had a good experience, and are self-sufficient enough to repeat.

Tip 18: Kaizen or Kaikaku: Redirecting Labor

As stated earlier, Bob made a no-layoff commitment at S&W. There were some volume-related reductions as they started operations in other nearby regions, non-replacements of staff, and some cutbacks in areas outside of those applying Lean heavily. However, there were no layoffs due to applying Lean.

That said, removing waste frees up time. Thus, the constant application of Lean thinking always frees up resources. Always. After several years of waste busting, S&W leaders did benefit greatly. Using only turnover, they were able to avoid replacing some staff and shift other staff to faster growth areas.

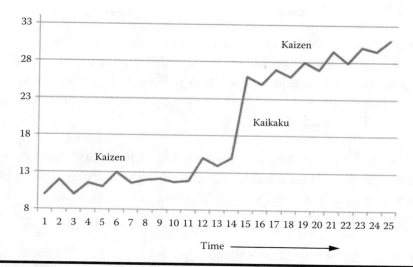

Figure 6.6   Kaizen periods followed by rapid transformation; both are needed.

In one of the best examples of dedication to no layoffs, hard-working, multi-shift laundry staff members were fully absorbed into the system when contracted laundry became viable (at a partner-owned contract laundry service). A key manager became a Lean coach.

Like most healthcare organizations, S&W had a lot of small base hit Kaizens, but very few major transformational changes, sometimes call Kaikaku,[*] or leapfrog change. From their simulation, leaders called these major transformational changes that doubled productivity "Round 4 Thinking."

Figure 6.6 shows lengthy periods of Kaizen, followed by rapid transformation. More rapid transformations were needed at S&W. The question was, could staff get there on their own, or would leaders need to force larger productivity gains? Sometimes incremental change is not enough.

The following outline shows more detail on the up-front budget and labor balancing process that was described in Chapter 5, Rebalance and Workshare in Huddles.

1. Update labor standards to match budget
   – Hospital departments use labor standards and budget (with high, medium, and low volume break points)
   – Clinics use budget (with volume break points)
   – Non-patient areas use five-year snapshot comparisons

---

[*] Ibid, Lean Lexicon, http://www.lean.org/Common/LexiconTerm.cfm?TermId=237.

2. Leaders review labor reports
3. Communicate labor levels to start fiscal year
4. Rebalance exercises commence in departments desiring help
   - Rebalance with leaders in advance; Workshare in huddles
   - Continuous cross-training to ensure maximum balancing; and discuss daily at huddles

Kaizen is incremental, small change for the better done daily by staff. Kaikaku is radical reform or innovation, mainly done by leaders. S&W needed systems and leadership vision in place for both. Until recently, their constructs for both were:

■ Kaizen: Huddles and Waste Walks
■ Kaikaku: Lean Projects and some leader-led restructuring

As in LMS-building, the leadership part of making rebalance exercises successful was larger than the actual analysis and Post-it moves. The following process shows what leaders do after the labor reports reveal any staff headcount changes:

1. Commission a champion
2. Rebalance work to new levels (rough):
   - Analyze supply vs. demand
   - Create pull signals and rules to flex staff
   - Ensure metrics in place to continue Workshare in huddles; elevate issues to leader huddles
   - Ensure cross-training plans are completed; post and update matrix on huddle board
3. Redeploy and retrain staff to growth areas
4. Repeat

At S&W, all ideas came from staff in Lean workshops. However, Lean coaches were still, at their core, engineers. They were capable of re-engineering work processes. This occurred when a new building or service line was started. However, it was rare.

In rebalance exercises, some areas at S&W were completely unbalanced. Structural changes were needed before any minor shifts in huddles could take place. Figure 6.7 shows the number of patients scheduled by hour in a busy specialty clinic.

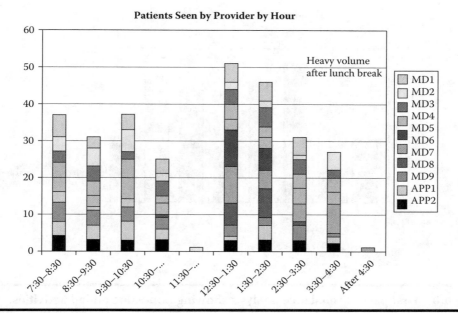

Figure 6.7 Patients seen by hour in a specialty clinic; unbalanced.

Schedule-wise, the department was not balanced at all. The supply of support staff could not possibly match the wide swings in patients to be seen (25 at 10:30 a.m. vs. 52 immediately after lunch). In this case, the doctors (providers) *caused* much of the imbalance by scheduling clinic patients into fixed slots in their own *preferred* schedules—sometimes all in the afternoon and on certain days of the week. This was because most of them reserved time out of the clinic in the morning for teaching, surgeries, or procedures. However, their fixed number of clinic support staff could not handle the peaks, and were underutilized during the "valleys."

Figure 6.8 shows, notionally, how a rebalance exercise might work. S&W's labor budget report showed that the number of a specific labor category (Clinic Technician) target was three, but the current actual was eight. Leaders discussed the clinic's growth and current staff assignments. They agreed the new level would be four. The department leader asked for Lean help to balance the workload for the four remaining staff.

The first "pass" of rebalance in Figure 6.8 showed a severe imbalance of work, and many NVA activities. A few of them are noted in call-outs.

Figure 6.9 shows the *after* picture, with rough rebalance of work. Department leaders rebalanced the value-added tasks, fleshed out a cross-training plan, and then reduced NVA tasks. For this clinic, some new *patient*

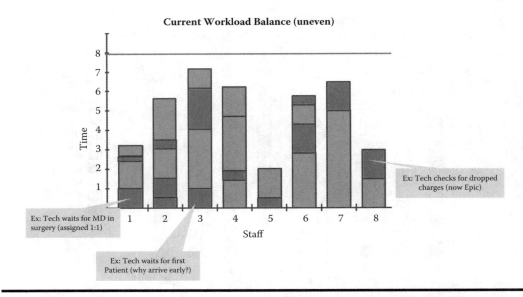

Figure 6.8   First pass of rebalance analysis showing non-value added activities.

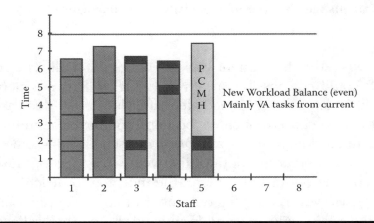

Figure 6.9   Rebalanced to 4-5 staff, mainly value-added work.

centered medical home (PCMH) tasks needed to be done, so the workload remained at five. They now had clear standard work to do the PCMH duties.

Flexing Staff to Other Sites

Another analysis Lean coaches did in helping departments get closer to Round 4 Thinking was how to "flex" labor better. The claim was, during any given day or week, some teams or silos had high demand when others were low.

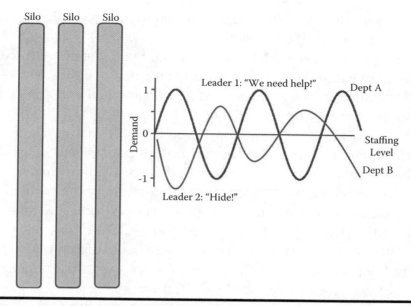

Figure 6.10 **Department silos—sometimes a department is busy when another is light.**

The Lean idea was to analyze them over several weeks and flex the staff within their department, and even outside their building if they were trained and capable (driving limited to 10 miles away). This type of flexing was common at S&W in the hospital for nurses. It was uncommon outside of hospitals and with other labor types.

Figure 6.10 shows silos—departments that do not share or communicate. The demand waves are notional. They show that department A was in high demand (understaffed) when department B was at low demand (overstaffed). A few hours later, it switched.

Even if they could help each other, they did not know the other departments' demand. In some cases, there were even disincentives for sharing. If a department shared a resource, even for a few hours, the resource was taken away from them in the next budget cycle.

This led some teams to beg for "help," while other staff responded to the call with "hide" (hide that they had some capacity for the next few hours). Somehow, those who willingly Workshare should be rewarded above and beyond those who do not because it is harder to develop cross-trained staff. This is much better than both departments hiring extra staff to cover the "peaks."

Once the analysis revealed departments that were naturally high when others were low, simple rules could be made to flex labor. An example might be nurses from same-day surgery flexed to a busy clinic in the afternoons and vice versa in the mornings.

All of these changes required cross-training. Even if staff were "certified," some tasks changed and improved. So, any task that could be Workshared needed cross-training. These tasks must be documented and completed with a high priority or they will not be done.

The best way to track cross-training is on a simple matrix. Figure 6.11 shows a cross-training matrix for support staff. It used pieces of a circle (pie) to show level of readiness to do shared tasks. Blank meant not trained. One piece of pie meant they observed the trainer doing the particular task. Two pieces meant they were trained with the supervisor a few times. Three pieces meant the person was fully trained and could do the work without referring to the standard work or manual. They could also produce at the quantity and quality needed. If there were four pieces of pie under their name for that task, they were the Master Trainer.

S&W kept pressing until they reached a certain number of qualified staff for each task (three or four quadrants). If there were less than three, they still needed cross-training. Staff were recognized when they reached level three or four.

These matrices were posted on the team's huddle boards. Somehow, posting the cross-training matrix encouraged staff to learn more, and leaders to allow time for them to do so. Remember, Workshared tasks need to be documented in the receiving and sending departments to maximize the possibilities for sharing. Again, these are posted and tracked on the huddle board.

	Sharon	Donna	Wendy	X Train Opportunities	TO DO:
Gift Shop	○	◕	●		Helpful Hints —
Kronos	◐	◐	◐		"Pinning" Excel Docs — don't have to dig in network to find
K Drive Access — Transport	○	●	○	✓	
K Drive Access — Pharmacy	○	●	○	✓	
Transport Progress Form	○	●	○	✓ (2014)	
Ordering Business Cards	●	○	○	✓	
Interview Process	●	◔	◐		
Travel Arrangements	◔	◔	◐		Interruptions: Visual Mgmt to Communicate
Rental Equipment & Charges	○	○	○	✓	
Recovery Care Report	◐	●	◐		

Not Trained	○
OBSERVED	◕
TRAINED WITH SUPERVISION	◐
FULLY TRAINED	◔
TRAINER	●

Figure 6.11 Cross-training matrix support staff.

Appendix A: Forms

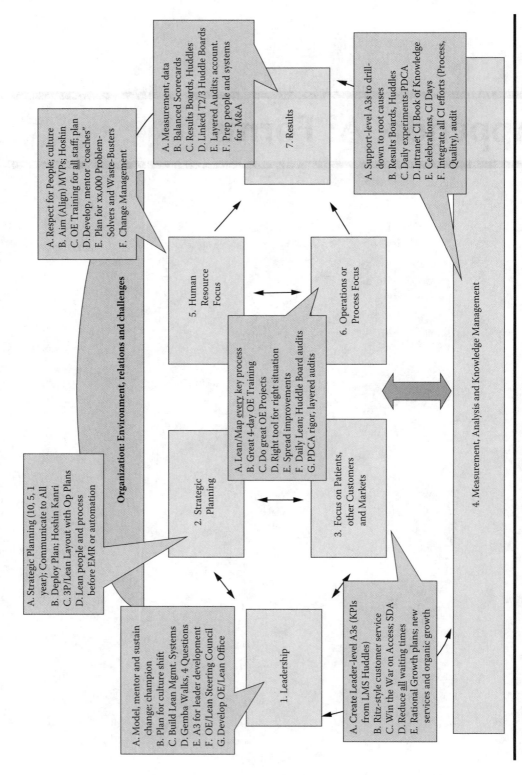

Figure 7.1 Baldrige framework with major Lean efforts for each box.

Waste Walk Checklist		
Waste	What do you see?	How to improve
Defects/Errors		
Overproduction		
Waiting		
Not Utilizing Employee Creativity		
Transportation		
Inventory		
Motion		
Extra Processing		

Figure 7.2 Waste walk form.

S&W Lean Steering Council's Project Selection Worksheet

(1) End Result - Select and prioritize the lean events that satisfy all Musts and rate among the highest scores on Wants.

(4) LIST ALL POTENTIAL LEAN PROJECTS

MUSTS:

CRITERIA (2)	1. ED - Patient in ED room to be discharged or sent to bed (VSM) INFO	Y/N	2. Temple Lab: From test ordered (ED) to resulted (excl. instrument processing time) INFO	Y/N	3. EVS-Laundry Delivery (Project on hold at request of DebS.) INFO	Y/N	4. Pharmacy: Inpatient medication administration for Adult patients in med/surg INFO	Y/N	5. Discharge patient from med/surg unit; planning from admit until room is ready for next patient INFO	Y/N	6. Temple OR: From Consult to Post-Op (increase capacity, schedule?) INFO	Y/N	7. EVS - OR Turnover (Project on hold at request of Deb S.) INFO	Y/N
Improves or maintains Patient access to healthcare		Y		Y		Y?		Y?		Y		Y		
Increases Staff Satisfaction w/Process		Y		Y		Y?		Y?		Y		Y		
Increases Operational Efficiencies		Y		Y		Y?		Y?		Y		Y		
Aligns w/Vision/Mission/Values		Y		Y		Y?		Y?		Y		Y		
Increases Patient Safety		Y		Y		Y?		Y?		Y		Y		
No competing current projects	roll into one project	Y	re-scope to avoid overlap	Y		Y?		Y?		Y		Y		No
A Champion exists	Dr. Steve S.	Y	Denise S.	Y	Name?	Y	J. P.	Y?	A. D.	Y?	Bob C.	Y	Name?	Y?
Goals:														

WANTS:

WANTS:	(3) HOW IMPORTANT (1-10)	1. ED INFO	(5) HOW GOOD (0-10)	SCORE	2. Temple Lab INFO	HOW GOOD (0-10)	SCORE	3. EVS-Laundry INFO	HOW GOOD (0-10)	SCORE	4. Pharmacy INFO	HOW GOOD (0-10)	SCORE	5. Discharge INFO	HOW GOOD (0-10)	SCORE	6. Temple OR INFO	HOW GOOD (0-10)	SCORE	7. EVS-OR INFO	HOW GOOD (0-10)	SCORE
Can be done quickly	8		2	16		6	48					10	80		3	24		1	8			
Capital costs	7		8	56		6	42					9	63		10	70	sched	2	14			
Highly Visible	8		10	80		6	48					5	40		7	56		10	80			
Data easily available	7		10	70		10	70					8	56		4	28		4	28			
Common/translatable across	6		7	42		8	48					9	54		9	54		4	24			
Increase Operational	10		10	100		10	100					6	60		9	90		10	100			
RELATIVE MERIT (Total Score)				364			356						353			322			254			
RELATIVE THREAT (from Risk Analysis)																						

Figure 7.3 Project selection worksheet.

SCOTT&WHITE
Healthcare

Inbound Domestic and Global Medical Process

Team Name:
Event Date:

Updated:
Created:

Problems/Case for Change:

Process Purpose:
Process Scope:
In Scope:
Out of Scope:

Central Steering Committee:

		TEAM		
Last Name	First Name	MD	Role (RN, IT, etc.)	Manager (Last, First)

AD HOC TEAM

Executive Sponsor
Executive Sponsor
Executive Sponsor
Process Owner
Process Owner
O.E. Coach
O.E. Coach

PROJECT TIMEFRAME
Kickoff/Scoping:
Scoping:
VSM Workshop
Followup Meetings:
1
2
3
4

Daily or Weekly Huddles (Loc?)

	GOALS/METRICS		
ITEM		CURRENT	GOAL

Figure 7.4   Blank charter form.

Suppliers	Inputs	Process	Outputs	Customers
Patients	Patients	1. Patient checks in, MA prints encounter form	Info into the EMR	Patients
	Med list	2. MA retrieves patient from waiting room and verifies name, DOB	Billing sheets	Providers
		3. MA takes patient's vitals	Rx	Billing staff
Hospitals	Data from hospitals, labs (test results)	4. MA starts a Chart Note. Adds complaint & vitals in note		
Reception	Phone messages	5. MA checks protocol (e.g., is patient due for immunization, foot check); reconciles med list; performs standard tasks (e.g., EKG for chest pain, urine test or urinary tract infection symptoms) if needed; collects test results. Does depression screening, etc.	Procedures that need to be referred and scheduled	
	Rx Refills requests	6. MA gives gown; starts paperwork for specimen		
Provider	Provider requests	7. Gives immunizations		
		8. MA exits, flips flag, and puts encounter form in bin outside of door		
		9. MA may return (e.g., to draw blood etc.) after provider sees patient		
EMR	EMR data (treatment/ symptom immunizations and tests needed as defined in protocols)	Between Patients, • Rx refills requests • Phone messages for provider • Flowsheet lab reports • Mail normal lab letter • Call patient when needed • Patient visits for just the MA		

Figure 7.5 SIPOC example.

Scott & White Alignment Tool

How will your team's performance affect our Value and Goals this year?

Name: _____
Leader: **Steve Hoeft**

(Boss' info goes up here)

S&W Mission:
Provide the most personalized comprehensive, and highest quality healthcare, enhanced by medical education and research.

S&W Vision:
Most Trusted and Most Valued name in American Healthcare.

S&W Values:
Teamwork, Patient-Centered, Innovation, Accountability, Excellence, Pride.

Legend:

No Alignment	
Indirect Alignment	0
Direct Alignment	X

OE	Pop Health	Growth	Institutes	Priority	Key Objectives	SMART Goals (through "catchball") FY14	Action Themes	Responsible
X	0	0	0	1	1.4 Implement Lean: Standardize and eliminate waste to reduce cost: **Do Great OE Training**	*(1.4.2) 90% of S&W Manager level and above attend 1 or 4-day OE Courses *4 OE Courses at Baylor or non-SW *8 full LMS Courses for S&W staff *3 full LMS Courses Baylor or non SW *(1.4.4) 120 staff attend LMS short courses	*Maintain Master Training Schedules-goal met well before end of FY14 *Track 1+ deliverable after every training session	SH
X	X	X	X	2	1.4 Implement Lean: Standardize and eliminate waste to reduce cost: **Do Great OE Projects**	*(1.4.3) 24 VSM/Kaizen workshops through workshop and results on-line *2 Institute or Pop Health projects *2 Lean Layout (full cycles)	*1D and facilitate workshops *Help develop Population Health processes	SH
X	0	0	0	3	1.4 Implement Lean: Standardize and eliminate waste to reduce cost: **Make Effective Tier-1,2,3+ Huddles**	*(1.4.5) 800+ Huddle Boards with at least 1 new team member idea tried out *50+ T2-3 Boards w/Issue Elevation system *Develop tool & process-do 60 Board audits	*Tailor/accelerate current/new Boards *Support all leaders we teach	SH
X	0	0	0	4	1.4 Implement Lean: Standardize and eliminate waste to reduce cost: **Coach up Huddle Leaders to deploy OE foundation tools**	*180 S&W Leaders thru A3 Wave *200 A3 problems (from Boards) documented on-line	*Guide Huddles to Problem ID/resolution *Deploy A3 Waves with instructor devel.	SH
X	X	X	X	5	1.3 Improve Patient Access: improve customer satisfaction	*Support 4 Access Improvement efforts/projects	Deploy **SDA Effort!** VSM/Kaizen/A3 projects	SH
	X	0		6	1.7 Financial-maintain Revenue-achieve $50MM Expense reduction	*Lead 6 'Round 4 Thinking' studies	Work Balance, cross-training, studies to support Round 4 Thinking before Additional resources are requested	SH
X	X	X	0	7	1.2 Implement EPIC: Improve efficiency of patient care processes	*Support EPIC Roll-out	Process and Problem Solving Support of EPIC	SH, DS
X	0			8	1.1 Retain high-perf staff: Improve Ee satisfaction: **Retain OE Staff**	*100%	Huddles, Engagement, Communication	SH
				9				

*Recommended number of goals is 5

System Strategies:
1. Operational Excellence*
2. Population Health
3. Growth (Rational and Strategic)
4. Nationally Competitive Institutes
(See FY2014 Strategic Plan Document for Details)

Figure 7.6a Hoshin (SWAT) form—Boss' form.

Name: _____ Staff Member: _____

Sr Lean Coach

*Operation Excellence Objectives:	Priority	Key Objectives	SMART Goals (through "catchball")	(ALIGNED-Employee's info goes down here) Action Themes	Responsible
1.1 **Retain engaged & hi-performing staff:** Improve Provider and Employee satisfaction; build strong service culture	1	1.4 Implement Lean: Standardize and eliminate waste to reduce cost: **Do Great OE Training**	*(1.4.2) 90% of S&W Manager level and above attend 1 or 4-day OE Courses *2 OE Course at Baylor or non-SW *1 full LMS Courses for S&W staff *2 full LMS Courses Baylor or non SW *(1.4.4) 30 staff attend LMS short courses	*Teach 25% of all 1 or 4 Day OE Courses (Baylor and S&W combined) *Teach OE Courses at Baylor or non-SW *Track 1+deliverable after every training session	DS
1.2 **Implement EPIC:** Improve efficiency of patient care processes					
1.3 **Improve Patient Access:** Extended clinic hours and alternate delivery channels to improve customer satisfaction	2	1.4 Implement Lean: Standardize and eliminate waste to reduce cost: **Do Great OE Projects**	*(1.4.3) 5 VSM/Kaizen workshops through workshop and results on-line*1 Institute or Pop Health projects*1 Lean Layout (full cycles)	*Work with leaders to ID workshops *Facilitate VSM/Kaizen workshops *Facilitate Pop Health Exemplar project *Help develop Population Health processes	DS
1.4 **Implement Lean:** Standardize and eliminate waste to reduce cost					
1.5 Provide highest levels of **Quality and Safety:** improve outcomes, costs, system revenue	3	1.4 Implement Lean: Standardize and eliminate waste to reduce cost: **Make Effective Tier-1,2,3+ Huddles**	*(1.4.5) 800+ Huddle Boards with at least 1 new team member idea tried out*50+ T2-3 Boards w/Issue Elevation system*Develop tool & process-do 60 Board audits	*Tailor/accelerate current/new Boards *Support all leaders we teach	DS
1.6 Improve **Customer Satisfaction:** increase market share and system revenue	4	1.4 Implement Lean: Standardize and eliminate waste to reduce cost: **Coach up Huddle Leaders to deploy OE foundation tools**	*5 S&W Leaders thru A3 Wave *8 A3 problems (from Boards) documented on-line	*Guide Huddles to Problem ID/resolution devel. *Deploy A3 Waves with instructor devel.	DS
1.7 **Financial:** Maintain Revenue-achieve $50 MM Expense reduction	5	1.3 Improve Patient Access: improve customer satisfaction	*Support 1 Access Improvement effort/project	Deploy **SDA Effort**! VSM/Kaizen/A3 projects	
	6	1.7 Financial-maintain Revenue-achieve $50MM Expense reduction	*Lead 1 Round 4 Thinking study	Work Balance, cross-training, studies to support Round 4 Thinking before Additional resources are requested	DS
	7	1.2 Implement EPIC: Improve efficiency of patient care processes	*Support EPIC Roll-out	Process and Problem Solving Support for EPIC *Lessons learned COE session (Sep/Oct '14) *Prepare Temple area Leadership Lean EPIC Go Live *Schedule COE team for Temple/Hillcrest EPIC Go Live	DS
	8	1.1 Retain high-perf staff: Improve Ee satisfaction: **Retain OE Staff**	*100%	Huddles, Engagement, Communication	
	9	Support Baylor OE Development	2 of every 3 weeks support onsite at Baylor *Map (VSM) key processes. Facilitate future state sharing BSWH processes *Assess OE levels and opportunities for A3 waves	Support OE Development at Baylor Provide Senior OE Coach Leadership	DS

* Recommended number of goals is 5

Employee's Major Initiatives: (list)

1) Create course content and deliver training to COE for Demand/Process/Operator Analysis (ACU EVS Room change example)
2) Return to Master's Studies - shift focus from MBA to an emphasis in Medical Informatics - 1st year Goal get accepted to program and finish 1–2 semesters of coursework
3) Write 1 article related to importance of Huddle (metric) boards - publish in medical media
4) Extend reach of Huddle Board learning by beginning a Huddle Board Blog/Twitter/Social Media
5) x
6) x

Figure 7.6b Hoshin (SWAT) form—Staff member's form.

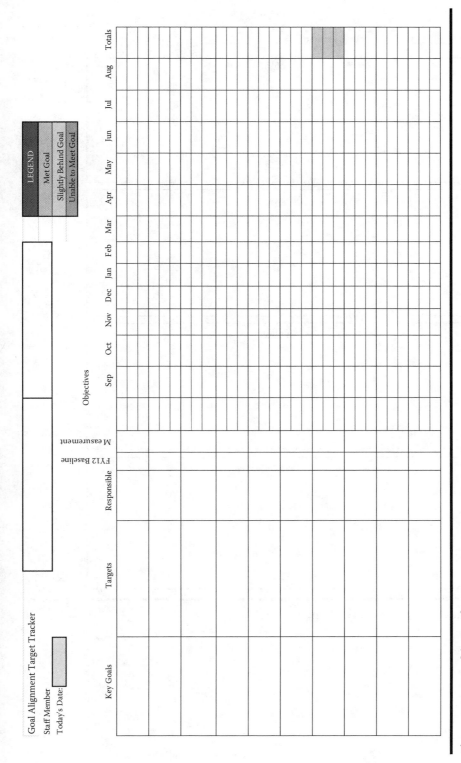

Figure 7.7   Hoshin tracker.

Leader Standard Work

Name:_____ Department:_____

Daily
1.
2.
3.
4.
5.

Weekly
1.
2.
3.
4.
5.

Monthly
1.
2.
3.
4.
5.

Gemba Time
1.
2.
3.
4.

Figure 7.8   Leader standard work form.

Huddle Tracking-FY14 Week-ending		7/1	7/2	7/3	7/4	7/5	7/6	7/7	7/8	7/9	7/10	7/11	7/12	7/13	7/14	7/15	7/16	7/17	7/18	7/19	7/20	7/21	7/22	7/23	7/24	7/25	7/26	7/27	7/28	7/29	7/30	7/31
VP/Admins		2014																														
Huddles (Planned)	19	1	1	1				1	1	0	1	1			1	1	1	1	1			1	1	0	1	0			1	1	1	1
Huddles (ACTUAL)	19	1	1	1				1	1	0	1	1			1	1	1	1	1			1	1	0	1	0			1	1	1	1
Goal: 90% of scheduled Daily Huddles conducted																																100%

July 2014

Goal: 90% of scheduled Daily Huddles conducted

Attendance:	% of actual	7/1	7/2	7/3	7/4	7/5	7/6	7/7	7/8	7/9	7/10	7/11	7/12	7/13	7/14	7/15	7/16	7/17	7/18	7/19	7/20	7/21	7/22	7/23	7/24	7/25	7/26	7/27	7/28	7/29	7/30	7/31
Ldr: Shahin M	68%	X	X	X				X	X		X	X											X		X				X	X	X	X
Matt B	58%		X	X				X	X		X	X				X	X												X	X	X	
Mark C	95%	X	X	X				X	X			X			X	X	X	X	X			X	X		X				X	X	X	X
Marshall C	68%	X	X	X				X	X		X											X	X		X				X	X	X	X
Michael D	84%							X	X		X	X			X	X	X	X	X			X	X		X				X	X	X	X
Cyndy D	37%	X		X				X															X		X				X			X
Betti G	63%	X	X	X				X	X							X			X			P	X						X	X		X
Candice G	79%		X	X				X	X		X	X				X	X	X	X			X	X		X					X		X
Ron H	58%		X	X				X	X													X	X		X				X	X	X	X
Jacki L	58%		X	X				X	X		X	X			X	X	X					X	X									
Susan M	95%		X	X				X	X		X	X			P	P	X	X	P			X	X		X				X	X	X	X
Thom M	95%	X	X	P				X	X			X			X	X	X	P	X			X	X		P				X	X	X	P
Tricia M	84%	X	X	X				X	X		X	X				X	X	X				X	X		X					X	X	X
Richard N	58%		P	P				X	P		P	X										P			P					P	P	P
Brian O	53%	X	X	X				X	X		X	X			X				X				X									
Sherry P	58%		X	X				X	X		X	X										X	X		X				X			X
Alita P	42%								X		X	X					X						X		X				X		X	
Karen S	74%							P	P		P	P			P		P	P				P	P		P				X	P	P	P
Stephen S	47%		X	X				X			X	X										X			X				X		X	
Scott S	79%	X	X	X				X	X		X	X			X	X	X	X	X			X	X		X							
Denise S	89%		X	X				X			X	X			X	X	X	X	X			X	X		X				X	X	X	X
McKinley T	100%	X	X	X				P	X		X	X			P	X	X	X	P			P	P		X				X	X	X	X
Invited guests																																
Mike A	11%							X															X									
Al A	95%	X	X	X				X	X		X	X			X	X	X	X	X			X	X		X				X	X	X	
Tim B	11%	X							X																							
Cheryl B	68%										P	X			P	P	P	P	P			P			P				P	P	P	P
Vince C	37%																					X	X		X				X	X	X	X
Annilyn D	84%	X		X				X			X	X			X	X	X	X	X			X	X		X				X	X	X	X
Nifty G	68%		X	X				X	X		X				X	X	X	X											X	X	X	X
Tom G	63%	X	X					X			X	X										X	X		X				X	X	X	X
Brian J	74%	X	X	X				X			X	X			X		X		X			X	X							X	X	X
Theresa K	5%																		X													
Ron K	11%																	X							X							
Nancy M	37%																X		X			X	X						X	X		X
Jennifer N	32%										X	X			X	X	X	X														
Kelsey O	37%								X			X			X	X	X								X							X
Harry P	16%								X							X							X									
Debby S	74%	P	P	P											P	P	P	P	P			P	P						P	P	P	P
Dave S (Lean Coach)	79%	X	X	X				X	X		X	X			X		X	X	X						X				X	X		P
Lonnie S	16%							P										X					X									
Travis S	42%			P												P	P	P							P				P	P	P	
Alex T	5%														X																	
Chuck V	84%		X	X				X	X			X			X	X	X	X	X			X	X		X				X	X	X	
TOTAL:		17	25	27				30	26		25	27			21	22	25	21	19			26	30		28				27	27	24	26
43		40%	58%	63%				70%	60%		58%	63%			49%	51%	58%	49%	44%			60%	70%		65%				63%	63%	56%	60%

Appropriate huddles include: Cascaded Huddle, Daily Temple and Central Clinic Huddle

X = present
P = on phone

Figure 7.9 Huddle and Attendance tracker.

Leader:		Scheduled Huddle Days and Times:			
Department:					
Board Location:		Audit Month:			

Go see the Huddle Board; Key Elements: Trend Charts, Analysis, and Implemented Ideas!				
	Goals (Yes, if > 75%)	Yes	No	Notes and Evidence
Q1. Are there metrics posted?	3-5 Metrics	☐ Yes	☐ No	
Q2. Are the metrics getting better over time? (Yes or No)	moving toward the Goal?			☐ Yes ☐ No (not scored yet for 'Year 1')
Q3. Are there Trend Charts?		☐ Yes	☐ No	
Q4. Are there clear Goals?		☐ Yes	☐ No	
Q5. Are the metrics tracked daily or weekly?	some monthly for T3 and T2 are OK	☐ Yes	☐ No	
Q6. Do the Charts align with their Leader's or System Goals?	show evidence of alignment	☐ Yes	☐ No	
Q7. Are the Charts current today or the most recent period?	daily or weekly	☐ Yes	☐ No	
Q8. Is there evidence of analysis of Metrics?	evidence = fishbone, 5 Why's, Why chart, list of reasons	☐ Yes	☐ No	
Q9. Is there a place to Capture Ideas?		☐ Yes	☐ No	
Q10. Have Ideas been captured in the last 2 months ?		☐ Yes	☐ No	
Q11. Have Ideas been Implemented?	NEW: please list implemented ideas as of current audit month	☐ Yes	☐ No	
Q12. Is there follow-up by leaders (an elevation system) for leaders to take up cross cutting Ideas and issues?		☐ Yes	☐ No	
Q13. Does feedback come back to the team on elevated Ideas or issues? (Yes or No)				☐ Yes ☐ No (not scored yet for 'Year 1')
Q14. Is there evidence the team is huddling at least weekly per huddle schedule?	evidence = huddle tracking log, attendance sheet	☐ Yes	☐ No	
		1	0	
Monthly Audit Score:		8%	0%	

Figure 7.10   Huddle audit form Year 1.

Huddle Leader: Audit Month:

Audit submitted by: Scheduled Huddle Days and Times:

Department: Submitt audit to XXXX by last day of the month

Board Location:

Question	Notes	Yes	No
Q1. Are huddle board metrics getting better over time (Trending data)?	IF YES - List metric that improved during the current audit month. Include metric details (i.e., Pt Sat improved from 51% to 73%)	☐ Yes	☐ No
Q2. Are there clear Goals on the Trend Charts?		☐ Yes	☐ No
Q3. Are the Charts tracked daily /weekly and current today or the most recent period?	Daily or weekly (Some monthly for T3 and T2 are OK)	☐ Yes	☐ No
Q4. How many Ideas were documented on your huddle board this month?		QTY:	
Q5. Have Ideas been Implemented in the current audit month?	IF YES - List implemented ideas	☐ Yes	☐ No
Q6. Is there follow-up by leaders (an elevation system) for leaders to take up cross cutting Ideas and issues and is feedback provided?		☐ Yes	☐ No
Q7. Is the huddle leader communicating regularly about system integration?		☐ Yes	☐ No

Ideas Implemented - Current Month	Ideas needed feedback from elevation
1)	
2)	
3)	
4)	
5)	

Metric Improvements - Current Month		
Metric	Metric at beginning of the month	Metric at end of the month

Figure 7.11 Huddle audit form Year 2.

Appendix B: Acronyms and Some Terms

The acronyms provided in this attachment have been largely derived from a variety of continuous improvement-related publications and programs.

5S: Traditional Toyota Production System tool to clean up, organize, and standardize a workplace: Originally five Japanese words starting with the letter S, translated to several combinations of English words. This is one interpretation:

> **Sort & Scrap:** (clear out rarely used items)
>
> **Straighten:** (organize and label; a place for everything)
>
> **Scrub:** (clean)
>
> **Standardize:** (make a checklist of the best-known way to do the first 3Ss)
>
> **Sustain:** (audit and reward the previous four items)

80/20: The 80/20 rule; Pareto rule (e.g., 80% of the problems are from only 20% of the possible causes).

A3: A problem-solving format; process and development tool.

APP: Advanced Practice Professional (usually includes Nurse Practitioners, Physician's Assistants, and Certified Registered Nurse Anesthetists).

ATP: Advanced Training Programs.

BSWH: Baylor Scott & White Health.

CAUTI: Catheter Associated Urinary Tract Infection.

CEO: Chief Executive Officer; the highest executive in an organization outside of the Board of Directors.

CI: Continuous Improvement.

CLABSI: Central Line-Associated Bloodstream Infection.

CLIP: Continuous Learning Improvement Program, an early name for Lean at Scott & White Healthcare.

CME: Continuing Medical Education.

CMS: Centers for Medicare/Medicaid Service.

CNO: Chief Nursing Officer.

COO: Chief Operating Officer.

CRNA: Certified Registered Nurse Anesthetists.

CTICU: Cardiothoracic Intensive Care Unit.

DOWNTIME: An acronym spelling out the eight categories of waste.

DRG: Diagnosis-Related Groups.

DRIP: Data Rich, Information Poor, for informed decisions.

ED: Emergency Department.

EMR: Electronic Medical Record, sometimes Electronic Health Record.

ES: Executive Sponsor.

EVS: Environmental Services.

Five Whys: A problem-solving analysis method to get at an underlying root cause by asking why several times.

FSM: Future State Map.

FTE: Full Time Equivalent.

Gemba (Japanese): The place where work occurs.

HAI: Hospital Acquired Infection.

Hansei (Japanese): Purposeful reflection with the purpose of improvement.

HCAHPS: Hospital Consumer Assessment of Healthcare Providers and Systems.

HMO: Health Maintenance Organization.

Hoshin Kanri (Japanese): Goal and effort alignment process.

House Model: Toyota house model for transforming all work processes; made up of a foundation, pillars, and roof and containing timeless, unchanging TPS principles.

HR: Human Resources (department).

IT: Information Technology department.

JCI: Johnson Controls, Inc. (specifically the automotive seat assembly division).

Jidoka (Japanese): Putting smart controls in the machine or process to stop the process when defects occur, so that the worker can avoid watching an automatically functioning machine.

JIT: Just In Time.

Kaizen (Japanese): Change for the good.

Kanban (Japanese): Signal card; used to pull materials to a process only when needed, not before.

LMS: Lean Management System.

LOS: Length of Stay.

MA: Medical Assistant.

MBO: Management by Objectives.

MICU: Medical Intensive Care Unit.

MVP: Most Valuable Player.

NP: Nurse Practitioner.

NVA: Non-Value Added, as in non-value-added tasks.

OR: Operating Room or rooms.

PA: Physician Assistant.

PCMH: Patient Centered Medical Home.

PDCA: Plan, Do, Check, and Act; systematic problem-solving process steps and cycle of improvement.

PM: Project Manager, also used for Plant Manager and Preventive Maintenance.

PMP: Project Management Professional (a certification level through the Project Management Institute).

PPE: Personal Protective Equipment.

PSS: Patient Service Specialist.

PT/OT: Physical Therapy/Occupational Therapy.

RIM: Research In Motion, inventor of the Blackberry phone.

ROI: Return On Investment.

S&W: Scott & White Healthcare.

SDA: Same Day Appointment.

SICU: Surgery Intensive Care Unit.

SIPOC: Suppliers, Inputs, Process, Outputs, and Customers for dissecting processes and inviting team members to a Lean workshop.

SMART: Specific, Measurable, Attainable, Realistic, and Time-bound, as in setting SMART goals.

SPC: Statistical Process Control.

SQDCM: Safety, Quality, Delivery, Cost, and Morale, the five typical categories of measures on a huddle board.

STICU: Surgery/Trauma Intensive Care Unit.

SVSM: System-Wide Value Stream Mapping.

SWAT: Scott & White Alignment Tool, S&W's version of Hoshin Kanri.

SWU: Scott & White University.

TOC: Theory of Constraints.

TPS: Toyota Production System.

TQM: Total Quality Management.

UDE: Undesirable Effect, or problems occurring in every process, as studied in a Lean project.

VA: Value Added, as in value-added tasks.

VAP: Ventilator-Associated Pneumonia.

VP: Vice President.

VSM: Value Stream Mapping.

WIP: Work in Process (inventory).

Index

About the Author

Steve Hoeft is the Chief of Operations Excellence at Baylor Scott & White Healthcare System. Since 2008, he has helped them build a strong *Culture of Continuous Improvement*, receiving national recognition for their transformation. He is a practitioner, teacher, author and thought leader applying TPS/ Lean principles. Steve has been called into dozens of board rooms to help integrate CI efforts into their overall strategic plans. Steve's strength is building the Lean Management Systems necessary to sustain and spread *Daily Lean* improvements.

Steve's book *Stories From My Sensei* won a 2011 Shingo Prize Award, and was translated into a dozen languages. His new book, *The Power of Ideas to Transform Healthcare: Engaging Staff by Building Daily Lean Management Systems*, comes out in spring 2015. He was also a contributing author to Dr. Jeffrey Liker's best-selling book *The Toyota Way to Continuous Improvement*.

Steve has successfully served as sensei to hundreds of healthcare leaders and internal facilitators. Steve also led successful Lean implementations in many different industries, including a key leadership role in the U.S. Air Force's effort for several years, winning multiple Shingo Prize Awards.

Before that, he helped lead Optiprise, Dr. Jeffrey Liker's Lean transformation consulting firm. His projects won many awards, including Shingo Prizes. He served as the Performance Improvement Manager for Johnson Controls, Inc. as they first learned to assemble automotive seating systems. During this time, he received significant coaching and training from Toyota in Georgetown, Kentucky. He co-authored and deployed the *JCI Manufacturing System*, winning the 1996 ASTD *Training Package of the Year* award. He helped apply for and helped win JCI's first Shingo Prize.

Steve's Lean experience began at the Delta (USA) Kogyo plant—one of Mazda's leanest suppliers. He was trained as a Delta Production System expert by Joe Shimada, Sensei. Steve started his career as a Production

Supervisor and engineer at General Motors. He received training and Jonah certification directly from Eli Goldratt (Theory of Constraints and OPT Scheduling). It was near the end of his time at GM where Steve first witnessed the superiority of the timeless principles of the Toyota Production System.

Steve and his wife Gena live in central Texas and still spend time in northern Michigan. They have three children: Megan, Erich, and Erin. Steve serves at Temple Bible Church in Temple, Texas.